Palgrave Insights into Apocalypse Economics

Series Editor
Richard Westra, Institute of Political Science, University of Opole, Opole, Poland;
Center for Macau Studies, University of Macau, Macau, China

The series offers a non-sectarian outlet for Marxist and critical heterodox economics scholarship on the tsunami of apocalyptic tendencies enveloping the global economy and society. Its guiding premise is that neoliberal policies from the 1980s not only failed to rejuvenate capitalist prosperity lost with the demise of the post-Second World War 'golden age' economy, but in fact have generated a widening spectrum of pathologies that threaten humanity itself. The series cultivates cutting-edge political economic analysis of the processes euphemised as 'globalization' and 'financialization', examining the impact of crises, austerity and inequality in the context of the recessionary, deflationary, inflationary, and stagflationary conditions that have beset the world economy in recent decades and into the 21st century. It covers themes such as the impact of monopolization and oligopolization in the new economy of information technologies, and the low wage production outsourcing and global social marginalization which accompanies that, as well as climate change, global environmental despoliation, disease pandemics, corrupted food systems and land-grabbing, rampant militarism, cybercrime and terrorism – all issues which defy mainstream economics and conventional political policy solutions.

The series invites work that is hard-hitting, inter/trans-disciplinary and multi-perspectival. It welcomes both theoretical and empirical writing with foci upon advanced and developing economies and encourages future-directed thinking on possibilities for another, better world. In particular, new and up-and-coming scholars are invited to submit their critical ideas and analysis. The series readership draws in academics, researchers, students, progressive governmental and non-governmental actors and the academically-informed public.

Achim Szepanski

Capitalism in the Age of Catastrophe

The Newest Developments of Financial Capital in Times of Polycrisis

palgrave
macmillan

Achim Szepanski
Frankfurt, Germany

ISSN 2523-8108 ISSN 2523-8116 (electronic)
Palgrave Insights into Apocalypse Economics
ISBN 978-3-031-57753-6 ISBN 978-3-031-57754-3 (eBook)
https://doi.org/10.1007/978-3-031-57754-3

Translation from the German language edition: "Die Ekstase der Spekulation – Kapitalismus im Zeitalter der Katastrophe" by Achim Szepanski, © Achim Szepanski 2023. Published by Galerie der abseitigen Künste (in Kooperation mit NON). All Rights Reserved.

Cover credit: Dina Belenko/Alamy Stock Photo

This Palgrave Macmillan imprint is published by the registered company Springer Nature Switzerland AG
The registered company address is: Gewerbestrasse 11, 6330 Cham, Switzerland

Paper in this product is recyclable.

Acknowledgements

I thank Jan Heintz for his work on the translation.

Thank you

CONTENTS

CHAPTER 1

The Ecstatic of the Excess in Bataille, Baudrillard, and Marx

In their *Panic Encyclopedia* from 1989, the authors Kroker, Kroker, and Cook interpret the phenomenon of the *excess* as a sign of ecstasy, saturation, and exhaustion. They list: "overfished, overrated, overcommunicated, overloaded with brands, over-aestheticized, over-medicated, surveilled, over-virtualized, over-medialized." (Kroker et al., 1999: 13) Today, it is particularly the speculative capitalization, which—inseparably linked with the rise of networked computers[1]—as a result of ecstatic escalation excesses has led to the *excess «over»*: Too much capital, but also too many images and too many signs, which neutralize any historical sense and exercise a white censorship through excess. This kind of simulation through excessive reality overload, which in turn can lead to reality denial,[2] triggers a new escalation of obesity (Baudrillard), which eventually becomes visible in all kinds of waste: nuclear waste, chemical waste, and industrial waste, but also the excess of opinions, laws, and texts, which drift like cadavers in the stream of decay and the pernicious. When Marx wrote, that capital is dead labor, whose function in the continuous and vampiric absorption of living labor exists, and that it as a vampire lives all the better, the more living labor it absorbs, then Marx had only a very faint idea of how capital with its expansion over two hundred years could generate a monstrous auto-cannibalism, in the course of which it wants to

A. Szepanski, *Capitalism in the Age of Catastrophe*, Palgrave Insights into Apocalypse Economics,
https://doi.org/10.1007/978-3-031-57754-3_1

absorb everything forever, until it eventually inflates itself to death (and destroys the earth).

We live today in a state of prolonged wakefulness and the ubiquitous and multiple work without a time limit. We enjoy the ever-accelerating excesses of over-information and delight in the voracity of electronic links, accept the obesity of the social body and the abundance of the derivative, drift deliriously through the high-speed economy and are mutants of satellite communication—we are caught and trapped in a hysteria of attention, where all aspects of acceleration, which indicate that at least a part of the world's population in the Global North is in permanent transit and mobile, meet decelerated scenarios, in which the surplus population in the Global South remains trapped in immobility. However, instantaneously, people are almost everywhere on the globe connected in 24/7 mode, seamlessly integrated into the ever denser networks of communication, information, and media representation, and they are fascinated by the scenario of media banality, which today underpins the real pornography, the real obscenity of triviality, indifference, and flatness, when we immerse ourselves in the delusional exhibitionism that characterizes social media, where quantity prevails over quality. All the over-information, which materializes in images, videos, and texts, becomes a tradable commodity, which tech capital extracts and capitalizes as data. All data are credit data. All differences (of content) are considered equivalent, or, to put it another way, any specific meaning dissolves in the ecstatic and infinite data stream. *Difference equals indifference*, so is nowadays the magic formula. This kind of rigid formatting goes back to an accumulation regime of financial capital, which in its short-term nature trades the *excess* of numbers, practices the ecstasy of speculation and at the same time must promise successful management of constantly present risk possibilities, no matter on which underlying values the insurances now refer. There is now a 24/7 non-stop operation of global production and circulation processes to report—the globe mutates into a networked and continuously open financial, trade, shopping and production center, with an excess of derivatives, products, things and information (and garbage) (Crary, 2013: 23). In the last instance it is speculative capital that cannibalizes even the number, to spit it out undigested as *over-more,* and it is in its peculiar emptiness the zero, which multiplies the fiction of always more (10, 100, 1000 etc.). Speculative capital finally short-circuits the structures developed in mathematics as socio-economic logic—its form of movement is, as will be shown, that of the empty *over-more*. Daniela Gabor has pointed out that contrary to expectations after the financial crisis of 2008, the hegemony of the global financial system has further solidified has, leading to what is aptly called the Wall Street consensus, which has revised and revived the neoliberal Washington consensus (Gabor, 2021).

To anticipate one thing here: Capital also suffers sui generis from a lack, namely the lack of surplus value or the more that determines the lack. There is also a lack of money, insofar as there is always a lack of purchasing power for outstanding goods and services. Thus the annual GDP as the total money value of all goods and services produced in the economy shows a surplus over the total wage and salary payments. These payments including the purchasing power of companies are always too low to absorb all goods. The gap between the purchasing power of households and companies and the outstanding market prices can be partly closed by households, companies, and governments receiving low-interest loans from commercial banks. The lending of commercial banks is the main way in which new money enters the economy.[3] This means that most money is provided by private banks through credit creation and not by the central banks. If no one were to go into debt in this way anymore, capitalism would immediately collapse. If it has become impossible to turn all the circulating money into to dissolve real goods or services, then money must always generate more money and credit must always generate more new credit. Debt repayment is then the infinite postponement of the redemption of payment promises, which always requires further loans. The postponement thus manifests itself in chains, multiplications, and proliferations, with no one knowing in the end who owes whom what (Röttgers, 2022: 146).

It is not money itself, but alongside industrial capital, it is fictitious and above all speculative capital, which creates the problem of the *excess* of debt. However, it is also necessary to limit this again. In 2019, approximately 17 trillion US dollars were in circulation in government and private bonds with terms of up to ten years and negative nominal returns (the lenders pay the borrowers money so that they take out loans). Thus, today we are also dealing with an abundance of money that is circulating faster and faster, especially on the financial markets.

Rapid progress, which in reality is Virilio's rapid standstill, is a figure of endlessly accelerating movement that has no goal because there is no end, and no end because the goal is missing. The "end of history", which Alexandre Kojève sometimes identifies with Napoleon, sometimes with the French Revolution, sometimes with communism, coincides with the capitalist modernity itself, whose "progressive thought" still perceives itself as infinite, as an uninterrupted final sprint of the seemingly new, leading to nothing or everything, depending on how you look at it. Precisely because there is no end in this sense anymore, we enter an endless crisis, into the infinite exhaustion of processes that nevertheless continue (Baudrillard, 2002: 50) (Kojève's mistake was mainly in the assumption that the post-historical man would live in harmony with nature, without suspecting that he could trigger a catastrophe of cosmic dimensions).

To propose the infinite ecstatic progress (of capital) as the only horizon is the same as inviting everyone to wait for Godot. Since we are modern, we live in times of the end or according to Baudrillard even after the end. Not that history has come to an end, but that it has no end in the sense of a finality, is up for debate in the course of eliminating an expectation horizon. The absence of a *new* future, which radically differs from the present, configures an end time of present, past, and future in contiguity.[4] We live for tomorrow and know that there is no new tomorrow. We want to move, always and everywhere, to charge ourselves with energies, to become faster and faster and to grow ecstatically into the infinite, yes to multiply our human capital congenially. That's probably why the enslaving robot is waiting for us. And there will always be someone, even if he has been locked up in his robotized bunker for 200 years and feeds on jelly and virtual sex, who will then say: "This is freedom". But even such end-time dreams, which the disaster porn fabulates around the clock today, are nothing more than simulacra. Even the apocalypse is over, says Baudrillard, it is today the precession of the neutral and the indifference (Baudrillard, 1994: 160). One should add, but also the precession of ecstasy (of more and less): Nothing is possible anymore, because nothing is impossible anymore.

This shows the retreat of an unpredictable, black, and new future, but at the same time points to the abundance of a risk-future. The operative condition of the speculative present seems to be the inherent uncertainty of the future. Any extrapolations into the future through calculation and financial speculation mean that strategies and designs that are made in the present, the unpredictability and uncertainty in calculable risks are transforming, and these risks continue to increase with the disintegration of the new future. The accelerating speculation and concentration of capital and the irreversible climate collapse reduce a truly new future to a null point and/or to the continuation of the already existing dynamics of a risk future. The historically founded formations and systems themselves pose risks for the future (for example, extreme inequalities in access to income and wealth, food insecurity, combustion of carbon dioxide, etc.). The future present that actually occurs remains unknown, but is determined in the present by the iterative calculation of a series of mainly financial risks, which in turn must remain subordinate to incalculable eventualities. In contrast to the time schemes of the linear chronology of progressive modernity (past → present → future) or the thesis of an infinitely extended present without a future (dystopias), the future present that will occur proliferates in the scheme of a present future that financially calculates the future as a risk. Nevertheless, for the speculative present future (of capital), which tries to include the future present, the premise of every historically realized future remains the unknown future present, which, however, by virtue of the present future, which is that of financial risk production, should at least be calculated. The fact that the present future, which calculates the future, wants to include the historical future present, but itself must assume an unknown new future that has not yet taken place, leads to a speculative time complex that displaces the time orders of both the forward movement of progressive modernity and the metastable present without a future, which each prioritize positive and negative semantic overdeterminations of the future present. The recurring calculations of the risk exposures of financial capital are an explicit operationalization of contingency. The exposure of the present to the future qua risk is on the one hand a retroaction of the unknown future on the present, on the other hand the risk exposure is the way in which the historical future present is generated according to the calculations of the present future, even if the latter is configured by the unknown future. The permanent calculation of risks in the future (speculation) is then a settlement and limitation of the abundance of future that affects the composition and semantics of the historical present, including a new and black future.[5]

At the same time, however, what Baudrillard calls the "spiraling cadaver of humanism" continues to proliferate: Even in the (always hypothetical) succession of humanity, the future will be human in posthuman discourses. Most current posthuman narratives, even those that refer to the development of a radical otherness of AI as an intended or unintended consequence of human strategies, are still modern versions of extinction fables that are rooted in the foundations of human rationality. No future is still a future—often a very specific one, fantasized to retroactively determine the current system. Thus, most narratives of posthumanism remain merely mutations of traditional Western religious narratives, intersected by modern progress mythologies in which humanity becomes the creator of the machine to which it develops itself: the DNA of what Baudrillard calls "the metaphysics of the code". The stochastic movement of evolution is coupled to the project of biotechnological control. Such evolution is, as Baudrillard says, indistinguishable from a socially and historically determined program.

Indeed, world capitalism seems to have entered a paradoxical, accelerating, and at the same time exhausting panic mode or a deadly excess in which the ecstasy of the *Over* as over-accumulation and over-speculation meet the destructive activities of capital, especially with regard to the capitalization of nature and the creation of a global surplus population. In the course of its expansive capitalization, the capital economy possesses a strangely phagic drive, as it prefers to always feed and *over* inflate itself further, insofar as finiteness is conceived as a limit that can be exceeded per se; the capitalist economy, in its omnipresent excess, seems to be driven by a desire for dissolution at the same time, which is an expression of a latent death wish that at least suspects the nullity of the self-generated void (in order to finally find a "redemptive" fusion with infinity).[6] In restricted economies (Bataille), where the generation of surplus value and financial returns dominate, however, the *over* can only be consumed in catastrophic events such as wars, devalued as capital in crises (or expropriated) or calculated. An economy that is filled with ever more demands and promises of payment for the future, which probably cannot be fulfilled, is a grotesquely inflated economy that will not be able to waste or unload the accumulated abundance and garbage within it. The current economic, social, and geopolitical disturbances, tensions, and conflicts, for which the term "poly-crisis" is used, point to a catastrophic capitalism, think for example of global financial capital and its bubble formations, the debt and inflation, Russia's invasion into Ukraine, which must be read against the backdrop of the conflict between the USA and China,[7] the Covid-19 pandemic, or also climate change. Even the term "disaster capitalism" (Callinicos) is now coming up. Nouriel Roubini has listed a whole series of factors that could trigger catastrophic dynamics in world capitalism beyond poly-crises: an inflation surge that forces central banks to a draconian tightening of monetary policy, leading to an unsustainable rise in interest rates; pandemics that are worse than COVID-19; a corporate debt crisis resulting from a credit crunch when interest rates rise; a new real estate bubble that bursts; a geopolitical shock like the war between Russia and Ukraine in 2022, which escalates and intensifies, leading to a further increase in commodity prices and inflation; the rising risk of another global recession and a return to protectionism or an economic and political decoupling between the USA and China, steering the two countries towards a geopolitical collision (Roubini, 2022). Currently, tensions between China and the USA in the Taiwan conflict are intensifying. An attack by China on Taiwan would be the beginning of a long crisis. The world would divide even more into blocks that are for or against China. The West would have to impose further sanctions, supply chains would collapse. It would be the beginning of a qualitatively new form of a highly technologized war. Not to be left unmentioned regarding these diverse polycrisis processes is the tendency towards new forms of state fascization and a new fascism.[8] And finally, climate change could lead to new wars over water and unforeseen waves of migration.

Long before the neoliberal turn, Adorno defined the *world spirit*, which stands for capital in his view, as the permanent catastrophe. Today, however, it is becoming apparent that we are in a period of live in a permanent poly-crisis, which can certainly also be described as a catastrophe, which means that the crisis is increasingly losing its purifying character for capital. This also changes the epistemic function of the crisis. While in earlier phases of capitalism, in the context of Schumpeter's creative destruction, it led to a new economic cycle, today, in the course of crises, the management of the flooding of the speculative boom-and-bust engine is driven or at least regulated, without being able to stop a whole series of symptoms of decay. What borders more on a catastrophe than a crisis is probably that the system has exceeded itself, i.e., it has already left its own goals behind and, precisely because of the ongoing acceleration, has little or no remedies left. Danowski and de Castro no longer speak of a crisis in time and space, but of a corrosion of time and space, a general collapse of spatial and temporal scales, with which historical time interferes with meteorological, ecological, and cosmological temporalities, in the sense of the interruption of cycles and the onset of cataclysms (Danowski & de Castro, 2016: 18).

In the new financial cosmology, time is engineered, not experienced. The current poly-crisis is very specifically temporal, possessing polyvalent and destabilizing uncertainties that can no longer be structured by a horizon of possibilities, but indicate boundaries, probabilities, and finality.

Temporality here is less a measure of a physical existence, but a technology with which systemic conditions of the economy are shaped. Time itself becomes a technical medium.

In times of catastrophe, reality and fiction merge. The global information war is currently in full swing in the face of the Ukraine and Gaza wars. Different versions of reality are increasingly openly clashing. There is no longer just one reality as in the old world. This is exactly what Baudrillard understands by hyperreality.

The catastrophe is equivalent to a continuous and intensifying polycrisis, in which collapses occur in the areas of economy, social, politics, and culture, and a return to normality is far off. Things are accelerated and at the same time halted before they end, in order to put them into the tension of their appearance for an indefinite period. The catastrophe jealously ensures the destruction of the illusion of eternity, but it also plays with it by fixing things to a second eternity. The catastrophe never completes itself, but more than that, because it never completes itself, it becomes the real, reality as a simulation of itself.

The word catastrophe originally means *kata* (down) and *streiphen* (turn) in Greek, to indicate a downward turn, a shift in temporal gravity, like a black hole reshaping the time period. It is now possible to distinguish between disaster, catastrophe, and emergency. The disaster is a crisis that suspends normal orders for a certain time. Normality is to be and can be restored. In the case of catastrophes, however, political functions, the economy, and the entire material and social fabric are disturbed or they are so far interrupted that a return to normality is far off. The catastrophe is a hole between before and after, which cannot be absorbed by the old rationality, while a new normality is awaited. One could also call the catastrophe a black box, in which the rationality of the modelable, the knowable, and the predictable collapses (Armand, 2023: Kindle Edition 128). The catastrophe is the result of lengthy multicausal processes from which the effects escape. It brings forth what one could call the "homo catastrophicus". However, talking about the catastrophe should not lead to the critical discourse falling in love with the idea of a permanently criticizable future, only to turn to preservation in the end, namely of the planet, humanity, and the culture of consumption (while speculative capital calculates the future coldly and rationally). One must not equate talk of the end (of the world) with the catastrophe. During the Corona crisis, states and central banks deployed exorbitantly high sums of money to exclude any possibility that the system could come to an end, while the crisis simultaneously scratched at the previous confidence in the system as a perpetuum mobile. Various symptoms of the catastrophe, such as the climate crisis, question the functionality of the system, while simultaneously proliferating and accelerating it.

It is important to further distinguish between catastrophe, apocalypse, and the end of the world. Apocalypse and extinction (end of the world) are not only different, but incompatible and contradictory terms. In short, while the apocalypse secures the meaning of an end, extinction anticipates the end of meaning. There will be film footage of the end of the world, and we are seeing it now, and its most striking feature is its obvious inability to draw a conclusion. Perhaps there will be footage someday and no one left to watch it. The apocalypse documents in advance the boredom of the digitized human in the face of the spectacle of this never-ending end. For Baudrillard, even the apocalypse does not exist more, and if so, it is merely the revelation of reality in a world where only its simulated form exists. And so, after the actual apocalypse is behind us, we are instead confronted with the virtual reality of the apocalypse, with the posthumous comedy of the apocalypse. With a silent yawn of our satisfied uselessness, we enjoy the war that has never taken place for us in the West. The idea of war as an event where something is at stake is behind us, so there is only the media event, making war an empty screen for itself. We have seen the war (and the end) so often that we have become weary of it. It comes, it goes: nothing changes. But of course, it never passes, which not coincidentally also contributes to our fatigue. Whether through deficit or excess, reality will inevitably continue the work of the apocalypse—by extinguishing it. The real apocalyptic event will then become the apocalypse of the apocalypse.

The lack (of capital) is never dramatic, for Baudrillard it is saturation that acts fatally, as it accelerates the cramp and immobility, analogous to Virilio's frenetic standstill or dromospheric pollution. To live every moment as if it were the last, that is for Virilio the paradox of post-modern futurism, a futurism of the moment that ignores the future. This also marks the loss of faith in the propaganda of endless progress (Virilio, 1988: 1).

For Baudrillard, it is the implosive tendencies that ultimately drive and accelerate the loss of power of the system. They are necessarily incalculable in their effects. The endpoint of these processes is the catastrophe, in which various crises connect, supplement and reinforce each other, resulting in devastating devastation in all economic, social and political areas, up to a high number of people being killed. For Baudrillard, however, the system is already haunted today by a constant feeling of crisis. And this kind of multiple crisis is not simply to be equated with the absolute limit of the system, on the contrary, it is immanent and omnipresent, with the system even constantly obscenely demonstrating its own crisis (news, disaster films, crime films, action films etc.). The crisis is also distributed in "homeopathic doses", in tiny amounts that are absorbed by other crises. Therefore, it does not lead to explosions, but is instead diluted and/or served to the masses on a drip. Possible explosions are also excluded by the various prevention policies, while the implosion, the death of the cybernetic, combinatorial world remains a constant threat.[9]

In this context, today's high-speed emergency capitalism always also has a biopolitical component. It concerns not only the mostly non-functioning remediation of disasters and the neoliberal management of climate change, but above all the disastrous management of the global surplus population, which has become superfluous for a largely automated, highly financed, speculative and at the same time implosive ultra-reproduction model of world speculation capital.[10] We can now also speak of a "reflexive biopolitics" that tries to manage the various risks that arise within capitalist modernity through local, regional, and global networks, in order to at least ensure the security of vital systems (health, disaster protection, infrastructure etc.). The tendency towards new forms of state fascization and new fascism should not go unmentioned in these diverse crisis processes.

Capitalist economies cannot develop a wasteful and useless handling of excess, as suggested by Bataille's General Economy, which includes a luxurious giving and a spending and at the same time useless consuming that ignores and exceeds all the miserable offers displayed by the (imagined) economic equilibrium, exchange, and profit production. Luxurious waste remains today largely a privilege of the super-rich as extravagant commodity consumption, which is by no means useless, but serves as the social distinction of an elite, as expressed for example in the political number that says that the currently annually accumulated expenses for the 6,000 operational super yachts could pay off the debts of all developing countries (Salle, 2022: 54). At the same time, as we will see, there is a permanent capitalization of excess, which, however, has absolutely nothing to do with the useless expenditure in the sense of Bataille, as it is subject to the necessity of constantly re-capitalizing the surplus (profit or return) instead of just uselessly spending it. Even waste products resulting from capital accumulation such as carbon dioxide emissions, plastic bags, illegal economy etc. can continue to be "productive" insofar as they have effects on various levels. Waste is inevitable and in some cases it is even desired in capitalism. Baudrillard shows using New York City as an example that waste products are essential for the functioning of the system.[11] New Yorkers draw an abnormal energy from the vices, evils, and excesses of the city (Baudrillard, 1992a). Yet modern rational logics and practices, as Baudrillard claims, fail to adequately consider the excessive effects of waste. It finds no entry into the official economic and social calculations. Finally, even Baudrillard's catastrophic events are swallowed up to capitalize them. At least the disaster is managed, it is provoked and at the same time normalized and instrumentalized. Even if the uncontrollable damages escalate so much that the "disaster capitalism" becomes a disaster for capitalism itself, the prospects for communist perspectives look bleak.

The principle of the restricted capitalist economy is based on the fact that there is never enough for everyone, while Bataille's principle of the General Economy is based on the fact that there is always too much for everyone; the latter is truly a risky, precarious, perhaps even an absurd organization, a project of destructive energy, an anti-economy, a prodigy, a consumption excess, a challenge to scarcity, which, however, hyper-speculative capital has long since overcome in its own way today. Bataille's General Economy is a quasi-science, a theoretical and written practice that examines a material as well as intellectual production of excesses, that cannot be used beneficially. Bataille calls this pointless loss the (impossible) "sovereignty", impossible insofar as every discourse or profit is now related to non-discourse or non-profit. Bataille's model of general economy also proves itself in its written elaboration as a concentration of expenditure on the irreducible loss (in writing), and thus also as an antipode to Hegel's system of restricted economy, which draws its inner value from the accumulation of meaning. Bataille's sovereignty thus also manifests itself in writing (as in the economy) as ruthless expenditure and thus as a loss of potential meaning (not an absolute loss, but effects and effects of the loss of meaning and non-knowledge), with waste being assigned a positive value.

Bataille substantiates the general economy with a bundle of entropy and energy metaphors. The basic thesis is that every living organism on earth receives more energy from solar energy than it needs to live (Bataille, 2021: 22). Bataille's general economies have subsequently found a way to get rid of the surplus through useless or superfluous expenditures. It is assumed that there can be no unlimited economic growth on earth in general, insofar as space is limited, so that a luxurious expenditure in ***manifold*** forms is necessary (ibid.: 37). The general economy is what Bataille also calls a "heterology", which is an important dimension of his theory, which he explores in his entire work (Bataille, 1985). To the time of profitability and acceleration, Bataille opposes a thoroughly heterogeneous time of unproductive expenditure, a time of individual and collective uprisings, to which the time of self-preservation, regeneration and work as productive consumption of energies is an abomination. However, what Bataille calls "unproductive expenditure", as practiced by the peoples colonized by Europe, seems to have become impossible today—the impossible in general. To live in the sovereign moment of self-loss, that is now the impossible, because a gift economy, a life that enjoys itself with unproductive expenses and pure waste, has become unbearable at least for the inmates Western civilization, who live a limited life in all possible dimensions. Any waste that does not obey the principle of commodity-consuming pleasure, not the movement of a recovery that compensates for the effort of work, serves, or regenerates the life force, must be excluded. A life that is not force, but act or celebration, a life that does not exhaust itself in the enjoyment of an ever-increasing self-movement, such a life has no place in capitalism.

According to Derrida, Bataille is concerned with the unregulated dissemination and the irreducible and non-assimilated remainder or residue that resists any form of containment and exposes every system to loss, as well as indeterminacy and heterogeneity, and all this makes the general economy and its configurations fundamentally uncontrollable (Derrida, 1988). The general economy brings with it a loss of all totalization, even though Bataille, like Nietzsche, speaks of the economy as a whole. But this "whole" is itself generally economic. A globalization without totalization, one might say, requires the irreducible general economic loss. Local configurations must in turn be considered economically as general, which among other things means that they can never be absolutely local. The general economy must therefore always refer to unproductive losses and expenditures—to expenditures without the retention of reserves. However, the wealth of general economies and its waste would be impossible without production.

When one examines the totality of wealth, one recognizes that in limited economies the manufactured products are used for productive purposes because they increase the material capacities of the producers. However, this is not unlimitedly possible, so a part of the wealth must necessarily be spent as a result of loss-making activities (Bataille, 2021: 22). Also, the energy of living matter, which it receives for free from the sun, is always excessive, so it is about the type of luxury waste, when the productive use of energy in an individual, a group or an entire economy reaches its limit. The General Economy implies that living organisms always already receive more energy (from Bataille only from the sun, without considering other forms of energy), than they need to stabilize their lives and therefore are almost dependent on excessive expenditure. This compulsion to excess has a naturalistic dimension in Bataille, as Baudrillard criticizes, but also a mythological dimension of sun worship. Moreover, Bataille strangely forgets in his writings the planetarization of matter and energy, which above and below the earth releases processes of energization (fossil, electrical, hydraulic, economic energy etc.). The anthropocentric orientation of Bataille is quite questionable as well.

Bataille often speaks of an "excessive energy" that cannot exist in an ontological sense, because it is not about what "is", but about what we can say about the "effectiveness" of energy. Effects are not causes, but events. The expenditure characterizes an illogical and irresistible energetic impulse to reject the purely rational monetary use of material or moral goods. It is not primarily about production and preservation or about a consumption that merely serves the continuation of productive activity, but about an excessive consumption that is associated with unproductive expenditures and loss: festivals, arts, potlatch, games, art, perverse sexuality etc. (Bataille, 2021: 24). It is important to remember that the surplus of energy, which does not serve the growth of organisms or economies, is useless from the outset (ibid.: 34). Although the existing energy fields, when human production extends living matter by techniques and apparatuses (inert matter), can be enlarged. On the one hand, technology absorbs excess energies, on the other hand it produces massive energy surpluses itself. But the growth generated by capital and specific technologies always reaches its limits in crises, so that energies must be wasted, in capitalist economies for example in the form of catastrophic events like wars. Bataille hopes that wars can be avoided in the future for expenditure. But for this, overproduction must be redirected, either into the rational expansion of an increasingly difficult industrial growth or one must waste in unproductive expenditures those energies that can in no case be accumulated.

The destruction of material goods and the subjugation to the inhumane chaos include forms of entropy, whereby the waste can also release a part of the energy circulating in a complex social network in a neganthropic way. This dynamic makes the dynamics of entropic loss simultaneously a dynamics of excessive production, indeed of quantum effect, which pays homage to the production of a multiple surplus, which in turn must be unproductively spent (Plotnitsky, 1994: 34). The General Economy must therefore always refer to a dynamics of loss *and* of production. The truth of the General Economy allows an opening for the improbability of what one could call the anti-anthropic quasi-cause[12] as opposed to the shallow anthropology of the (neoclassical) utility economy, insofar as technology is no longer thought of as a means or as an instrument, but as that which reveals the true general production in a neganthropic manner, namely as "exosomatic différance" (Stiegler, 2017: 246).[13] This goes beyond Bataille's construction of dualistic oppositions such as work versus play, production versus consumption or commodity versus gift, although Bataille himself did not believe in the purity of excessive consumption or ecstatic play, so that the différance or the instability of the oppositions always resonates with him. The exosomatic différance would refer to a technique that is transductive in the sense of Simondon, that is, it promises a successful interplay of the relationship to oneself, the relationship to others and the relationship to the world through technology.[14] Stiegler sees with Bataille a cosmic totality emerging, which is conceived neganthropologically, that is, it includes the knowledge and the power to create manifold bifurcations within entropy. Each quasi-causal branching goes back to a cosmic potlatch that destroys large amounts of differences and orders, but this in turn happens through the projection of a very large difference on another level, which represents another "order of magnitude" against the disorder in the cosmos, because without this projection of a coming, the universe would be without any singularity (ibid.). Such a neganthropocene would, however, require more than the elaboration of a new speculative cosmology, namely a destruction of the logic of capital itself, into which it is inscribed. Through a positive neganthropic feedback spiral, which recovers the negative movement of entropy as a (positive) object of knowledge, Stiegler takes up the concept of *negentropy* as a redemptive recovery of the loss of the world, by simply converting negative into positive feedback. Such a productivism always runs the risk of constructing a conceptual Ponzi scheme (pyramid scheme) instead of promoting waste.

If one brings time into play here, one would have to define it as a "source"—as that of the mutually inhibiting or impelling effectiveness of negentropy and entropy, and thus one would speak of a force that is both productive and expenditure or destructive. In these two aspects—productive and expenditure—the effectiveness possesses an enormous anti-epistemological potential. A General Economy therefore relies on consumption and expenditure, profit and loss, preservation and waste, it is not simply conflictual or contradictory, but it is multiple and complementary (Plotnitsky, 1994: 34f.). In doing so, the General Economy must establish a relationship of dominance to the restricted economy, but does not completely destroy it, insofar as it always remains necessary that certain energies be productively used. For Plotnitsky, Bataille's General Economy is characterized as a complementary intraplay between expenditure, production and conservation (without productive result), in stark contrast to Hegel's figure of sublation, which simultaneously negates, conserves and overcomes (ibid.: 36). Radical transgressions can however never be absolute.

Plotnisky goes even further and tries to bring Bataille's General Economy closer to quantum theory, insofar as both pay homage to a fundamental indeterminism, which is deeper than any aleatoric or stochastic (ibid.: 18). A fundamental uncertainty or an abyss of "more-or-less" within (non-)systems characterizes this economy, indeed an irreducible loss, which however itself possesses a kind of diversity and complementarity. De-formalizations and de-systematizations, which are also re-formalizations and re-systematizations, show the connection of the irreducible loss and the incompleteness with the an irreducible diversity or heterogeneity of a system or non-system. In quantum mechanics, the relationship between uncertainty and multiplicity is equally important, as one is confronted with an irreducible, infinite multitude of all systems considered (ibid.: 30). In relation to Derrida and beyond him, one might perhaps go a step further at this point and surrender both levels of the de- and the re- to a negation, an infinite negative division and a negative difference without any presence.

General Economy at least makes clear that non-usable surpluses and energies are produced and at the same time non-reproducible losses must occur and it must relate its theoretical knowledge especially to these losses. For Plotnitsky, who refers here to Niels Bohr,

General Economy shows the complementarity between representation and non-representation (ibid.). It is supra-statistical in its complexity, which precedes simplicity, and avoids any statically underpinned causality through its différance. The global or extensive dimension of General Economy, which never neglects the phenomenon of locality, Plotnitsky relates to the complex relations of local and global configurations in quantum theory, which indeed has not only a microscopic but also a macrophysical dimension (ibid.: 33).

Derrida aligns with Bataille's General Economy when he writes that it, so to speak, keeps the non-reserve in reserve. He mentions as an example of a restricted economy a company that makes a profit from its investment, and in contrast the différance, which misses its profit and may even "pay" for this with the absolute loss, death (Derrida, 1988: 19). However, Derrida relativizes the opposition between a restricted and general economy again, insofar as he sees that in both economies production as reproductive consumption remains tied to a cybernetic program. The entropy occurring in both economies is always associated with the work of dissipation, and this work incurs costs and enforces a value, even if it stands under the sign of a non-value, to which the system of waste can only refer. The general dissipative economy appears as a system of positive and negative feedbacks, in which growth is determined as the accumulation of dissipative effects. Dissipation generates more dissipation in the mode of an economic struggle for maximization.

Of course, it is obvious to connect Bataille's General Economy with the various versions of luxury communism. However, when talking about fully automated luxury communism, it is already necessary to consider today that the pushback against climate change will also bring with it extensive labor-intensive tasks. Think, for example, of the construction of high-speed rail connections as a replacement for air travel, the care of hundreds of millions of traumatized, displaced people, or the pushback against pandemics. These tasks will probably absorb more than 100% of the workforce freed up by automation. This somewhat relativizes Bataille's notion of waste.

Unlike in the General Economy, the situation with the production (and waste) of the *excess* in capitalism is different. The *excess* today is far beyond the (industrial) overaccumulation of capital, shaped by the circulative logic and ecstasy of financial capital. We will show this in detail below. It was Baudrillard who used the term ecstasy particularly in the context of the expansive increase and overheating of communication and information in all media (Baudrillard, 2012a, 2012b) When all social functions are eliminated except for one dimension, namely that of communication, then we are already dealing with ecstasy in Baudrillard's view. It has two aspects: On the one hand, it shows pure circulation and excessive increase, a "Either-Or" no longer exists. Consider metastases and their acceleration and aimlessness of growth (ibid.: 27). The only thing that matters is that communication takes place and must lead to further communications. On the other hand, it also heads towards deceleration, inertia, towards the end after the end and survival in standstill or catastrophe, which however remains without consequences and at the same time is considered the purest form of the event.

For Heidegger, the term "ecstatic" has nothing to do with rituals and wild states and the like. Heidegger derives ecstasy from the Greek word ἐκστατικόν, which means "stepping out of oneself in time"[15] (Heidegger, 2005: 329). Since time is the direction of being, existence as the enactment of being in ecstasy consists precisely in "stepping out of oneself". Following Heidegger, Baudrillard expands and specifies that ecstasy should by no means be associated with passion, desire or lust, all of which lead into the hot universes. Rather, one should analyze ecstasy in the context of the cool universes of fascination, obscenity, and communication (Baudrillard, 2012a, 2012b: 29). While Heidegger refers ecstasy to a decidedly non-classical temporal subject (Dasein), Baudrillard's reference point—thought of quasi system-theoretically—is the optimization of possibilities within a purely operational system. Today, it is the artificial neural networks in which learning as adaptation and as feedback of internal parameters is realized as an optimization procedure on computers. The ecstatic optimization of the cybernetic system includes the phenomenon of acceleration. Therefore, Baudrillard can write: "Everything that is traversed at insane speed is a desert" (Baudrillard 1994: 114). One can indeed see the desert as a kind of homogeneous trans-space that remains without origin and reference point, a space that today increasingly consists only of screens. Analogous to the natural desert, which is always the same and to whose landscape we have no access precisely because of its homogeneity, there is today an artificial desert-like space characterized by speed and networking, and which eludes us because of its instantaneity, think for example of the desert-like form of the social, which is fed by endlessly accelerating communication and information, and the desert-like form of the economic, which is driven by ultra-fast speculative capital. All horizons have already been crossed, according to Baudrillard, we have already confronted all other worlds, and all that remains is to fall into ecstasy in a decidedly melancholic way (Baudrillard 2012a, 2012b: 40).

Baudrillard writes: "The only revolutionary transformation in things today comes not from their dialectical transcendence, but from raising them to the power of x, whether it be the revolution of terrorism, irony or simulation. It is not dialectics that are happening today, but ecstasy. Thus terrorism is an ecstatic form of violence, the state an ecstatic form of society, pornography the ecstatic form of sex, the obscene the ecstatic form of the scenic and theatrical, etc. It seems things have lost their finality and critical determination and can only repeat themselves in their exacerbated, transparent form. This is the case with Virilio's ›pure war‹: the ecstasy of unreal war, potential and omnipresent. Even space exploration is a mise en abyme of this world. Everywhere the virus of virtualization and self-reflexivity is on the upsurge, carrying us on towards an ecstasy which is also the ecstasy of indifference" (Baudrillard, 1990: 29–30). What Baudrillard strangely does not mention here: *Speculation (financial) is the ecstatic form of surplus value.*[16]

So Baudrillard writes in his book *The Transparency of Evil* even from a trans-economy, in which financial speculation no longer leads to any (classical) surplus value, but instead demonstrates a kind of ecstasy of monetary surplus value, detached from industrial production and its real conditions; it refers to a pure, empty form, which Baudrillard calls the "purified form of value", which, like a spiral, works with nothing other than its own rotational movement, indeed its own orbital circulation (Baudrillard, 1992b: 33ff.). The profit (monetary surplus value) that arises as a result of speculation is therefore by no means to be equated with Marx's surplus value. Financial speculation forces a barely controllable and regulatable, indeed a catastrophic logic of linkages, which with the securitization of derivatives (CDOs) before the financial crisis of 2008 had already occurred and set in motion a monstrous excess of escalation.[17] Baudrillard sees here the overcoming of classical economics by an aleatory, dizzying form of speculative multiplication of capital in progress (Baudrillard, 2002: 28). The escalating nth degree and its escalating power stands for Baudrillard in diametrical opposition to the dialectical figure of sublation, which for him remains a movement of transcendence (Baudrillard, 2012a, 2012b: 50). The spiral movement of the increase of speculative capital has left every reference point behind and lost all transcendence and reference, it eliminates every balance and leads to the potentialization of the derivative by means of the codes connected/disconnected and profit/non-profit. Baudrillard speaks of a "surmultiplication" (ibid.: 69), which is to be understood as immanent, namely as the multiplicative more of the same from the same (G-G'): *More speculative than speculative, that is the ecstasy of speculative capital.* It is a potentializing, delirious, and instantaneous process, an indifferent and transfinite pornography of money, which captivates us in a totalitarian manner.[18]

One could conclude at this point that financial speculation represents at least an exaggerated, hysterical form of Marx's surplus value production. But the ecstasy of speculation ultimately amounts to a destabilization of classical political economy and a comprehensive transformation of industrial capital, which now monstrously and somehow ironically also makes all possible alternatives impossible. Indeed, it will be necessary to examine to what extent the surplus resulting from financial speculation differs from Marx's surplus value. But at least capital does not lose the property of continuing to operate the instruction for future profit. This shows the time of capital as the homogeneity of the coming as the return of the same, with which circular and linear time condition each other (Lenger, 2004: 157). Hans-Joachim Lenger writes: "Unceasingly, capital writes itself from its own future, designs the present towards a delta G, which it is not and cannot become. Always ahead of itself, the ›real‹ capital is always retrospective. But in such a way out of itself, its ecstasy remains without event: cold ecstasy of a mediation that arises from the erasure of difference and always only finds its way back to itself in a circular manner" (ibid.).

The ecstasy of speculation, which consists in the at least formally boundless increase and the escalation of the power of speculative capital X (more x than x), now becomes the new super-superlative and also swallows in the energy of real capital in the whirl of its ecstatic indifference (more of the same, money). It is no longer primarily the mode of production that is interesting, but the way and manner the flourishing and easy circulation of monetary capital, with which the classic Fordist factory production is increasingly disappearing, at least in the global North, but continues to live on in all possible proliferations (in the Global South). Disappearing here primarily means that industry, at least in the capitalist core countries, despite all attempts at reindustrialization, is becoming increasingly insignificant and increasingly invisible in purely quantitative terms. However, the ecstasy of speculation, which is already that of financial capital, is still crossed by the detours of an industrial temporality and those of an industrial spatial topography. Speculative capital requires the media of communication and transmission in coded, symbolic, and technical terms, without being able to fully control them. Thus, speculative capital continues to depend on the general conditions of production or on material, operational and political infrastructures in order to be able to economically stage itself as circulation in real time. In and with the orgy of accelerating speculation, however, belief in it can also fade, because financial activity in real time contributes to unreality, similar to how one asks oneself in a splatter film whether that really happened. At the same time, the endless repetition of financial activity has long since been transferred to accelerated automation, into a nanosecond seriality, at the end of which one no longer knows what it is for or where it leads, because the last secret has been moved into the black box of the machines. Nevertheless, it must be noted: Although speculative capital in the sign of escalating circulation speeds detaches itself from territorial boundaries, it still requires technical and material infrastructures that make its speeds registrable, without being able to produce these infrastructures itself.

The circulation of speculative capital no longer needs to directly correlate with the production and circulation of goods and services, although the connection, contrary to what Baudrillard assumes, never completely breaks off.[19] For LiPuma, for example, the growth of the dollar, which far exceeds the growth of production results today, as well as the fact that the circulation speed of money in production decreases, while it increases in the financial markets, indicates a fully circulative capital, which often moves largely independently of production, without completely losing its connection to it (LiPuma, 2017: 79). But what is actually circulating? Marx was interested in the produced table as a commodity that circulates in the markets, and noted that the table is both actor and played character when the table as a commodity in circulation begins to speak. A table may still be a thing for providing a meal today, it may be a speaking commodity and possess an exchange value, but when factors like the interest rates of loans from table-producing companies, options and insurances on the wood price and finally currency fluctuations are overlaid with the various factors in production, and this in the context of the production of further goods and services, a global feast of monetary capital is placed over the extremely modest table (as a physical object and exchange value).[20] *It is always important to consider that the»value« of a financial investment (value of the monetary capital) is not subordinate to the capitalist production process, but precedes it (logically).* It does not exist because either surplus value was produced or another type of income or wealth was realized in the markets, but because financial capital is confident to a certain degree that the realization of returns occur within the framework of the production/circulation of capital in the future and will repeat itself according to the standards of the expanded reproduction of capital.

But it is also necessary to discuss again whether this actually means that the classic surplus value no longer plays any role at all, and has, so to speak, lost its significance with the ecstasy of speculation. In late capitalism, there is a gradual transition towards a parallelization of a slight growth of industrial capital and an ecstatic growth of financial speculative capital.[21] Where the growth of real capital stagnates, speculative capital ecstaticizes in the quantum cosmos. The pure ecstasy is now the (virtual) quality inherent to financial capital, which spirals within itself to run hot in its pure form, but its circulation, which is always in motion, becomes "cool", fascinating, and obscene with the acceleration, with what circulates more than the circulation itself. However, indetermination and uncertainty also penetrate into every circulating and calculable financial risk, challenging the abstract mathematical structure that prevails in the logic of capital, so that the already failing hyperdetermination of capital in the rush of an abundance of money as bubbling volatility/liquidity in the circulation of circulation is turned up another notch.

Wherever there is nothing left but the relations of pure money capital, hyper-accelerating and simultaneously saturated speculative capital forms; in a system where the circulation of capital is increasingly exposed to speculation, the surplus is a multiplicative quantum delirium that includes hyper-speculation with even the smallest amount of money in the metastases of circulation. Quantum mechanical determination orientation-capital. The quite logical exaggeration, this escalation of floating money, polycentrizes capital, makes it shoot in waves in all directions, and creates quantum wave capital that circulates at light speed, this last reference point that still needs to be overcome, until there is finally no (rational) measure left with which the capital flows could still be measured—this ecstaticizing without measure translates Marx's formal measurelessness of capital[22] into the hyperreal of speculation, which is visible only on screens, telematic capital. The accelerating hyperspeculation makes capital also sluggish and saturated. No metastasis without stasis.

The fictitious/speculative capital must circulate. Gravity and any fixed point must disappear in the circulation channels; the chain of investments and reinvestments must never stop, the capital must radiate endlessly and in all directions, without ever losing itself. Thus, analogous to quantum theory, two capitals can overlap or overlap immanently despite and in competition, and their identity is preserved even when they produce a third capital, which is not to be understood as a synthesis of the first and second capitals nor as a destruction of both capitals, but as an expanded capital of the same type. In the state of superposition, the capitals virtualize and thus precisely avoid their principal distinction. The concept of superposition takes over here the role of ecstatic immanence, which constantly absorbs its own transcendence and transforms it into a new level of hyper-immanence.

The circulation time of capital, whether it is commodity, production or money capital must always be further reduced. But if the circulation time of capital were equal to 0, the system would enter into a kind of paralyzing standstill. In order to "be" what it will have been, as Lenger puts it, capital would have overtaken itself (Lenger, 2004: 228). Marx therefore wants the possibility of a speed that could stage the cancellation of various times, although he addresses it, does not allow it.[23] Although capital has this "dromological" (Virilio) tendency, certain limits are evident. If the circulation of capital were "absolute", i.e., if it no longer had to bridge any temporal or spatial distances that would allow it to iterate, it would have made itself impossible. For the télos of capital is to return richer, which means it depends on a quantitative difference that it must at least also pass through temporally in order to multiply as money. But even the speed of light in high-frequency trading can be too slow in a certain sense, so that geographical distances play a greater role again, which means that in a business deal that a trader in New York offers simultaneously to a trader in London and Frankfurt, the trader in London is preferred because the signal sent at the speed of light takes longer to reach Frankfurt than London. So time cannot be completely abolished for capital. Nevertheless, according to Marx, it remains the necessary tendency of capital to strive to set the circulation time = to zero, i.e., to abolish itself, since for capital the circulation time causes costs and is set as a moment co-determining the production time. To remain capital, the immanent tendency to release infinite speeds must constantly be suspended and induced.

The utopian goal of limitless accelerating growth at least indicates that the economic is totally obsessed with itself and becomes its own perversion and obsession—hyperreal and overcapitalized, it becomes fat feeding on itself. The obesity of capital—capital stuffed with capital, as if capital were pregnant with itself—is evident in the fact that every financial transaction must be stored and recorded on media in order to keep the system operational and at the same time to pay homage to a monstrous potentiality in lost motion towards the (never ending) end run. Capital, according to its own logic, projects a future that it has long since predetermined for itself, thereby denying and betraying its openness and blackness. Under the conditions of a "destruction of space", as Marx writes, it is also time that capital devalues, insofar as circulation causes costs that reduce surplus value. To become what it will have been, it will still have to break through the horizon of this space–time to reduce it to zero (which cannot succeed).[24] Financial speculation in ubiquity and real time is today becoming the dominant parameter in which capital not only rushes towards its own future, but also wants to catch up with and overtake the horizon of its own future. It wants to leave this horizon behind in order to fulfill the promise of "absolute self-presence" that is inherent in its formal sliding process.

Capital is now always also the spaceless space and the timeless time, the present quantum catastrophe. Capital overtakes itself in the rhythm of communication and information technologies and requires ever deeper digital networks. It raves in the inflation of derivatives and constantly peddles its own hysterical hypostasis—it becomes hypertelic according to Baudrillard (Baudrillard 1991: 13). Capital has always been at least telic: "Desire is desire of presence. Eros too is thought from the perspective of presence. Like movement. Hegel calls the telos, which sets the movement in motion and directs becoming towards itself, the absolute concept or subject" (Derrida, 1988: 70). The tautology of capital consists precisely in always aligning itself in its becoming only with itself. But financial capital wants to increase itself to the x-th power in its ecstatic period and even overtake itself. In the end, the speed would become negative, or would be a contra-operationalization to acceleration. Let's assume, an object orbits the Earth and is so fast that it overtakes itself, even multiple times, and this self-overtaking continues to increase, then the effect is that the object is slower than itself, namely n-fold.

Capital requires a technical economy of performative sentences, where pronouncing them already means having realized them. And in this, a scenario emerges for Lenger as well as for Baudrillard, in which speculative capital ecstatically overdrives itself, has left the "Globe" and has entered an orbital satellite space. But with such a destruction of times and spaces simultaneously, insoluble non-simultaneities break open on the globe and drive new conflicts, which are still to be located in the context of the internal boundaries of capital. Deleuze and Guattari write: "The difference therefore does not cancel itself out in the quotient, which constitutes it as an essential difference, the 'tendency' has no end, no external boundary that it could reach or even approach. The tendency only has an internal boundary, which it crosses, but by shifting it, that is, it reconstitutes it as an internal boundary that must be crossed again by shifting it, reinvents: thus the continuity of the capitalist process is generated in this constantly shifted incision of the incision" (Deleuze & Guattari, 1981: 296). In the midst of the globalizations, spaces and times are thus torn open, which are characterized by a lack of code and profit, they are according to Lenger "uncodable incisions of barbaric inscriptions, which return ungovernable" (Lenger, 2004: 229).

The moment of (temporal) infinity of capital is in itself nothing new. Capital is in a certain sense the infinite, since at least formally and without any interruption the end of a capital cycle forces the beginning of a next and expanded cycle, and this both at the level of individual capital and at the level of total capital. The self-realizing capital is thus initially empty growth. If capital accumulation is an increase in emptiness, or to put it another way, a tautological increase, then this is formally so for C. Arthur (Arthur, 2022: 204). Capital must always be in a process of infinite becoming in which it manifests itself, but always also disappears in a new specific negation.[25] Capital exists only as the process of negation of its current form in favor of an expanded future form. Its movement is the self-representation of capital through its negative.[26] In reality, capital has a double existence, because in addition to itself as a boundless form, it can only accumulate by seeking an adequate content in the economic metabolism. The Hegelian Marxism of a C. Arthur speaks with regard to the latter aspect of a negation of the negation, in which the negative, the labor power, with its integration into the industrial production process and its subordination to the movement of capital is negated again. The spiral of accumulation generates in industrial capital also a wealth of new material contents, e.g. new productive forces, further commodity production and so on.

This kind of negativity has disappeared in fictitious and speculative capital, as we have already hinted at with remarks on the concept of ecstasy and the power set. The ecstasy of capital as metastasis is more speculative than speculative, it implies a quasi deterritorialized and de-temporalized money capital, which as exaggeration accelerates through itself, up to the realization of the pure form, to its ecstatic glow. Capital now requires as the realization of the formally boundless movement an excessive About. As a purely formal sliding process, capital already produces systemic scarcity as a lack of more, or inaugurates the famous excess, whereby the anticipation of more, oriented towards the future, dominates scarcity and not vice versa, so that a representation of the economy oriented towards the explication of scarcity is excluded from the outset. The excess (as anticipation of more) of capital, or more precisely the more of money capital, dominates scarcity and not vice versa. In this procedure, capital establishes itself as an absolute process not only in relation to itself, yes, it even sets its environment as an autoreferential system and thus first attains its characteristic ultra-stability, which, however, cannot be separated from its cyclically moving ultra-instability or susceptibility to crises.

The latter is manifested today in the fact that global speculative capital jumps from "bubble to bubble", is trapped in the cloning of derivatives, the effects of which today permeate all technologies, real estate markets, and government bonds. Financial activities also keep real capitalist production running. As will be soon seen. Financial capital and its instruments are now the systemic driving forces. While bubbles in the past were both temporally and spatially a rather isolated phenomenon (when bubbles burst, they made way for new cycles of real accumulation), today a bursting bubble in the course of a persistent crisis transitions into another bubble (inflation of bubbles) (Vighi, 2022: 115). But this also means that the bubble formation process theoretically does not have to find an end, which can also be supported by the mathematics of fractals, because the fractals generate their basic structure anew at each stage of its reiteration. In this process, a loose monetary and credit policy leads to excessive borrowing and the purchase of assets that are rising in price, leading to further purchases of assets and increased spending on goods and services. Eventually, this cycle reaches a point where it becomes unstable. Loose monetary policy leads to overheating and inflation and forces central banks to interrupt this policy.

Modifying a Baudrillard quote about the all too willingly voting masses, one could now write: The financial industry sprinkles and infects the excited and at the same time exhausted nervous system, makes the involved actors invest until they themselves want to invest more and more often, and they would actually like to invest even more. This does not mean that they possess a trivial greed or believe in the meaning of finance—on the contrary, it expresses a bulimic and quasi-capital-generated and automated desire for money: The financial system becomes voracious through itself and it is incrementally swallowed and digested. It empties itself and rids itself of itself through a surplus—the whole system transforms into a huge white financial belly. The financial simulation sucks up all the energy of the real and spits it out again as an excess of the hyper-real. The system suffers incurably from the circulative repetition, indeed from the ecstasy of the same from the same.

This can be illustrated briefly at this point by the circulation and securitization of derivatives such as CDOs. These contain hierarchically structured claims to payments, in tranches that are assumed to be safe, and in uncertain tranches, even the risky papers of which were bought up again before the financial crisis of 2008 and packaged into new promises of payment. If a company buys the papers threatened with default in sufficient quantity, the risks can be bundled again and financed through further tranched securities, thus creating third-degree CDOs, etc. However, the packaging of CDOs into CDOs of CDOs and into third-order CDOs does not eliminate the non-linearity and diachrony of risk structuring, but instead leads to an implosion of the CDOs and at the same time intensifies the interdependence of financial institutions, through the successive increase in mutual credit claims.[27]

Baudrillard speaks in the context of trans-economy about the enormous masses of floating, even flying money, that whirl around the Earth in an orbital cycle (Baudrillard, 1992a,1992b: 33). Speculative financial money is today the most important artificial satellite. As a pure artifact, it enjoys truly astral mobility and is instantly and universally convertible. Money has now found a non-place, which is much more fluid and wondrous than the stock exchange, namely that of the orbit, where it rises and sets like a sun (ibid.). The credit system, the financial world, the technosphere, communication—all have become satellites in an inaccessible space and have left the real economy to stagnation or even decay. According to Baudrillard, we are in the age of the weightlessness of money, which circulates in an orbital motion at the speed of light, which threatens to become eternal.

For Marx, however, there were still "natural barriers" to this lightly floating movement, initially addressing agriculture and nature in general, which resist the real-time movement or the absolute speed of capital. Technologically induced speeds can reduce these barriers to nanoseconds today, but not completely dissolve them. Marx seems to expect a certain resistance of the "real" that cannot catch up with or dissolve itself in "real time". Here, Baudrillard's Real should be referred to as the limit of the system, which is to be distinguished from the Real, which the system itself produces and integrates (Butler, 1999: 17). The first Real would resist the dictate of performative sentences or the speeds at which capital wants to realize itself in absolute presence and thus perhaps even overtake itself. The second Real, on the other hand, sneaks economically into the system via the money symbol, which has the status of a "reality", and this could enter a hyper-accelerated stage via credit and derivatives. With regard to industrial production and circulation, Marx further relativizes: "The circulation artists, who imagine that by speed of circulation they can do something other than shorten the obstacles to its reproduction set by capital itself, are on the wrong track (even more crazy, of course, are the circulation artists who imagine that by credit institutions and inventions, which abolish the duration of circulation time, not only to eliminate the stay, the interruption in production, which requires the transformation of the finished product into capital, but to make capital itself superfluous, against which the producing capital exchanges; i.e. to produce simultaneously on the basis of exchange value and to want to eliminate the necessary conditions of production on this basis, to bewitch away" (Marx, 1974: 450). With today's technical-media speeds, the circulation time of industrial capital can indeed be shortened, but never reduced to zero. Only when the goods are realized on the market can the money be reinvested. The end of one cycle is separated by an irreducible, even if minimal, caesura from the beginning of a new cycle. We have already mentioned this.

Not because of acceleration by means of transport and transmission technologies, but under the conditions of credit, stocks, and derivatives, a new production cycle can start before the surplus value of the previous cycle is realized. With credit, a time-technique is established that allows new production while the product of the previous cycle is still in production or circulation and is not realized yet. The credit is granted on the not yet realized surplus value and enables its production. Thus, capital anticipates the future and breaks through its horizon. Marx sees this very well:

"The necessary tendency of capital therefore *circulation without circulation time*, and this tendency is the basic determination of credit and the credit contrivances of capital. [...] This is a form of the *Circulation without circulation time*. Money itself is a product of circulation. It will show how capital in credit creates new products of circulation" (ibid.: 561). With credit, capital is relieved of certain restrictions of space and time, insofar as production can now be continued directly in a new cycle without having to wait for the realization of the surplus value that comes from the previous production cycle. Times and spaces are advanced or anticipated, with "future" production becoming seamlessly "present" (Lenger, 2004: 234). Thus, credit and derivatives introduce time techniques that outperform all communication and transport technologies. Options even allow for capital investment in future productions, which are still in question whether they will take place at all. Here, the determination of money capital in itself is articulated, which now becomes the pure instruction for future work and capitalization. With credit, future work, which is still pending in the horizon of realization, becomes "real" insofar as it can start again, even though the previous production cycle is not yet completed, on the other hand, "real" work itself becomes speculation, insofar as future production is negotiated on the financial markets.

Credit and derivatives thus not only appropriate the present, but above all a future that is monetized as "present". In this respect, there is no future that would still be black and incomprehensible to the present and could open up a horizon of possibilities, because the future becomes an element of a present that discounts it. Capital has overtaken or at least caught up with its own "future" and thus destroys the last retreats of time that had still opened up in the horizon of possibilities (ibid.: 236). Nevertheless, according to Derrida, this kind of presence always comes too late and demands a time that drives the ecstasy of money capital, and precisely in this excess, every future otherness becomes again the hostage of an expanding "present", which nevertheless always faster, finally today with the help of quantum technology, must capitalize the future.[28]

However, just as capital accumulation cannot completely free itself from the restrictions of spatialization through a dromology of traffic and communication processes, it is not possible on the level of credit (and derivatives) to make all restrictions disappear. At least for Marx, credit is still dependent on "work", even if it does not have to be expended in the present and is therefore postponed. "The ›product‹ of credit economy is always already dead, present and not yet born" (ibid.: 238). Credit refers to future surplus value, today one must add especially also to a future monetary capitalization. Although the deferral can always be stretched anew, insofar as one credit can be replaced by another and integrated into a chain of securitizations. While credit thus discounts a potentially infinite future, it must nevertheless preserve its own viability and repayability in each individual case.

With equity capital, property titles are created in which capital, at least according to Lenger, is copied or cloned in the imaginary. Thus the sum of money circulates twice, namely once as money, and again as an instruction for money. The lack of more is thus doubled.[29] This semiocracy, as Baudrillard or Lenger call it, seems to have detached itself from the real as well as from the symbolic. Lenger writes with reference to Baudrillard, that the share capital would circulate as an imaginary in a mirror stage, and equates this with the simulacrum, which has rid itself of all relations to the real as well as to the symbolic. Share capital represents a title that, like a copy, relies on the "reference" of its mirror stage. Lenger writes: "In a certain way, the imaginary capital thus quotes what has been silently delivered to it as a lack, in order to condense this lack into a positive given and let it float ... Imaginary or fictitious capital is not only the ›last word‹ of an Oiko-semiotics of expression. In a certain respect, it is rather its ›first‹. It merely expresses that the logic of expression and symbol is always and inherently 'dominated' by the dictate of the imaginary" (ibid.: 240).

However, neither fictitious nor speculative capital is to be understood as essentially imaginary, especially not with reference to Baudrillard. For he has assigned the mirror and its duplications to another epoch than the current epoch of simulation and speculation with reference to Lacan's mirror stage. Baudrillard writes that reality today is no longer the reflective truth of the mirror, but the manipulative truth of the test, which tests and questions, of the laser, which probes and cuts, of the matrices, which store sequences, of the genetic code, which controls combinations, of the cells, which inform a sensory universe, and one must add, of speculation, which multiplies money (Baudrillard, 1976). So it is not about the doubling of the real/reality in the imaginary, but about the transformation, generation and reconstruction of reality in and through simulation, and exactly this hyper-reality appears particularly real, because it also contains the principles of perception and actions as construction factors of reality as well as the construction methods of the models themselves.

Even if the financial claims are realized, they can also cause economic devastation that makes everything on which the claims for the future had been set already destructive in the present. We have already spoken of the destructive creativity of derivatives and loans. For example, the claims on the indebted countries in the Global South can never be fulfilled by them, because the interest burden alone overwhelms their economies, but these claims can also not be cancelled or even deleted. This would cause the prices of certain assets to crash and trigger global crises.

Against this background, it is by no means paradoxical for Baudrillard that the economy triumphantly returns to the agenda—although it is questionable whether one can still really speak of economy in the classical sense, insofar as its engine is now financial capital, which can at any time in the context of floating risks also bring about the destabilization of the real economies. With the escalations of speculative capital, which indeed have something of metastatic capital clones about them, inflationary surges on the financial markets (asset prices) are today the order of the day, and in times of boom there is an ecstatic proliferation of financial simulacra. Financial capital announces the victory of a weightless digital economy, which on the one hand has largely freed itself from the "real economy" and indulges in pure speculation, but on the other hand must also repeatedly control, test, and regulate the real economy on the financial markets, so that one cannot speak of an absolute detachment of financial capital from industrial capital (Milios, 2003). The distinction between "real" and fictitious/speculative capital therefore does not mark an absolute break that would have completely torn speculative capital away from a "referent" and transformed it into a purely free and purely circulating and floating movement. Marx seems to follow this line in certain passages of *Capital*, with which the fictitious capital separates itself from the "real" capital, even floats self-referentially, without maintaining a relationship with real capital. In this respect, he speaks of fictitious quantities, probably rather derogatorily referring to them as 'crazy'. If today the accumulation of money capital is understood, among other things, as the accumulation of claims (assets) and promises of payment on future production, of which no one knows whether it will ever take place, and furthermore also as the accumulation of claims on the production of further assets, then the reference to industrial real capital actually becomes increasingly fragile (Lohoff & Trenkle, 2012) Both capitals also differentiate themselves from each other through a different rhythm—where the "real" capital constantly repeats the exchange with labor, the fictitious and speculative capital continuously repeats the financial trade of its instruments (stocks, bonds, derivatives). Thus, speculative capital only indirectly exposes itself to living labor, and it can at least for certain periods limit itself to multiplying as money capital in relation to other money capital (via assets and derivatives). It designs and designs options and futures on production cycles that may never take place or calibrates a future on the financial markets that can become impossible through other strategies and options. The nature of the relationship and non-relationship of the two economies and their relationship to each other will need to be examined more closely later. For Baudrillard at least, today we are dealing with the dominance of a virtual trans-economy that has separated itself from the real economies and destroyed the classical political economy to transform it into an A-economy of speculation, which only simulates the old economic logic (law of value, market, production, surplus value etc.) (Baudrillard, 1992a, 1992b: 33f.). For Baudrillard, the classical political economy is slowly coming to an end and is also continuing as a remnant through the intensification of its own logic.

The current dominance of the financial industry confronts us, according to Baudrillard, with the nakedness of the capitalist symptom, which is no longer anchored in the modern architecture of liberal-democratic values that were installed to protect industrial capitalism. As a rule, it is said, capitalists invest in the financial industry when the rate of profit in the industrial sectors falls, while the prices of assets rise. The expansion of speculative capital allows companies and the state to maintain the appearance of general prosperity to a certain extent and for a certain period of time, but this prosperity also depends on debt—a paradoxical situation that has taken on a whole new ecstasy of debt in the last three decades. The massive increase in global liquidity in the form of bank loans, securitized debts and especially derivatives (from 150% in 1990 to 350% of global GDP in 2011) inevitably leads to financial bubbles, with states and central banks having to save their banking systems since the financial crisis of 2008 by increasing their own borrowing. The rising private debt (in relation to GDP) was absorbed by the public sector after the financial crisis of 2008, which rushed to the aid of highly indebted companies to prevent a collapse. The result of this maneuver was a significant expansion of public debt. As the McKinsey Global Institute reported in August 2018, global (private and public) debt in relation to global GDP has continued to rise despite the temporary reduction of private debt after 2008, also due to the growing public debt[30] (McKinsey, 2018).

Baudrillard notes an obesity of the current systems, which are so saturated with information, debts, and financial simulacra that they are good for nothing. The system, in the course of overproduction, has even dissolved the use value, if one connotes it with the need (Baudrillard, 2004: 15). This kind of uselessness ironically reduces the neoclassical theory of marginal utility to absurdity. Baudrillard writes: "With this wonderful uselessness comes a specific disgust. The disgust at a world that grows and proliferates and accomplishes nothing. All the memories, all the archives, all the documentation that no longer produce any idea, all the plans, programs, and decisions, that can no longer bring about any event, all these high-tech weapons that can no longer unleash any war!" (Baudrillard, 1992b: 40). The obsession with optimization, the ecstasy of optionality and differentiation creates systems of high complexity and magnitude, which can hardly hide their dysfunctions anymore. Trapped in the paradoxical logic of accelerating metastasis and inertia at the same time, Baudrillard sees a significant risk of exceeding the inertia threshold, the danger of a gravitational collapse by exceeding the critical information and money mass, especially thanks to the absorption of all negative elements by the system: crashes, errors, scandals, conflicts, and crises—everything is absorbed and sucked up. Even the microelements, which despite all fragmentation carry all the characteristics of the macro-structures, now serve Baudrillard only for fractal multiplication (ibid.: 10). Baudrillard speaks of a mad metastability, which however, provokes a whole series of virulent and destabilizing abreactions and crises.

In any case, Baudrillard sees no longer any possibility to spend or productively use all that we have accumulated, even if we recycle parts of the globalized waste and can digest various disturbances in the economy. Lurking in prospect for us, according to Baudrillard, is a creeping or even brutal decompensation, in which every vector and acceleration factor serves to generate inertia and brings us even closer to absolute inertia. To conceal this, chaos must be invoked at every opportunity to then worship the emergency cycle, which since the financial crisis of 2008 increasingly proves to be the gushing tap of central banks. What we call crisis is for Baudrillard always also a premonition of absolute inertia. Ultimately, attempts are made to mitigate or even eliminate the crisis, because when it appears as a financial crisis and could lead to a grand devaluation of money capital, central banks today immediately mobilize enormous sums of money capital to keep the banks, the shadow banking system, and ultimately the entire economic system running. This is referred to as "emergency capitalism" (Vighi), which is perpetuated by ever new disasters, be it financial bubbles, inflation, stagnation, wars etc. Most of the time, it is then provisionally instructed emergency programs and political interventions that are introduced ad hoc in latent or manifest crisis phases to avoid devastating breaks and implosions. Baudrillard speaks of an energetic dead end, the inertia fate of a saturated world, in which the phenomena of inertia accelerate and growth turns into stagnation. Baudrillard ties the instability of the system at the same time to the implosion, suggesting that the system could collapse in on itself (and not explode through a nuclear war or through the revolution). It is in a state of involution, so it could suddenly collapse in on itself at one point. For Baudrillard, the system today is increasingly accelerating towards its culmination point or its limit, whereby it is the increasing density of simulations that ultimately destroys it (Baudrillard, 1991: 70). The implosion also goes hand in hand with a destruction of meaning in the whirl of the visible and obscene. The crisis-ridden nature of the economy, indeed its general uncertainty, is supposed to be overcome by the constant reinforcement of the artificial evidence of the derivative as well as the government interventions, without however preventing curvatures and deformations up to the implosion. The implosion is for Baudrillard the secret of hyper-telia, whose end, however, is not foreseeable (ibid.: 13). For, as Baudrillard also sees it, it must never be forgotten that capital is formally a blind process that abhors stagnation. Once things are liberated after the orgy, money begins to float freely in speculation.

It is not at all said that capital implodes due to its own gravity, at least it can release media escape velocities and a cheapening of the fixed capital with digital technologies, so that it continues to exist, even if it escapes itself. Its existence as a perpetuum mobile today always results from the mechanization of codes and simulation models, which capital appropriates as a war machine. For Lenger, in contrast to Baudrillard, it is not about the problem of whether these techno-financial accumulations and cycles could eventually die in an implosion or discharge in a deadly crisis. Indeed, Lenger argues, a curve could be drawn according to which the mass of the surplus value produced due to automation and the replacement of living labor power would no longer be sufficient at a certain point to continue the expanded capital accumulation, insofar as the technologies have in a certain way liberated themselves as means from their respective ends and the highly technologized accumulation rate has reached a level that shows that the living (classical) surplus value is exhausted and the system implodes under its own gravity. Following Henryk Grossmann, Robert Kurz also surrendered capital to the fate of an inevitable collapse due to the dwindling of surplus value. The system would have entered an insurmountable phase of its own agony. But for Lenger, this is not sustainable. We have also discussed and criticized this extensively elsewhere. It is precisely the case that a system that so fanatically defends its own implosion could have many more shocks in store for us. In the current regime of simulation and the fractal, social and economic realities are increasingly generated by derivatives, codes, signs, and models, technologies that are enforced with shock strategies and precede the real, indeed the technologies produce the real as hyperreality, which is both the medium and the message. As a result, the models, codes, and signs refer to nothing more than themselves. In the hyperreal, obsession circulates as the outbidding and ecstasy of signs by signs, and above all as the outbidding and ecstasy of money capital by money capital.[31]

It is far from certain whether the system cannot continue to shift its inner limit. At least the following can be said: The famous immoderation (as anticipation of the more) of capital means that the more dominates the lack and not the lack the more. Thus, capital as a process not only sets itself, yes, as an autoreferential system and at the same time as a turbulent quantum system, it even sets its environment and thereby first attains its peculiar ultra-stability, which, however, cannot be separated from its general ultra-instability (susceptibility to crises) (Schwengel, 1978: 201). The processes of ultra-stability-in-ultra-instability (of total capital) must be thought of as virtualized superimpositions that actualize as strategies of individual capital. Contrary to the exclusive foundation of surplus value in the exploitation of living labor power, we also assume the possibility of a machine, an algorithmic and a monetary and financial surplus, which arises from the exploitation of differences and quantum superpositions, which flow into the pure addition of the more.

Finally, there remains the "discourse" of economics, which subsumes technology. Lyotard writes: "The acceleration of the time beat and generally the oversaturation of the community's schedule result from the extension of the economic discourse to sentences that are not subject to the exchange rule [...] There are now possibilities to completely subject the actually uncatchable téchne of machine language programs to the dictate of economic expressions" (Lyotard, 1989: 288). Capital invests en masse in digital technologies of codes, algorithms, and a-significant semiotics, which not only increasingly operate automatically, but also simultaneously write new reservoirs of what is "free" for capital.

Notes

1. Questions of digitalization, artificial intelligence, automation, and platform capitalism are dealt with in more detail in the upcoming book "In the Delirium of Simulation: Baudrillard Revisited" (Szepanski, 2024).
2. The denial of reality as a reaction to the simulation and artificial intelligence, which confronts us with the final stage of post-truth, manifests itself in the following: If I am no longer able to understand where the deception is hidden, I can believe in nothing of which I am not a witness myself. Then there is only the delusion of immediacy.
3. Money is recorded in figures and sums on accounts, it exists as a measure in these pure numbers. At the same time, money is endowed with a very special power, namely the power to be exchanged for any kind of something. As a quantified, non-substantial thing, money is the comprehensive power of access to x-anything. Bockelmann writes: "Rather, it becomes the measure itself, a measure in itself, pure quantum as a quantity existing purely for itself between commodities. And money becomes this according to the following, now well-known logic. Money, as the one and pure medium of exchange that can be exchanged for virtually any commodity, can itself only be determined quantitatively, as a pure quantity. And since it must stand for virtually all commodities, it must itself appear in virtually every possible quantity, it must be able to assume all numerical values in a freely scalable manner. And this is the result: Money as the one thing—exchanged for virtually all goods—and therefore as a pure quantity in freely scalable numerical values" (Bockelmann, 2020: 215).

   As a pure quantity, money inherits the reproduction of an abstract unit, it is the pure number. One calculates and measures in the abstract unit, with the number one being fundamental, and in this abstract unit of calculation, money is the measuring entity. Money is the calculating unit of the many, insofar as it accomplishes the unity of the economic system of the many (Brodbeck, 2023: 50) Because it serves as a measure, it is, it can not be measured in turn, that is, money has no value. It is the unit in and with which all market participants quite naturally calculate; the unity of the many qua the many must be realized as a process of social validity, which in turn is recognized by all money subjects.

As a multiplication of this abstract unit, money can take the form of the infinite number series, 1, 2, 3, 4 etc. Money must be distinguishable as a discrete entity, and there must be a similar multitude of this entity. It is thus always also pure quantity. Money as an abstract measuring unit is always related to something, to measured non-money or goods. In calculating with money all things are measured in an abstract unit or with the same measure—money is the abstraction of a number, the one, in calculation (Brodbeck, 2013). It shows the structure of quantitative relations that then become the form of thought of social and thinking calculation to mathematics. One now counts and pays. The monetary transactions and their networks need not be backed by anything material (they represent, for example, no gold); they take place today as difference in the digital code in the form of algorithms.

But zero must definitely be added to one, as Brodbeck has shown (ibid.). Zero gives the numbers a position, it is a placeholder that leads to an ordering of the numbers in a system of counting, which is infinite (Brodbeck, 2009: 921). A number like the 3 gets a higher rank through zero: 30, 300, 3000 etc. Zero multiplies the social fiction given in the unit of calculation and assigns a higher rank to a digit in validity.

4. On the question of the end of history in Baudrillard, see Szepanski (2024).
5. The future 2 shows itself here in that money in the present is valued by what it is supposed to have been worth in the future. Since one cannot calculate in advance what the money will have been worth in the future, the money can only be calculated purely speculatively in its relation to itself, or in other words, the speculative calculation with the money is its own permanent temporalization, which actualizes the money regime and at the same time always pushes it further forward, in other words, present futures and future presents are not identical, i.e., as soon as a future present actually becomes current, the difference to that future that capital expected (present future) and whose prospects it once used, also updates, and so always different futures than the expected ones return to the

present (Cf. Esposito, 2010: 177f.). The temporal circularity of the financial economy, according to Elena Esposito, consists exactly in the fact that the present is dependent on the future, which in turn is referred to the present, which is oriented towards it (ibid.: 28). This means that we are dealing with an extension of the present into the future, in a very twisted sense, with the future perfect tense of "It-will-have-been". This also means that capital, so to speak, always already goes into the future with its back—it relies on its own undeniable uncertainty and unavailability, but also on the fact that things will always have gone well (for capital) from behind. And this view of the future presents the future as a closed future, precisely because the future is determined exclusively from a horizon of expectation that wants to eliminate the truly new, and not only that, capital is its future, it has already stipulated its future and it has determined it, which immediately indicates that this ominous occupation of the future, which is devoid of any anti-axiomatic surprise and virulence, can only be written from the perspective of the future perfect tense, although even this time is to be overcome again and again—the continuum of capital therefore insists on rushing towards its future in perfect neutrality, on the one hand, and on constantly having to overtake its own future, its trauma par excellence, which is to be caught up with through the capitalization, which in the context of its future research relies on absolute self-presence or actuality, but cannot be caught up with.

6. The economy slides into an abyss, accelerates in the void and multiplies through the endless circulation of money. For Baudrillard, money is the equivalent of the universal circulation of nothing and speculation is a kind of ecstasy of value, indeed a pure, empty form (Baudrillard, 1992b). The surplus in the context of the void is to be understood in a similar way to Heidegger's "grounding abyss" as fundamental. It stands for the non-counting, the non-one, when it is only about the intensive multiplication, for which the quantity is simply irrelevant. The name of this economy is the void. After all, global debt consists of debts that will never be repaid.
7. Military conflicts like Gaza open new possibilities for profit. Wars followed by reconstruction fuel profits not just for the military industry, but for engineering, high-tech, and energy, all combined with the transnational financial centers of the global economy. In 2022, leading US corporations such as Lockheed Martin,

Raytheon, Northrop Grumann, and General Dynamics were the most successful companies in terms of their stock price increase and market capitalization. In particular, the war in Ukraine was an excellent business for Western companies.

8. For Maurizio Lazzarato, the new fascism is a mutation of historical fascism in the sense that it appears national-liberal instead of national-socialist (Lazzarato, 2021). The left-wing political movements are so weak today that the fascists don't even need to pick up their demands and twist them, as the fascists and the Nazis did in the 1930s. The new fascism no longer needs socialist disguises, on the contrary, it is ultra-liberal: It is for the market, capital, and individual initiative, even though it demands a strong state for the exclusion of minorities and "foreigners", a state that at the same time must absolutely secure the "free" market, business, and above all capital.

   The new reactionary libertarians go even further in restricting the role of the state than the neoliberals: The state should not only be deprived of the education system, health system, and infrastructures, but also sovereign powers, by further promoting the privatization even of the army, the police, and the judiciary. Nevertheless, economic libertarianism or the avant-garde of the second financialization (asset managers and hedge funds) on a political level has extremely authoritarian tendencies. When an ultra-hard austerity policy must be pursued, which no longer knows any financial and social redistribution downwards, it is necessary to prevent any potentially emerging social movements in advance by staging the restriction of freedoms and rights, and possibly only the use of violence remains to regulate social life depending on the situation. Freedoms are cashed in to preserve the fundamental freedom of the right to property and capital.

   People now also speak of Neo-Illiberalism, which is based, among other things, on the fact that neoliberalism has lost its ideological appeal after the financial crisis of 2008. In an increasingly lawless gig economy, where capital replaces social contracts with offshore anonymity, the transnational capitalist class even manages to buy up governments. The neoliberal endgame is accompanied by breaks and recompositions within the elites, both at the national level and on a global scale. Although neoliberal technocrats like to rant against oligarchs who turn states into plunder zones, neoliberal politics by no means question the power of the oligarchs, whose fortunes are driven to unimaginable heights with the help of central bank politics. This is accompanied by a political illiberalization, which relieves the executive of various constitutional restrictions (ibid.). While the preceding waves of neoliberalization remained more or less within the bounds of legality defined by liberal-democratic norms, rules, and procedures, neo-illiberalization is characterized by an executive machine that increasingly also uses illegal tactics to establish political functional systems that threaten to steer authoritarian neoliberalism into totalitarian tracks through unrestrained digitization. The dismantling of liberal democracies brings about the alliance between authoritarian states and large, data-rich IT monopolies, with the symbiosis between political power and capital accumulation having progressed furthest in China. China promotes parallel processes of market development and political consolidation. The introduction of data-driven technologies increasingly requires the repeal of liberal rules and laws to make way for a political economy based on mass surveillance and AI. The rise of neo-illiberalism recalls that totalitarian and thus illiberal current against which the liberalism of the twentieth century defined itself: fascism. Today's pre-fascism is the result of a capitalist system that escapes its liberal principles of order and in which financial capital is increasingly absorbed by technology. Fabio Vighi also speaks of an illiberal meta-emergency world system that is currently emerging .

9. For Baudrillard, the implosion is always also a consequence of the disappearance of the causes and effects of power. With the principle of causality, the cause generates the effect. Causes therefore always have a meaning and an end, they never lead to catastrophe (they only know the crisis). The catastrophe, on the other hand, draws its energy from the abolition of causes, by flooding them under the influence of the effect and hurling the causal connection into the abyss, thus giving things back their pure appearance or disappearance. The causes have now disappeared, but the effects have become immense—for example, when a local catastrophe causes a global standstill. It is never the causes, but the effects and appearances, which, when they connect with each other, lead to catastrophe. Unlike the crisis, which is only a disorder of causes, the catastrophe is the delirium of effects and appearances. There

is no coincidence at work in all this. For Baudrillard, it is rather a formal connection of the highest necessity.

Once certain limits are crossed, there is no relationship more between cause and effect, but only viral relationships between one effect and another, and the whole system is driven solely by inertia. The development of this force, this speed, and ferocity of the dead, is the modern history of the cursed share. It is not up to us to explain this, according to Baudrillard, but we must be its mirror image in real time. We must overtake the events, which in turn have long since overtaken liberation. The rule of incoherence, anomaly, and catastrophe must be acknowledged.

This creates a problem: The warning of the catastrophe should itself be the catastrophe warning. Whoever thinks this logic through to the end, ends with a tautology: only the real apocalypse is the perfect warning of the apocalypse; only the accomplished disaster would be the proof of a truth that becomes evident as a complete realization in reality; only with self-destruction would humanity have achieved its goal.

10. In capitalist economies today, the phenomenon of the "*over*" as *excess* appears as a catastrophic dystopia:

 - A worldwide debt of 380 trillion dollars, which is growing exponentially.

 - Rapidly increasing deficits in the core countries and the emerging countries.

 - Inflations in the stock, bond, and real estate markets.

 - Hyper-inflation in the derivatives market.

 - Rising inflation with the potential for hyperinflation.

11. Catastrophe systems, like New York City, are vital and alive when the waste energy continues to be productive or when the cursed share is integrated into the system. However, some systems can gain strength, accelerate, and shift into a catastrophic state. In this state of superfusion, the energy resists the rules of regular operation. Instead, it exceeds the principles of this operation, becomes unpredictable and threatens the system that first released the energy.
12. In Deleuze, the quasi-cause refers to the relationship between two or more (incorporeal) effects. In Stoic philosophy, however, only bodies, i.e. material things, can be causes in relation to each other.

For Deleuze, effects are not causes or even properties, but events (Deleuze, 1993).

13. The term energy comes from the Greek and means something like "*acting force*". Energy has the ability to do work, give off heat, or emit light. So it is necessary when something is to be set in motion, accelerated, heated, or illuminated. The oldest source of energy for humanity is the sun. According to the laws of thermodynamics, energy flows tend towards increasing dissipation, while the universe expands towards a complete disjunction. Without movement, there is no thermodynamics and no entropy. Heat and energy are merely terms that describe the movement of matter and have no existence independent of it. The energy of the sun allows plants to grow on earth, which in turn release energy in the form of oxygen, which is then used as energy for the respiration of animals, which as waste is excreted, and so on. By constantly fleeing from itself, nature increases the total entropy in the universe.

    The second law of thermodynamics merely states that motion tends to increase disorder, but not that this must be the case in every instance. Since motion is stochastic, it is also possible that a new order or negentropy can arise, although this is less likely. Negentropy, by negating entropy, stands for novelty and thus also for the complexity of information. Implicit in this is the idea, derived from the information theory of Claude Shannon, that entropy not only releases a dissipation of energy through work, but that it corresponds to an information potential that is transmitted from a signal giver to a receiver.

14. However, exo-somatization can also be interpreted as the externalization of a global power regime, which continuously drives forward resource exploitation, expropriation, and expenditure under growth imperatives. It would then correspond to the neoliberal economy with its postulate of continuous growth (an apparent refutation of what Marx formulated in a reformulation of the second law of thermodynamics as the law of the tendential fall of the profit rate).

15. Heidegger speaks of three ecstasies, the ecstasy of the past, the present, and the future, i.e. the thrownness ("already-being-in-the-world"), the fallenness ("being-with"), and the projection ("being-ahead-of-oneself"). These ecstasies are always already intertwined with each other. Each ecstasy is, according to Heidegger, a rapture

towards something, insofar as temporality is already outside itself and is raptured within itself as past, present, and future (Heidegger, 2005). This is a plea for openness within the respective ecstatic horizon.

16. Or should one say of the more-than-surplus-value? The term "speculatio" does not aim at the gaze, but at the panoramic view and the inverse reflection in the sense of a view (speculare from specula, lookout tower, observation post). In the philosophy from Augustine to Hegel, speculation was presented as a thinking or reflection of the whole or later as a method that produces relevant knowledge, as Whitehead says, a thinking that demands a "system of general ideas" (Whitehead) to enable us to interpret the elements of our experience. In contrast to Hegel, Whitehead's conception moves away from practical and formal reasons and directs the reason towards the question of final causation, it goes less in the direction of critical, but instrumental justification. The term speculation takes an ironic turn in the 1990s with authors like Baudrillard or Kroker, who almost in unison claim that economic speculation in a completely parodistic way puts an end to political economy, inflates it into a trans-economy, which finally operates an ecstasy of value without any reference to production; speculation now no longer pushes for surplus value, but is from now on "more than value". In this sense, speculation is ecstatic. If today derivative contracts not only cut whole units into smallest parts, but also cut and divide the flow of time or the metric, then the distinction between short and long periods, with which one tries to analytically separate investment from speculation, tends to implode. For the French broker Elie Ayache, absolute speculation and contingency is identical, where one encompasses the other, insofar as speculation is an expression of absolute risk (Cf. Ayache, 2010a, 2010b). Beyond the continuous trading of securities, absolute speculation remains infinite, it transforms the ordinary end into an end that can always start anew, it masters the complicated task of producing a medium or a surface at the moment when the complication turns inward as an implication, and this at the same time as it is thought. Implication here means two things: (a) the speculative mode, which depends solely on the thinking/writing of the derivative, which Ayache calls contingent demand, (b) the speculative speed, which tears thinking directly into the medium of

contingency, which for Ayache represents the market. Speculation becomes as dependent on thinking as it becomes independent of it, so that thinking reaches a critical phase where its own stake is at stake, indeed the analytical separation between theoretical and economic speculation is at stake.

17. If more and more money transactions are constantly being linked to an existing series of transactions or if a transformation of transactions into securitized claims takes place, then the multiplication of capital continues as the multiplication process of money capital flows in the form of quasi-postal procedures, so that with each new link a new fictitious capital is created (Lohoff & Trenkle, 2012: 134f.). The integration of various money capitalists into the chains of money and payment flows, all of which include the creditor-debtor relation, leads at least temporarily to the additive increase of the initial capitals; money capital functions in these processes/flows as a self-referential relation, whose code is profit/non-profit.
18. Normally, potentiality refers to the defined and countable amount of possibilities, so that certain events can occur within the framework of laws. However, when the power set comes into play, the whole numbers in their infinity, countability, and totality are problematized. For Cantor and following him Badiou, both the thinkable and the observer-independent contingent are not totalizable.

    The power set axiom according to Zermelo-Fraenkel allows to form the set of all subsets of an original set [for each set (A) there is a set (P), whose elements are subsets of (A)]. Thus, each set can always exceed to the larger power set by regrouping its subsets, leading to an unfinishable multiplication of quantities. If we have a set A of elements (a, b, c), the power set P (A) can be written as follows: [(a), (b), (c), (a, b), (a, c), (b, c), (a, b, c)]. It consists of single sets, subsets and the maximum subset, which is identical with A. It is easy to see that the number of elements of the power set is always greater than the number of the original set, so that a constant exceeding of quantities takes place, insofar as each power set can in turn serve as the base set of a new power set. A constant surplus is created by recombination of the elements. For purely formal reasons, the power set axiom ruins any form of closed whole or totality, since the power set is always larger than the original set, even if it were infinite. Therefore, it also seems possible to have an infinite series of infinite sets. to form, which in turn means that a set (Z) defined as a totality cannot contain the quantity that can be formed starting from the set of the totality (Z) (Meillassoux, 2008: 140f.).

Russell has already demonstrated the logical inconsistency of a set of all sets. It is not possible to construct a set of all objects without including this total set itself as an object, for which one would again need another total set to integrate that object and so on. Therefore, with the power set, a larger set than the previous one can be generated recursively. At least this indicates a possible axiomatization with which the non-totality of a conceivable is defined. However, the question arises whether Cantor's transfinite, which points to the significance of the (necessary) contingency of every law, which can change quickly or rarely in terms of its frequency, or whether this kind of transfinite is actually accessible to ontologization, as Badiou or Meillassoux following him assume, the latter aiming at the incompleteness of nature.

By making it fundamentally possible to think of the incalculable surplus, a speculative economy could come into play beyond the positions of Meillassoux. Assuming that the number of possibilities is not totalizable, it can be assumed that virtually anything can happen on the derivative markets, at any time and in any place; the market would then virtually (virtually inscribed in it) contain the prices of all derivatives of an unfinishable set n, which in turn would indicate the error of the statistical model n – 1. This includes the definition of an absolutely contingent market as a radical alternative to statistics, in which a kind of continuous unfolding of an incalculable more appears. In this situation, the agents on the markets are at the mercy of the system's reality. Ayache links this moment to what Ray Brassier calls stochastic noise or Meillassoux calls the transfinite (cf. Meillassoux, 2008: 140); it is about the detotalization of the number, which ultimately does not allow the trading of derivatives on the financial markets to be automated, as it operates beyond the regions of a calculative reason. However, this is merely an axiom that concerns the virtuality of the market or the unfinishability of profitable activities.

19. In *Capital* Volume 2, Marx starts from three circuits of industrial capital, namely money capital, productive capital (constant and variable capital) and commodity capital, and he captures the

entire cycle of capital in the process formula G - W (PM, AK) ... P ... W' - G'. (MEW24) In the circulation sphere, capital is in the forms of money and commodity capital, in the production sphere in the form of productive capital. Marx refers to these forms as functional forms or functional modes of existence. The entire cycle includes, in addition to the production time (P), two phases of circulation, namely the preparation time (G-W) and the realization time (W'-G'). Marx uses the term circulation not only for the two phases of selling and buying goods (circulation sphere), but also for the entire duration of the capital turnover, which also includes production. Marx then speaks of the total circulation time of a certain capital (MEW 24: 154).

(In the latter, production, marketing, and financialization are increasingly intertwined today; ever larger shares of wage labor are used more for logistical, marketing, and financial activities than for production activities. The accelerating dynamics of these circulations are driven by the rotation speed of the globalized circulation of capital and in turn drive it. The technologies that both the product as well as the cause of this intensification of circulation are provided by the revolutionizing of industrial processes by capital, think of mobile communication, 5G high-speed networks, artificial intelligence, and advanced automation. At the population level, it is now necessary to secure the movement of bodies, goods, and information through network circulations, which are increasingly necessary for a new political economy of accumulation.

The circulation of money capital is the circulation of the capital advanced in the form of money. (Freiburghaus & Müller, 1973: 62) It expresses the driving motive of capital. Money capital must be constantly reinvested and realized at a higher level in each cycle. The circulation of money capital is decisive for the entire circulation of capital, insofar as the latter, as a circulation process, comprehensively structures, represents, and integrates the circular and spiral movements of capital, as it also implies disturbances within the cycles, insofar as it itself functions as a constantly shifting center (MEW 24: 31ff.). Capital Circulant, as Marx also wrote, is not a special form of capital, but it *is* capital (Marx, 1974: 514). The becoming of capital is its self-positing process. This formula of the monetary circulation of capital is the primary mechanism of the capitalist economy, which constantly accompanies and includes commodity production as production-for-profit and production-for-circulation. Although, as Marx notes (MEW 25: 406), money capital is also a transitional moment of the entire reproduction process of capital, but once capitalization is set as the formation of fictitious capital, i.e., the form of capital most developed for Marx, then all qualitative differences of the industrial and commercial individual capitals, their production processes, and their commodities have become secondary. Marx writes: "The circulation of capital is at the same time its becoming, its growth, its life process. If anything was comparable to blood circulation, it was not the formal one of money, but the substantial one of capital" (Marx, 1974: 424). And further: "The circulation of capital is price-setting, not only formally, but really, insofar as it sets the value" (ibid.: 423).

20. William I. Robinson writes that in 2018 only 17 global financial conglomerates together managed $41.1 trillion, more than half of the GDP of the entire planet, and that these conglomerates are so interwoven transnationally that a distinction into clearly delimited companies is impossible (Robinson, 2022: 10).
21. Moreover, financial speculation is an expression of a meaningless a-subjective passion, whose object is fetish-money, whereby economic activities for Baudrillard no longer align with a single purpose and even the simple reproduction of capital is no longer in the foreground, but rather are oriented towards a measure without measure, towards signs and numbers that explicate the meaninglessness of the economy and economic action. It is now always also the means that formulate the ends. So at least Baudrillard (Baudrillard, 2020: 173). In this context, he also speaks of money as a substitute finality, which allows a universal compromise between sense and nonsense to be concluded (ibid.: 175). After a phase of simulation, in which the object becomes a sign, the sign now becomes an object again, but not a real object, but a fetish object, a pure, exchangeable object, which can be any object.
22. The multiplication of money knows no saturation point, because it is not tied to psychological factors of humans, it is a subjectless process.
23. The circulation time remains indispensable for industrial capital to realize surplus value, but everything must be done to make it tend towards 0. When Marx hypothetically sets the circulation

time equal to 0, he outlines the scenario of a shattering of periods that still know a circulation time. He generates an economy with a self-outpacing speed, which now floods the networks of communication media, transport systems, and media. Because circulation costs are to be accounted for as production costs, capital aims at "the télos of infinite speeds of their own realization" (Lenger, 2004: 227). This requires a-human temporalities and aims at topographies of an instantaneous globalization. It could now be a mediality that rushes towards its own dissolution, because the circulation time is supposed to tend towards zero. So it would be about a mediality that is so perfected that it collapses into itself, to achieve an extreme mobilization that would find its télos in a kind of ubiquitous realtime, but even this it strives to overcome (ibid.). What is crucial is not just space, but all resistances of space and time, which oppose the circulating capital. The spirals of capitalization must be run through in ever smaller time quanta. Marx writes in this regard that it is crucial that "these sections are run through in certain *periods* (even the local distance dissolves into time; it is not about the spatial distance of the market, but the speed—the time quantum in which it is reached)" (Marx, 1974: 443).

However, this excess of speed also has an enormous destructive force, which deprives the globe of certain spatial horizons, insofar as globality can now be instantaneously "everywhere" without however, being able to find itself anywhere on this globe. To be everywhere at the same time becomes a dictate for the system (Lenger 2004: 227). "For the simultaneity, which the concept of the ›Global‹ implies, wants to catch up in a technically generated temporality, which it must at the same time minimize" (ibid.: 227–228).

24. Virilio speaks of a transition from the geopolitical to the chronopolitical space, which he understands as the result of an increased "speed-production" (Virilio, 1988: 14). Deleuze and Guattari describe this new type of space as "smooth" space, which in contrast to "striated" space is open, unlimited and not territorially divided (Deleuze & Guattari, 1992: 524). The light-speed information technologies, logistics, and transport techniques have created a chronopolitical type of space, in which all places are at the same distance, insofar as the ecstatic speeds relativize the physical distance. With Marx, Virilio assumes that speed annihilates space

in its extension. We now inhabit time and no longer the earth; chronography replaces geography. Like Baudrillard, Virilio sees in the new communication technologies not only the accelerationist, but also the inertial moment: "We return to a zero point, where no longer the surface of the earth is populated and no longer the real space of the planet is urbanized; rather, the ›real time‹ is populated., their mere appearances and the sporadic fading out of the ›communication partners‹, to which we have all become." (Virilio, 1993: 60)

25. For Arthur, time is a necessary concept of capital, because capital in its logic of negativity needs time to complete its movement through various phases. (Arthur, 2022: 203 ff.). Capital must therefore constantly transform and overcome itself, as an endless change that positions itself in a movement of multiplication. Thus, it constantly denies what it was, only to set and project itself as what it will be. The movement of its time is its reality (ibid.: 205). Its infinite becoming also requires the moment of finiteness in order to determine the rate of accumulation. The time continuum is finite in the interval between two times, over which an accumulation rate can be composed. The movement of capital in its immediacy is abstract in the relationship of capital to itself as it then concretely articulates in its accumulation rate. The measure of the moving capital is therefore not simply a continuous increase of its mass, but its accumulation rate in a certain period of time. This also allows for the comparison of one capital with another; the capital that most closely corresponds to its concept is the one with the highest accumulation rate.
26. What Marx defines as surplus value is for Lacan a sign of surplus jouissance, which coincides with the intervention of a new master signifier that marks the body of the worker as valorized working time (Vighi, 2022: 54). Fabio Vighi similarly assumes, like Baudrillard, that Marx with his concept of surplus value reduces work to a countable, accumulable unit without recognizing that the capitalist signification of work qualifies it as the negative substance of capital, which at the same time functions as the energetic engine of its drive for reproduction (ibid.: 17ff.). In the *Grundrisse*, Marx comes close to understanding the negative of work, so Vighi, when he writes that capital can only position itself by appropriating labor power as non-capital, as pure use

value and thereby making it productive, while labor power as an isolated being is not productive (ibid.: 18). In this sense, Marx speaks of the worthlessness and devaluation of the wage worker as a prerequisite of capital. These remarks coincide with what Marx writes at the beginning of Volume 1 of the *Capital*: "Human labor power in liquid state or human labor forms value, but is not value. It becomes value in a coagulated state, in an objective form" (MEW 23: 65). The crucial point, however, escaped Marx, because primarily surplus value is created as a meaningless splinter of a symbolic/formal operation through which capital calculates the intrinsic worthlessness of labor. Labor power as non-capital, for Marx, is ultimately a positive entity as a producer of use values. For him, labor power enjoys the ontological status of an affirmative potentiality and ecstasy, while at the same time he also considers labor power as non-capital and as pure capacity, as potential for work, which is already present before its capitalist mediation. For Marx, labor power is a plus, which, when appropriated by capital, creates a surplus for the capitalist. In the Hegelian (and Lacanian) sense, however, labor power is a minus, a negative (impossible, uncountable, unconscious) substance, which precisely as a minus triggers the self-valorization of capital (ibid.: 20). If abstract (wage) labor provides the basis for exchange values and profits, the crucial point of Hegel is not only that production itself is mediated by circulation, but that the essence of labor power proves to be groundless. What Marx misses, according to Vighi, is that labor power not only represents a negation of capital, but above all a negation of itself as a negation of capital. Marx also overlooks the groundlessness of the substance of labor in its justifying function.

Marx indeed also understood labor as a negative anthropological constant and ultimately as a third party that remains within the system of political economy, but is also withdrawn from it. In fact, it was initially the citizen who attributed supernatural creative powers to work, while for the late Marx it was not an essential determination of man that he had to perform certain work under certain economic conditions. Neither essence nor capacity, neither substance nor entity, work eludes any determination. If political economy says that labor is the source and measure of value, then the question would be what the value of this source consists of—as a source, this value would be immeasurable or unmeasurable, and would thus plunge the entire economy into its own immeasurability (Lenger, 2004: 122ff.).

27. For Baudrillard, every derivative would not only be a copy, but would also carry a copy of itself within it and could be exchanged for any other derivative at any time. However, the derivatives are worth different amounts, so they can also be seen as a representation of themselves, and yet they perfectly represent each other, so they can reproduce in any fractal environment. This type of approach is also used with great success by fast food franchise chains, which offer the same environment in every restaurant.
28. The first users of quantum computations are wealth management firms, for which this hardly incurs higher costs. The Spanish company Multiverse Computing has conducted successful pilot projects with customers such as BASF and Bosch, showing that its quantum algorithms can double profits in foreign exchange trading and detect almost four times as many errors in production. Highly technologized economies are always riddled with optimization problems that can be processed ultra-fast by quantum algorithms in the future, thus saving time, energy, and resources. Quantum deep learning algorithms differ from classical algorithms, meaning they can be trained faster, try out more strategies, and have a much higher capacity to recognize important correlations from a large amount of data. Tech companies like Google or Amazon as well as the USA, China, and the EU are fighting for technological supremacy in this area. According to an analysis by the International Data Corp., the global quantum computer industry will grow from $412 million in 2020 to $8.6 billion in 2027. IBM plans to bring a 1,121-qubit processor to market in 2023 and deploy 4,000 qubits by 2025 by developing modular quantum circuits that connect multiple processor chips in a computer (Campbell, 2023).
29. A doubling is found not only in credit but also in the trade of fictitious capital. This happens concretely when a money owner buys property titles such as shares, bonds, or securities, and does this purely with the aim of making more from his money. Quite contrary to the purchase of standard goods from industrial production, which serve either consumption or industrial use, the purchase of a property title implies the specific use of the secondary

use value of money capital, That is, the buyer of the property title uses the secondary or meta-use value of his sold sum of money to generate returns in the future, while the seller of the share, bond, etc. is by no means excluded from the capitalization of the money capital, because, as with the sale of ordinary goods, issuers of shares or bonds, for example, have real control over the money that the sale of the property title brings them (Lohoff & Trenkle, 2012: 131f.). The sellers of the securities now find themselves in a position to apply this new money capital as purchasing power by hiring labor and buying machines, raw materials, auxiliary materials, etc. for the expansion of production, while at the same time the buyers of the property titles trade fictitious capital on the money markets. In addition to the sum of money achieved by the issuer, the fictitious capital of the buyer of the bonds or shares comes into play. This type of business relationship does not merely ensure a mere forwarding of already existing money capital, because (a) in the concrete disposal of a company as an intentionally negative value—capital—it forms the prerequisite for further profit-making production processes, and (b) the buyer can trade the share or bond with the aim of obtaining a surplus on the financial markets.

30. What would happen if capitalism were to implode in and with the cycles of financial circulation by folding into itself, think here of Nick Land's cyber-positive feedback loops, teleonomy, etc. (Land, 2010), and at the same time move with such vector force that they would increasingly trigger the power potentials of (industrial) capital? This gives rise to two hypotheses about virtual-financial capital as pure circulation: On the one hand, the future of capital as empty and end-running—as Baudrillard writes, no unlimited production, no necessary consumption, no romance of use value, no exchange value, no dialectic, only a cycle of digital exchange processes that move with the hyper-speed of financial circulation (i.e., thoughts, light, etc.), or a hyper-capitalism as an explosion of production and a feast of consumption, a period of alternating excess and recession, fetishes everywhere and always, changes of all signs without stability, because the speed of capitalism has reached the speed of economic dizziness. The former is probably more likely.

31. The categories of classical economy lose their dialectic in favor of categories that represent a distributed economic field. The derivatives marked by spreads are relational spaces that allow simultaneous movements in different directions. These movements through time-spaces, where transactions in nanoseconds simultaneously show the disappearance and importance of time, are fractalized under temporal aspects as intervals or times of evaluation, characterized by speed, liquidity, volatility, and realization. This ultra-mobile configuration replaces the usual immobile configurations of points and positions. If one examines the economy more from the point of view of the spread or the spread of speculative capital, then there is no hard opposition between production and circulation, material wealth and financial assets, investment and speculation, because all terms are mutually conditional dimensions of capital. This type of spread includes a specific implementation of the social, which in turn mobilizes a ritual to transform uncertainty into security. Finally, it is about an immanent understanding of the sciences, insofar as the analysis of the financial markets must have a reference to the methods and practices of the agents who construct such markets.

References

Armand, L. (2023). *Entropology*. London.

Arthur, C. J. (2022). *The Spectre of Capital: Idea and Reality*. Leiden.

Ayache, E. (2010a). *The Blank Swan: The End of Probability*. London.

Ayache, E. (2010b). The Turning. http://www.ito33.com/sites/default/files/articles/1007_ayache.pdf

Bataille, G. (1985). *Die Aufhebung der Ökonomie*. Berlin.

Bataille, G. (2021). *Der verfemte Teil*. Berlin.

Baudrillard, J. (1976). *Der symbolische Tausch und der Tod*. München.

Baudrillard, J. (1990). *Cool Memories*. London/New York.

Baudrillard, J. (1991). *Die fatalen Strategien*. München.

Baudrillard, J. (1992a). *Das perfekte Verbrechen*. München.

Baudrillard, J. (1992b). *Transparenz des Bösen. Ein Essay über extreme Phänomene*. Berlin.

Baudrillard, J. (1994). *Simulation and Simulacra*. Michigan.

Baudrillard, J. (2002). *Paßwörter*. Berlin.

Baudrillard, J. (2012a). *Von der Verführung*. Berlin.

Baudrillard, J. (2012b). *The Ecstasy of Communication*. Cambridge.
Baudrillard, J. (2021). *Der verfemte Teil*. Berlin.
Bockelmann, E. (2020). *Das Geld. Was es ist, das uns beherrscht*. Berlin.
Brodbeck, K.-H. (2009). *Die Herrschaft des Geldes: Geschichte und Systematik*. Darmstadt.
Brodbeck, K.-H. (2013). Phänomenologie des Geldes. https://khbrodbeck.homepage.t-online.de/phaenom.pdf
Brodbeck, K.-H. (2023). *Phänomenologie des Geldes*. Zürich.
Butler, R. (1999). *Jean Baudrillard: The Defense of the Real*. London.
Campbell, C. (2023). Quantum Computers Could Solve Countless Problems—And Create a Lot of New Ones. *Time*. https://time.com/6249784/quantum-computing-revolution/
Crary, J. (2013). *24/7: Schlaflos im Spätkapitalismus*. Berlin.
Danowski, D., & de Castro, E. V. (2016). *The End of the Worlds*. Cambridge.
Deleuze, G. (1993). *Logik des Sinns*. Frankfurt/M.
Deleuze, G., & Guattari, F. (1981). *Anti-Ödipus. Kapitalismus und Schizophrenie*. Frankfurt/M.
Derrida, J. (1988). *Randgänge der Philosophie*. Wien.
Esposito, E. (2010). *Die Zukunft der Futures. Die Zeit des Geldes in Finanzwelt und Gesellschaft*. Heidelberg.
Freiburghaus, D., & Müller, H.-P. (1973). *Zur Struktur des Krisenproblems bei Karl Marx*. In: Mehrwert. Beiträge zur politischen Ökonomie 5. Berlin.
Gabor, D. (2016). The (Impossible) Repo Trinity: The Political Economy of Repo Markets. *Review of International Political Economy, 6*, 967–1000.
Kroker, A., Kroker, M., & Cook, D. (1999). *Panik-Enzyklopädie*. Wien.
Lazzarato, M. (2012). *Die Fabrikation des verschuldeten Menschen. Ein Essay über das neoliberale Leben*. Berlin.
Lazzarato, M. (2021). *Capital Hates Everyone: Fascism or Revolution*. Cambridge.
Land, N. (2010). *Fanged Noumena: Collected Writings 1987–2007*. London.
Lenger, H.-J. (2004). *Marx zufolge. Die unmögliche Revolution*. Bielefeld.
LiPuma, E. (2017). *The Social Life of Financial Derivatives: Markets, Risk, and Time*. Durham/London.
Lohoff, E., & Trenkle, N. (2012). *Die große Entwertung. Warum Spekulation und Staatsverschuldung nicht die Ursache der Krise sind*. Münster.
Lyotard, J.-F. (1989). *Der Widerstreit*. München.
Marx, K. (1974). *Grundrisse der Kritik der politischen Ökonomie*. Berlin/DDR
Meillassoux, Q. (2008). *Nach der Endlichkeit*. Zürich/Berlin.
McKinsey Quarterly. (2018). A Decade After the Crisis, It's a Different World. https://www.mckinsey.com/~/media/McKinsey/Industries/Financial%20Services/Our%20Insights/A%20decade%20after%20the%20crisis%20its%20a%20different%20world/A%20decade%20after%20the%20crisis%20its%20a%20different%20world.pdf

Milios, J. (2003). *Zur Darstellung von Marx' Krisentheorie im dritten Band des Kapital* (pp. 47–60). Beitrage zur Marx-Engels-Forschung. Neue Folge 1998.

Plotnitsky, A. (1994). *Complementarity: Anti-Epistemology after Bohr and Derrida*. Durham.

Robinson, W. I. (2022). *Can Global Capitalism Endure?* Atlanta.

Röttgers, K. (2022). *Monetäre Textualität*. Marburg.

Roubini, N. (2022). *MegaThreats: Ten Dangerous Trends That Imperil Our Future, And How to Survive Them*. Boston.

Salle, G. (2022). *Superyachten. Luxus und Stille im Kapitalozän*. Hamburg.

Schwengel, H. (1978). *Jenseits der Ideologie des Zentrums. Eine strukturale Revision der Marx'schen Gesellschaftstheorie. Reihe Metro. Bd.1.* Marburg.

Stiegler, B. (2017). *Automatic Society. Volume 1: The Future of Work*. Chichester.

Szepanski, A. (2024). *Im Delirium der Simulation. Aufsätze zu Baudrillard*. Hamburg.

Virilio, P. (1988). *Geschwindigkeit und Politik. Ein Essay zur Dromologie*. Berlin.

Virilio, P. (1993). *Revolutionen der Geschwindigkeit*. Berlin.

Vighi, F. (2021). The Cental Bankers' Long Covid: An Incurable Condition. https://thephilosophicalsalon.com/the-central-bankers-long-covid-emergency-noise-and-conspiracys-best-kept-secret/?fbclid=IwAR1Nus3syvTQeO2W9w2xCvFDh9C-mTeXxS7YHdWbkooMPl8kYf3iWUnf9Zc

CHAPTER 2

Overaccumulation and Crisis

For Marxists, the phenomenon of *over* is primarily associated with the development of the concept of overaccumulation by Marx, which is certainly not new territory. In this context, Marx speaks of "overproduction crises" and explains: "Overproduction of capital (= plethora of capital), not of individual commodities, (although overproduction of capital always includes overproduction of commodities) means nothing more than overaccumulation of capital" (MEGA II, 4.2: 325). And further: "Overproduction of capital never means anything other than overproduction of means of production—labor and means of subsistence—which can function as capital, i.e., can be used to exploit labor to a given degree of exploitation; in that the fall of this degree of exploitation below a given point causes disturbances and stagnations of the capitalist production process, crises, destruction of capital" (MEW25: 266). Limits to accumulation arise initially because the capitalist economy cannot generate a higher accumulation rate than the one at which the entire economic surplus is reinvested.[1] The mass of value produced is the sum of the transferred value of the means of production (constant capital), the value of the labor force used (variable capital), and the surplus value produced. The surplus value to be accumulated is the driving force of capitalist investments and thus of employment and income growth. Profitability is also the strongest indicator of an impending collapse of

A. Szepanski, *Capitalism in the Age of Catastrophe*, Palgrave Insights into Apocalypse Economics,
https://doi.org/10.1007/978-3-031-57754-3_2

capitalist production. Profits arise from the margin between production costs and selling prices. Technological innovation is related to the compulsion to realize a rising relative surplus value (productivity). New technologies open up new possibilities to maintain and increase the profit rate for individual and total capital, and on the other hand, they enable the valorization in a geologically or biologically significant way.

It is the competition between companies that leads to ever further investments in newer and better machines and technologies. Companies are forced to increase productivity and produce more products per capita. A company must make profits so that money is available to finance further investments. The actual investment of companies is determined by their "internal profit" and their "internal rate of profit", which can each be influenced by the external financing of companies and their leverage effect. (Internal profit = surplus value minus the distributed interest). If investments are the main locomotive for the economic movement, then the rate of internal profit is limited by the rate of overcapacity. Investment decisions are considered dependent in the macroeconomic sequence on: (1) production, which is based on bank financing or credit creation by commercial banks; (2) validation of production through expenditure; (3) distribution of a part of the validated surplus value to external financiers; and (4) the resulting internal rate of profit (Reuten, 2019).

Also with regard to the aspect of external financing, profitable investments are important insofar as banks only lend to a company if its planned investment projects appear profitable. These are future profits that enable loans to be repaid and interest payments to be made (Binswanger, 2019: 47). Through the credit creation of commercial banks, the financing of new investments is made possible without having to save beforehand. It is a necessary condition for growth, but not a sufficient, insofar as pure money creation without investment in real capital can lead to inflation. There is a close correlation between money creation, growth, and profits. We have discussed this in detail at other places (Szepanski, 2014a, 2018a, 2022).

Economic growth requires on the one hand increasing money capital and on the other hand higher employment or increasing labor productivity, which is always tied to a growing and qualitatively improved capital stock (gross fixed capital formation). The slowdown in investment growth and the decline in the investment rate as well as the accumulation rate (growth rate of capital) are to be understood as important indicators of a stagnating capital accumulation. From the perspective of individual capital, it does not matter whether the capital increase results from an investment in functioning physical capital or in financial assets. In order to be able to assess the accumulation tendencies, it is necessary to examine all forms of capital.

Moreover, a "healthy growth" requires a relative balance between the rhythms of the three cycles of capital, which together form the "reproduction schema" in *Capital* Volume II, where the cycle of money capital corresponds to the rhythm of valorization, the cycle of productive capital to the rhythm of accumulation and the cycle of commodity capital to the rhythm of realization.

Overaccumulation occurs with the entry of means of production, which can no longer function as capital, i.e., in the code of profit/non-profit fall on the right side, that is, in interaction with the variable capital, they can no longer guarantee the necessary profitability. Crises are thus characterized by an abundance of capital (constant and variable capital), but it is often overlooked that it is primarily an overaccumulation of money capital, which is accompanied by an overproduction of means of production and unsold consumer goods. With the overaccumulation of capital, there is also a stagnation of demand (consumption restriction) and a falling general rate of profit (of industrial companies), or, to put it more precisely, both factors must be understood as moments of overaccumulation and crisis.[2] It is not easy at this abstract and general level to assume a complementarity of the two factors that characterize overaccumulation. In contrast to the theses of underconsumption theory, it is important to point out that the arrow of causality runs from capital production to demand and not the other way around. It is therefore necessary, to insist on the validity of Marx's thesis that "the size of the accumulation is the independent variable, the size of the wage the dependent variable and not vice versa" (MEW23: 648). The dynamics of capital accumulation determines effective demand and the respective level of employment.

Another important factor for crises is the divergence between the rate of profit and the rate of capital accumulation, insofar as the long-term investments in fixed capital increasingly lead to declining returns. This is reflected in the increase in the ratio between the net operating surplus of a given total economy and the net investments in fixed capital. The reaction of capital to this problem is a decline in investments in fixed capital and instead the search for other investment opportunities such as in the financial industry. Short-termism now begins to dominate long-termism, and the question arises whether this changes the crisis processes qualitatively.

Classical capital accumulation also enters a crisis, when functioning capital is overaccumulated through credit financing, where the production set in motion hits its limits due to the falling rate of profit and goods can no longer be profitably realized due to declining demand. An overaccumulation crisis can therefore begin with the bursting of a credit bubble. In this case, the production of surplus value or its retransformation into additional constant and variable capital is reduced, investments and the employment of wage workers decline. In the crisis, overaccumulated capital and commodity capital are destroyed and devalued until the capacity utilization no longer decreases and the investment processes stabilize again.

The crises of relative overaccumulation, according to Marx, only lead to temporary destabilizations of the capitalist expansive reproduction process and simultaneously implement purifying processes of capital devaluation, which lead to the restoration of a level of profit rates sufficient for companies. Marx thus initially configures a cyclical situation in which enormous amounts of capital have already been accumulated in one economic cycle, but this capital finds no productive possibilities for reinvestment. Thus, for Marx, the capitalist crisis represents an "organic a-rhythm". The factors that determine the outbreak of the respective historical cyclical crisis are always a question of concrete historical analysis for Marx and cannot be reconstructed solely from the tendential fall of the general profit rate, as some Marxists assume who adhere to a monistic crisis theory.[3] Among Marxists today, there should at least be agreement that Marx himself did not present a sophisticated systematic crisis theory. In traditional Marxism, the disproportionality theory was first adhered to, later in the 1930s the underconsumption theory dominated and was replaced in the 1970s by the theory of the falling profit rate. In each phase, it was generally assumed that the prevailing theory was Marx's authentic theory.

Marx thus only dealt with periodic or cyclical crises, while the discussion about structural crises or long-term economic waves (Kondratieff waves), which presuppose a long capitalist history, only began after Marx's death. For Marx, the function of a periodic crisis is the restructuring and potentiation of the economic system. In the *Grundrisse* he also mentions the break with the capitalist system as a "function" of the crisis. Similar to

Bataille, the crisis would then be a radical caesura or a drastic event that could open the gate for a new communist economy of expenditure and luxurious waste.

In this context, Marx also speaks of absolute overproduction. He writes: "There would be an absolute overproduction of capital as soon as the additional capital for the purpose of capitalist production = 0." (MEW25: 261) At a certain point, the system would therefore no longer have sufficient capital available to continue the accumulation profitably and to follow its own télos, to appropriate unpaid labor. The determining factor would now be the fall of the surplus value rate to zero. The system would have entered an insurmountable phase of its own agony. This would be the absolute dystopia for capital.

The following remarks should be made: Cyclical crises may only affect certain countries or regions, while structural crises infect the entire world economy. During the twentieth century, capitalism was in two major structural crises, namely the Great Depression of the 1930s and the stagflation crisis of the 1970s. The financial crisis of 2008 marked the beginning of a new structural crisis of world capitalism.[4] This last major economic event permanently implemented the crisis as a permanent political-economic governance device, which has taken the form of an administration of the economy by financial markets and central banks and thus itself has become a monstrous form of political judgment. (Gentili, 2020: 22)[5] What is now referred to as a "permanent crisis" is no longer a cyclical crisis but affects a new form of societal reproduction. That is, the crisis has become a new general form of the social, political, and economic. We will return to this in the context of the discussion of the poly-crisis.

Historically, the phenomenon of over-accumulation can be classified for the second half of the twentieth century, in which the hegemony of globalized financial capital and new types of accumulation and crisis established themselves, as follows: After the Second World War, the USA became the leading imperialist power in the world and maintains this status despite the rise of China and an increasingly multipolar world order in the international geo-economic and geopolitical comparison to this day, mainly due to military strength, the internationally dominant financial system, and the international reserve and key currency dollar. In the long period of prosperity after the 2nd World War until the beginning of the 1970s, US companies invested 70% of their profits in the internal production processes in their own country and financed 90% of their capital expenditures from internal financial resources. This changed at the latest when the companies' profit rates began to stagnate in 1973, leading to a severe over-accumulation crisis.[6] In addition, the intensifying competition with companies in Japan, Southeast Asia, and Germany led to a reorganization of American capital. The structural crisis of the 1970s, characterized by "stagflation", the combination of stagnation and inflation, was attempted to be overcome by the US capital through factors such as financialization, real wage reduction, and globalization (export of goods and capital). As more and more US companies shifted their production capacities to Asia, the demand for industrial capital in their own country stagnated, leading to a further internal over-accumulation of capital. Thus, financial surpluses were generated that could no longer be reinvested in production and long-term investment capital at least in their own territory. These factors led to a significant increase in investments in the financial sector by large US companies, be it high-leverage financial transactions, massive share buybacks, and bond trading.

The rise of the financial industry in the core countries in the second half of the twentieth century was also promoted by the emergence of petrodollars. In the early 1970s, there was a constant flow of petrodollars into the hard currencies of Europe and the USA, mainly because Saudi Arabia had little opportunity to reinvest the capital raised in its own country. The historically high oil prices, driven by the new demand from India and China, in turn exacerbated the problems of falling profit rates and over-accumulation of industrial capital in the centers. In addition, the high-interest phase, with which inflation in the USA was combated at the beginning of the 1980s, promoted the rise of the financial industry, insofar as the interest rate level, which at times rose to 18 percent, led to an enormous flow of capital also from foreign capital to the US financial markets, while deindustrialization continued in the Rust Belts in the USA.

The problem of over-accumulation of industrial capital was thus answered in the capitalist core countries with the creation of new fictitious and speculative capital and the reorganization of the financial markets as the decisive spaces for financial investments. Added to this were factors such as globalization and logistics. The starting point for the rise of the global financial sector, starting from the liberalization of exchange rates after 1971 over the deregulation of the large banks to the growth of the shadow banking system and the derivatives and foreign exchange trading as well as the explosion of public and private debt was thus the exhaustion of productive dynamics in the industrial sector in advanced economies, leading to a stagnation of profit rate levels. There was a reorientation of capital, away from domestic productive investments towards the search for higher returns in the global financial sector and in globalized production chains. Derivatives and other securitization instruments have forced the transfer of surpluses, which were previously invested in longer-term capital investments, into the financial industry.

Indeed, since the 1970s, there has been a transfer of idle money capital into the financial sector. Consider the transfer from the stagnating industrial areas in the Midwest (Ohio Valley) of the USA to capital-hungry California, where new technology companies, financial institutions, and the logistics industry settled. It was financial companies like Salomon Brothers that created financial instruments such as mortgage bonds and "Collateralized Mortgage Obligations" (CMOs; the packaging of various types of credit such as student loans, credit card debt, loans for home and car purchases, etc.) and organized their distribution in the USA (LiPuma, 2016: 129). The derivatives were now no longer directly tied to production, but to the circulation of money flows. The underlying asset of the derivative is now involved in an abstract relationship. The derivative deals with the volatility of this abstract relationship, which in turn produces derivatives on this abstract relationship. A speculative economy emerged, in which CDS and CMOs began to circulate ecstatically, their connection to the "real economy" for example consisted in homeowners learning to treat their homes as financial assets. However, financial capital also drove the growth of the entire economy. Samir Amin insists: "Financialization is therefore not only the only way to absorb excess capital, but also the only stimulus for the faltering growth in the USA, Europe, and Japan since the 1970s. Consequently, a pushback of financialization would only weaken the growth of the ›real economy‹ even more." (Amir, 2012: 60)

Consumer loans also boosted consumption beyond what workers could afford with their stagnating real wages. The financial system of the neoliberal period has enabled the transfer of future demand of wage earners into the present through the increase in debt, which in the long run increasingly undermines the part of their wages available for consumption. If debts are a claim on the value of future wages, the expiry date approaches as soon as the markets begin to doubt whether the accumulated rights to these wages will ever be redeemed.

So how is the relationship between financial crises and crises in production to be understood? Sometimes financial crises open a period of overaccumulation of capital, sometimes they mark the end of an overaccumulation crisis, and sometimes financial crises manifest relatively independently of real business cycles, i.e., they have no significant influence on the movement of industrial profit rates and employment (Sotiropoulos et al., 2013: 55). In any case, the crisis movements of financial capital cannot be fully synchronized with the cycles of industrial profit rates, as traditional Marxist theory has often tried, because the development of financial crises and their bubbles always has a certain autonomy. Carlota Perez has attempted to explain the connections: In expansion phases, innovative companies have problems financing themselves because companies using the already established technologies absorb the available capital, while then, when these technologies have reached their highest efficiency and profitable investment opportunities for these technologies are lacking, sufficient money capital is available. In the downturn phase, financial capital can intervene by financing new innovative projects or the modernization of existing sectors, while unprofitable industries are liquidated (Perez, 2002). However, the establishment of new technological-economic paradigms and productive forces remains an unstable process, as the realization of new projects is uncertain, regardless of the creation of new institutional conditions, which support the new developments through research. Technological innovation remains inscribed in capital transactions (Durand, 2017; Kindle Edition, 1776).

Notes

1. In particular, Anwar Shaikh strives for the reconstruction of macroeconomics based on classical economics, where the concept of real competition plays a central role. (Shaikh, 2016) An important thesis of Shaikh's is that the growth rate of (industrial) capital is determined by the expected net profit rate (difference between the expected profit rate and interest rate) (Ebd.: 40). In contrast to Keynesianism, where the profit rate is, so to speak, hanging in the air, the expected profit rate is tied to the current profit rate and this in turn remains tied to average profit rates. (Ebd.: 268) In a boom, the expected profit rate rises above the current rate, in a recession it is the opposite. Both rates fluctuate around each other in a turbulent manner. The concrete and relevant profit rate is the return on the new investment approaching the current incremental profit rate (Ebd. 978).

If the profit rate in the financial sector is greater than in the industrial sector, then capital flows at an accelerated rate into the financial sector. In this process, expectations affect the current prices, these in turn affect the fundamental data, while expectations are in turn affected by the movements of the current prices and the fundamental data. The current prices thus oscillate in a turbulent manner around the gravity-oriented values. Since expectations can affect the fundamental data, the gravity-oriented centers themselves must be path-dependent. Thus, the future is not a stochastic reflection of the past, but it is non-ergodic. (Ebd.: 545) However, expectations cannot create any reality that only confirms them, rather the gravity-oriented centers such as the general profit rate continue to act as regulators of the current economic events, so that boom phases lead into recessions, and vice versa. Competition leads to the turbulent equalization of profitability or return rates in all areas. However, this is doubtful when it comes to returns due to financial speculation.

In the context of a growing economy, it is also necessary to consider the ratio of supply and demand, which is regulated by profitability: The production supply is based on profitability, while demand or consumption depends on wages and the interest rate; dividends are parts of the profit and the demand for investments is regulated by the expected profits. Marxist macroeconomics, as Shaikh summarizes, is neither supply nor demand oriented, but profit oriented (Ebd.: 6). Furthermore, the savings of companies are not independent from investments, because both sizes belong to the same entity. If savings increase in such a way that they can finance any increase in investments, then there is no multiplier. Every company's savings rate responds to the difference between investment and current savings. This rate is endogenous.

In the long term, the financial situation of companies will correlate with the equalization of profit rates and the normal interest rate with the price level and the normal profit rate (Ebd.: 464ff.). Furthermore, bank credit offers the possibility that expenditures can exceed given revenues. Banks can create new purchasing power, so that investment rises faster than savings, and consumption rises faster than income. For Skaikh, however, the profit rate remains the pivot of the system, although banks can influence the ratio of expected and current profit rate, of supply and demand, and of output and capacity (Ebd.).

In a growing system, the nominal growth rate increases when demand exceeds supply, the growth rate of capital stock increases and when output exceeds capacity. Capital flows more strongly into the financial sector when the current interest rate exceeds the normal interest rate. This always takes place in the context of turbulent compensatory movements, where in the short term the ratio of supply and demand dominates, but in the long term the relationship between capacity and output, between current and normal interest rates, and between current and expected profit rates. This synthesizes Keynes' remark that demand could be relatively autonomous in generating purchasing power, with the classical thesis that accumulation depends on net profitability, and the classical thesis that expected profitability depends on normal profitability and that current capacity utilization fluctuates around normal utilization. The level of savings and investment depends on the interest rate and the level of output, with the interest rate in turn being determined by the profit rate, and the savings rate is linked to the investment rate. Because current growth rates fluctuate around equilibrium, the level of output will have a stochastic and a deterministic aspect, it is path-dependent. Even a temporary increase in the profit rate will increase the level of output and employment. This is the classical response to Keynes' multiplier (Ibid.: 348).

2. The technical revolution of the means of production does not always and constantly coincide with an increase in their value share. The profit rate would then not automatically, at least not constantly, fall.
3. On the question of the connection between the tendential fall of the general profit rate and crisis, see John Milios (2003) and Szepanski (2014a). In it the chapter: Average profit rate and the law of the tendential fall of the general profit rate. On the law of the tendential fall of the profit rate, see Stamatis (1977). According to Stamatis, any increase in productivity leads to a percentage increase in the technical composition and thus also the value composition of capital, while at the same time in the wage goods sector a decrease in the value of the means of reproduction, plus, if the growth rate of productivity is higher than that of real wages, a decrease in the value of labor power can be observed. However, the resulting increase in the relative surplus value rate is far from sufficient to compensate for the increase in the value composition of capital, so that in the end the general profit rate must fall. But there are indeed

"new" capitalist production methods (ibid.: 305ff.), which Marx himself briefly points out in the Grundrisse in connection with the presentation of the problem of ground rent; methods that increase the relative surplus value rate due to specific productivity increases, while at the same time the value composition of capital remains the same or even falls (among other things due to the cheapening of machinery, which can indeed be the case today in digitized industries): By definition, this increases the general profit rate. Even with an increasing technical composition of capital and to a lesser extent the value composition, the profit rate can therefore rise if productivity grows in percentage terms more than the value composition of capital—and this seems decisive for the introduction of these new capitalist production methods. Insofar as cybernetic systems make machines run faster and at the same time reduce their technical wear and tear, the value of such innovations is to be assessed as lower from the outset than the one they replace (cheapening of constant capital). And it should be taken into account that machinery as hardware today is subject to efficient control by software, which translates and iterates the rhythm of time. And in these processes, even specific reserves of production are taken up and used, which are to be considered as parts of communal work and cooperation (affects, cognition, language etc.) or as free services for capital.

4. The years 2008 to 2020 were characterized by a steady increase in underutilized production capacities and a global stagnation of industrial production. The international profit rate fell after 2010, but the mass of profit at large companies has grown enormously. Transnational corporations recorded record profits in the 2010s, while at the same time corporate investments declined.
5. William I. Robinson identifies three types of crises in the course of Marx: The cyclical crises or recessions, which occur approximately every 10 years and last 18 months, the structural crises, which occur every 40-50 years and lead to restructuring of technologies, institutions, class relations, and capital accumulation (Kondratieff cycles). Robinson then further assumes a new type of crisis, which bears traits of the global structural crises of the 1880s, 1930s and 1970s but takes on new dimensions, be it the ecological limits for the reproduction of the system, be it the lack of new territories that can be integrated into the capitalist world system. The commodification and capitalization of natural resources up to wars

has reached an unprecedented level, and new investment opportunities are becoming increasingly difficult to discover (Robinson, 2022b: 11f.).

Anwar Shaikh, on the other hand, assumes three to five-year cycles that are aligned with a company's inventory, seven to ten-year cycles that are related to fixed capital, and longer structural cycles (long waves). All these cycles are pervaded by accelerated and decelerated capital accumulation (Shaikh, 2016: 723 ff.). The Great Depression of the 1930s was characterized by high unemployment and high prices, while the stagflation crisis in the 1970s resulted in halved unemployment compared to the Great Depression and high inflation rates due to Keynesian policy. From the 1980s onwards, we are dealing with a new boom; a permanently low interest rate increased the net profit rate on capital (the net difference between interest rate and profit rate). Falling interest rates led to a widespread distribution of capital around the globe and to an increase in consumer credit and eventually to intensifying financial crises and bubbles. At the same time, there were neoliberal attacks on real wages, which fell in relation to productivity. The fall in interest rates and real wages led to an increase in net profit rates. Normally, this would have had to lead to a stagnation in consumer demand, but due to the fall in the interest rate, consumer credits could be granted on a massive scale, and so consumer demand continued to rise due to debt until the great crisis of 2008. The capital's response to the stagflation of the 1970s was thus an attack on real wages and a drastic reduction in interest rates, which had a positive effect on net profit rates. This is where Shaikh sees the secret of the boom since the 1980s. But this boom was inherently inconsistent for Shaikh. The expansion of cheap finance led to high debts in all sectors of the economy, especially households compensated for the fall in real wages by taking on consumer credit (Ibid.: 736ff.).

6. For Joshua Clover, too, the year 1973 marks a pivotal crisis that engulfed the entire US industry and led to a new metacycle, which now obeys the sequence "circulation-production-circulation" (Clover, 2021: 19). It then begins a long-lasting phase of the crisis of production, which is overwritten by financialization and the increase in world trade (logistics and globalization), i.e., by the "circulation". The above sequence is in turn overwritten by the sequence

"Riot.Strike.Riot". If, according to Clover, before the industrial revolution the riot was the prevailing conflict paradigm, which from the nineteenth century on until the 1970s was replaced by the strike, then the riot reappears and parallel to the shift towards circulation, which is determined by the period of the disintegrating hegemony of the USA at the end of the twentieth century.

References

Binswanger, M. (2019). *Der Wachstumszwang. Warum die Volkswirtschaft immer weiterwachsen muss, selbst wenn wir genug haben*. Weinheim.

Clover, J. (2021). *Riot.Strike.Riot: Die neue Ära der Aufstände*. Hamburg.

Durand, C. D. (2017). *Fictitious Capital: How Finance Is Appropriating Our Future*. London/New York.

Gentili, D. (2020). *Krise als Regierungskunst*. Leipzig.

LiPuma, E. (2017). *The Social Life of Financial Derivatives: Markets, Risk, and Time*. Durham/London.

Milios, J. (2003). Zur Darstellung von Marx' Krisentheorie im dritten Band des Kapital (pp. 47–60). *Beitrage zur Marx-Engels-Forschung*. Neue Folge 1998.

Reuten, G. (2019). *The Unity of the Capitalist Economy and State. A Systematic-Dialectical Exposition of the Capitalist System*. Leiden.

Robinson, W. I. (2022b). *Global Civil War: Capitalism Post-Pandemic (Kairos)*. Oakland.

Shaikh, A. (2016). *Capitalism. Competition. Conflict. Crises*. New York.

Sotiropoulos, D. P., Milios, J., & Lapatsioras, S. (2013). *A Political Economy of Contemporary Capitalism and its Crisis*. New York.

Stamatis, G. (1977). *The "spezifisch kapitalistischen Produktionsmethoden" und der tendenzielle Fall der allgemeinen Profitrate bei Karl Marx*. Berlin.

Szepanski, A. (2014a). *Kapitalisierung Bd.1. Marx' Non-Ökonomie*. Hamburg.

Szepanski, A. (2018a). *Kapital und Macht im 21. Jahrhundert*. Hamburg.

Szepanski, A. (2022). *Financial Capital in the 21th Century*. New York.

CHAPTER 3

The Hypertrophy of the *Over*: Speculative Capital and Derivatives

The importance of speculative capital, whose main instruments are derivatives, as well as of fictitious capital, which includes credit, stocks and bonds, grew with the global reorganization of financial markets and the introduction of computer and information technology in these markets.[1] In the early 1970s, speculative capital in its pure form first appeared in the USA and then in Europe, with a relative decoupling of the financial system from industrial capital and the state regulatory authorities over time. Arbitrage, hedging, and speculation on currencies was in turn enabled by the end of Bretton Woods in 1973.

It should be noted that the expansion of credit creation by the private banks today is an important resource for speculative capital,[2] which fuels the derivative markets and can also stimulate the real economy, but does not have to. The expansion of credit lending leads to increased investments in derivatives, whose valuation increases with rising demand; the derivatives that have risen in price serve as collateral for further loans, thereby setting in motion a feedback loop in which the loans increase the positive valuations of assets and at the same time the assets as collateral increase credit lending. The illusion of the eternal ecstasy of liquidity expansion implies that the leverage of money capital to purchase assets, which serve as collateral for further loans, remains the ultimate for fictitious and speculative capital.[3] However, the derivative markets must be

A. Szepanski, *Capitalism in the Age of Catastrophe*, Palgrave Insights into Apocalypse Economics,
https://doi.org/10.1007/978-3-031-57754-3_3

profitable, liquid and volatile enough for the financial companies themselves to invest speculative capital, but the companies must know how to prevent the moment when the elasticity of volatility can become dangerous for them: derivative markets generate so to speak the disease against which they have to immunize themselves (LiPuma, 2017: 54). The logic of speculative capital consists in the ongoing reinforcement of the motive, to create opportunities for the differential profitable monetization of returns, or, to put it differently, it includes the capitalization of the difference and must generate a corresponding leverage.[4] And this logic necessarily takes place in the mode of monetary circulation, which implies the risk in its derivative form, but it also refers to industrial capital accumulation. Although financial circulation cannot replace industrial production, it gives it a new shape.[5] It should be taken into account from the outset that in these processes of capitalization the asset is not subordinate to the capitalist production process, but logically precedes it, i.e. capitalization does not exist primarily because surplus value has already been produced and as the company's profit and interest were not realized in the markets, but because financial capital is confident to a certain extent that the realization of profits will take place in the future and will repeat itself according to the standards of expanded reproduction.

Securitization is a synthetic form of circulation that occurs through derivative instruments, which are based on calculating, hedging, and capitalizing on facts and figures such as interest rates, currency risks, and derivative prices. Derivatives are not rooted in production, but in circulation—in and through the capitalization of cash flows, which in turn depend on liquidity. In the production sphere, money is considered the general equivalent that measures the value of goods according to Marx, in the world of derivative circulation, which must always be realized in money, money is entirely self-referential, with not only derivatives circulating self-referentially in relation to themselves, but even the underlying/base value can be integrated into their relations.[6] Since all market participants work with a similar range of mathematical models, diagrams, graphics, concepts, and motivations, they imagine the fabrication of derivatives as a simple expansion of a recurring type of instrument, which in turn demands from the financial community the need to manage derivatives as a resource for profits at all times efficiently, precisely because derivatives are an accepted instrument that seemingly accurately predicts the volatility of prices or the behavior of market participants.

The allocation of capital is increasingly dominated by financial and derivative interests today. *It is not the real economy that drives the financial economy, but rather the financial economy that structures the real economy.*[7] That is, derivatives organize the flows of money capital in the context of various securities, currencies, and bonds and thus also have regulatory capacities by taking over state codings, tasks, and functions themselves and integrating politics into the economy. The latter is particularly evident in the fact that governments have switched their policy from establishing social security to guaranteeing the liquidity and solvency of financial markets (bailout) (Meister, 2021: 130).

The metaphor "central nervous system of capital," which Tony Norfield uses in his book *The City* to characterize the current financial system, accurately refers to the financial constellation of capitalist economies. If the capital principle is the energetic engine of the breathing capital monster, then the financial system is its brain and central nervous system (Norfield, 2016: Kindle Edition: 168). The financial system executes to a not insignificant extent the competition, coordination, and regulation of companies (in all sectors), which in turn presupposes total capital, which enables the real competition of companies, which for Marx is not a ballet, but a war, by setting the framework conditions. Analogous to quantum theory, the possibilities that total capital sets for individual capitals are determined, it sets a binding framework, while the actualization of these possibilities by individual capitals is burdened with contingency.[8]

Since the interest-bearing, fictitious, and speculative capital in the form of loans, bonds, stocks, and derivatives is growing much faster in absolute numbers today and has assumed a much larger nominal volume as the industrial and commercial capital, the growth of the wealth and profit masses of the financial industry cannot primarily feed on the capital accumulation of the "real economy", but must be generated and accumulated by financial capital in self-referential processes[9] (Lohoff & Trenkle, 2012). Financial capital employs enormous credit sums, fictitious and speculative capital, and other multiple capital equivalents, which are characterized by high liquidity, mobility, and flexibility. Today, it is the derivatives that, as forms of speculative capital, possess a higher effectiveness due to their profitability, energy, and multiplicity in time than fictitious and industrial capital, and this also in the sense that they determine as well as open up possibilities and set conditions.

However, the financial sectors are not exclusively speculative activities completely detached from production, as for example both the construction and maintenance of global supply chains are very finance-intensive activities that heavily strain both the operating capital of companies and the supply of short-term bank loans. The decline in industrial profitability not only leads to investments in speculative financial assets, but can also require investments in increasingly complex industrial plants—including automation and division of labor within companies, but it also leads to a refined and spatially distributed division of labor between companies -, which in turn requires the use of increasingly complex financial investments.

Nevertheless, we borrow money from a future that does not exist and will never exist, precisely because it consists of speculative iterations of a fictitious and speculative capital that is increasingly decoupled from human labor. In view of the artificial intelligence emerging on the posthuman horizon, living labor will continue to be pushed to the margins in absolute numbers, and the growth prospects of the entire economy will increasingly depend on the financial industry and the large tech companies. The global volume of financial instruments traded daily on the world's financial markets is already out of proportion to the mass of values produced in the real economy. This should prompt us, according to Fabio Vighi, to thoroughly rethink our nostalgia for a world built on "concrete" capitalist wealth (Vighi, 2022: 121ff.). It is estimated that the three major asset managers (BlackRock, Vanguard, and State Street), which together employ only about 35,000 workers, will soon control a financial mass equivalent to half of the global GDP. Vighi goes to the extreme with Baudrillard when he writes, in essence, that if we hold the allegedly parasitic financial capitalism responsible for the fragility of our system, we deny that the real economy is already dead, although its ghost still haunts us (ibid.). Vighi assumes that the relative strength of the old capitalist symptom still forces us to cling to a socio-economic narrative that has long since passed its expiration date. He, like Norfield, Milios, Meister, and us, comes to the conclusion that finance is not a tumor or a parasite (rentiers) of the late capitalist system, but its essence.

However, the institutional analysis of the financial system, to which we will now briefly turn, is not to be conducted exclusively as that of an autonomous financial sector, but rather it must assume that today all major capitalist companies without exception must carry out important financial operations. The French economist François Chesnais distinguishes in his book *Finance Capital Today* between finance as a highly networked and interdependent conglomerate, consisting of insurance, pension and investment funds, large, shadow and central banks, asset managers, transnational industrial and commercial corporations, and powerful wholesalers (organizational level), and finance qua finance, the structural processes of expansion of fictitious capital and derivatives, which are held, shaped, and traded by large banks, investment funds, and hedge funds on the financial markets (processual and functional level)[10] (Chesnais, 2016: 36).

Regarding the former organizational aspect, a stratification of the companies and institutions of financial capital is to be assumed. The first area of financial companies includes commercial and investment banks that are active in the secondary derivative markets or capital markets. These companies own internal hedge funds that speculate with company-owned capital, that is, also with the capital of the shareholders, and use leveraged strategies to increase returns. Other players are the independent hedge funds that benefit from the decline of long-term investment strategies and the transition to short-termism and the associated increasing volatility in the capital markets. A relatively new actor are the financial departments of large multinational companies that grow faster than their industrial departments and speculate on the money and capital markets even as non-banks.[11] Other important players in the financial markets today are large asset managers like BlackRock, which are based on passive trading management. BlackRock manages hyper-large sums of money and is connected with other financial institutions that bundle thousands of individuals, groups, and institutional investors, while the company itself invests in leading corporations in all areas. There are two types of institutional investors, on the one hand the asset owners, which include pension funds, insurance companies, and foundation funds, and on the other hand the asset managers, such as private equity firms, hedge funds, and investment companies, which in turn manage investment funds, exchange-traded funds, and passive funds. These two forms of organization are not strictly separated, but interconnected: The latter not only attract money from private investors, but often also manage the assets of the former, creating a hierarchy of financial power that is increasingly dominated by companies like BlackRock, which bundle and capitalize large sums of assets. The systems of specialization create concentrated nodes of financial power, which are also capable of regulating industrial capital from a financial perspective.

For about 20 years, the shadow banking system has been becoming increasingly important and represents an extremely important area of the overall economic system. The global shadow banking system, which deals with the mediation of loans and the trading of securities, currently has a trading volume of 200 trillion dollars annually, which is more than 50% of all assets traded worldwide. With a growth rate of 6–9% annually, it is growing significantly faster than the traditional banking system (Wullweber, 2023). Within the financial system, more and more loans are now being granted by shadow banks, which are not traditional banks and are not subject to their regulation. The main actors are hedge funds, investment banks, insurance companies, and money market funds. Actors who are not traditional banks are thus granting more and more loans today, but unlike in the bank-based credit system, no funds are created, rather it comes to the mediation of money and securities through the market. Instead of classic bank loans, the lending is done via repos. Securitization of loans and repos are important functions of the shadow banking system. Securitization is a tool that allows loans (including mortgage, car, or student loans) to be bundled and transformed into tradable securities. To understand the shadow banking system, we will explain the functioning of repos in more detail below. The procurement of liquidity is cheap here and the restrictions are lower than in the bank-based credit system. To finance the portfolios, short-term investments are usually used, allowing for a flexible mix of payment promises with various risk profiles and investments with different maturities.

Shadow banks are to be understood as poles and relations that operate outside the accounting of regular commercial banks and thus also outside state and transnational regulatory bodies. This is also due to the fact that global supply chains, in which complex derivative and securitization chains constantly take place, are becoming increasingly important for capital. It is estimated that shadow banks had already handled a third of the global volume of financial transactions in 2011. Shadow banks are therefore financial companies that conduct credit business relatively independently and pursue bank-like business models, but do not have a banking license themselves. They are therefore not bound by banking regulation and supervision and can take on higher risks to achieve even higher profits than commercial banks. Most shadow banks have their legal headquarters in offshore centers and tax havens. According to the report of the European Systemic Risk Board (ESRB, 2016) from July 2016, shadow banks in the EU alone had invested capital worth 37 trillion euros in the fourth quarter of 2015. This represented about 36% of the total assets of the European financial system (ESRB, 2016: 3). Shadow banks cannot create bank deposits like commercial banks. Credit is usually granted via repo transactions. The actors of the shadow banks buy securities with funds they raise themselves. They use leverage to flexibly exploit price spreads and shift the money available in the economy between the actors. The loans granted by the shadow banks are not recognized as state money. They receive money from money market funds, but not from their own balance sheet transactions like private banks.

Derivatives and all other exotic and synthetic financial instruments, which on the one hand are to be understood as power technologies (Sotiropoulos et al., 2013: 155ff.), and on the other hand as speculative forms of capital with which returns are achieved (LiPuma, 2017: 11), today represent a necessary condition for the constant implementation of capitalization into the entire economic field. Derivatives are considered instruments that create the speculative chapter and its agents in complex (constructive and destructive) processes and use them particularly within endogenous cycles to dig deeper into the processes of industrial production through a machine of securitization/insurance that operates the creation, design, and distribution of the risks of derivative trading, as a kind of informal supervisory authority. This process is often seen by various economists as a contamination of the "real" economy, although speculative capital embodies a kind of conductor who sets the pace and thus the conditions for their capitalization and strategies for individual capitals, regardless of the sector they belong to. The idea that financial capital strangles the real economy does not therefore correspond to reality.

Derivatives are forms and instruments of speculative capital, with which the cycles of a global, nomadic, and opportunistic capital are managed[12] (ibid.: 28). The derivative is not a thing, it is relational sui generis, rather, it is a relation of relations (ibid.: 31). First, the volatility of the derivative in relation to the volatility of the underlying asset should be mentioned to characterize the derivative. In a derivative contract, two contracting parties initially speculate on what will happen to an underlying asset (underlying value) in the future, for example, the currency changes between dollar and euro. This bet applies for a specific time period, which is clearly defined in the contract. The crucial aspect of the replication of the derivative itself is its size and the speed of its volatilities.

Options, for example, are derivative contracts that include the right to buy (call) or sell (put) underlying assets or goods at a predetermined price until a certain point in time (maturity), without the need to exercise the option. If the price of the goods increases in the future, the buyer of the option has made a profit (minus the price of the option). Unlike futures, with options, if the price has not increased, the purchase does not need to be executed. He then only loses the price of the option. Buyers and sellers of the option have different expectations about the future price, which include assessments of risks, interest rates, and market development of the goods. This type of information production remains uncertain, yet it is not a mere bet. Derivatives are generally financial instruments or contracts that promise payments resulting from speculation (not as a bet, but due to organized information procurement) on the future value of something else, the so-called "underlying asset", which can be anything, prices, indices, objects, goods etc. These derivatives can be resold or derivatives and default risk insurances can be developed on them, so that the difference in price of the derivatives to the prices of the underlying asset can always become larger, provided there are buyers for these financial products. A financial product should rather be referred to as a financial process, the value of which is subject to quantum uncertainty, making the value itself a process based on a permanent and usually accelerating metric (Harney & Moton, 2022: 169). This process involves several kinetic moments: speculation on the movement of the underlying asset, on the relations between the underlying asset and the derivative, and on the internal movement of the derivative (compared to other derivatives) over time.[13] The procedural design of a derivative contract is determined by the variables time, price fluctuation, and volatility. On the one hand, the volatility of the derivative in relation to the volatility of the underlying asset must be taken into account, on the other hand, however, the relations of the derivative to itself must be considered (the internal price movements of the derivative, which are themselves volatile). Derivative pricing generates a mode of volatility and optionality with respect to the second aspect, which intrinsically refers to the operations on the derivative markets themselves (Malik, 2014; Meister, 2021: 2). According to Malik, there is a triple contingency to report in derivatives: The derivative contract (contingency that already arises with the act of writing), the variability of derivative pricing (contingency of revision, price movement is subject to constant revaluation, which depends on the movements of the prices of the derivatives and the underlying assets) and the future absolute volatility of price formation, which is based purely on the internal price movement of the derivatives themselves (thetic contingency) (Malik, 2014). The latter means that the valuation of the derivative is contingent and could already be different. To put it in the words of Elena Esposito: If present future, which expresses what one expects from the future, and future present, which denotes the future that actually occurs, are not identical, then in the course of the use of mathematical calculation methods, a future present is always realized, with which the difference to that future is updated, which one expected and whose potentials one may have used (Esposito, 2010: 178).

If one brings quantum theory into play at this point, then one could understand derivatives as virtual "objects" that need to be actualized, namely in money. One could also describe derivatives as intensive objects, whose quantity is not fixed, but variable—it is about rates and price movements, by constantly transforming one relation into another. Prices always result from the interactions of relations with other relations. The derivatives are thus not stable objects, but rather already relational processes and as such they are at least quantum loop objects, that is, relational stages of indeterminate processes that repeat, but always differently. In this respect, they are not even objects, but rather events. If objects are monotone processes that loop themselves, then the derivative also repeatedly loses the status of the object. Or, to put it another way, derivatives are indeterminate processes, insofar as all kinetic movements of the relations always entail further relations in the future. From the relations, the relata/objects emerge again. To then sharpen it quantumly, are derivatives as potential objects statistical possibilities (waves), which actualize in discrete stages as money (particles).

It is always about the efficiency of the process, which must be measured anew to increase it. This even subjects the measurement of the metric and kinetics of the process, on whose profitability is now speculated. The ecstatic increase in profitability is the credo of financial speculation. Harney/Moten talk about the flow of the line or the assembly line now becoming speculative itself. Kaizen or improvement is at the center of a financial speculation that occurs on the derivatives in their flow. The currents of financial processes themselves become moments of speculation. Hedge funds no longer buy companies, but business processes, which they constantly divide and reassemble with a view to improving and accelerating profitability (Harney & Moten, 2022: 171).

In a certain way, with derivatives, as Edward LiPuma says, speculation is on the volatility and a tango with time is played[14] (LiPuma, 2017: 28). The volatile price movement of the derivative takes place in time intervals, that is, time is pressed into the period between the start and expiration of the derivative contract, or, to put it another way, the derivative cuts out a certain time interval from the constant film of time and shapes it—it is an interval that is directed towards the future, which in turn has an effect on the present. Or, to put it another way, the valuation and interpolation of the future is in question, which leads to the expansion of the present, but also to its destabilization. The derivative consists not only in predicting and calculating the future, but it also serves to control the present. As a machine derivative, it is essentially recursive: It continuously evaluates the past to anticipate the future, which as such in turn disciplines the present[15] (ibid.: 37). In the face of an ever uncertain future, it requires the calculation of expectations, which are calculated and capitalized in the present, which is equivalent to a reversal of causality, insofar as the cause now lies in the future and the effect in the present. It is no longer the present that capital appropriates, but the future, which is already being plundered in the present. In this respect, there is no longer any future that would stand against the present as black and indeterminable and could open up a horizon of possibilities. The future now becomes an element of a "capital present" that expands and contracts within itself. Capital has now definitively overtaken its own future, and this is what Lenger could call its "annihilation" (Lenger, 2004: 236).

The traders are doomed to anticipate a future they cannot know, and in doing so they follow the guidelines of financial theory, which tries to determine the future as a probability-theoretical distribution and stochastic phenomenon. This use and this kind of determination of time distinguish the derivative significantly from the classic commodity. The buyers and sellers of a classic commodity can agree on a price because they attribute different value formats to the goods they exchange. While the seller realizes a profit, the buyer wishes to satisfy his needs with the consumption of the goods. Unlike the derivative, which is not a classic commodity and does not have a transparent price in the here and now, because the only measure that motivates the transaction lies in the realization of a profit by means of the calculation or discounting of its future value.

Furthermore, the metaphor of the tango correlates with time and speculation. Speculation possesses two signatures of time, which refer to risk:

There is an intra-temporal dimension, which consistently assigns risk to the production, movement, and marketing of the product, and there is an inter-temporal dimension, which ensures the continuity of the systemic conditions necessary for logistics, circulation, and financial markets. Speculation knows the rope of both time registers, which in turn correspond with two further registers: That of concrete risk, which affects the entire social life of the trader, and that of competitively organized abstract risk in the derivative markets themselves.

Derivative contracts are intrinsically performative, in that they create the conditions of their own existence, just as saying the word "promise" brings about the real promise under certain conditions. The use value of the derivative lies in dynamic replication, or, to put it another way, derivatives exist in the interval between inception and expiration, and in doing so they continuously create a new now as a price, by opening the gap between a price and a possible future and closing it at expiration (LiPuma, 2017: 37). Thus, derivatives fill a period of time, in which wealth is created as a consequence of trading volatility, as a dispersion of what they represent as the imaginary center of the spreads. The design of the derivatives shapes the kinetics of this volatility, with convexity here meaning that the variation of the price of the underlying and the derivative do not have to be symmetric. The question would be whether the derivative does not hint at that horror that would lie in the infinite replication of itself.

A minimal variation in the price of the underlying can lead to a disproportional variation in the price of the derivative, consider that in the subprime crisis of 2008 a relatively small number of mortgage defaults led to high losses in the CDOs or CDSs. Thus, the price movement of the derivatives can be disproportionately higher than that of the underlying assets. This is called the "Jensen inequality". The derivative cannot be reduced to an anticipated income stream or a future return, because the size and speed of its volatility also determines the level of return. The price therefore refers to the expected future volatility of the derivative, which is measured as the degree of variance of the price between the moment of transaction and its maturity. The derivative price is thus centered around the relation between the expected volatility and the maturity.

Derivatives not only differ from classic commodities, but also from other forms of capital such as fictitious capital, for example from a corporate bond in a significant way. Thus, derivatives do not yield accumulative profits like bonds over time. While with the bond the profits accumulate over time, the value of a derivative decreases with time or towards the expiration of its maturity date. The derivative is tied with its price to an underlying, but it also prices out aspects that the underlying itself cannot price out, such as the specific risks of the underlying in relation to the risks that relate to the market as a whole. And derivatives can form prices that refer to errors of the clearinghouses, to an accelerating inflation or to a decline of profit curves.

Without volatility, no derivative is conceivable, that is, if derivatives do not constantly circulate, then they are worthless. Derivatives capitalize on the volatility, which they actively create. In the derivative, a gap opens up between the price and the value, since the partners have to agree on a price in the derivative contract, but differ in their expectations and speculative calculations about the future value (in a certain time interval). The derivative aims at the future, it can only be priced because the market participants assume a different bid-asked spread (buying and selling price) (ibid.: 28ff.).

Moreover, volatility must necessarily be volatile itself and thus one is always also trading volatilities. Instead of assuming volatility as given and determining the option price, one assumes this as given and determines the expected volatility, which retrospectively makes the price formula of the option true. The value that is now added by optionality is a product of unexpected changes in expected volatility. It is about the reflexivity of the paradoxical effects of predictions on the future, namely on that, what the future will be (and will have been) (Meister, 2021: 194). Nevertheless, trading with these prediction models such as the Black-Scholes formula can fail, namely when the actions of the participants falsify the prerequisites of the models. When the financial participants price out the volatility of their own expectations about volatility, then they are always trading the uncertainty about the models. It is at least recognized that their evaluations are based on a future uncertainty, which is based on the fact that constantly data about the past are updated to revise the own assumptions about the volatility of the future. It is about to what degree the future will be like the past. But this is again rather a question of calculable risk and not of uncertainty, and because this difference is often not considered, the economists' forecasts fail again and again fulminatingly, as Karl-Heinz Brodbeck has also elaborated in his book *The Rule of Money* (Brodbeck, 2009).

The general problem of financial markets is to generate as much volatility as possible without the resulting volatility impairing liquidity. Thus the immanent and differential dynamics of market participants lie exactly in the necessity to arbitrage volatility through financial transactions and at the same time to calculate the level of risk (using leverage), which is necessary to again generate exactly the liquidity and volatility that allow the arbitrage to continue to function. This implies a tendency towards crisis processes, in which just a decrease in volatility, which leads to stability in the markets related to industrial production, can intensify instability in the derivative markets. An expected decrease in volatility reduces the profitability of arbitrage, which in turn motivates traders to compensate for the stagnation of profits by increasing leverage, so that outstanding positions can be hedged more difficultly and small changes in the underlyings cause high changes in the prices of derivatives. If the derivative is systematically transformative, then because it is a self-realizing and expanding form of money capital. That means speculative capital.

Furthermore, a dynamic replication between volatility and liquidity is necessary for the derivative. The ability to exploit volatility is absolutely dependent on the liquidity available in the financial markets.[16] In general, the derivatives have to follow a difficult path, namely to increase volatility without becoming so excessive and uncontrollable that it leads to a loss of liquidity (LiPuma 2017: 40ff.). The collective trust of market participants in the future liquidity of the market is essential here. Therefore, derivatives inherit the performative power of a ritual to exactly set in motion collectively what each individual agent unconsciously presupposes. But the liquidity in the markets also evaporates again and again, because the actors cannot remember their previous mistakes. New contagion risks constantly lurk in the financial system which is based on dense networks. In a time when, for example, dollar debts become more expensive due to rising interest rates, the default of a globally networked bank or a distress sale of financial assets are concrete events that can lead to collapses in the markets. Liquidity is also often used as a synonym for the social relations that allow agents to construct the collective enterprise that is the market: A market that always has a counterpart for a contracting party, a market that is homogeneous and constantly provides liquidity, which in turn enables the recalibrations of derivative price movements necessary for the continuation of the market. For example, when a market for assets becomes illiquid (market liquidity), and these assets are used as collateral for repos, then a lack of market liquidity, which generally leads to falling prices, turns into a lack of financing liquidity. This is based on the market value of the assets with which the actors refinance.[17]

Especially in the shadow banking system, in the context of high financial leverage (leverage), a lack of market liquidity can lead to so-called "liquidity spirals", where a decline in prices leads to a deterioration of financing liquidity, which then affects and impairs market liquidity.

However, liquidity is more than just a metaphor for the monetary fluidity of financial markets. Because it is generally the capacity of the economy to circulate capital, i.e., the relatively free-floating circulation of money capital is a necessary condition for the existence of the economy in the twenty-first century. However, there are a number of legal restrictions, laws, and codifications to consider that also influence, channel, and regulate money capital flows. We will come back to this later. Constitutive for today's economies is therefore the circulation of speculative capital, which in turn is unimaginable without the new information technologies, which channel, shape, and accelerate capital flows and finally advance the technologically supported production of knowledge. There is also a necessary connection between the contingent and often unpredictable financial events and the construction of the market as a totality. The derivative markets are therefore absolutely dependent on liquidity.

For Robert Meister, liquidity is an abstract form of power that correlates with global financial capital (Empirie/Norm), and this in the same way as state sovereignty is an abstract form of power that correlates with the national modes of capitalist production (Meister, 2021: 3). Liquidity is therefore the basic prerequisite of transnational money and capital markets, although the liquidity of a financial investment cannot be guaranteed sui generis. Thus, the buyer of an asset must endure the ups and downs of prices in the markets. There is no guarantee of liquidity in the commodity markets. But in the capital markets today, the guarantee for liquidity can be bought or sold by paying an option price. This guarantee can therefore be priced out and traded as an asset on certain markets. Full liquidity for an asset can then be guaranteed if there is an "asset repurchase agreement", the right to buy it back at its original purchase price (ibid.: 111). There are also institutional traders who can provide liquidity if they are willing to buy when others sell, or to buy when others sell. Because they are indifferent to buying or selling, and provided they can do this at different prices, they can even achieve a spread between bid-ask-price. However, a collapse of liquidity can arise precisely from the actions of these traders. Then asset prices fall rapidly because no buyers can be found. This can in turn be ended if states provide liquidity to the asset markets from the outside, e.g., when the Fed buys up debt securities that no one else would buy anymore.

The relationship between liquidity and optionality was first developed by Keynes. The value of the optionality that money provides lies in the various possibilities of transferring it to make a profit or avoid a loss, assuming that the future will be like the past (ibid.: 6). Modern financial theory generalizes the possibility of pricing options independently of the market prices of the underlying goods, starting with the fact that liquidity premiums arising from any asset can be split and valued as a distinct asset class. It essentially essentializes uncertainty (the fact that financial markets currently cannot distinguish between information and noise), so that optionality as such can have a marketable value, namely as a measure of the influence of new information on liquidity. If there is a future to buy or sell at a price known in advance, in response to information and price movement that cannot be known in advance, then it includes a valuable right, for which it can be expected that one will pay an amount above the liquidity premium that exists when holding cash.[18]

Trading with speculative capital has the autopoietic and ecstatic effect of generating markets with increasing volatility and higher risks. In doing so, the circulation of speculative capital achieves a certain autonomy, characterized by the invention of derivative instruments, the transformation of uncertainty into quantifiable risks, and the proliferation of speculative capital itself. These processes trigger accelerated complexity and increasing connectivity, so that financial institutions become increasingly dependent on each other, although this largely remains invisible. The resulting "quantum interdependence", in which the fate of the individual actor is tied to the fate of the collective, is also a result of traders' demand for ever higher liquidity. And this liquidity in turn allows for higher leverage. If lenders have positive confidence in the liquidity of the markets, then the costs of leveraging transactions fall, while at the same time the opportunities for speculative capital increase. And the connectivity, which is based on the collective trust of market participants in the smooth functionality of the markets, will also increase. Today, 90% of derivatives are traded on the unregulated OTC markets, which means they are not standardized products.

Derivative markets are historically determined and at the same time contingent spaces of capital, where a risk is attributed to the price of the derivative, with the derivative markets in a certain way separating circulation from production and at the same time generating new modes of mutual relations, dependencies and connectivity. This refers primarily to the fact that derivatives in their quantities are not limited by the structures of industrial production and are not completely dependent on them. Each derivative has a generic design scheme based on a time-related calculation of volatility, the division and recombination of capital, and the mixing of variable and incommensurable forms of risk, which ultimately results in an abstract number that in turn functions as a social mediation. (For an economy driven by derivatives, indicators such as GDP are meaningless.) One could say that derivatives represent the economic totality of markets as an indeterminate, disparate aggregation of globally replicating contracts based on abstract risk. Today, the size and the principle limitlessness of the derivative markets and their production and circulation also have enormous consequences for the organization of national labor markets and the conditions of collective reproduction of the entire economy.

The more one knows about past risks, the faster one recognizes that much of what happened in the markets was not calculated or expected. Only the unexpected happens with certainty. Therefore, information about the future becomes essential, and this shows that one can speculate with derivatives for both profit and loss. And the more data there is in the markets, the more urgent and delirious the search for more data becomes. And the greater the desire becomes to insure against the growing uncertainty, against the fact that the future is now not like the past, the sooner there will be someone who prices exactly this insurance based on data. The data is the medium to evaluate one's own option, which consists of the fear of uncertainty in the future, which in turn is created by the data, because they always come from the past.

Another function of derivatives is therefore to monetize risks for a certain period of time. The capitalization of the derivative pricing process is only possible on the condition that a multitude of specific risks exist in the financial markets. Thus, over the last 40 years, various generative and classificatory schemes have emerged (interest rate risks, credit risks, transaction risks, direct risks, counter risks, liquidity risks, etc.), and ultimately, any financial variable that can be identified can be transformed into a specific risk. This nominalization implies that finance can translate any type of risk into a real object. In these contexts, market makers design derivatives to compare and liquidate the risks that arise in various specific financial situations, so that derivatives are ultimately understood as the objectification of abstract risk. With this, the financialized risk is separated from its social contexts and concrete relations to translate it into an abstract, purely analytical and mathematical space (Sotiropoulos et al., 2013: 161). Capitalization, a method for calculating and valuing future payment promises, always also involves a specific way of representing, regulating, and anticipating future economic events, which must be distinguished from each other in order to identify them as concrete risks and finally to trade them as derivatives embodying abstract risks. There is no capitalization without the specification and comparison of risks. Today, the concept of risk is sui generis integrated into the logic of capital.

So, the respective types of concrete risks are translated into an abstract form, or to put it another way, the incommensurable and variable forms of concrete risk are transformed into a singular form: abstract risk (LiPuma 2017: 32 ff.). Speculative capital now inevitably takes the form of derivatives because they unify various concrete risks in a single instrument, even if they merely mask the uncertainty that appears on the financial horizon. Derivatives thus introduce a formative perspective on concrete risks, make them commensurable with each other and reduce the heterogeneity of concrete risks to a single abstract attribute, namely that of abstract risk, which the derivatives embody. Think of swaps, for example.[19] The abstract risk only counts insofar as it has a quantitative dimension and a price as a derivative. After all, derivatives always have to be realized in money. However, the distinction between concrete and abstract risks does not mean the existence of two types of risks, but the presence of two inseparable dimensions of risks within a single risk complex. In contrast to uncertainty, risk is calculable and can be determined with a stochastic probability function. Thus, in recent decades, new derivative products have repeatedly emerged, which detached the concrete risks from their previous context, so that they could be quantified as abstract risk, that is, sliced, diced, liquefied, and circulated as speculative capital.[20]

For example, the default and interest rate risk (specific risks) can be extracted from the original security and then traded in a new derivative context. This "repackaging" of specific risks includes trading in abstract risks through derivatives. Although the interest and default risk can already be understood as a bundling of various specific risk components, it seems more sensible to understand these risks in their new derivative form (abstract risk). Thus, CDS and CDOs can be understood as a condensation of certain cash market transactions into singular derivative instruments (Cf. Szepanski, 2018, 2022).

In a given market, a specific risk (for example, the fluctuation of currencies) is particular and is generated by a fluid, heterogeneous circularity, but as an abstract risk it is merely an individualized dimension of a homogeneous and systemic mediation, which aims at the reproduction of the market as a totality. The abstract risk precisely targets what the agents invariably and unconsciously do, namely to imagine the market as a whole, which always remains liquid, through the countless iterations of price setting and under circumstances that are constantly changing, especially those which enable the recalibration of prices.[21] All the relations included in these relations are priced out on the financial markets, they circulate and are speculated upon. In these processes, the economic agents constantly misrecognize the social dimensions of risk, precisely because the market appears to them as an objectified and formal construction. To summarize at this point, the abstract risks subsume the specific risks and act as mediator for the liquidity that makes the derivative market possible in the first place. Without the abstract risk, there is no liquidity and no derivative market. And the risk-driven derivative is the new tool, which constantly stitches the circulation, by objectifying the risks (through abstraction and monetization) and thus precisely establishing and trading that connectivity which capital needs, so that completely anonymous agents and organizations can be brought together on markets that are based on risk-based transactions.

In particular, John Milios refers to derivatives as a power technology, which is inseparably linked to risk management (Sotiropoulos et al., 2013: 162ff.). The derivative has in this context the function to constantly evaluate and control the various market participants (companies, households and states) in terms of their future prospects and expected profitability. It is precisely the financial markets that generate a fluid structure for calculating the effectiveness of the individual capitals of all sectors—they are to be understood as a kind of supervisory authority over the capital movements, so that the individual capitals have to constantly adapt their strategies to the respective requirements, rules, and optimization strategies of the financial markets within the framework of competition. It should be noted that the control of companies by the financial system, however efficient it may be, is a fictitious control, insofar as the calculation, forecasting and evaluation of complex production processes of companies by analysts, rating agencies, and financial markets always have to include a multitude of contingencies, which the markets also produce on their part.

To clarify once again, derivatives and the other modern financial instruments and innovations are the necessary prerequisite to implement financialization comprehensively on all markets. They allow it, to relate and compare specific risks, to formalize them and to reduce their heterogeneity to a uniform calculable to reduce property. Already as a result of Marx's theory about the capitalist mode of production and its systematics, financialization is by no means to be understood as a deviation or distortion of a supposedly "good" industrial capitalism, but as a historical development in which form determinations come into play that are inherent in the capitalist mode of production from the outset. The rise of finance does not threaten industrial capital, nor is it merely to be understood as an indication of its weakness (its inability to secure adequate accumulation rates), even though this circumstance should not be neglected. Finance, rather, represents a special technology of power (along with a special kind of financing economic activities) that corresponds thoroughly to the nature of capitalist exploitation (Sotiropoulos et al., 2013). For Milios, the key role of financial markets lies in a kind of monitoring of the effectiveness of individual capitals of all sectors as well as in enabling companies to implement effective valorization strategies, that is, to reward profitable and competitive companies and at the same time to punish those that are not sufficiently profitable (Milios, 2023). For example, if a large company is dependent on the financial markets for its financing, any suspicion of insufficient future profitable valorization increases its financing costs and reduces the possibility of obtaining financial resources, thereby depressing its share and bond prices.[22]

The balance sheets of today's commercial banks, in which differently timed payment promises are recorded, are to be understood as dynamic and open fields of relations in which the debts of others (loans as assets) are opposed to one's own debts (loans as liabilities). The balance is disturbed and restored by permanent financial activities. The assets and liabilities consist on the one hand of derivatives and securities (capital market instruments) and on the other hand of repos, certificates and deposits (money market instruments). Due to factors such as securitization and lending, shadow banking and deposit trading, the activities on the two markets are often no longer completely separable today. In this context, the leverage that we have already discussed above is a distinct form of financial power. To briefly explain the concept of leverage again: Profitable transactions appear on the asset side of the bank's balance sheet.

If the bank wants to carry out the transactions, it must first provide monetary resources—consisting of equity or borrowed capital—whereby equity only makes up a small part of the liabilities (the part that is not borrowed from other owners, but is held by the owners of the bank itself; the company's debts to its owners). This is where the leverage effect comes into play. "Leverage" refers to the leverage effect that can be achieved by controlling the difference between the cost of external financing and the return (on borrowed and equity capital). In other words: Leverage indicates the real ratio between equity and external financing of investments. By using borrowed capital, the return on capital can be increased precisely when the interest rates on borrowed capital are lower than the total return on capital.

From the 1960s onwards, US banks increasingly shifted their activities from the "credit and investment" relation to the active creation and trading of assets on the capital markets, while they also increasingly became borrowers on the money markets. The European banks had to take over the construction of the assets designed in the USA via external financialization on the Euro-Dollar market. The excessive leverage of the European banks was driven by the ultimately not very successful attempt to compete with the US banks on a financial market denominated in dollars. Thus, before the financial crisis of 2008, the European banks borrowed money on the US money markets in order to invest it on the US capital markets to establish and use the purchased CDOs and MSBs as collateral for their financing in the money markets. Therefore, European banks had to engage in risky leverage in the US capital markets, buy CDOs and other derivatives, and then use these as collateral for their financing in the money markets. The leverage in the capital markets ultimately created the conditions for "deposit-taking" in the money markets (Beck et al., 2022: 33ff.). Balancing the leverage taking place in the capital markets to ensure financing in the money markets is also a process of transforming the long-term assets in the capital markets into short-term liabilities of the money markets, i.e., a liquidity transformation (ibid.: 39). The leverage in the capital markets generates the conditions for financing in the money markets (and vice versa). Therefore, the financial activities that can insure the activities in the money markets take place in the secondary markets or capital markets, and thus the banks systematically expand their balance sheets and create a power that inflates and simultaneously keeps the financial markets liquid.

The liquidity transformation is a relatively simple procedure, when it comes to safe papers like government bonds that serve as collateral. However, the CDOs and MBSs had to be divided and repackaged as collateral to make them appear as safe assets. Although the trading of CDOs has changed after the financial crisis of 2008, for European banks, financing in the money markets always remains a consequence of investments in the capital markets.

The financing problem is central for commercial banks and shadow banks. It arose with the growing importance of liability management in the money markets. As the costs of bank financing increased due to rising inflation and interest rates in the 1970s, because the borrowers' capacities to repay their debts decreased, the profits of the banks also decreased. The banks therefore switched to a much riskier business model, based on active asset management and corresponding liability management. Thus, the pursuit of high profits in the capital markets, which now also served to meet the liabilities in the money markets, became increasingly important. For this the transformation of asset trading was initiated, that is, the banks had to increasingly switch to riskier assets, whereby the search for these risky assets had to be underpinned by securitization to make the former appear safer. Those companies that had the chance to beat the average with their investments to secure their financing activities, now had the largest shares of market liquidity, which serves to generate further assets in the secondary financial markets. This resulted in an overproduction of circulating money, so the profits continued to fall.

However, as European banks gained power, they still had to continue to align with the business practices of US banks and the rules of the US financial markets. Currently, European banks have to take on expensive FX swaps to transform the Euro financing into a dollar financing, because their demand for dollars does not meet a complementary demand from US banks for euros (ibid.: 43). This increases the costs for dollar financing. But since this financing through the dollar is important, the European banks are forced to rely on higher leverage in the capital markets and to intensify their search for dollar-denominated assets that can be used as collateral for financing. This relative weakness of the European banks compared to the US banks was a motivation for the former before the financial crisis of 2008 to constantly increase the excessive leverage in the capital markets. The search for CDOs and MSBs was for dollar-denominated assets, which were considered relatively safe, were liquid and at the same time were supposed to bring high profits (ibid.).

The hegemony, various variants to create CDOs, but remained in the hands of US banks, while European banks largely traded in synthetic assets, meaning that the underlying assets of the CDOs were not cash-based, but were themselves derivatives and indices. In the year 2004, of the 160 trillion traded CDOs on the European market, 140 trillion were synthetic CDOs, as European banks did not have enough monetary reserves that could be used for the purchase of cash-based CDOs (Ebd.: 45). With synthetic CDOs, the limit is pushed out, as the speculative value here can be much higher than that of the underlying assets. European banks were thus operating in a much higher risk area than US banks. One would expect that European banks, which had a higher leverage, also generated higher returns on equity. But that was not the case, insofar as European banks not only invested in assets, to make higher profits, but had to produce or buy usable assets to hedge their dollar financings. Complex and profitable CDOs could only be produced in Europe by a few large banks.

Money itself is the most liquid asset that can be defined within the financial logic of capital, because it is the only "medium" that fully satisfies the demand for means of payment. From this aspect, it shows a premium of the money markets over the assets, financial instruments and derivatives that must always be realized in money. The exchangeability of money with financial assets on the money markets also testifies to the ability of institutions to create new financial products such as derivatives, in which value can be preserved and accumulated. By creating a negotiable security, an illiquid thing or a future state in the world can be transformed into an asset or promise of payment that is priced because it can be pledged as security to generate funds today.

Finally, it is important to point out a further development in the derivatives markets. The catastrophe itself is now tradable and it is monetized (Zhexi Zhang, 2023). Statistical models that collect data on storms and flood risks to estimate the damage that will be caused by future disasters are now indispensable. However, millions of synthetic floods or storms must be simulated to obtain a sample of sufficient size to estimate potential future damage. With various time scales from 10 to 100 years, the possibility of future floods or storms is simulated to indicate a period that allows the threatened clients who purchase the evaluations to estimate how high their future losses could be. The risk simulated with these models is a threat and a resource at the same time. Scientists who model disasters make scientific findings understandable and usable for organizations in the financial sector. It is insurance companies that transform their policies into financial instruments that circulate as catastrophe bonds or "Cat Bonds" and sell them in high-risk classes. An American pension fund can then speculate on a coming flood in Pakistan or a wildfire in California. Upcoming natural events are understood as uncorrelated with the markets, but at the same time used to diversify the portfolio. Investors, for example, put up a sum of money to buy a bond called "Pakistan Flood". If the flood actually occurs under certain conditions and within a certain time span, then the money is lost. And one may even have to pay for damages. If nothing happens, then the holder of the bond is paid out with profit. Cat Bonds are an alternative investment that primarily trades with the volatility of natural conditions and assets.

In Miami, for example, the use of risk capital since the year 2010 has responded to the threat of a rising sea level with increased market liquidity, which even allowed the construction sector to expand. Here, one must speak of a divergence between the short-term interests of the developers of catastrophe bonds, the medium-term risks of the owners of real and financial assets, and the long-term natural conditions of Miami. However, the market for these financial instruments is currently in a crisis (ibid.).

It is the money robots of high-frequency trading that dominate automation on the financial markets today. They are actually nothing more than complex algorithms that analyze and process data at enormous speed and are able to learn by means of feedback processes in order to ultimately generate new outputs (Ehrenhauser, 2018). Today, around 90% of all financial transactions on the markets are carried out by money robots (ibid.: 36). They are materialized ecstasies of high frequency, of raging speed at milli- or even nanosecond intervals, which often enough promise a trip into the unknown.

Today, the high-frequency trader *Virtu Financial* uses its complex algorithms to trade around 12,000 different financial instruments 24/7 on 235 different trading venues in 36 countries, constantly flooding the global computer exchanges with orders (ibid.: 17). Ehrenhauser writes: "But not only has the speed increased dramatically, the number of orders has also increased. Ten years ago, a trader would send seventy orders a day to a single exchange; today there are a million orders on five different trading venues. The needs of the real economy play no role in this. The motto is buy quickly and sell immediately, even on the stock market. In

1980, the average holding period for shares was just under ten years, in 2000 it was six months and in 2013 just 23 seconds" (ibid.: 99). With the acceleration of financial cost-cutting transactions and the complete conversion of capitalization strategies to short-termism and the future, the production of risk and uncertainty is now systemic and systematic. Any thought of a speed limit on the markets, which could have a positive effect on the system as a whole, seems anathema to traders.

Money robots such as *Flow Financial* or *Virtu Financial* are referred to as "liquidity providers," which are supposed to ensure liquid (fluid) trading on the financial markets through enormous volumes of buy and sell orders. This is the first of four strategies cited by the SEC (*U.S. Securities and Exchange Commission*) to explain the functions of the money robots. This strategy is that of the digital market maker, which permanently places buy and sell offers on both sides of the order book, whereby the profit arises from price differences (spread) and commission payments from the exchanges.

The second strategy is arbitrage, which aims to realize a risk-free profit through the simultaneous execution of certain financial transactions on at least two (or more) markets. A share is bought on one stock exchange—whereby it has different prices on two or more stock exchanges—at a certain price and then immediately sold again on another stock exchange at a higher price, thereby realizing a risk-free profit. Arbitrage is a means of keeping the volatile financial field in which the assets are traded liquid, but as soon as the arbitrage opportunity arises, it is immediately closed by the very players who profited from it.

A directional trading strategy, the third strategy, involves the rapid collection of relevant information that affects prices on the financial markets, with the money robots exploiting speed advantages by being able to react to price movements faster than the competition.

Finally, "latency arbitrage" or "front running", in which special computer programs identify financially strong interested parties on the market and the high-frequency traders then buy the shares in demand themselves in milliseconds on the various stock exchanges and sell them on to the original interested parties at a higher price. Although the profit per share is not high here, it is replicated millions of times over due to the high transaction volumes and is also considered safe. Front-running is usually financed by large institutional investors such as investment and hedge funds or pension funds, and ultimately also by pensioners and small investors.

In addition to these four strategies, there is a whole range of other manipulation techniques, such as "quote stuffing", in which an enormous number of orders are sent to the stock exchange and then deleted the very next moment in order to delay trading for fractions of a second. This drives market prices in the intended direction in the short term, only to profit from the countermovement in the next moment. The company Nanex, which specializes in researching trading anomalies and provides software for the real-time analysis of stock quotes, has analyzed these strategies in detail.

Crises are welcome opportunities for money robots to increase their profits—for example, the debt crisis in Greece, which led to high price fluctuations, especially in derivatives on the financial markets, and thus to increased buying and selling decisions, with the increased demand causing spreads (the difference between the buy and sell price; the amount that money robots collect for the liquidity offered) to rise. The increased trading volume plus higher spreads therefore led to higher profits, which ordinary savers, pension investors and insurance policyholders, among others, also had to pay.

The companies that use money robots usually work with a mixture of different strategies; they create time advantages over other institutional investors thanks to their powerful technologies and infrastructures. The speed excesses and the enormous number of transactions, which usually only have a small spread and therefore lead to low margins individually, result in high profits for the money robots overall, especially when volatility (price movements on the stock exchanges) is high. However, companies not only profit from price fluctuations, but also trigger them in order to spread and amplify them in seconds via the global financial markets, which are to be understood as extremely networked systems, precisely by constantly increasing speeds and trading volumes. Iterations occur in a matter of seconds, with each node of a network can itself be seen as a network, just as the overarching structure of fractals repeats itself. In 2016, however, profits of the US company *Virtu Financial* and the Dutch company *Flow Traders* fell significantly; they recorded a drop in profits of almost 50%, despite the enormous technological arms race that is being organized with the money robots in order to obtain the relevant information faster than the competition (ibid.: 46). There has long been an asymmetry in the competition between money robots and institutional investors (insurance companies and pension funds), which could also jeopardize retirement provision in the long term.

Even small signals—triggered by tweets, certain messages or manipulative strategies—are enough to cause systemic disruption via a variety of chains of effects. In 2013, for example, the Twitter account of the US news agency *Associated Press* was hacked and the news of two explosions in the White House was then spread. The Twitter feed signaled an imminent price collapse for the algorithms of high-frequency traders and triggered an enormous number of automated sell orders within a very short time, resulting in an extreme price collapse or flash crash (ibid.: 49).

Despite these extreme price fluctuations on the stock exchanges, algo-traders insist that they use their money robots to smooth out volatility on the markets, especially in crisis situations when prices plummet because many players try to sell their products at the same time, thus reinforcing the price trend. Especially in such critical phases, a price would be set, signaling to market participants that they can buy and sell at any time, which would tend to calm price movements. However, a 2016 study by Deutsche Bank states that high-frequency traders often withdraw from the market in particularly volatile phases and reduce their liquidity supply, thereby creating an increased risk of extreme volatility, which in turn could encourage strong fluctuations in prices and even flash events. According to Ehrenhauser, in times of high volatility on the financial markets, the money robots would tend to exacerbate the excessive price movements (ibid.: 77). The ideological mantra of eternal liquidity on the markets also lurks behind the position of automated companies.

Notes

1. In this context, the computerization of the financial sphere, which is based on the Platonic idea that the financial markets perfectly integrate information about the real economy, is a fitting example of what Baudrillard called a "techneme", i.e., a reconciliation between theory and reality through a technical artifact.
2. Richard Werner's empirical studies have shown that the vast majority—about 90%—of the world's money supply is created by commercial or private banks. Every time a bank grants a loan, it creates new money, which is added to the total money supply of the economy. (See in detail about the credit creation by private banks in Szepanski, 2018, 2022). For growth to occur, more transactions must take place each year than in the last. This can only

happen if the amount of book money available for these transactions increases, in other words, if the commercial banks grant more loans.

Whenever a commercial bank decides that a customer is creditworthy (he must hold collateral and ideally have the potential for future capital realization), he is given a loan and thus a certain amount of money is credited to his account. These deposits, provided they arise from the loan itself, are called book money, which is credited as a number at the push of a button (hence the term keystroke capitalism) on an account and is processed with today's mostly electronic payments. What is lent are thus digital money signs, which represent the book money and are credited as a number on current accounts and always also entail a claim to (state) cash on the part of the borrowers, provided that they make the contractually fixed promise to repay the loan within a certain period of time plus a certain interest rate (the price of the loan). When the commercial bank grants a loan, it has to deliver the money, which represents a liability for it, to the customer immediately and at the same time it owns an asset, insofar as it collects interest over a certain period of time, while the customer also has an asset/balance on his bank account, but also incurs the obligation to repay the loan plus interest. These balance sheet relationships are essential for the relationship between creditors and debtors. The credit balances on the accounts of the debtors resulting from the loan can be referred to as "fictitious deposits", as they do not depend on the current cash holdings of a private bank.

With the granting of credit, the commercial bank has on the asset side of its balance sheet a loan claim against the customer, who on the liabilities side has the customer's deposit as a liability of the bank opposite, whereby this, and this is the crucial point, but is not offset by a payment on the part of the bank, rather, book money simply arises through the bank's granting of credit, by extending its assets (repayment promises of the debtor) and obligations (towards the debtor) on both sides of the balance sheet. No other account of the bank or an external account is reduced by the loan amount granted, rather the bank can always pay their loans with their own payment promises. Over the entire term of the loan, the bank's promise to pay out the granted loan amount remains a promise, and only when the customer withdraws parts of the amount in cash, the bank has to reduce its cash reserves. The bank books a loan on the asset side of its balance sheet and a numerically identical credit on the liability side or the current account of the borrower. So while on the liability side of the bank's balance sheet the liability appears as a deposit from the loan issuance, on the asset side the balance sheet total has increased by an amount that roughly corresponds to the loan (minus reserves). In technical jargon, this is called "balance sheet extension". The liability appears in the bank's balance sheet simply as "customer credit". The question of whether the amount is deducted from another account when it is booked, leading to a reduction of other sizes in the balance sheet—either the reserves (partial reserve theory) or other funds (bank as financial intermediary)—can therefore be denied.

If new bank loans are used for productive corporate investments, jobs are created and sustainable economic growth without inflation is achieved. If new loans, on the other hand, are used for purposes such as trading in financial assets (including bonds, stocks , and futures) or real estate, this leads to an inflation of asset prices, which can trigger a banking crisis, if the boom is big enough. If bank loans are mainly created to support private household consumption, this can lead to an inflation of consumer prices. Today, banks' lending has significantly shifted from lending for productive corporate investments to lending for the acquisition of assets. Since large banks want to make extremely profitable businesses, lending for the purchase of assets today makes up the largest part of lending.

3. Knowledge about the current monetary system must be assumed. It consists of two money circuits: Private banks create book money through the issuance of loans, while central banks create central bank money. Private banks demand central bank money to comply with minimum reserve requirements, to meet the cash demand of bank customers and to secure interbank transactions within the framework of the interbank market. The amount of central bank money is based on the demand for reserves expressed by the banks. Central banks cannot directly control the lending of private banks via the amount of central bank money but only indirectly by setting the base interest rate (interest rate at which banks borrow central bank money on a short-term basis). Banking crises can occur when private banks have a deficit of reserves and lack refinancing options.

To prevent a crash of the banking system, central banks take on the role of lender of last resort, by meeting the demand for reserves from banks today without restriction, against collateral.

4. Leverage indicates the real ratio of equity and debt financing (of assets). By using debt capital, the return on capital can be increased precisely when the interest on debt is lower than the total capital return. If the total capital return rGK is higher than the interest rate on debt rFK, the return rEK on the used equity (return on equity) increases with increasing degree of indebtedness V (ratio of debt and equity).
5. Pure 24/7 circulation as a condition and as a product of the virtual-financial model of circulation of cycles. Cycles of production, cycles of consumption, cycles of exchange and cycles of distribution, all linked and overlapping. The cycles of circulation connect in the mode of quantum uncertainty with the multiple circulation of cycles, and this must be so, because the stocks of goods and capital are constantly being recoded, recombined, replicated, and cloned. In circulation, something flows out and comes back in, over and over again, that is, it is a continuum, and in this respect it is at the same time inside and outside. It is a multiply folded system with relative inside and outside states without absolute exclusions and inclusions, rather both are folds of the same continuous process. Circulation not only reproduces a flow qua a network of multiple folds, but allows them to expand when they come together. It is the controlled reproduction and redirection of movement. Circulation is about quantities, liquidity, speed, and vectors.
6. The circulation of capital is not an accidental determination of its production. This kind of mediality is an unconditional prerequisite; capital now circulates in things that do not exhaust themselves in their physical determination.
7. The relationship between financial economy and real economy is for LiPuma one of disruptive interdependence (LiPuma, 2017: 48). While the real economy depends on interruptions and volatility being avoided as much as possible, volatility is, so to speak, the lifeblood of finance, insofar as it must be capitalized and increased, which often enough serves the real economy, which at least benefits when volatility in the financial markets is gradual and predictable, while jumps in volatility can advance the financial markets, provided

they do not restrict liquidity. Derivatives thus also reconfigure the values of classic goods, reprice them, with respect to their uncertain future prices. And this also affects the structures of labor markets and the capital distributed in production. When a good is already sold before it is produced as a worldly thing, then derivatives infiltrate the circulation into production, precisely by being able to attribute floating prices to the good. Speculation on a derivative-driven good (real estate) means speculating on the spread between the directionality of prices and the spread that the derivative markets produce.

The exchange value of the derivative is by no means a function of abstract labor, rather it is the expression of a social abstraction (of risk) that is generated in a certain time interval. Moreover, the price of the derivative is based on information and the conditions that are codified in the contract—it is not in a commodity based on abstract labor, but among other things in the labor required to establish the interconnectivity of capital, which circulates globally.

8. We use the term "quasi-transcendental" to explain the concept of total capital (Szepanski, 2018, 2022). We must distinguish between capital in general (the movement of categories) and total capital. In relation to total capital, the effects of connections between "effect entities" must be examined, without referring to an organic or Hegelian conception of totality. Rather, the effects are to be related to the concept of the transcendental total capital. Total capital is not to be thought of as a unifying system, but as a determination and at the same time as a virtual potentiality, so that it does not follow any plan in relation to the latter, not even in the sense of Adam Smith's invisible hand.

The total capital is primarily understood in its transcendental constitution, namely as an a priori assumption to which the individual capitals passively refer, insofar as they must follow the a priori of the total capital and its axioms without exception. At the same time, the total capital is secondarily the result of effects (the active price-setting and cost-reducing strategies of individual capitals, which take place in competition) and even of contingent economic strategies, which can always fail. As a result of considering the second moment, we only speak of the "quasi-transcendental of capital", to which it must be added that the effects for many Marxist authors appear as causes, and therein lies also the possibility of misrecognizing economic structures. The transcendental determination of capital is not a Kantian-inspired subjective transcendentalism, but must be understood sui generis as an objective or objectifying (and historical) determination. Here, economic events are given or caused, i.e. they are effects of objective economic structures, but this always requires the conceptual analysis of real or empirical economic events. The concept of total capital does not function here as totality or even as a superorganism, but as a framework and historical transcendental. Moreover, the prefix "quasi" emphasizes that there is no availability of structure without a genesis (and a series of contingent actions).

9. For Lohoff and Trenkle, financial capital has been at least since the 1980s the engine for the expansion of global commodity production, which has been taking place since the 1960s at a high level of productivity and on the basis of advancing process automation. The authors speak here of "induced value production" (Lohoff & Trenkle, 2012: 147f.) or of "inverse capital". First, because value production is based on the extraction of surplus value through the use of labor by capital. Second, because the growing accumulation of fictitious capital increasingly drives production, which is essential for capital accumulation. Without the production of fictitious capital, the functioning capital (the capital invested in the "real economy") would have long since had to enter a cycle of significant devaluation. The financial volume has grown significantly within the framework of global economic transactions. The corresponding figures reflect this financial deepening in the developed economies of the western countries: Bank deposits today on average have a value of 200% of the gross domestic product (Sahr, 2017: Kindle Edition: 4902). The Global Wealth Report estimated the financial assets (excluding derivatives) in 2010 at 231 trillion dollars, four times the global GDP. The total volume of derivatives grew from 72 trillion dollars in 1998 to 673 trillion dollars in 2008, twelve times the then global GDP. Accordingly, the debt of non-financial actors (states, companies and households) in the OECD countries increased from 167% in 1980 to 314% of economic performance in 2009. The increase of 147% is distributed to the state with 49%, companies with 42% and households with 56% (ibid.: Kindle Edition: 4916). Worldwide, the debt overhang in 2015 compared to global GDP was 286% (Pettifor 2017: Kindle Edition: 85).

At the same time, the profits of the financial sector in relation to corporate profits in the developed economies have doubled since 1980. These figures sound quite impressive: The total nominal value of derivatives was already 694.4 trillion US dollars at the end of 2012, while the value of global GDP was 71.1 trillion US dollars. The "over-the-counter derivative markets" accounted for a total of 642.1 trillion dollars (Bank for International Settlements, 2013). However, there are some limitations in the evaluation of the statistical sizes, as the reported sums of money only represent the nominal value of the derivatives (the amounts that could be payable; they can also be referred to as virtual, as the derivatives have not yet been realized here). In 2012, the "gross market value" of the derivatives (the market price of the derivative contracts) was estimated at 24.7 trillion dollars; it thus corresponds approximately to the combined GDP of the two largest economies, the USA and China. In addition, the derivative contracts offset each other through hedging, so that the net credit volume of the OTC derivatives at the end of 2012 was estimated at 3.6 trillion dollars, a sum that corresponds approximately to the GDP of Germany (ibid.).

10. Chesnais characterizes financialization with eight aspects: (1) The multiplication of capital as intellectual property. (2) Higher capital concentration. (3) Financialization of non-financial multinational corporations. (4) The multiplication of the credit system through the shadow banking system. (5) The automation of financial capital in relative independence from material conditions. (6) The valorization of money capital, which he attributes solely to fictitious capital, in relative independence from industrial production. (7) The gluing of social life through money fetishism. (8) The subordination of labor under the financial system (Chesnais, 2016).
11. In many cases, certain companies are assigned to the manufacturing industry, although they are much more likely to be considered financial companies. Take the example of Apple. Apple has a market capitalization of 750 billion dollars. As for the assets, Apple has 27 billion dollars that are exclusively attributable to equity, production facilities, and equipment, while the financial securities amount to 170 billion dollars. Apple's Braeburn, a company based in Nevada, is today the largest investment fund in the world. In addition, since 1998, Apple has massively bought back shares to increase the share price and dividends. The transactions from derivative trading have

a volume of 120 billion dollars (nominal on the contracts) (Cf. Norfield, 2016).

12. We refer to assets (commonly understood as assets) as specific forms of credit, fictitious and speculative capital. We start from a progressive differentiation of three different classes of financial assets: (a) the generic asset, (b) the synthetic asset and (c) the securitized synthetic asset. The category of generic asset includes forms of credit (loans, mortgages etc.), fictitious capital (stocks and bonds), and vanilla derivatives (forwards, options, futures), while the category of synthetic asset includes complex derivatives (CDS, TRS etc.) (Cf. Lozano, 2014). Synthetic derivatives are to be understood as a form of speculative money capital in latency, as they always have to be realized in money. Securitized synthetic assets like CDOs can contain securities, loans and credit default swaps (CDS).

    The nomadic capital as a concept is the processual unit in the process of stages and special forms. If this unity is not maintained, the capital is negated and devalued. Capital is thus a constant becoming. The crisis occurs when this becoming not only stagnates or is interrupted, but when stagnations and interruptions continue to assert themselves. Ideally, capital circulates at the speed of light. However, capital is also a material process. If the capital is a takes on an economic form, it must invest in matter, in something, that can indeed resist it. The movement of capital thus depends on the economic and material form it takes, and the transfer is always faster than the transport.
13. Even hedging includes a speculative element, insofar as it refers to the trajectories of future volatility of the underlying. The correlation hypostasized in hedging—if y develops upwards, then x develops downwards—is not understood by the market participants as a parameter of the model, but as real. The hedge can therefore also mutate into a speculation. The aim is not to reduce risks, rather they are only hedged for the purpose of increasing speculative capital, which means that risk only counts quantitatively, as a calculation of a price, which is assigned a number. In this process, the risks are separated from the conditions of their realization and this has certain implications: Risk can now be defined in terms of volatility and measured as the probability of the relative variance of the derivative price. Volatility itself is incorporated into a logic of

production. The derivatives now capitalize on the volatility, which they actively create.

14. In the game of derivatives, according to Baudrillard, it is not about a transgression like in potlatch, that would still be Bataille's transcendental utopia. The obscenity of this kind of "gambling" with derivatives is total for Baudrillard, because there is no appeal to any depth or value: Here money is naked, stripped as pure circulation, pure fascination, formal passion as transparent, cold, and superficial money lust. But the secret of the game is also total: It consists in the fact that money does not exist. It is like the secret of power, that there is none. Money exists at least neither as essence nor as substance nor as value. The "gambling" leads it back to its specific non-existence as value. This is for Baudrillard exactly the opposite of political economy and exchange, where money is still charged with the symbolic operations of value. Today, money is distributed as a pure simulacrum. The secret of the game is that money has no meaning. It only exists as an illusion.

    Not only Baudrillard, but also LiPuma identifies a structural similarity between the financial trader and the poker player, which consists in a socially generated desire that is exclusively directed at money, with there never being a limit to the desire to continue acquiring money, because this itself is the means to keep the game running (LiPuma, 2017: 243ff.). This form of greed, generated by socio-economic processes, which dominates the behaviors and thinking of market participants, is based entirely on the acquisition of money. It is a performative creation of the financialized subject through the permanent repetition of acts of money acquisition, driven by a deep-seated, unconscious compulsion, whose appearance in the everyday practices of financial actors takes the form of an asocial drive event.

15. This time logic can also be illustrated using an asset like a home. Mortgage payments on houses are determined by a speculative logic in the derivative and asset economy. They do not primarily serve repayment or payoff, but rather enable households to invest in the promise and the future potential of asset appreciation.

    This means that the owners of assets like a house must ensure a flow of liquidity in the present to meet their fulfilling payment obligations, which in turn promise future increases in wealth. The owners of a house burdened with a mortgage can be somewhat certain that their asset will gain in value and that as a result of their investment, their household wealth will likely increase in the future. However, they still need to access liquidity in the present to meet their structured debt obligations. They are already disciplined by allocating their wages for certain goods and by taking out loans in the present. There are temporal delays between the accumulation of wealth, the increase in the value of assets, and the realization of future capital gains, which can have significant consequences. For example, a temporary lack of liquidity in the present due to wage decline or unemployment can have far-reaching effects and make the difference between speculative boom or death-like fear and stagnation. In this sense, liquidity through wages and credit is to be understood as the lifeblood of households, enabling them to buy the time they need to make their investments in homeownership successful in the future.

The pandemic led to widespread disruptions of economic activity and mass layoffs and dismissals of workers. These factors posed an immediate threat to the boom of households burdened with mortgages, as they could cut off a crucial source of liquidity (wages) and thus the ability of households to meet their structured debt obligations. The economic standstill therefore raised the specter of stagnation for households burdened with mortgages and even threatened them with the forced liquidation of their real estate assets. However, in stark contrast to the financial crisis of 2008, Western governments responded with a series of emergency measures that helped to keep asset and wealth values, and especially residential property values, afloat. These measures not only enabled homeowners and investors burdened with mortgages to retain their wealth, but also to hold on to the prospect of future capital gains. Through various distributions of liquidity to households and the facilitation of a deferral of mortgage payments to mortgaged homeowners and investors, states kept homeowners and their assets, and thus the prospect of future wealth increases, alive and thriving. In this way, the government measures gave this population group time to ensure that their investments in future homeownership will pay off.

16. We define liquidity as the nominal relation between maturity and value. If liquidity means money that is virtually or latently present in a financial asset, this is only possible if the asset is not currently

in monetary form. If liquidity is actualized or transformed into money, then the liquidity of the asset is liquidated. Consequently, the investment can never remain perfect in its liquidity, and in this sense, liquidity appears as the intensive consequence to the extensive property of the security, which is denominated in money. Thus, liquidity is a functional relation between a time of delay and the time of realization of the asset.

17. Financing liquidity includes the possibility for investors to obtain financing. Financing liquidity is high when it is easy to borrow money. Market liquidity is low when the sale of the asset lowers the selling price. Market liquidity is synonymous with the possibility of finding someone who will take the other side of the trade.
18. For Meister, the "value" of financial theory lies in its ability to price options, which is done through models, mathematics, and texts, often enough via standardized contracts that co-reference certain sequences of financial events and points of parity between them. Such a point of parity could be a spread between the prices of two commodities at a certain point in time. But it could also be a parity between non-comparable units such as an average price and the measurement of an average temperature. This moment of co-referentiality, which is located in the derivative contracts, is priced and traded on the secondary markets. The secondary markets of derivatives include the way the economy reflects itself, they contain a meta-economy (Meister, 2021: 13).
19. We have extensively examined the workings of abstract risk (Szepanski, 2018, 2022). Take an example. Security A contains a variable interest loan and security B a fixed interest loan. If a swap here realizes the comparison between two resulting future income streams, then it is not a comparison of the exchange values of two commodities (or between commodity and money), but a comparison or exchange of two future money capital streams, which in the best case are profitable for both parties if they can both realize future income streams. Derivatives are therefore to be understood as a specific form of speculative money capital, as the currently most profitable form of money capital and at the same time as powerful instruments with which the conditions, structures, and processes of the current capitalist reproduction processes can be relatively effectively observed and shaped, without however leading to a

long-term elimination of the crisis-ridden processes in the capitalist economy.

Another example: Assuming that the swap itself is considered an important form of derivatives, a fixed-for-floating-rate-swap is introduced here as an example. In the contract, certain conditions for the exchange of future cash flows (cash flows, income or revenue streams) are agreed upon. Asset A is a government bond issued by a sovereign, developed capitalist state and guarantees a fixed return rate Ra. At the same time, B is a loan held by a capitalist company with a variable interest rate Rb. The fixed-for-floating-rate-swap involves the comparison of two future money capital streams (two different income streams are exchanged):

x-Ra = y-Rb (Sotiropoulos et al., 2013: 176).

The future income streams Ra and Rb are already commensurable at a monetary level. But how are the economic relations to be understood that are necessary for a quantitative comparison of the rate x/y? The two income streams can only be exchanged in money if the economic relations, namely those of state control in case A and those of private surplus production in case B, are represented to the satisfaction of financial capital and its analysts. A completely liquid and efficient market is assumed.

20. The ongoing evaluation of subjects by credit institutions is today a process of differentiated-hierarchical division of economic positions as well as access to financial flows. This capitalization and control not only evaluate products, but increasingly every aspect of human life. Balibar calls the capitalization of life a total subsumption, which only wants to consider any outside as a useless residue or as a field of further capitalization. Whether the capitalization as the comprehensive integration of the surplus population into the financial field through microcredits is successful remains open to this day.
21. It is necessary to deconstruct the semiotic hierarchy present in speculative transactions. Every speculative intervention begins with a sign or an instance. It is about how the difference present in the derivatives makes a difference. One cannot identify and manage risk by considering only a singular event, rather one must typify the event or sign. To make a calculation, the actors must accept the sign with Peirce as the "indexical icon" of a type. The reproducibility of the sign as a type is immaterial and aims for unlimited

repetition regardless of its material marking. And the relation between sign and type must be transparent, so that, for example, a currency swap can be analyzed with a mathematical model that was created for swaps. However, the mathematical derivation of the pricing of derivatives always requires the concept of an efficient market as a totality. The provision of a closed, secure, and efficient space called a market separates the forms of risk from their generative contexts, so that, for example, political events that influence derivative price movements can be treated and mixed with other market-oriented risks. Only this kind of decontextualization allows actors to bundle and price out incommensurable concrete risks, the result of which can then be referred to as abstract risk. If one assumes an efficient totality, it can be assumed that all instances of price models are "indexical icons" of a type. A derivative, e.g. a currency swap, can typify the projected volatility based on the fact that the future volatility reproduces the past volatility of the relationality contained in the derivative (e.g. dollar or euro). The technology of risk is based on leverage and convexity; the object of speculation is the volatility function of abstract risk.

22. In a certain way, even the stock price can be understood as a derivative related to the underlying "company", with the options running on the stock price being understood as derivatives on derivatives, so that trading in derivatives on the financial markets co-determines the future of the companies. In contrast to fundamental analyses, which are supposed to capture the basic business of a company, the technical-financial analysis generates the company solely on the basis of the trajectories and volatility of its stock price. Especially for tech companies that do not yet produce products, technical analysis is a welcome tool to measure the risks implemented in the companies already now. A major conflict of interest in the twenty-first century will take place between speculative capital and the managers of industrial and commercial companies, and this goes far beyond the disruption of Fordism as assumed by most production-oriented theorists of Marxism like Harvey.

References

Bank for International Settlements. (2013). https://www.bis.org/publ/qtrpdf/r_qt1312_de.htm

Beck, M., Samuel, K., & Sgambati, S. (2022). Leveraging Financial Claims: Transatlantic Bank Struggles and the Power of US Finance. In B. Braun & K. Koddenbrock (Eds.), *Capital Claims: Power and Global Finance*. Taylor & Francis.

Brodbeck, K.-H. (2009). *Die Herrschaft des Geldes: Geschichte und Systematik*. Darmstadt.

Chesnais, F. (2016). *Finance Capital Today: Corporations and Banks in the Lasting Global Slump*. Leiden.

Ehrenhauser, M. (2018). *Die Geldroboter: Wie Hochfrequenzmaschinen unser Erspartes einkassieren und Finanzmärkte destabilisieren*. Wien.

Esposito, E. (2010). *Die Zukunft der Futures. Die Zeit des Geldes in Finanzwelt und Gesellschaft*. Heidelberg.

Harney, S., & Moten, F. (2022). *Allseits unvollkommen. Plantokratie und schwarzes Studium*. Wien.

Lenger, H.-J. (2004). *Marx zufolge. Die unmögliche Revolution*. Bielefeld.

LiPuma, E. (2017). *The Social Life of Financial Derivatives: Markets, Risk, and Time*. Durham/London.

Lohoff, E., & Trenkle, N. (2012). *Die große Entwertung. Warum Spekulation und Staatsverschuldung nicht die Ursache der Krise sind*. Münster.

Lozano, B. (2014). Of Synthetic Finance: 3 Essays of Speculative Materialism. http://speculativematerialism.files.wordpress.com/2012/12/ofsynthetic-finance-complete-text.pdf

Malik, S. (2014). Ontology of Finance: Price, Power and the Arkhéderivative. In R. MacKay (Ed.), *Collapse Vol. VIII: Casino Real* (pp. 303–480).

Meister, R. (2021). *Justice Is an Option: A Democratic Theory of Finance for the Twenty-First Century*. Chicago.

Milios, J. (2003). Zur Darstellung von Marx' Krisentheorie im dritten Band des Kapital (pp. 47–60). In *Beitrage zur Marx-Engels-Forschung*. Neue Folge 1998.

Norfield, T. (2016). *The City. London and the Global Power of Finance*. London/New York.

Pettifor, A. (2017). *The Production of Money: How to Break the Power of Bankers*. London.

Report of the European Systemic Risk Board (ESRB). (2016). https://www.esrb.europa.eu/pub/pdf/ar/2017/esrb.ar2016.de.pdf

Sahr, A. (2017). *Das Versprechen des Geldes. Eine Praxistheorie des Kredits*. Hamburger Edition HIS.

Sotiropoulos, D. P., Milios, J., & Lapatsioras, S. (2013). *A Political Economy of Contemporary Capitalism and its Crisis*. New York.

Szepanski, A. (2018). *Kapital und Macht im 21. Jahrhundert*. Hamburg.
Szepanski, A. (2022). *Financial Capital in the 21th Century*. New York.
Vighi, F. (2022). *Unworkable. Delusions of an Imploding Civilization*. New York.
Wullweber, J. (2023). Der neue Staat-Finanzmarkt-Nexus. https://makroskop.eu/spotlight/bankenbeben-fehlverhalten-oder-systemcrash/der-neue-staat-finanzmarkt-nexus/
Zhexi Zhang, G. (2023). *Catastrophe Time!* London.

CHAPTER 4

The Transformation of the Shareholder Concept and the New Asset Managers

Since the year 2005, the competition and power struggle between the external shareholders and the internal managers of large companies has significantly intensified, with the latter gaining more and more power. This process was organized by a group of investors who, in the competition for the allocation of money capital, transformed both the internal operations of the companies and sought new external opportunities for outsourcing and external financing. The restructuring of the company from a production system to an investment system has three dimensions: (1) The transformation of top managers into actors of speculative money capital[1]; (2) the reorganization of corporate planning as an internal capital market; and (3) the strengthening of (external) financial functions over other areas of the company (Maher, 2021).

The so-called "General Managers" of a company are increasingly concerned with financial investment tasks, while the operational tasks are transferred to subordinate managers. The development of internal capital markets contributes to the expansion of financial operations within the company, which is evident in the transformation of the "Corporate Treasurer" into a powerful "Chief Financial Officer". This indicates even in the large industrial companies a restructuring from a "production system" to an "investment system", leading to the emergence of an investment group that is responsible in the competition for the allocation of money

A. Szepanski, *Capitalism in the Age of Catastrophe*, Palgrave Insights into Apocalypse Economics,
https://doi.org/10.1007/978-3-031-57754-3_4

and capital both for internal operations and for new external opportunities for capitalization. In this way, the increasing size and complexity of the corporate organization has not suppressed capitalist competition in the internal factions, but intensified it. The increased financial discipline exerts a new pressure on the company which consists of increasing efficiency, reducing costs, and increasing profit margins.

The shareholder concept is now to be expanded in such a way that the managers of non-financial companies can to a certain extent also instrumentalize the shareholders and lenders for their own leverage strategies. Today, the availability of financial resources has further increased due to the low interest rates, so that the indebtedness of companies has increased significantly in recent decades because firms can borrow money cheaply. Large corporations are now also heavily financed through retained earnings and income. The scarcity of financial resources for companies, on which the power of shareholders is based, insofar as they have the necessary money capital, seems to be decreasing in importance (Duta, 2022: 51).

Most often, the main focus of corporate theory is still on the dominance of external shareholders and financial capitalists, who use their economic potential in the capital markets to put pressure on the managers of companies to drive up stock and asset prices. But the managers of non-financial firms have long been active in the financial markets. Therefore, it makes sense not only to look at the relationships between lenders and borrowers, but to consider the power relations between the different classes of debtors (ibid.: 54). The managers of non-financial companies, who themselves work with high leverage, are now able to enlist the shareholders, customers, and workers for their interests. They use the infrastructural power of valuation practices, reduce costs, adopt optimistic forecasts about future claims, borrow money from banks and in the money markets to finance acquisitions and intellectual property rights. In doing so, they are increasingly moving away from active and productive capital investment, rather their strategies often rely on passive asset management, with the operational financial debts always facing thinner portfolios of material assets, so that the promises of future cash flows are secured by balance sheets that often enough only rely on the goodwill of valuations that are purely immaterial.

The financial restructuring of the large industrial companies reached its first peak in the early 2000s, namely with the transition from the organizational form of the multi-divisional conglomerate to the multi-layered subsidiary. The latter has the function of a "system integrator" that transforms a secondary layer of subcontractors as well as internal business areas into highly flexible and competitive global production and investment networks. Like the internal business areas, the strategies of the subcontractors are entirely focused on the competition for the investments of the large multinational corporations, whose global power is often secured by the possession of two crucial, state protected assets: intellectual property and brand rights. It is obvious that a globally integrated financial system is a crucial prerequisite for the development of this form of corporate organization.

This dynamic within the non-financial corporations was further intensified by the formation of closer and more comprehensive interconnections between these companies and the financial institutions. The result is an institutional regime that encompasses and permeates financial and non-financial companies and has further solidified the power of the financial sector in the structure of global capital accumulations. During the neoliberal period, various constellations of competing financial institutions already exerted a far-reaching influence and discipline on industrial companies. But only after the financial crisis of 2008 did external investors take on an even more active role in corporate governance, which also characterizes the new financial capital.

The decisive factor for the transition to the newly organized financial capital was the increasing power of a certain group of financial institutions after the financial crisis of 2008. This happened through three interconnected shifts within the financial system, all of which aimed at a weakening of the traditional banking system and a turn towards a new model based more on passive asset management: (1) The historical shift towards new asset managers and passively managed investment funds; (2) the emergence of new types of hedge funds; and (3) the significant growth of private equity firms. Even though the firms in each of these categories were not "new" themselves, they did develop innovative organizational forms and closer relationships with the industrial companies.

People now like to talk about an asset manager capitalism, which is dominated by the new asset managers. Asset managers like BlackRock are private financial companies that manage large sums of money on behalf of the wealthy elites and institutional investors such as pension funds and insurance companies, with which they primarily invest in the bond and stock markets and thus control large industrial corporations and certain geographies of the global economy. In recent decades, an increasingly larger part of the funds of institutional investors has been invested not directly, but indirectly, through the new specialized asset managers, who charge fees for their services. The global money capital is now less parked in industrial or tech companies or actively managed via certain hedge funds and banks, but it is managed by the large asset management corporations like BlackRock, State Street, and Vanguard (and passively managed), which have become an important faction of transnational capital after the financial collapse of 2008, taking on new investment and control tasks at a global level (ibid.: 54). These asset management firms follow with their diversified portfolios increasingly passively the stock indices, instead of actively trading stocks, bonds, or derivatives; they act more as financial intermediaries when they take on the function of shareholders in corporations, and provide financial channels in which the wealthy elites invest. In addition, they are interested in a generalized extraction of aggregated resources and generate a general asset inflation. In 2020, the value of indirect investments managed by asset managers was about 100 trillion US dollars (Christophers, 2023: Kindle Edition 148).

Following the financial crisis of 2008, there was also an expansion of passively managed investment funds, so-called index funds. They are important for asset managers insofar as they serve as a tool to pool the money capital of third-party investors and invest it in their interests. It is usually not the asset managers themselves, but their funds—which can take various forms—that carry out the transactions. Some asset managers maintain hundreds of such investment funds. These are to be understood as aggregations of capital owned by various investors. Asset management is therefore about the creation and management of investment classes in which the money of several investors is pooled. Over the years, these collective investment classes have received various names and legal forms—funds, trusts, partnerships, etc. Some of these funds hold shares indefinitely and only trade when the weighting of companies in a certain index (e.g., NASDAQ, S&P, etc.) changes. Since these funds cannot exercise direct discipline on industrial companies through stock trading, they have resorted to more direct methods of influencing the companies in which they are involved. The increasing frequency of contacts and institutional connections between the investment funds and the industrial and commercial companies is an important aspect of the new financial capital, which distinguishes it from the previous neoliberal period. The enormous concentration and centralization of assets within these passively managed funds has simultaneously promoted the rise of a new group of activist hedge funds such as Elliott Management, Starboard Value, Carl Icahn, and ValueAct Capital. These funds try to influence underperforming companies by putting pressure on the boards. Since the reforms driven by these actors allegedly benefit all investors, they often also find the approval of the passive funds, which hold much larger share packages and represent ideal "external directors" who can also sit on the boards of the companies and monitor reforms that internal areas might oppose.

A large part of the money collected by asset managers is invested in financial assets such as stocks and bonds (BlackRock etc.), but not all of it, and increasingly less of it. Some asset managers (Blackstone, Harrison Street, Safanad, Foresight Group etc.) invest more and more of the funds entrusted to them not in financial assets, but in two other important types of assets (ibid.: Kindle Edition 6506). The first area concerns real estate, the second area includes infrastructures, from physical water supply networks to roads and hospitals to power transmission networks. These asset managers now own real estate and infrastructure assets worldwide worth at least 4 trillion dollars (Ibid.). They own schools, bridges, hospitals, roads, and wind farms that are essential for the life of the population.[2]

Until the 1980s, asset managers invested exclusively in financial assets such as stocks and bonds. This changed when asset managers began to invest their money not only in pure financial assets but also in tangible assets and physical infrastructures. The possibility that the ownership of asset managers of these physical assets rose from the 1980s to today to trillions was created by the privatization of companies and infrastructures by the state. Before the 1980s, it would have been difficult for asset managers or other private sector investors to accumulate extensive holdings of residential real estate and infrastructures because there simply wasn't much to buy. Infrastructures and to varying degrees rental apartments were indeed owned by the state. But when governments around the world began to privatize infrastructures and housing, numerous opportunities for private investments arose. The modern asset management industry is geared towards maximizing profits from real estate and infrastructure. When purchasing infrastructures and real estate, asset management companies typically receive two types of fees: a recurring management fee, which is based on the amounts paid by investors into their funds, and a share of the profits made with their funds. The individual investment managers who manage the funds are directly involved in these profits.

This motivates them to maximize investment returns. To satisfy institutional investors, managers of infrastructure and real estate funds must squeeze the maximum profit out of everything they buy. Otherwise, they risk investors leaving and missing out on business.

The asset managers in this area are hardly interested in long-term investments. The faster the infrastructure and real estate investments bought and sold by asset managers are turned over, the higher the returns. For fund managers, it is not worth buying the asset and holding it for a long time, rather it is worth buying it and then quickly selling it for a profit. Asset managers also implement measures and projects to increase the revenues (e.g., from rents or water fees) generated by the assets. They cut the costs incurred for the operation of these facilities. In their endeavor to sell the assets quickly, they have little interest in long-term maintenance or repair of the facilities. Dependence on a real asset acquired by an asset manager for accommodation, energy supply, water, or transport—usually means higher costs and poorer service quality, followed by significant disruptions when the owner changes just a few years later.

The almost unnoticed takeover of the built environment by asset managers has already profoundly changed the lives of hundreds of millions of people around the world. By buying large parts of the infrastructure and housing construction, asset managers are increasingly replacing the governments that used to own and manage these things.[3] There is one area where this trend will continue, the climate, because the climate crisis is also a crisis of infrastructure. The Climate Finance Partnership, for example, is a new investment fund managed by BlackRock, which has raised 673 million US dollars (ibid.). Of this, 130 million US dollars was so-called catalytic capital, provided by development banks, which take on any losses before BlackRock itself and its private investor clients. The fund will invest in climate infrastructures, including renewable energies, in the Global South.

BlackRock operates in both areas of asset management. This asset manager does not only conduct purely financial asset management, but also invests in tangible assets. BlackRock is to be considered a general manager; it invests in the full range of asset classes — in private and government bonds, commodities, currencies, in infrastructures, real estate, and other investment opportunities such as private debts. Compared to the very specialized asset managers who only operate in one area, there are asset management firms that are affiliated with large banks or investment banks, and are considered financial service companies, which are often also customers of the large asset managers. It is also generally necessary to distinguish between the more passive asset management firms, which hold bonds and shares of listed companies, but do not control them, and such active, operational companies that own the physical assets and decide in what form the asset (electricity, houses, roads etc.) is exploited. Via interposition of various investment funds, the incomes of active asset management firms are generated from the respective assets, be it parking fees, rents, water, and electricity charges, etc. The asset management firms themselves, which are involved in the funds, in turn generate their revenues from fees they charge to institutional investors, as a percentage of the capital managed or invested. The activities of the asset managers and the respective risk profile of the investments play a role in determining the level of the percentage of fees.

It should be noted that profit rates in the area of tangible asset management are higher than in the area of financial investment (ibid.: Kindle Edition 6506 f.). While the asset manager BlackRock, which is mainly active in financial investment, is about 50 times larger than the asset manager BlackStone, which invests in tangible assets, the latter's profits are lower in absolute terms, but higher in relation to the managed sums of money. In 2020, BlackRock managed a sum of 8.7 trillion US dollars, while Blackstone only managed 187 billion US dollars. BlackRock's net income (profit) was 4.9 billion US dollars, and Blackstone's was 1.7 billion US dollars. These figures show that Blackstone's profit rate was significantly higher. To earn one US dollar, BlackRock needed 1770 US dollars, while Blackstone only had to invest 110 US dollars (ibid.). This is also a result of the macroeconomic developments since the financial crisis of 2008. Western central banks have continuously lowered interest rates until 2022, so that returns on government and corporate bonds have declined. In addition, the talk of the so-called infrastructure gap—the difference between the amount invested in infrastructure and the amount that must be invested in infrastructure in the future (among other things because of climate change)—has led to the various infrastructures being transformed into a lucrative asset class of asset managers. In 2016, 45% of private investment firms' infrastructure deals were with renewable energies, the generation of which costs less labor than coal or gas (ibid.: Kindle Edition 1631).

The new constellation of financial control is reinforced by the growing power of private equity funds, which are managed by firms like Blackstone and Apollo. These firms gain a high level of control over the companies in which they acquire shares, often also dissolving and reselling these companies. Here, the connection between financial managers and industrial managers is the most intimate case of merging. Moreover, it shows a particularly close parallel to the organizational form and strategic practices of the multi-layered subsidiary, whose relationship to its internal operating departments reflects a similarly close intertwining of finance and industry.

As a result of these developments, there is no longer a clear distinction today between large industrial and financial companies—both are tokens of financialized capital, primarily focused on managing and increasing their portfolios of financial investments. While the global restructuring that accompanied these developments has made the lives of the working classes more precarious, the emergence of the new financial capital has not come at the expense of the competitiveness of American multinational companies. Instead of a capitalist decline, the new financial capital has constituted itself through the formation of dynamic, competitive, and flexible networks of global production, investment, and capitalist class power.

Notes

1. Within the companies, there is a vertical line where the line managers stand high up. In "algorithmic institutions", their main function is to operate the algorithmic metric (Raunig, 2018). Instead of proceeding strategically as before, the task of this part of management is now to prevent the susceptibility to error and slowness of human decisions, including at the top management level. These managers try to keep the line moving in order not to disturb the algorithmic leadership, whereby the algorithmic metrics can become so pervasive that line managers themselves are deskilled and can only act as enforcement and surveillance bodies within the company. They no longer set directions or goals and no longer have an explanation for the direction the organization is taking. They are consequently defensive, bullying, insecure, and limited to reproducing solutions from the institution's management. They seem busy with micromanagement, but in reality, the metrics have taken possession of them and operate through them.
2. Various forms of US pension legislation in the 1970s significantly expanded the pool of capital available for investment. The increase

in retirement savings did not initially guarantee that this capital was invested through asset managers: Pension funds could choose to invest directly and avoid external managers. However, the 1980s saw a trend towards outsourcing investments and companies. There were also significant changes within the asset management industry itself. In the 1960s, asset managers expanded their market by offering their services not only to wealthy clients but also to the public. In the 1970s, they further expanded this market by introducing a new type of investment fund—market-based index funds—which operated with low fees and thus broader access. This set the stage for another crucial development: diversification.

3. In the years of Covid-19, there was a return of government intervention. Although governments borrowed and spent on a relatively large scale, the ownership and control over what they spent the money on remained the same. Governments have abandoned ownership and financing of housing and other key infrastructures for decades. Despite all the hype about the return of the state, Covid-19 has not changed this. The state that has allegedly returned remains a neoliberal state, serving capital in the economic sphere and particularly the capital of asset managers.

References

Christophers, B. (2023). *Our Lives in Their Portfolios: Why Asset Managers Own the World*. London.

Duta, S. J. (2022). Countering Financial Claims: On the Political Economy of Definancialisation. In B. Braun & K. Koddenbrock (Eds.), *Capital Claims: Power and Global Finance*. London.

Maher, S. (2021). The New Finance Capital: Corporate Governance, Financial Power, and the State. https://journals.sagepub.com/doi/full/10.1177/0896920521994170

Raunig, G. (2018). Dividend. https://transversal.at/transversal/0318/dividend/en

CHAPTER 5

Financial Capital: Leverage Power and Financial Infrastructure

Financial claims as claims to future monetary resources and payment promises now dominate the portfolios of institutional investors and the wealthy elites. The leverage shows the power of financial companies, which now have the capacity to increase their balance sheets by borrowing cheap money to buy assets and derivatives whose profits far exceed the cost of credit. When banks create an account or borrow money in the money markets, they already exercise a certain "leverage power" (Braun & Koddenbrock, 2022: 15f.). But also institutions of the shadow banking system such as investment or hedge funds or transnational companies use debt as a tool to increase returns for themselves and their investors, while risks are supposed to be minimized. However, the claim of the business models of the shadow banking system to create dollar-denominated assets that are simultaneously safe and liquid and also supposed to enable high returns proves to be a chimera (Braun, 2021). States and central banks act as issuers of safe assets, the scope of which is virtually limitless at least in the imperialist states of the Global North, and are thus to be understood as an important part of the global financial machinery. In contrast, the states of the Global South, which often have to borrow money in foreign currencies, do not have this power at all and are completely tied to the financial cycles of the global financial industry. China, on the other hand, is subject to few restrictions due to its high foreign currency reserves.

A. Szepanski, *Capitalism in the Age of Catastrophe*, Palgrave Insights into Apocalypse Economics,
https://doi.org/10.1007/978-3-031-57754-3_5

The global financial infrastructure, which is now provided by systemically important actors such as private service and index providers, clearing houses, and payment system companies, only enables the systemic creation, i.e., the production and circulation of financial claims and promises of payment. Infrastructural power is exercised by those actors who do not themselves own monetary claims, but offer various services and infrastructural services so that the creation and trading of assets and promises of payment can be exercised at all. Think, for example, of index providers, central counterparties, and payment services. These are quite profitable activities that are based on the collection of fees. Index providers are universal sorters and provide the criteria for whether companies or states are included or excluded from certain indices. Today, financial companies usually operate in an environment with abundant financial resources. They can borrow large sums of money cheaply and thus a sudden financial shortage seems to be increasingly neutralized. However, these conditions have not led to an increase in productive investment or higher real growth of economies.

An important factor of infrastructural power today is based on financial companies that create and maintain large stock indices (Fichtner et al., 2022: 106ff.). Large companies like MSCI, S&P Dow Jones Indices and FTSE Russell (they hold together about 75% of global index revenues) dominate this market and are important institutions of global capital and part of its infrastructural power (ibid.: 107). Their central position in the index investment system gives them the power of a private regulatory instance that can regulate and partly control the financial claims and assets of companies and states, for example by influencing domestic regulatory authorities, controlling investors' access to the indices and manipulating international capital flows. This also has to do with the trend and the shift from active to passive investment. The latter means that asset owners such as pension funds and the wealthy elites increasingly invest their money in financial products or companies that merely replicate and replicate the well-known and dominant benchmark indices, think of the MSCI World Index, Dow Jones, and Bloomberg Barclays Global Aggregate Index. Passive index funds also charge lower fees than active hedge funds, while they generate the same or even higher returns on investments.

Since 2006, there has been a migration of financial owners of money capital from active to passive wealth funds, the most important of which today are BlackRock, Vanguard, and State Street. In the years from 2006 to 2018, 3200 trillion US dollars were managed by active funds, while

3100 trillion US dollars were managed by passive funds (ibid.: 108). We now speak of the age of passive asset management, with which the role of index providers within the global investment chains has also changed. In the past, these providers played different roles for various funds merely played an informational role, while now especially index funds increasingly delegate parts of their investment decisions to the index providers. These guide the global flows of money capital insofar as they decide on the inclusion or exclusion of companies and countries in the important indices, causing trillions of dollars to flow into the indices or exclusions to occur. Index investment is to be understood as a delegated investment, insofar as the inclusions and exclusions of private companies or states are based on the decisions of the index providers. For example, they set the criteria that states, especially emerging markets, must follow to qualify for index membership, while at the same time investors increasingly delegate their investment power to the index funds and providers. These therefore offer an essentially important infrastructure that enables the creation and trading of passively allocated claims.

Indices are numerical instruments that allow a comparative evaluation of, for example, stock prices over time. They are supposed to represent the performance of an economic entity such as the Dow Jones Index at a certain point in time in a single number (ibid.: 109). Indices are offered and also calculated by exchanges, index providers, or rating agencies. The best-known index providers include MSCI, S&P/Dow Jones, STOXX, and FTSE. Such indices are based on a series of corresponding data and numbers, with the evaluations providing the series of stock and bond prices with specific weights, the sequence of which also shows the performance of the evaluated assets. Successful financial performance at the company level and a positive investment environment at the national and international market level support the attraction of money capital and influence what type of investment is made in the respective markets. Due to the ability to decide which economic entity is included in or excluded from an index, and how it is evaluated and calculated, index providers play an important role in standardizing and interpreting what is worth investing in a company in the global financial markets. This gatekeeper role of the index providers for capital (ibid.: 106ff.) has developed with the increasing presence of the capital markets, within which they initially only took on an informational role and set the benchmarks. The providers were merely supposed to make the performances of companies in the various markets comparable and transparent, especially for actively managed funds, which used the information from the providers as a basis for comparing their performances.

From the year 2005, however, the index providers began to actively influence the global capital flows, with both the financial concentration of the providers playing an important role and the trend towards passive investment, with which they influenced the investments of the large asset managers and index funds. Money capital is now no longer only actively managed by the fund managers of hedge funds, but is increasingly flowing into passively managed index funds. Over a longer period of time, the actively managed funds can no longer beat the benchmark of the indices, while they charge higher fees than index funds like BlackRock Advisors. Today, the passive index funds (not traded on the stock exchange), which replicate a reference index like the DAX as accurately as possible, constitute a large proportion of the passively managed capital, thus setting a normalizing standard power in the global financial markets and at the same time determining the benchmarks for the actively managed funds. This is intended to tame the ecstasy of speculative capital, whose investments are associated with high risks and can inevitably lead to financial crises, as we will see, according to the lessons learned from the financial crisis of 2008. Whether this can succeed will be shown by the future.

Index providers do not hold any financial claims themselves and do not own any shares or bonds, but they influence the investment decisions of large asset managers like Black Rock and have a steering effect on the holdings of passive index funds and EFTs. But they also have an influence on the actively managed funds, insofar as these draw upon the benchmarks offered by the index providers as a comparison for their own performance. Similar to clearinghouses and financial payment systems, they are understood as important private financial actors who today organize the infrastructural arrangements and environments necessary for the existence of global financial markets. An index provider specifies through the setting of benchmarks for investors which assets are worth holding, and thus influences the composition of investors' portfolios.

In addition, index providers are understood as intermediaries between lenders and borrowers. A financial claim is an asset that allows the lender to receive funds or other resources from the debtor, so each claim corresponds to a liability (ibid.: 112). The large index providers bundle large sums of financial claims in their indices and are therefore powerful institutions that co-determine whether new funds are made available to private and public debtors. Thus, the company MSCI World decides which criteria states must meet in order to be included in the index, which in turn influences the actors of domestic financial regulation, international capital flows, and the influx of investors. Countries are now sorted according to specific criteria to be excluded or included or entered into watchlists. Thus, index providers constantly shift the boundaries for inclusions and exclusions, indicating which countries are worth being included in the indices and thus defining as reflectors the hierarchy for the global financial markets. Today, S&P DJI is the largest index provider, when revenues are used as a criterion, and this is mainly due to the S&P 500 Index. MSCI, on the other hand, is the most important index provider for the equity indices of emerging markets, countries that are classified and hierarchized according to the criteria of their economic development, size, and liquidity, and in terms of access potential for investors (ibid.: 115).

Derivatives as claims on future income and return flows are the hallmark of speculative capital. They are also the central instruments of private risk management, allowing financial actors to assess and trade volatility and profitability in the markets. This is not about mere betting, but about informed risk management that allows, through specific derivatives, to hedge an uncertain future and thus create calculability in the midst of a volatile financial environment. For a financial speculator who enters into a derivative contract, there always needs to be a counterparty that ideally should not go bankrupt; there must therefore be actors who provide this kind of stability and ideally bear the risks associated with entering into the contract. So which actor is able to guarantee a low risk and a low probability of non-fulfillment of the contract? The system of financial risk management today, due to the ecstasy of derivative trading, absolutely needs certain central agents whose balance sheets allow volatilities to be limited by the agents guaranteeing a certain financial stability as central counterparties in the derivative contracts. In the aftermath of the 2008 financial crisis, this became necessary to increase the resilience of the financial system through calculated private risk management (Thiemann, 2022: 130 ff.). These are forceful regulatory attempts to reconcile the empirics of the financial system with the theory of financial equilibrium by making insurance and hedging against all types of risks real. The legally secured new private systems and the support of liquidity supply by the central banks greatly reduce defaults in the financial markets. This kind of non-insolvency also depends on large clearinghouses being strengthened as central counterparties vis-à-vis the banks as counterparties in terms of risk distribution. At the same time, systemic risks are transferred to the central banks, which must provide comprehensive liquidity in the markets in case of crises. We will come back to this.

Before the financial crisis of 2008, it was mostly the large banks that counterparty risks were absorbed by contract partners for a fee, using their balance sheets to offset all possible types of risks due to the operation of the law of large numbers and the networking of various claims. Banks and funds were also "too big to fail" and operated without far-reaching restrictive regulations. When Lehman Brothers went bankrupt, it became difficult for American regulatory authorities to even read its balance sheets due to the high degree of networking of the company and the complexity of its derivative transactions, to sort out, untangle, and locate swaps and other derivatives in order to trace the viral contagion paths and untangle the bankruptcies of the counterparties. The central counterparties or clearinghouses ("central counterparties", CCP) suffered hardly any losses from the crisis. After 2012, the hitherto rather insignificant central counterparties (for repos and derivatives) became increasingly important and expanded their balance sheets immensely, so that the profits for the owners increased significantly. The trading of credit default swaps, over-the-counter FX derivatives, and repos was increasingly impossible without these actors, so that in 2021 about 80% of interest rate derivatives and 55% of CDS were settled by these actors. Their average profitability of 36% was three times higher than that of banks (ibid.: 131–132).

Thiemann argues that these central counterparties represent a new regulatory regime in the financial markets, which, together with the supply of liquidity by the central banks, generally reduces default risks and in particular reduces the defaults caused by bankruptcies of counterparties to almost zero (ibid.: 130). As we will see further below, the central banks remain responsible for dealing with systemic risks, while the central private counterparties in the financial markets are increasingly expanding their regulatory power.

The latter actors, whose owners are usually exchanges, take the counterposition for certain customers in the derivative revenues, where they also assume the risks of a contract for a fee. When the volatility of their contracts increases, clients must add additional hedges. The advantage for clients, such as large companies, is now that the risks that arise when it comes to hedging their position in the contract, which requires a solvent counterparty, are reduced, as the central counterparties have large portfolios of derivative contracts, with which they can constantly balance certain positions (ibid.: 132). Overall, the costs for the hedges and the risks are reduced, insofar as these actors are woven as central nodes into a network of derivative contracts and are not dependent on bilateral clearings. Based on the law of large numbers of trades, there is a network effect to report here, which generally increases the resilience of financial companies. The profit per trade for the central counterparties is rather low, so high profitability can only be guaranteed with high leverage and a high number of trades. These actors have little equity.

It is the so-called clearing banks that hold internal contracts with the clearinghouses and collect the derivatives of their customers and offer these clearings, which they settle together with the central clearinghouses, to reduce the necessary hedges for both the customers and the clearinghouses. For example, CCH Clearnet in London is surrounded by some clearing banks that collect and channel their customers' derivatives. This leads to a constant struggle between the clearing banks and the central clearinghouses, which take over the risks in the event of a counterparty default and also take care of the enforceability of claims. However, it is the clearing banks that bear the higher risk. First, the amount of damage of an insolvent party must be reported. Then the exchange, which stands behind a central counterparty as an owner, provides the desired amount, with the involvement of clearing banks being necessary.

The higher an actor stands in the hierarchy of the financial capital order, the less regulated are the insolvency rules in case of crises. Today, it is the task of private lawyers to write and code derivative contracts and assets in such a way that their owners have priority on claims, that the enforceability of claims is secured, and that the owners can avoid possible insolvency proceedings. Definitely, fictitious and speculative capital today needs coded organizations and contracts and does not always move freely floating in the form of freely tradable assets on the markets. Rather, capital can also be fixed in certain companies, so that it is transformed into property, that is, a non-tradable claim on future income of a company. Advantages for financial companies can also be granted by public law, and this with regard to the risks and the organizational form of the companies. This also applies to central counterparties as important financial players who play a not to be underestimated role in the transformation processes of the transnational shadow banking system towards a resilient market-based finance. These organizational and regulatory changes are not only the product of an organic development in the markets, but also based on regulatory measures by certain institutions after the financial crisis of 2008, to establish a resilient market-based financial regime in the world markets. This form of risk management, which is supposed to make the factors of volatility and uncertainty in the markets calculable, absolutely also requires quasi-public infrastructures that escape private risk management and are based particularly on the public nature of central banks.

Today, infrastructures that point beyond national and territorial borders are needed, for which payment systems play an important role. They serve the creation, the smooth flow, and the collection of claims. In recent decades, the Belgium-based form SWIFT has established itself as the most important institution for cross-border records of financial transactions. Today, payment processes are based on a multitude of electronic messages between the various financial institutions, with the companies for payment systems acting as intermediaries between the sender and the receiver of a payment. The payment traffic between the two different financial institutions of sender and receiver requires a financial infrastructure including an internationally functioning payment system. Here, we distinguish between retail and wholesale payments and between clearing (transfer) and settlement as current transfer. However, and perhaps precisely because of the exclusion of Iran and Russia from the Swift payment system, the BRICS countries are intensively dealing with the development of a SWIFT-independent, common payment system and their own reserve currency in 2023. So far, there are 13 confirmed candidates who want to join the BRICS countries — including Asian countries like Iran, Saudi Arabia, and Indonesia. Goods, services, raw materials, and financial assets could be traded in the future with the ruble and especially with the renminbi (RMB). If China's power continues to rise, its trading and financial partners could decide to value their goods and services with the renminbi as the primary unit of account. In parallel, the RMB will increasingly serve as a means of payment in world trade, as a reserve currency for central banks and as an investment instrument for private investors.[1]

In the future, artificial intelligence, machine learning, big data, 5G, and the Internet of Things could further accelerate the transactions of payment promises, reduce costs, and increase reliability. Companies in the United States and China dominate the industry when it comes to transfers with mobile applications.

Notes

1. The new protectionist industrial policy, especially of the USA, but also of Europe, is in tension with the agenda of development-oriented states in Asia. These are using the new political leeway that has opened up to enact non-WTO-compliant measures such as demands for local shares in production and export bans. Indonesia's President Jokowi banned the export of raw nickel from the country in 2023. His government demands that Indonesian minerals remain in the country for processing and that foreign companies instead transfer technologies such as high-pressure acid leaching for the production of battery-grade nickel there. This policy has helped attract Chinese investments for Indonesian processing and battery production.

References

Braun, B. (2021). Asset Manager Capitalism as a Corporate Governance Regime. In J. Hacker et al. (Eds.), *American Political Economy: Politics, Markets and Power*. Cambridge/New York.

Braun, B., & Koddenbrock, K. (2022). *Capital Claims: Power and Global Finance*. London.

Fichtner, J., Heemskerk, E., & Petry, J. (2022). The New Gatekeepers of Financial Claims: States, Passive Markets, and the Growing Power of Index Providers. In B. Braun & K. Koddenbrock (Eds.), *Capital Claims: Power and Global Finance*. London.

Thiemann, M. (2022). The Benefits of Network Centrality: Central Counterparties, the Enforceability of Claims, and the Securing of Extra-Profits. In B. Braun & K. Koddenbrock (Eds.), *Capital Claims: Power and Global Finance*. London.

CHAPTER 6

The Financial Crisis as a Temporal Crash of the *Over*

The phenomenon of the *excess* manifests itself in financial crises in a very specific form. The crisis generally interrupts every production, distribution, and circulation of an economy or exposes it to the constant possibility of being interrupted. Every sentence that Marx writes about the crisis proves this difference (Lenger, 2004: 35). If classical capitalism was characterized by a kind of creative destruction (devaluation of capital) in production during recession and crisis times, today speculative capital derails in crises through destructive creativity (LiPuma, 2017). This drives the dynamics of risk production incessantly and cyclically through derivatives, with which one should constantly liberate oneself and grow beyond oneself in times of neoliberalism, not only in the economy, but in other areas of life, but precisely to generate that *excess* that leads the stability in constant growth or the growth as stable ad absurdum. To maintain growth at all levels, more and more superfluous, that is also broken and useless must be produced. At the same time, the classic commodity, which once expressed class affiliation and distinction, transforms into the universal network commodity (Beller, 2021: 113) and is finally integrated into the mode of destructive-creative derivatives. The capital based on derivatives and its agents, however, still do not possess comprehensive techno-economic-logical capacities to assess the values and effects of the strategies that cyclically generate the *excess,* instead, neoclassical

A. Szepanski, *Capitalism in the Age of Catastrophe*, Palgrave Insights into Apocalypse Economics,
https://doi.org/10.1007/978-3-031-57754-3_6

economists stubbornly continue to insist that the financial markets are inherently stable and the economic models that are supposed to stabilize the markets only need to be adjusted to prevent crises in the future.

The gigantic surplus of surplus capital, which today circulates in trillions of US dollars around the globe, characterizes the crisis-ridden structure of the financial circulation of fictitious and speculative capital, the non-producing and continuously expanding pool of a mobile floating and yet coded speculative capital at light speed, which the financial institutions and their actors negotiate for profit maximization by playing the volatility of the derivatives. Now finally the circulation of G-G‘ comes to itself. Marx writes: “The circulation of capital is at the same time its becoming, its growth, its life process. If anything was comparable to the circulation of blood, it was not the formal one of money, but the substantial one of capital” (Marx, 1974: 424).

The global financial crisis of 2008 played the *excess* in dimensions, processes, and quantities of money capital beyond what we knew or could remember. It also showed that the processes of financial capitalization have replaced industrial production as the most important dynamic engine of capital and at the same time have implemented a creative destructiveness into the social economy that goes far beyond the allocation of capital for the purpose of increasing the production of value and commodities,[1] insofar as it is now particularly about the promotion of the (crisis-ridden) excess of profitable speculation of money capital, the acceleration of the flows of a nomadic capital through the creation of constantly new innovative derivatives up to the generation of systemic violence in the context of a financial collapse, which plunged large parts of the populations, especially in the Global South, into new miseries, impoverishment, and financial uncertainties.

The same process can always be observed: The expansion of credit mobilizes money for derivatives, whose positive rating increases with rising demand; these derivatives then serve as security for further borrowing, thereby setting in motion a feedback loop in which, in a double movement, loans promote the creation of assets and the assets as collateral further mobilize lending. In the illusion of eternal liquidity expansion, the leverage of capital to purchase assets that serve as collateral for further loans is systemically crucial. And as long as the self-fulfilling spiral movement continues, the securitization of loans and derivatives (promises of payment) can be continued. However, when interest rates rise and promises of payment and collateral decrease in price, borrowers start to falter and begin selling assets, which soon leads to herd behavior. With the deterioration of collateral, there is a risk that the assets will fall below the values of the outstanding debts, causing liquidity to dry up and eventually the bubbles to burst. This is the stage we are moving towards again today: asset valuations are falling, collateral is shrinking, loans are collapsing (Cf. Vighi, 2022).

Bubble inflation promotes "hot air" in the form of borrowed liquidity. The lung capacity of the system is the capital markets, non-places where assets are traded. When money capital must be raised for the investment of assets, as collateral or to finance government spending (including wars), bonds are issued among other things, obliging the issuer to repay them at a negotiable maturity date and interest rate. Companies issue bonds, as do governments. The capitalist system is now existentially dependent on the exploding masses of assets with which investors also secure the loans they need for their speculations on the financial markets. Aggressive borrowing to invest ecstatically is the risky strategy known as leverage and which constitutes the DNA of today's ultra-financialized capitalism. In 2019, the global financial system was once again on the verge of a nervous breakdown because toxic derivatives behaved hysterically and interest rates on the repo market rose sharply. COVID-19 was also a response to this catastrophic risk (ibid.: 127).

The more extensive extremely high profits are realized on the financial markets, the more speculative capital flows into these markets, thereby intensifying the competition between financial companies, which in turn drives their motivations to increase leverage. LiPuma calls this the pathological, progressive impulse of modern derivative markets (LiPuma, 2017: 149). It is therefore not surprising that financial institutions constantly preach the promise that the return on derivatives (returns) will be much higher than that on government bonds or investments in productive capital. This actually channels more and more participants into the financial markets, thereby increasing both the demand for derivatives and their volatility, through the injection of extremely mobile speculative capital, euphemistically referred to today as "fast" or "hot" money.

It is a characteristic of financial markets that there is a temporal compression in which the acceleration and increase in the number of trades makes the margins and returns of companies thinner. The response of professional traders to this is to further increase their leverage, to which the mass of traders must respond by applying the same strategies, which in turn reduces overall leverage in the long run.[2] Thus, the temporal and quantitative progression of the market requires market participants to constantly increase their risk appetite. Unforeseen risks that arise in the markets themselves, and external social and political problems, however, can lead to gigantic swings in volatility, which mutually amplify each other and lead to the bursting of bubbles. These swings in volatility become risky when, for example, hedge funds that operate with high leverage rely on long-term securities such as mortgage loans, but primarily possess quick money that is to be invested in the short term.

With the treadmill effect, which LiPuma identifies as responsible for the dynamics of financial crises (ibid.: 24), two tendencies are at odds, namely on the one hand the inherent necessity for the individual actor to increase risk, and on the other hand the general necessity that the integrity of the market as a whole remains secure. These two opposing tendencies produce an intrinsically structural tension, which is crisis-prone in itself, carries a tendency towards market entropy within itself and at the same time lies in the logic of speculative capital itself (ibid.: 146). The central argument that LiPuma develops in view of the temporality of speculative capital, states that the derivative markets self-referentially set in motion a temporal progression that drives abstract risk to a level where even small turbulences in the markets can lead to a systematic collapse. The tendency towards instability, which induces the crisis, is also based on the temporal dynamics of the markets. There is a directional dynamic, which points to an increasing complexity and instability of the markets which LiPuma tries to explain with the "treadmill effect" (ibid.: 144ff.). In this context, the issue of time, namely the discrepancy between the abstract time of the markets and the concrete time of the agents must be negotiated, insofar as these are essentially different times. In addition, the financial field possesses a multitude of temporalities, which are closely intertwined.

What may be rational for the actors in the short term in this context, becomes a problem for the market as a whole. Financial crises are not simply consequences of random outbreaks, as Nicholas Taleb has assumed with his "Black Swans",[3] but they are results of a structural tension or disruption, which is immanent to the various temporalities and logics of the financial markets. However, external news from politics or other areas can also accelerate the crisis processes.

Central to the temporal dynamics in the financial markets is the category of risk, as this is an important factor for the specific form of transactions that articulate for speculative capital with derivatives. And this dynamic creates a socio-economic field, which is characterized by the fact that the market participants must necessarily incorporate the risk structure into their habits. The systemic risk is evident, for example, in the loss of confidence in the solvency of the counterparties and is realized as a mutual restriction of liquidity. Precisely for this reason, the power of the central counterparties was strengthened after the financial crisis of 2008. No matter what happens in the markets, ultimately it is always the systemic dimension of risk, which is related to the market as a whole, which can trigger a crisis among other things. This is the modus operandi of finance and derivatives, where risk is at the same time a concrete speculative and a socially generated activity, which permeates the market in its systemic cohesion. However, the price decline of derivatives during a crisis is by no means due to incorrect pricing by the agents, rather the falling prices of concrete risks express the temporality of the systemic, abstract risk. Here, two necessary tendencies are at odds, namely the necessity to increase the concrete risk, and the necessity to maintain the integrity of the market. This immanent and at the same time torn logic of speculative capital does not imply that the market follows a linear logic and must systematically collapse, but it establishes the possibility of crisis processes that are immanent to the financial markets.

In terms of time, circulating capital perpetuates the treadmill effect. What may be rational for traders in the short term may be irrational and destructive from a systemic perspective. The structural dynamics of securitization chains are known, they result in the necessity to constantly increase the leverage of portfolios by borrowing short-term funds at low interest rates in the money markets to finance for example, longer-term CDOs with higher returns in the capital markets. This was possible during the last financial crisis of 2008 because two cycles of leverage were related: The homeowners leveraged their houses as financial assets and the managers their portfolios, driving the two interlinked markets into a mutually fueled instability through the directional dynamics. If every high reached in the various financial markets represents a new plateau from which speculative capital wants to exclude the possibility of falling profits, then this leads to the crisis as a systemic error, although various insurance companies keep claiming that there are no systemic errors.

LiPuma identifies several factors that were decisive for the financial crisis of 2008: The strategies of securitization were inherently tied to a phase of euphoria in the markets, starting from mortgage loans to derivatives. Since all systems in which human actors are involved, intrinsically contain socio-economic logics, the potential for errors, which the system contains, cannot be reduced to individual actions or the dispositions of agents (ibid.: 158f.). Finally, the current financialized capital economy is fundamentally tied to the treadmill effect insofar as the pressure generated by the competition of various actors in the financial markets pushes capital ever closer to its own abyss. In doing so, social collective dispositions are also created, which guide the behavior of individual actors in a certain direction.

In the CDO markets, the treadmill effect took a very specific form before the financial crisis of 2008. The multitude of derivatives was supposed to principally provide a higher return than the risk-free return of government bonds or that of production-related profits (the "risk premium" is the difference between the returns of the CDOs and the interest rate of risk-free government bonds), and this increased the demand for these instruments as well as their volatility. For the actors with their short-term perspectives, it is rational not to miss profitable positions, no matter how high the risk of derivative management may be in the future. Due to the good ratings and high returns, the demand for CDOs in the years since 2005 in the capital markets grew exponentially. A high demand for CDOs tends to lower the "rates of return" of the buyers because more participants are buying the same CDOs, leading to a fall in profitability (ibid.).

It was now imperative and logical that the strategies for maintaining high profits for market participants consisted in increasing the leverage of their portfolios and thus their risk tolerance and this was also facilitated by the enormous quantities of money, which were pumped into the markets by the loose monetary policy of the central banks. This worked as long as the returns and income streams generated by the CDOs were greater than the costs of the borrowed money. Thus, the demand for CDOs increased at an ever higher speed, which in turn also led to an acceleration and multiplication of the supply of underlying, secured, and unsecured mortgages. It was therefore also necessary to force an increase in the demand for new mortgages, and in the end, it didn't matter what the solvency of the borrowers was, and whether in particular the unsecured mortgages ultimately lowered the "risk premium".

This set in motion a movement with which the now, which marks the realization of a certain level of profitability at a certain point in time, became the base level of that temporal of a framework that had to be referenced in the future (ibid.). However, this could not function infinitely, so to speak, in a bad infinity, which Hegel countered by elevating the lack to potency. What might have seemed rational for the actors in the short term in this context, became a problem for the market as a whole. Similar to how rationalization or the replacement of labor by new technologies is rational for individual industrial companies, but for capital as total capital it becomes a problem, insofar as the processes of technologization induced by competition reduce the general profit rates in the sectors. As the barrier for the realization of profits continued to rise, speculative capital compensated for the prospect of falling profits with highly leveraged investments, which turned into a systemic error, even though companies like AIG developed complex derivative instruments like CDS to further hedge the high risks.

This process was possible because, as already mentioned, two cycles of leverage fed each other and led to instability: While homeowners leveraged their houses, fund managers leveraged their portfolios. Rising interest rates, falling real wages, stagnation of demand, defaults, and the lack of ability of households to repay the accumulated debts led to the price increases of houses and the assets referencing them gradually fell. The demand for new housing therefore declined, which also slowed the inflation rate of real estate prices. This in turn led to many houses eventually having more mortgage debt outstanding than could be generated by the sale of the house. Financial institutions also used assets as collateral for loans, and when their prices fell, more collateral had to be provided for the same loan. At the same time, actors who had taken on high risk and borrowed large sums of money had to sell their assets to maintain their margins. There were sudden and far-reaching stops in liquidity.

In the financial crisis of 2008, liquidity in the financial markets evaporated almost completely in a short time. The financial institutions hoarded the money instead of investing it, as they feared that their counterparts might already be insolvent and thus the pricing of derivatives could be inefficient. The systemic risk manifested itself in the loss of confidence in the solvency of the counterparties and was realized as a mutual restriction of liquidity. Even the market makers were seized by the fear that the next financial event could already signal the insolvency of the competitors. The loss in value of the assets prompted a further tightening of the credit markets, which in turn led to further defaults. When a series of assets could no longer be valued, this led to a liquidity crisis at the major financial institutions. Unforeseen risks and problems can thus lead to gigantic swings in volatility, which amplify each other (ibid.).

But it was not only the mortgages that triggered the financing difficulties at the major financial institutions, but the fact that they had to finance their holdings of assets through constant purchases and sales on the repo markets. If one loses access to these markets like Lehman Brothers did due to a collective loss of trust, one inevitably drifts into insolvency, unless there are state supports and bailouts.

By providing comprehensive liquidity, states and central banks can revive the financial markets, no matter how catastrophic the bubbles are, see the financial crisis of 2008. The main concern for a financial system is not primarily that those who hold the assets preserve their wealth, but above all that economic contagions and their destructive effects on the derivative and credit markets are prevented, and what is even more important, it is about preventing or compensating for negative effects within the market allocation of profitable assets, when in falling markets every investment must be priced at its liquidation value (Meister, 2022). Ultimately, it is about preventing a non-accumulation of already existing wealth. And if the bailouts are made too late or not at all, this can only increase the cost of future bailouts.

In 2023, following the economic upheavals of the Corona pandemic, the question of an impending financial crisis is again more pressing. People are now even talking about "poly crises" that go far beyond the financial sector. In the poly crisis, the various shocks that run through the economic, political, and social fields are differential and of varying intensity, but they work together and mix, so that as a result the (open) whole drives even more overwhelmingly into the crisis than if the crisis were only a result of a sum of partial crises. Today, authors such as Adam Tooze[4] or Michael Roberts (Roberts, 2023) speak of a completely new dynamic of a global "poly crisis" looming on the horizon, which the former attributes with the following characteristics (Tooze, 2022a)[5]:

(1) Several separate crises occurring simultaneously in various sectors of the economy as well as in social and political institutions. This is, for Tooze, the most general characteristic of poly crises.
(2) There are cybernetic feedback loops that cause the individual sub-crises to interact with each other in both predictable and unpredictable ways. This also points to the way in which the various crises relate to each other.
(3) We are dealing with the quite excessive moments of escalation and amplification of sub-crises, with various interactions leading to

the individual crises accelerating further and potentially leading to symptoms of uncontrollability. The way in which these crises, which have different temporal progression forms, are connected leads to an intensification and deepening of the various crises.

(4) In poly crises, one is confronted with the problem of boundlessness: each singular crisis can no longer be clearly delineated in time and space, as the problems associated with it spill over into other crises and merge with them. It becomes increasingly difficult to distinguish where one problem ends and another begins.

(5) There is a stratification and a dynamic of crises, which Tooze associates with the overlapping strategies and tactics of various interest groups, thus also bringing new dimensions of social problems to light: current problems mix with historical problems, concrete interest problems with ideological problems, political problems with non-political problems; finally, the problems overlap and superimpose themselves in multidimensional variations.

(6) There is a collapse of a common socio-political sense, which results from the fact that crises are interpreted differently and yet interact with each other in complex ways. To the extent that each crisis merges with or connects with the other, it becomes more difficult to invent a clearly defined and precise meta-narrative and a comprehensive narrative for each individual crisis or for the overall crisis.

(7) There are overlaps, where each individual crisis can hinder the solution of another crisis, as each sub-crisis claims certain dynamics, attention potentials, and resources for itself.

(8) The totality of these crisis dynamics, which all exhibit a high degree of feedback effects, the sum of their parts is exceeded. As in quantum theory, the whole is now more than the sum of its parts, which can ultimately only be explained by the potency of possibilities inherent in the entanglement of processes. The concept of entanglement shows that a holistic overall state exists, which, as a result of superpositions of parts, encompasses many more states than would follow from a mere addition and sum of the parts. This is due to the quantum-multiplicative composition of the whole. Thus, the current poly-crisis is much more than a collection of smaller, separate crises. Instead, it inherits a version of the "Fujiwhara effect," a term used to describe when two or more hurricanes come together, overlap, morph, and even

> merge.[6] However, the whole must not be thought of spatially or even as a being, not even as an encompassing that originates from a totality, but must be understood in the sense of quantum theory as a structure of relations. Mathematically, in classical physics, the state manifolds are composed additively, but in quantum theory multiplicatively ("tensor product of the state spaces").

If one follows the arguments under point 8 using quantum and complexity theory, the term "poly-crisis" in the strict sense would not simply stand for the addition of various crises, but for a globalized system characterized by diverse networks, interactions, and interrelationships—for a complexified crisis that is much more effective than a crisis that is merely composed of the addition of various crises. An economic world system struggling with a poly-crisis mutates into a kind of nightmarish "emergent" system, whose causalities and effects proliferate in all directions. Tooze initially sees this crisis as a deviation from the normality of a quite functional world market. Nevertheless, the poly-crisis is a situation of escalating complexity, novelty, and radicality. We have been in the midst of the escalation for some time now.

The question that arises here is whether one can still speak of separate crises that connect and branch out, or whether one should rather speak of sewn or overlapping processes of financial, geopolitical, and other ecstasies that lead to an increasing eco-economic, systemic chaos in the capitalist world system. Using an impact matrix, it would then be necessary to connect different crisis-ridden processes with each other, such as the hegemony of the financial system with its bubble formations, the imbalances in the trade balances of large industrial exporters like China or Germany, the interruptions of global supply chains, the increase in global warming and pandemics caused by zoonotic coronaviruses, the state fascism, and the strength of capitalist blocs based on the extractivism of mineral resources, land, and fossil fuels. We would then be talking with Alex Callinicos about the "Age of Catastrophe" (Callinicos, 2023), a "multidimensional crisis" that, as already mentioned, is based among other things on factors such as global warming, problems of industrial stagnation, social inequality, and financial instability.[7] From a geopolitical perspective, the struggle for global hegemony between the USA and the EU on the one hand, and China and Russia on the other hand, should be mentioned. From a political point of view, the erosion of the center of globalized neoliberalism as a result of right-wing populist eruptions. The war in Ukraine is a compressed expression of these overlapping crises of economy, ecology, and imperialism. It only makes sense against the backdrop of growing competition between the USA and China. The USA, as a hegemonic imperialist state, is currently trying to disentangle western capitalism from the relationships that have been important for the maintenance of economic globalization since the 1970s, by reducing Europe's and North America's dependence on China as a supplier of industrial goods and on Russia as a source of cheap energy.[8]

Furthermore, when considering the system solely against the backdrop of the logic of financial capital within the framework of the American boom-bust-bailout economy, it becomes apparent that its continued existence constantly requires ad-hoc interventions by the state and the central bank, with this moment of state sovereignty repeatedly proving disappointing in its successes. Financial capital continues to show such an extremely strong hegemonic dynamic that short-term regulations fizzle out in their effect or the interventions of states and central banks even initiate the next round of expanded accumulation, which from a certain point again requires ad-hoc interventions. Such perpetuated uncertainty could indeed escalate into the catastrophic.

The prevention of financial crises was answered by the central banks with lowering interest rates to zero, they intensified quantitative and credit-related easing by purchasing long-term bonds and mortgage-backed securities. Thus, the ecstasy of credit was staged and talk of "QEinfinity" began. Households, companies, and governments began to drive debt to even greater heights due to low interest rates, until from 2014 corporate debt exploded, especially in risky and leveraged companies. The Collateralized Loan Obligations (CLOs), which securitized bundles of corporate loans, resembled the infamous securitized Collateralized Debt Obligations (CDOs) from the subprime crisis. These corporate debts were not financed by banks, but by shadow banks, hedge funds, and private equity funds. By mid-2017, the Fed had begun to slowly raise interest rates, but private and public borrowers were so heavily indebted that small interest rate increases caused a furor in the markets. The stock market fell by 20% in the fourth quarter of 2018, prompting the Fed to intensify quantitative easing again. Almost a year before the Covid-19 crisis, the Fed could not even carry out a modest tightening of its policy. In March 2020, the stock market crashed, every lender hoarded cash and there was little money in circulation to keep the economy going. Banks, shadow banks, hedge funds, small and medium-sized enterprises, and mortgage creditors could not pay the lenders due to their high debt burden. The bond markets went into free fall. The Fed's response was to continue to let money flow quickly and heavily, at a speed, pace, and scale that was much larger than ever before, even larger than in 2008. Quantitative and credit policy easing massively reduced borrowing costs for public and private borrowers, while at the same time fiscal measures supported the shares of technology companies, real estate prices, private equity, SPACs, cryptocurrencies, government bonds, and exotic credit instruments such as Collaterized Loan Obligations (LOs). The Fed's rescue operations from March 2020 drove up prices for all types of assets.

By the end of 2021, we had left the pandemic behind us, with tons of debt, rising household deficits, and looser monetary policy than ever before in history. The monetization of debt promotes bubbles that threaten to burst everywhere, be it cryptocurrencies, risk-loving hedge funds, or real estate. With the emerging inflation and the tightening of central banks' monetary policy, a new phase of crisis processes was initiated. We will return to this below.

Finally, let's examine the rise and the crisis-ridden Expansion of China's economy over the last three decades. When considering China's economy in conjunction with its financial system, one must analyze the process of crisis-ridden credit deterioration over the years. In China, the GDP is an input that is politically determined at the beginning of a period. Once China has announced its GDP target, local authorities are responsible for generating enough economic activity to close the gap between the GDP growth target and what is referred to and measured as high-quality growth (the growth rate of the private economy, which consists of consumption, exports, and corporate investments). Bridging the gap between the two has not been a problem for the Chinese economy since the 1980s, mainly because China had a significant backlog of investments in real estate, infrastructure, and production capacities, so the investments required for the GDP growth target were largely considered productive.[9]

This began to change ten to fifteen years ago when China had largely closed the gap between existing investments and the investments that the economy could productively absorb. When this happened, China should have drastically reduced the share of reinvestments in production, but to achieve this without causing a drastic decline in economic growth, the economy would have had to switch to more consumption, which in turn means that income from previously successful parts of the economy would have to be transferred to the household sector. Politically and institutionally, however, China was not able to manage this transfer comprehensively. Instead, it kept investment growth rates high and began to systematically over-invest in projects that less increased the profitability of the economy but led to higher costs. The result was a drastic increase in the country's debt burden. When debt is used to finance unproductive investments, debt rises faster than a country's debt service capacity, for which GDP is an indicator.

The Chinese financial system is completely dominated by banks, and decisions about lending are determined administratively and politically, largely through various forms of control by the People's Bank of China, the State Council, and local governments. The increase in debt was either reflected in the banks' balance sheets or in the companies supported by the banks. While the increase in debt in the banks' balance sheets was accompanied by an increase in the book value of assets, the actual economic value of these assets was often far below the book value, so that seemingly healthy balance sheets were often heavily burdened and contained hidden losses.

All these problems were exacerbated by developments in the Chinese real estate sector, which is a reflection of total infrastructure spending. The real estate sector absorbed a significant portion (about 25 to 30%) of China's high investment rate (investments account for about 40 to 45% of Chinese GDP) over extended periods. Thus, the real estate sector is a major engine that has enabled Beijing to achieve its growth targets, but it required enormous debt that quickly exceeded the value of the associated projects, and this arrangement depended for many years on an implicit guarantee (in this case by constantly rising property prices), which gave developers free rein to leverage.

In addition, the strains on the Chinese banking system were exacerbated by the way households, companies, and financial institutions systematically took on too many financial risks in their balance sheets. Normally, companies that take on too little risk perform worse and are eventually pushed out of the market, while companies that take on too much risk initially perform better, but then run into trouble during corrections. A problem arises when an economy like China's has been a rapid growth, increasing liquidity, and rising real estate and asset prices. Under such circumstances, companies that tend to take on too many risks are hardly disciplined and systematically perform better than companies that take on a more cautious level of risk. In such a system, as Hyman

Minsky knew, over time all households, companies, and banks are forced to take on similar risks if they do not want to fall behind their competitors.

At the individual level, households and companies thus take on excessive debt, but do not adjust their balance sheets. At the same time, systemic risk unfolds, insofar as there is a close correlation between the debt of private households and that of companies, all of which take on excessive debt in a similar dynamic and unbalance their balance sheets. This resembles the treadmill effect as described by LiPuma (LiPuma, 2017). Bankruptcies and balance sheet collapses do not occur individually and randomly, but in coordinated waves at a multitude of companies at the same time. When forms of excessive risk-taking are strongly correlated among a large number and variety of companies, this leads to an increase in systemic risk, i.e., the risk of a collapse of the entire financial system. For this reason, Minsky considered the correlation between the balance sheets of the overall economy and the financial system to be more important than the risk of individual balance sheets.

Households and companies adjust their strategies to their operational environment, so that conditions or distortions that have characterized the economy for many years are integrated into the processes of these actors. In parallel, the financial conditions that have been maintained for many years are anchored in the balance sheets of households and companies. After many years of stable or improving exchange rates, consistent monetary policy, falling inflation, rising asset prices, and increasing liquidity, financial institutions begin to structure increasingly riskier financial activities that implicitly or explicitly assume these risks. When finally, the prices of assets rise faster than the underlying economic growth, this can even have a procyclical effect on the economy.

Since real estate prices in China had been continuously rising, even companies that invested too much in real estate relative to their operational requirements performed better and eventually displaced those that did not, while banks that directly or indirectly granted loans for real estate tolerated excessively risky loans in the assumption that their risks would be mitigated by constantly rising real estate prices. With China's increasing urbanization and the growing productivity of its companies, real estate prices began to rise. As long as real estate prices reflect the basic demand for current use, rising real estate prices serve an important economic function. In the case of China, however, the year-on-year rising real estate prices have changed the behavior of companies in a way that led to price distortions. After a phase of rising prices, companies with a higher risk appetite and more optimistic prospects will eventually begin to anticipate their future real estate needs. Assuming that real estate prices will continue to rise indefinitely, they buy more land than they need for operations, thus speculating on future price increases. Under such circumstances, the most successful companies are often not those that manufacture and market products most successfully, but those that speculate most aggressively with real estate. If real estate prices continue to rise, companies that are willing to take on excessive real estate risk consistently outperform their more cautious competitors, and over time the former begin to displace the latter. Over time, the purchase of real estate goes from a largely fundamental approach, based on the operational requirements of the company at the time of purchase, to a partially and eventually largely speculative approach. This gradual and procyclical transformation of the market began in China probably in the 1990s, when the surge in demand triggered by speculative purchases led to prices rising faster than they otherwise would have, thereby inhibiting the economic function of prices in the efficient allocation of land. Instead of favoring the most productive land users, the price mechanism began to favor speculators.

Real estate prices can rise rapidly over the years, and since the mixing of speculative profits and operating profits cannot be easily resolved, speculative profits inevitably begin to affect the GDP growth as a higher value-added component, as wealth effects further increase spending on real estate. Even GDP growth is further boosted over time by rising real estate prices and speculative real estate developments, which in turn are boosted by high GDP growth expectations, with the individual elements reinforcing each other. There are further examples of this type of speculative financialization: When the central bank guarantees liquidity and lowers interest rates, the costs of maintaining high inventory levels decrease, and companies adapt by maintaining the level of production regardless of demand development. When companies expect a stable and undervalued currency, the export sectors effectively bet on currency stability and exports increase relative to imports and domestic demand. Under these circumstances, companies are rewarded for individual behavior that makes the system as a whole riskier, and they are punished with consistently poor performance compared to their competitors if they do not participate in this behavior.

The implicit value of liquidity increases when an increasing proportion of economic balance sheets are adjusted in this way, so that any degree of incongruity becomes increasingly risky. If more and more financial companies have to tighten liquidity at some point by taking on illiquid balance sheet positions, they reduce liquidity in the operational part of the economy. The problem of liquidity is now notoriously undervalued. Therefore, the consequences of a liquidity shock, which must eventually occur, can be unexpected. As households, businesses, and financial institutions then rush to convert their risky assets into cash and other liquid instruments, the price of risky assets falls and the value of liquidity rises. When this happens, companies can get into a squeeze where asset prices and returns fall while financing costs rise—until the central bank is forced to intervene to absorb the liquidity imbalances in the economy.

Long periods of rapid growth are, as seen in the development in China, associated with a kind of financial ecstasy that almost always leads to overvalued asset prices and usually also to higher real estate prices. But when this escalating positive trend reverses and the overvalued asset prices are corrected, companies and homeowners face a decline in their booked assets, and the negative wealth effect prompts them to drastically cut their spending just when the economy is already weakening. This exacerbates the downturn, which in turn can cause the prices of a variety of assets to fall even faster. In the case of China, three decades of rising real estate prices, increasing liquidity, and high real estate and infrastructure investments were key conditions for the entire economy. Chinese households, businesses, and financial institutions have incorporated this into their operational and financial assumptions. The problem now is that they have incorporated too many risks in a similar way, so that any adjustment or shock affects a large part of the economy at the same time and in the same way.

There are always feedback loops involved. In the case of China, the first relevant feedback loop ran from rising real estate prices to increasing real estate development and increasing state revenues to increasing state spending on infrastructure and services, to rising growth expectations, which were generated by real estate development and government spending, and to further rising real estate prices. A reversal of this loop can lead to an opposite, self-reinforcing process with falling real estate prices, slower growth, and lower government spending. The rapid responses of Beijing to contain the financial contagion due to the problems of the company Evergrande in the year 2022 show that Beijing has clearly recognized that this is a systemic problem and not just a few poorly managed banks. China must slow down the pace of its investments in the long run but this is associated with further costs. A longer period in which the debt rises faster than the country's debt serviceability increases the risk of a disruptive financial adjustment. Unlike Western states, however, the Chinese state is able to intervene more deeply in market processes.

Notes

1. Capital accumulation generally means that purposes become means to achieve further purposes and the means become ends in themselves, so that the question of "why?" becomes superfluous (Röttgers 2022: 20). The ultimate purpose is solely to maintain the process of capital multiplication. Capital multiplies without sense and purpose according to its own developmental logic.
2. In these financialized processes, copying successful strategies and ideas is a common pattern of market participants' actions, so that a few lucrative trades can quickly become the trades of the masses (crowded trades). For the smaller actors in the markets, the short-term, competition-driven trading is entirely rational, as they often simply copy the trading strategies and positions of companies like Citigroup or Goldman Sachs and at the same time expect high returns, like those of hedge funds Greenlight Capital or Citadel Investment Group.
3. The algorithms are always on the hunt for what lies outside their territory and its (im)probabilities, they are defined by what they are not yet and what they may never be able to become. And with them, traders hunt the Blank Swan, when they create, write, and sign derivative contracts seemingly out of nowhere: While white swans are based on probabilities, the Blank Swan is the creature of the unknown, what lies beyond any probability calculation. For ex-trader Elie Ayache, the Blank Swan is the non-knowledge of the future that has become the market (Ayache, 2005). The human factor of machine capitalism, from this perspective, lies in creating the event of the drawing: The work of traders consists in writing and drawing the derivative as an alleged creatio ex nihilo. The image of the presuppositionless tabula rasa permeates their fantasies. Without prior knowledge, foresight, or predictions, they transport themselves into the future according to Ayache.

   And still, the relationship to the future is central. Even if it is supposed to be a future without predictions, the traders, in their frantic hunt for the future, forget the present. The Black Swan, like the white swan, remains trapped in the logic of algorithmics and logistics, always on the hunt for what it is not.

4. In 2023, Tooze distinguishes between crises that (1) are triggered by fiscal and monetary policy decisions, (2) arise from exogenous macroeconomic shocks (instability of supply chains due to global energy price shocks) or the Fed's interest rate policy, (3) are attributable to high levels of debt, and (4) are finally understood as implosions of complex financial instruments (derivatives, CLOs, etc.) (Tooze 2022c).
5. Even the elites are aware that global capitalism is confronted with a series of interconnected crises—a phenomenon now also referred to as a "poly-crisis" by the annual *Global Risks Report of the World Economic Forum* in Davos for 2023 (Global Risks Report, 2023). According to the report, the world is facing "inflation, cost of living crises, trade wars, capital outflows from emerging countries, widespread social unrest, geopolitical confrontations, and the specter of a nuclear war". These risks are "amplified by relatively new developments in the global risk landscape, including unsustainable debt, a new era of low growth, low global investment and deglobalization, a decline in human development after decades of progress, a rapid and unrestricted development of dual-use technologies (civil and military), and the growing pressure from the effects of climate change" (ibid.). Taken together, "these factors will shape a unique, uncertain, and turbulent decade," the report concludes.
6. At the beginning of the year 2022, there were turbulences in the global energy markets, which confronted energy importers, especially in Europe, with cost increases and rising bills for energy subsidies. Within a few weeks, energy supply companies in both Germany and England were driven into bankruptcy because there was a mismatch in their balance sheets between the long-term energy supply contracts with consumers and the sharply increased prices on the spot markets. Some of these companies were saved with government assistance. In 2023 the volatility in these markets has settled down again. (Tooze, 2022b).

Rising interest rates, decreased risk appetite, and the disillusionment with the "tech companies" also triggered a crisis in the crypto economy in 2022. However, it was no more systemically relevant than the debt crises in developing and emerging countries (ibid.). There may also be dozens of economies currently approaching a debt crisis, but the affected economies are usually poor and small, so they make up a small share of the world economy. We live in an imperialist world economy, in which a large part of the world's population is excluded from the "systemically relevant" cycle. For Tooze, the question arises whether an economic calculus that is primarily oriented towards shares in global GDP, still does justice to the complexity of an increasingly multipolar world order (ibid.).

A high risk has existed since the beginning of 2023 in the global real estate market. With 258 trillion dollars worldwide, real estate represents an important asset class. The vast majority of this sum circulates in the USA. Real estate is also traded with high proportions of borrowed capital. Even before 2020, there were fears that real estate prices in the world's crisis areas could escalate and during the pandemic, there was an unprecedented increase in the real estate markets which has increased global wealth by several trillions. As interest rates have been driven up since 2022, the question arises whether a global real estate crash will occur. If this were the case, the impacts would be enormous. The real estate markets in China pose a significant problem.

If these assets dissolve, there will be a massive recessive shock. The rise in mortgage rates and/or the collapse of real estate prices is a major problem for the world economy. To cushion these risks, the wealthy economies have a welfare state that secures home ownership through tax benefits, subsidized home loans, and protective measures.

As mortgage rates in the USA had more than doubled within six months in 2022, the sector has run into difficulties (ibid.). Rising prices and rising interest rates result in a decline in real estate purchases. The index of US housing costs in 2023 is as high in relation to income as it has been since the era of Paul Volcker. Given this pressure, it is not surprising that the demand for mortgages is collapsing (ibid.).

The US market for government bonds, on the other hand, is not only important because of its size, but also because of its function in the organization of global liquidity flows. If there were to be liquidity problems in the US investment markets, as was the case in 2020, this poses a danger to the functioning of the entire global financial system (ibid.).

Finally, there are significant cross-country connections between creditor and debtor countries worldwide. In 2022 Russia, China, and Saudi Arabia saw their trade surpluses swell. But the reserves are not rising at the same pace. Russia has been effectively excluded from the global financial system following its military intervention in Ukraine.

As far as global financial stability is concerned, Japan is an important factor. Although Japan no longer generates large trade surpluses, it is an important global player due to its accumulated foreign assets. Moreover, the pursuit of returns by Japanese asset managers means that Japan is a potent buyer of international assets regardless of its trade balance. Japanese pension funds and savings banks are important owners of US Treasury securities and European government bonds, particularly French government bonds (ibid.).

7. The idea of catastrophe originates from the French mathematician and topologist René Thom, who invented a theory of accidents based on qualitative discontinuities found in the world, where random variations can be channeled in a dynamic topological landscape. Thus, the progressing complexity of an organism can be understood as maintaining structural stability through the catastrophic generation of discontinuities in a continuous medium. When dynamic, unbalanced systems accelerate, however, uncontrollable, and even deadly forces can be unleashed.

   This theory provides a set of methods to analyze how a system undergoes sudden behavioral changes of one or more variables. Catastrophe theory is considered a part of geometry, insofar as its variables and their changes can be represented as surfaces or curves. The theory is used to explain natural disasters, uprisings, discontinuous fractures, or social movements. Critical points occur in various areas when the conditions of possibility for a positive circulation of values are destroyed: One could describe these breaks as anagrammatic, insofar as the logic and grammar of modernity lead to a collapse. What remains of the catastrophe is anagrammatic, because we are forced to think of new arrangements as impossible and non-operative—ana—in the sense of "against" and "non" renewable. The catastrophe leads into a nihilistic abyss. This could be called the end of the world, with all dualisms such as inside and outside being destroyed and only uncertainty about the future remaining.

As such, a catastrophe is first and foremost a radical break, an interruption of the temporal continuity of history, which can announce a destructive and unexpected end. This seemingly simple temporality of the catastrophe, which can also be referred to as the temporality of the event, however, conceals a number of complicated and persistent questions about the multitude of temporalities that play a role in the conception and meaning of the catastrophe.

8. It seems that China will emerge as the winner of the technological arms race. According to Nicholas Chaillan, the Chief Software Officer of the Pentagon, the USA has no chance against China in 15 to 20 years (Roubini, 2022).
9. A more detailed analysis of Chinese state capitalism cannot be provided here. In China, since the 1980s, a form of state-controlled companies has emerged, characterized by a hybridization of private and state ownership structures and governance processes. It is therefore said that the Chinese state, which certainly comprises various groups, remains a central actor in domestic and foreign economic processes and thus the economy in its orientation towards long-term positive capital accumulation has particularly integrated the state. A partly private accumulation of capital, but especially the state organization and control of the Chinese financial sector, were an important condition for the industrialization processes and the technological upgrading of the Chinese economy. Factors such as the influx of Western capital, the establishment of large companies, and access to the world market, which contributed to the establishment of an export-oriented industrialization and accumulation regime as part of the market-oriented reform processes initiated by the state, were particularly important. However, important sectors remained in the ownership of national capital and are managed by private and state companies. Today, the privately organized tech sector plays an increasingly important role.

   Nevertheless, the highly financialized Chinese economy and the Chinese banking sector are largely under state control. Especially since 2017, the state and the CCP of China have subjected the financial sector to an institutional reorganization, in which the operational leadership was transferred from state agencies to the Central Committee of the CCP. The largest financial institutions—commercial banks, investment banks, insurance companies or asset managers—are controlled by the state. According to the Global

2000 ranking of Forbes Magazine, the Industrial and Commercial Bank of China (ICBC), a state-owned Chinese bank, is today the largest publicly traded company in the world. Wall Street's own JPMorgan Chase is only in fifth place.

The nominal concentration of power does not exclude organizational fragmentation, fragmentation of organizations, and occasionally even a certain disorder. Greater rivalries take place between the public institutions themselves, both horizontally (between the central bank and the regulatory authorities) and vertically (between the State Council and the provincial governments). China's financial industry is an important battlefield for the most powerful political and economic actors who try to benefit from their control over state assets. The financial industry can therefore be treated as an integral part of the political system.

After the financial crisis of 2008, the importance of the export sector declined, while the state simultaneously initiated the development of an internationally competitive private high-tech sector. In addition, credit lending on an international scale, which mainly relates to infrastructure projects, was massively promoted. However, since 2010, overcapacities in the infrastructure sector and industrial production have also become apparent. State-owned enterprises and municipalities today have a high level of debt and bubbles are increasingly forming on the real estate and stock markets. From 2016 onwards, a slowdown in Chinese economic growth and a simmering financial crisis can be observed.

References

Ayache, E. (2005). The "Non-Greek" Non-foundation of Derivative Pricing. http://www.ito33.com/sites/default/files/articles/0509_ayache.pdf

Beller, J. (2021). *The World Computer: Derivative Conditions of Racial Capitalism*. Durham.

Callinicos, A. (2023). *The New Age of Catastrophe*. Cambridge.

Global Risks Report. (2023). https://www.weforum.org/reports/global-risks-report-2023/

Lenger, H.-J. (2004). *Marx zufolge. Die unmögliche Revolution*. Bielefeld.

LiPuma, E. (2017). *The Social Life of Financial Derivatives: Markets, Risk, and Time*. Durham/London.

Marx, K. (1974). *Grundrisse der Kritik der politischen Ökonomie*. Berlin/DDR

Meister, R. (2021). *Justice Is an Option: A Democratic Theory of Finance for the Twenty-First Century*. Chicago.

Roberts, M. (2023). Polycrisis and Depression in the 21th Century. https://thenextrecession.wordpress.com/2023/01/05/polycrisis-and-depression-in-the-21st-century/

Röttgers, K. (2022). *Monetäre Textualität*. Marburg.

Roubini, N. (2022). *MegaThreats: Ten Dangerous Trends That Imperil Our Future, And How to Survive Them*. Boston.

Tooze, A. (2022a). Polycrisis—Thinking on the Tightrope. https://adamtooze.substack.com/p/chartbook-165-polycrisis-thinking?utm_source=%2Fsearch%2Fpolycrisis&utm_medium=reader2

Tooze, A. (2022b). Finance and the Polycrisis (5) The Hunt for the Next Market Fracture. https://adamtooze.substack.com/p/chartbook-179-finance-and-the-polycrisis

Tooze, A. (2022c). Finance and the Polycrisis (1): What Bends? What Breaks? What Implodes? https://adamtooze.substack.com/p/chartbook-170-finance-and-the-polycrisis

Tooze, A. (2022e). Zugzwang—Are We on the Brink of a Central Banking Paradigm Shift? https://adamtooze.substack.com/p/chartbook-151-zugzwang-are-we-on

Tooze, A. (2022f). The Bond Market Massacre of September 2022. https://adamtooze.substack.com/p/chartbook-157-the-bond-market-massacre?utm_source=%2Fsearch%2FLiability%2520Driven%2520Investment&utm_medium=reader2

Vighi, F. (2022). *Unworkable. Delusions of an Imploding Civilization*. New York.

CHAPTER 7

State and Financial Market

A money-issuing state has the ability to monetize its own debts at least virtually infinitely by abolishing the distinction between issuing and borrowing money. The general use of state money accepted by the population gives the state absolute liquidity, as also assumed by the Modern Money Theory. Here, the relative liquidity of the financial markets always appears as the product of political decisions. However, this thesis needs to be restricted, insofar as the economic strength and power of states are negotiated on the secondary financial markets. The functioning of a relatively autonomous pricing of financial derivatives by speculative capital is today constantly renegotiating and managing the relationship between publicly created and private, market-based liquidity, under the dominance of the private war machines of capital.

Katharina Pistor shows in her book *The Code of Capital*, how various agents and actors of capital can bring state power to their side, for example by influencing the law, and thus also the code for capital, without having to take over the state apparatus as such (Pistor, 2020).[1]

There are four factors or properties for Pistor that ensure that a certain good or a class of goods becomes capital. These must, and this is crucial for Pistor, be legally secured in order to transform property into capital: (1) The priority of private property over competing ownership claims, which is legally guaranteed. The attribute of priority protects the capital

A. Szepanski, *Capitalism in the Age of Catastrophe*, Palgrave Insights into Apocalypse Economics,
https://doi.org/10.1007/978-3-031-57754-3_7

owner from the access and insolvency of other owners. (2) The permanent legal protection of private property. (3) Capital requires universality. Although private contracts can establish a priority and durability protection between the contracting parties. However, as long as only the two contracting parties are bound by it, there is a risk that a third party will also claim the property. The universality of the law now ensures that claims and entitlements are not only valid between the contracting parties but that the state defends claims against everyone. (4) Convertibility. This attribute gives the owners the right to convert their goods into state money when no private buyer can be found. Since state money is the only "good" whose (nominal) purchasing power is certain, convertibility allows capital to not completely lose its value even if private demand disappears. An example of this property is the willingness of central banks to purchase certain securities and in return provide central bank money (ibid.: 32ff.).

The legal code is thus differentiated by Pistor into four modules: the prioritization, which includes advantages for creditors in terms of obligations, the permanence, which protects legal positions from access can be shielded and capital can potentially have an infinite lifespan, as well as universality, which enforces permanence and priority for all, and finally convertibility, meaning the convertibility of private values into state money.

Pistor writes that it is precisely the owners of wealth who today invoke contractual freedom for their projects, without acknowledging that these rights are ultimately guaranteed by states. According to Pistor, the English common law and the law of the state of New York are internationally leading in this coding of capital. And it is of course no coincidence that these legal systems correlate with the financial centers of London and New York, where the important law firms are also located (ibid.: 25–26). So there is no central globalized law of a single world state, but there are powerful and privileged national laws that are connected by certain rules. The transnational corporations are very flexible in this context and then choose the rights that are most favorable to them in order to assert their interests.

However, Pistor's concept of capital has some ambiguities. On the one hand, in explicating her concept of capital, she speaks of the "correct" legal coding as a privilege that transforms goods into capital, thereby "intensifying" the "tendency" to create wealth (ibid.: 17), on the other hand, she speaks of a fundamental legal coding as a condition of the possibility of wealth creation in the first place (ibid.: 18). Capital owes its wealth-creating ability to legal coding (ibid.: 32), and does not set itself, as Marx had assumed. At least it can be stated that even for self-setting capital, there remains a necessity to demand at least a latent-threatening enforcement of any claims or rights by the state.

Nevertheless, Pistor also tries in newer texts to demonstrate a relative autonomy and dominance of the global financial industry over states based on certain functional mechanisms. An important function of financial power is to create enforceable claims on an unknown future, by capturing and retaining the profits now, while shifting the risks to other actors (state, central banks, counterparties) (Pistor, 2022). This requires the creation and coding of rules (e.g., by private large law firms) as well as the ability to enforce contracts, laws, and accounting rules in one's own interest, and this with regard to the ability to transform future cash flows into current cash flows, by insuring the production of the assets, drawing new lines between assets and liabilities, and demarcating asset pools against each other—it is about money creation as simultaneous creation of future assets and current liabilities, which is recorded by double-entry bookkeeping and requires the demarcation by law from the assets of other owners.

The relation between finance and state is regulated by laws, contracts, and certain regulatory procedures. Various state functions that concern regulation are today, for example, outsourced to private rating agencies. In addition, assets can be designed with the help of international law firms without referring to the existing law of a particular country. The ability to exploit certain national laws and recombine this with new assets, thereby drawing benefits from new coding possibilities, is enhanced by the fact that countries today usually formulate their laws in such a way that the private autonomy of financial actors remains untouched or is even strengthened, whose power then in turn extends far beyond certain territories. Through factors such as leverage, instrumentalization of infrastructures, and enforceability of legal claims, the relative autonomy of financial capital is mobilized, enforced, and anchored. Leverage also transforms the legal private power of financial capital today into a put on the state (bailout) (Meister, 2021). Its general infrastructural conditions also enable large-scale financial systems especially away from the state, although not without any reference to it, and ultimately, the collection of legally secured claims is also instrumentalized by financial capital for its purposes. Although for Pistor, the relative autonomy of financial capital remains bound to the legal regulations and codes of states, these in turn create autonomous spheres for capital, with which it can exert its dominance over the state (Pistor, 2022: 251f.). The financial crisis of 2008, however, not only demonstrated the ecstatic and simultaneously disastrous power of speculative capital, but also the despotic power of imperialist states, which saved financial companies with massive bailouts, which only further strengthened the autonomous power of finance.[2] Internationally positioned financial actors can thus continue to create new assets without having to assume the liabilities actually included therein.

The confidence of companies, which can be understood as the capitalists' calculation of future threats to profitability, suffers when reform-oriented state managers try to make redistributions for the workers. The class struggle capitalistsfight forces the state to use state resources to enable a smooth flow of capital investment into new areas, with the hegemony of companies over state policy being diminished in times of great instability, in which the government must respond to social demands. Most countries are integrated into collateral-intensive financial systems that are organized around bond/stock, derivative, and repo markets. There are also new cooperations between capital and state: The highly controversial public–private partnerships make social infrastructures investable for private capital. Private capital commits to financing and managing public services—hospitals or renewable energy facilities, highways, student dormitories, water and sewage, prisons or airports etc.—as long as the state assumes or shares the risks. Daniela Gabor speaks of a "Derisking State" when it comes to the structural constraints that subject the state to the hegemony of capital (Gabor, 2016).

Shadow banks and offshore markets are to be understood as important examples of the financial power of private capital over the state. But even the offshore markets require a number of laws for their smooth functioning. The ability of gatekeepers like index providers, who create exact statistical criteria for who is included in an index or not, and grant or deny states access to private credit markets, among other things, shows the dominance of globalized financial power. The transfer of direct investments often involves financial innovations and requires legal protection in the respective country, which enables the claim to future value, which ultimately arises through operational global activities. The major players in the global financial markets can outsource parts of their activities from their own country of origin and seek legality from those states that improve the conditions for their creation of profits. This is about the manipulability of private legislation by finance, that is, one can also use the law to save costs and generate returns. Due to the bifurcation of currency and law (so claims can be denominated in dollars, while enforcement is under British law, see the Eurodollar market), potent borrowers can increase their leverage in good times when they borrow money from offshore money markets, while resisting the power of certain laws in bad times. Offshore dollar loans have lower interest rates, the markets are hardly regulated and the companies pay lower taxes than in the domestic markets, which further increases their leverage power. For domestic claims, the bank holding the claim, the law, and currency are identical, while for an offshore claim, the bank, law, and currency can be subject to different jurisdictions. There are three relations to report here: (a) Between the borrower and the bank that holds the claims. (b) Between the borrower and the state, which enacts the laws and regulations. (c) Between the borrower and the country that issues the currency and in which the claim is denominated (Pistor, 2022: 256f.). The financial services of offshore centers are mostly provided to foreign participants, there are little or no taxes to pay and the owners and their financial flows and liabilities become invisible, thereby eliminating national borders.

An important significance of the state's provision of liquidity through the issuance of government bonds is that it thereby has the option to support the maintenance and valuation of assets in the capital market and to keep the money market liquid, and in doing so, it also holds the political risk that this option will be maintained by preventing the non-accumulation of capital. By providing liquidity in various ways, states and central banks can revive the financial markets in times of crisis, no matter how catastrophic the bubbles develop, see the financial crisis of 2008. The former through the issuance of government bonds, which serve as collateral in the money markets, and the latter through their interventions (purchase and sale programs of government bonds) in the secondary markets. The aim is not only for the states, but also for the financial actors primarily not to preserve the wealth of those actors who hold the assets, but above all to prevent economic contagions and their destructive effects on the markets during crises (Meister, 2021: 127ff.).

Of course, government bailouts can also fail. Then the question arises whether the potency of capital to destroy or devalue itself in crisis processes is a sign of its weakness or the basis of its strength. The flight of financial companies into good securities such as government bonds during the financial crises increases the demand for liquidity issued by the state, while privately issued assets as collateral suddenly become less accepted. If states can borrow at low interest rates from the financial sector to issue more secure collaterals, then the government bailout is definitely also at stake. In a situation of credit shortage and private financial instruments, there can also be a shortage of state-guaranteed liquidity, which is now in higher demand. It seems to be an illusion that newly created private financial instruments are as liquid as the state's bonds. Here it is important to distinguish between liquidity and moneyness (ibid.: 124). This means that securities can be liquid and stable in their prices at any maturity, but only the shortest IOUs can really quickly meet the demand for money. Only these instruments are as liquid as the state-issued money.

For Robert Meister, it is important at this point to analyze the interactions between the money markets, the shadow banking system, and the states. The states provide both good collateral and the interactions between the capital markets and the money markets, which supply the money markets with financial liquidity. The money markets increasingly also rely on the existence of safe and liquid collateral, such as US Treasury Bonds. These are considered safe because they are convertible into cash. The guarantee of a risk-free government bond, i.e. the assurance of its full liquidity, reveals a paradox of the money markets, which consists in the fact that cash pays no interest, but interest-paying bonds are traded for cash (ibid.)

When investors burn the private assets on the markets in certain cycles, there is an increasing demand for government bonds, while usually at the same time the supply of good collateral that can be bought or sold to generate funds grows. US government bonds have this function in the money markets, by pricing the difference between cash and the safest collateral that can be traded for money. It is the money markets that keep the financial markets liquid today. Meister asks himself at this point whether there is a financial value when the financial system is kept alive by state bailouts, which can be priced into the value of an asset—a macroeconomic put (ibid.: 128). For Meister, the aim is to show that under the condition that states restore systemic liquidity and reduce the spread of differential liquidity, it can be assumed that this liability, in the face of falling asset prices, is the same as if a put is sold. The state's ability to do this can be priced as a financial asset, an option that is sold for a price.

The function of issuing government bonds and thus of debt is no longer primarily in the Keynesian dimension of countercyclical fiscal and monetary policy (the Modern Money Theory also argues in a Keynesian vein), but in the production of a supply of safe collaterals demanded by the money markets in certain economic situations (ibid.: 130) (The Modern Money Theory is wrong in assuming that states primarily spend money to stimulate the economy and then collect taxes and borrow money to prevent inflationary effects). The state is now a factory for the production of securities, especially for the shadow banking system. In this scenario, government bonds for market-based finance have the function (which is analogous to the function of central banks for bank-based finance) of creating base assets with which the growth of payment promises of all kinds in the markets can continue to increase. Although the state continues to privatize banks and companies and has left macroeconomic governance to independent central banks, its economic importance has become greater again today in the context of global finance. Government debt is an important factor of the modern financial system, as a benchmark for pricing assets, with which positions in the income markets can be hedged and insurances for the creation of credits of the shadow banking system can be created. Meister assumes a temporary financial dominance of the state when there is asymmetric support of the financial system through bailouts in a situation of falling asset prices (ibid.: 130f.).

If the governments of the capitalist core countries can borrow money interest-free on the financial markets in order to issue even more secure government bonds, then they increase their economic relevance for financial capital. The power of governments, when they simultaneously issue government bonds and the currency with which they are paid, has put them in the position of a market dealer also in the shadow banking system, which Meister then calls the dealer of last resort (ibid.: 131). The market is now also guaranteed by governments that trade their own debts, which are covered by the currency they issue themselves. Meister refers at this point to the economist Daniela Gabor, who points to the epistemic shift away from Keynesianism and towards a new austerity policy, where less state money is spent (public expenditure) and at the same time more bonds are issued at low interest rates, because the creation of these collaterals is exactly in the interest of the state, insofar as the financial system can be stabilized with it. The state creates the ultimately safe asset with the issuance of government bonds, which in turn guarantees the growth of payment promises also of the shadow banking system (ibid.: 130). We will return to this in the chapter on central banks. The global financial sector today has no doubt that the liquidity of the asset markets is guaranteed by the powerful Western governments, which also trade their debts, which are in turn secured by the currencies they can produce themselves.

However, Meister does not want to accept that the public pays for the state bailouts, rather he warns that the capital markets themselves should make a financial contribution, namely for what they receive from the states that restore their liquidity (ibid.: 132ff.). This would not even have to be cash, but could also be a financial asset, such as a long call, which increases when the market rises and contains a growing claim on accumulated wealth. This long call could even be leveraged to finance the reduction of existing inequalities.

Notes

1. This dominance of financial capital over the state influences its structure itself. It seems that capital is becoming less and less interested in the democratic variant of the state constitution and is quite willing to accept or even promote forms of state fascism (Szepanski, 2018b). From a certain period in the history of capitalism, capital was no longer satisfied with maintaining an equal alliance with the state and its war machines. The construction of its own war machine by capital integrated the state, its political, military, and symbolic sovereignty, and all its administrative apparatuses, and modified them under the imperatives of financial capital.

   The coming 'fascism', which should be put in quotation marks as such, is being forced by the state policy of preemptive crisis and risk management, which, driven by prevention policies and hyper-technologized paranoia aggregates, suspects a system enemy or chaos everywhere and nowhere and therefore has to intervene with ever more drastic means to prevent what the state considers to be the worst. In conjunction with the global war machine of capital, the state no longer addresses only the terrorists as enemies, but in the form of a company and a motorized executive machine of directives, it functions as an instrument of exploitation, control, and discipline of a long-globalized workforce. The keyboard of racisms and nationalisms institutionalized by the state itself after the financial crisis of 2008 is increasingly being played by right-wing populist movements today, which want to drive state fascism towards an open civil war, which defines its primary enemies as refugees, Muslims, and generally foreigners. When the management of the financial crisis in the capitalist core countries, which consisted particularly in Europe in the transfer of the debts of private banks to the taxpayers, was accepted by the public in 2008, it was clear that both the transnational war machine of capital and the states had to initiate a new wave of internal and external colonization of certain population groups in order to catch up on the state debt through a tightened austerity policy on the one hand and to find an enemy on the other hand who could be held responsible for the misery. The dismantling of the welfare state and the stagnation or reduction of real wages led to the further integration of private households into the debt economy and they had to "speculate" on their incomes in financial terms. And debts must be understood as power apparatuses that particularly affect women, blacks, and the poor. Racist policies, especially institutionalized racisms, were part of austerity policy from the beginning. After the crisis of 2008, racism and nationalism were finally elevated to the level of state power.

If one refers to Giorgio Agamben at this point, one can speak of a state of exception that on the one hand manifests the break between constitution and government (legitimacy and legality), and on the other hand forces the creation of a zone in which the two components can no longer be distinguished. The government promotes the suspension of law and the associated creation of an exception zone, while the government continues to claim to act lawfully. While the state of exception suspends the legal order, it is stubbornly claimed that it still has a relationship with it. However, with the state of exception, a legal state is put into force in which on the one hand the law de jure prevails, but de facto loses power, and on the other hand measures and regulations that have no legal force quasi gain legal force. Today's administrative state has established the state of exception as a permanent and not just a temporary political paradigm for Agamben. State and government, according to Agamben, now reflect each other without articulating themselves (Agamben, 2023).

2. This dominance of financial capital over the state influences its structure itself. It seems that capital is becoming less and less interested in the democratic variant of the state constitution and is quite willing to accept or even promote forms of state fascism (Szepanski, 2018b). From a certain period in the history of capitalism, capital was no longer satisfied with maintaining an equal alliance with the state and its war machines. The construction of its own war machine by capital

integrated the state, its political, military, and symbolic sovereignty, and all its administrative apparatuses, and modified them under the imperatives of financial capital.

The coming 'fascism,' which should be put in quotation marks as such, is being forced by the state policy of preemptive crisis and risk management, which, driven by prevention policies and hyper-technologized paranoia aggregates, suspects a system enemy or chaos everywhere and nowhere and therefore has to intervene with ever more drastic means to prevent what the state considers to be the worst. In conjunction with the global war machine of capital, the state no longer addresses only the terrorists as enemies, but in the form of a company and a motorized executive machine of directives, it functions as an instrument of exploitation, control, and discipline of a long-globalized workforce. The keyboard of racisms and nationalisms institutionalized by the state itself after the financial crisis of 2008 is increasingly being played by right-wing populist movements today, which want to drive state fascism towards an open civil war, which defines its primary enemies as refugees, Muslims, and generally foreigners. When the management of the financial crisis in the capitalist core countries, which consisted particularly in Europe in the transfer of the debts of private banks to the taxpayers, was accepted by the public in 2008, it was clear that both the transnational war machine of capital and the states had to initiate a new wave of internal and external colonization of certain population groups in order to catch up on the state debt through a tightened austerity policy on the one hand and to find an enemy on the other hand who could be held responsible for the misery. The dismantling of the welfare state and the stagnation or reduction of real wages led to the further integration of private households into the debt economy and they had to "speculate" on their incomes in financial terms. And debts must be understood as power apparatuses that particularly affect women, blacks, and the poor. Racist policies, especially institutionalized racisms, were part of austerity policy from the beginning. After the crisis of 2008, racism and nationalism were finally elevated to the level of state power.

If one refers to Giorgio Agamben at this point, one can speak of a state of exception that on the one hand manifests the break between constitution and government (legitimacy and legality), and on the other hand forces the creation of a zone in which the two components can no longer be distinguished. The government promotes the suspension of law and the associated creation of an exception zone, while the government continues to claim to act lawfully. While the state of exception suspends the legal order, it is stubbornly claimed that it still has a relationship with it. However, with the state of exception, a legal state is put into force in which on the one hand the law de jure prevails, but de facto loses power, and on the other hand measures and regulations that have no legal force quasi gain legal force. Today's administrative state has established the state of exception as a permanent and not just a temporary political paradigm for Agamben. State and government, according to Agamben, now reflect each other without articulating themselves (Agamben, 2023).

References

Agamben, G. (2023). Die zwei Gesichter der Macht: Anarchie und Politik. https://non.copyriot.com/die-zwei-gesichter-der-macht-anarchie-und-politik/

Gabor, D. (2016). The (Impossible) Repo Trinity: The Political Economy of Repo Markets. *Review of International Political Economy, 6*, 967–1000.

Meister, R. (2021). *Justice Is an Option: A Democratic Theory of Finance for the Twenty-First Century*. Chicago.

Pistor, K. (2020). *The Code of Capital: How the Law Creates Wealth and Inequality*. Princeton.

Pistor, K. (2022). The Rise of Autonomous Financial Power. In B. Braun & K. Koddenbrock (Eds.), *Capital Claims. Power and Global Finance*. London.

Szepanski, A. (2018b). *Imperialismus, Staatsfaschisierung und die Kriegsmaschinen des Kapitals–Drei Essays*. Hamburg.

CHAPTER 8

Central Banks as Crisis Actors of the Over

Paradoxically, in the last decade, central banks have tried to cure the *excess* of speculative, fictitious, and industrial capital, which leads cyclically to crises, through the *excess* of their expansive monetary policy. Undoubtedly, central banks today are significant crisis actors, securing, prolonging, and expanding the profitability of fictitious and speculative capital through various dispositions, rules, and interventions into the circulation of money in the financial markets, thereby also bringing about new destabilizations.

Central banks are located at the intersections of state apparatuses and financial systems. They are, on the one hand, bureaucratic state institutions and, on the other hand, bank organizations that operate on privatized financial markets. Over several decades, they have built a global financing infrastructure with a focus on their activities in the repo markets, which contributed to nourishing and solidifying a liquidity illusion among financial actors, namely the conviction that balance sheet positions in market-based systems can be refinanced at any time. Participants in the financial markets expect financial support from central banks in the event of possible defaults and crises in the markets as well as expansive measures to maintain the boom. Debtors thus rely on favorable financing conditions from central banks to extend large amounts of existing debt and to issue more. These expectations are already factored into the prices of assets and in debt management strategies. What central banks do under

A. Szepanski, *Capitalism in the Age of Catastrophe*, Palgrave Insights into Apocalypse Economics,
https://doi.org/10.1007/978-3-031-57754-3_8

these circumstances is to confirm the maintenance of expectations in order to keep the financial regime alive. In addition, the issued inflation target of two percent prompted central banks to focus their policies in the face of uncertainty on creating predictability, which led market actors over the years to expect a stable development of inflation and interest rates in the future. Moreover, central banks are the main regulatory and supervisory authorities for the money markets and the banks' reserve management.

With the large-scale purchases of assets, central banks in the twenty-first century (as lenders to market participants) developed a new instrument, a form of credit provision, which during the financial crisis of 2008 and later also due to the ongoing economic stagnation and the austerity measures of the state became an important instrument of macroeconomic control. The policy of Quantitative Easing (QE) was until recently, as the Covid-19 crisis has once again shown, still very much in demand with its massive interventions. Through the massive purchase of government bonds (and also of mortgage-backed and other private securities) central banks lower the costs for these bonds. This also led to a reduction in the long-term borrowing costs for governments and for private companies and households. Central banks not only buy government bonds, but also securities of other private issuers. The convergence of fiscal and monetary policy objectives signals a certain erosion of the independence of central banks. During the COVID-19 crisis, the direct monetization of household deficits and debt has de facto become the norm. The expanding shadow banking system and an unprecedented level of debt have made it necessary for central banks to act as ultimate insurers for the financial and economic systems. The threat of market collapses, debt crises, and secular stagnation make their nearly unlimited balance sheet capacities indispensable. At the same time, however, central banks with QE have exhausted their capacities to achieve certain macroeconomic outcomes. Central banks contribute namely, to make the financial markets more unstable over time and to intensify a financing-dependent development that produces unmistakable structural problems for the economies. Central banking is thus an endemic feature of a system whose instabilities and inequalities are becoming increasingly noticeable today.

Already in the neoliberalism of the 1980s, central banks proved to be hyperactive political decision-makers, constantly adjusting interest rates to changing financial and macroeconomic conditions and the associated expectation dynamics. At the same time, the financial markets were able to continue expanding in the period before the 2008 financial crisis because they were based on the politically induced expectation that macroeconomic processes would remain stable in the future. This led to an illusion of stability in the markets. The money markets, driven by private profit motives, were a crucial factor in the failure of liberalism and post-war regulation (Eurodollar). With the introduction of new techniques for implementing their policy, central banks learned to exploit the strategies of private banks and the arbitrage relationships that had arisen in market-oriented financial systems. The consolidation of an appropriate architecture of the money markets required active support from central bankers, who intervened in the formalization of important legal, regulatory, and operational agreements. Where the activities of the central banks were most intense (in the repo segment), market liquidity also grew the most (Gabor, 2016). For a certain period of time, central banks were able to promote credit growth and stabilize the prices of assets and derivatives in times of crisis, while ensuring in conjunction with broader institutional configurations that there were no inflationary effects. However, it is important to refer in this context to a crisis process that was also effective in the 2008 financial crisis: The shadow banking system, which helped trigger the crisis, issued money by short-selling safe collateral on a prepayable (repo-based) basis, with this collateral in turn having to be secured. The Fed did this with the help of repo transactions, thereby issuing liquidity by short-selling its own debt and thus acting as a shadow bank for the shadow banking system.

At the same time, central banks contributed to massive instabilities, such as the growing inequalities in income and wealth. The expansion of the financial system today is accompanied by the expansion of an extremely wealthy class. This class is confronted with the problem of capital surplus: Where to invest in economies where there are no lucrative investment opportunities that are not themselves products of financial activities? The capital surplus has led to secularly declining interest rates for safe investments, a process that has further intensified the aggressive search for returns. In addition, only fragile islands of wealth were created for the upper middle classes, as the households in question usually hold all or a large part of their wealth in just one asset, namely their own home. Losses in value of real estate then lead to over-indebtedness and deleveraging, which in turn reduces overall demand.

For the powerful financial actors, however, the policy of the central banks was more than advantageous. Precisely because the financial companies anticipate the state bailouts and the policy of the central banks, they then take on even greater risks in the financial markets in order to maximize their returns. They fundamentally rely on the policy of "too big to fail". Thus, the largest lenders, the banks on Wall Street, were even encouraged by the anticipated security of state bailouts to charge too little to the largest borrowers, the hedge funds on Wall Street, for the risks they were taking. When private banks become seemingly weaker in their power due to state guarantees, the power of states increases, while at the same time governments also increase due to their obligations weaken, which in turn is a feedback that the banks have become weaker. These negative feedback loops can successively increase through the interconnection of shadow banking systems, states, central banks, and insurance conglomerates (See Meister, 2021: 122).

The state and the central banks are transforming today with various methods and instruments into factories for the production of securities, and this also for the shadow banking system (Wullweber, 2021: Kindle Edition 1755 ff.). The state eventually becomes a shadow central bank itself. Although the state continues to privatize its own companies and has left macroeconomic governance largely to independent central banks, its activities for financial institutions have gained weight again during and since the crisis of 2008 and the Corona pandemic. Government bonds are today an important cornerstone of the modern financial system, and also as a benchmark for pricing assets.[1]

Regarding the central banks, it should first be said that central banks do not have to secure their activities with their own capital if their liabilities are denominated in legal tender (they can create additional money at any time), but they can only seemingly work with (negative) capital indefinitely. As Adam Tooze and Joscha Wullweber show in their new books, the power and functions of central banks were strengthened in 2020 by their new role as "market makers" (Tooze, 2019: Kindle Edition 2348; Wullweber, 2021: Kindle Edition 2371). Daniela Gabor also writes that central banks have expanded the "holy trinity" of their objectives—price stability as the primary goal of the central bank, central bank independence as an institutional arrangement, and the short-term interest rate as an operational goal—by a fourth function, namely that of large-scale interventions in the secondary markets for government bonds (monetary financing). These aim to facilitate private financing in the money markets, support the liquidity of the secondary government bond markets ("Market-Maker-of-Last-Resort function") and lower yields (a macroeconomically motivated intervention) (Gabor, 2016: 967ff.). For central banks, maintaining full employment has now taken a back seat to stabilizing financial markets and controlling inflation. This policy of the central banks is supplemented by the states issuing government bonds to provide enough cash and good collateral in the form of risk-free debt also for the shadow banking system and to keep the money markets liquid, which are of paramount importance for the financial system. For Gabor as well as for Meister, the state and the central banks are increasingly becoming a security factory for the shadow banking system (ibid.: 969).

When it comes to the macro-financial role of government bonds, one should also consider the monetary policy derisking of central banks with the specification of inflation targets and the associated institutional updating from lender to market maker of last resort. Central banks keep the price of interbank money close to the prime rate and try to control the price of government and private loans in such a way that total demand is maintained at a level that is consistent with the inflation target. Market imperfections—such as the sudden disappearance of liquidity in the markets for systemic collateral—disrupt the transmission of price signals from the prime rate to the interest rates of government and private bonds. The control of the price of government bonds is structurally necessary to protect the systemic security function for price and financial stability. However, central banks can also exacerbate price distortions in collateral when providing emergency loans against collateral that is valued at market prices on a daily basis. When the collateral falls in price, commercial banks must meet the central banks' margin calls for additional collateral or cash and resort to further distress sales of securities, which further depresses liquidity and prices.

In times of crisis, private actors are exposed to financing liquidity risk and market liquidity risk. They may not have sufficient collateral to meet margin calls (increases in margin requirements). Counterparties might also not extend a repo transaction. As the last central counterparty (dealer of last resort), central banks can guarantee the price of assets or collateral. However, loans granted in the shadow banking system due to optimistic risk assessments during a boom cannot be regulated by the central banks, as they lack intervention options in the shadow banking system. Central banks now also secure shadow banks, without having control over their expansive tendencies. In times of crisis, central banks intervene by taking bad assets onto their balance sheet. This validates these investments retrospectively as an authority.

The shadow banks and the institutional investors, who received a large part of this support from the central banks and states, used the trillions of dollars after the 2008 financial crisis for new speculative activities, contrary to the Keynesian expectation that the flood of cheap money would stimulate a productive upswing in industrial companies. If private financial firms do reinvest the money received from the state, the Keynesian idea is that the real economy is stimulated by granting more loans. However, financial firms used the money in the years after the 2008 financial crisis to restructure their portfolios. This included a higher demand for assets such as derivatives, stocks, corporate bonds, and real estate. Especially in the USA, the money also flowed heavily into high-yield corporate bonds, which drove up the indebtedness of companies and led to the existence of zombie companies that could only make the interest payments on their outstanding debts. If even banks become zombified, then the toxic effect spreads to those companies that are kept alive by the banks (Tooze, 2022d, 2022e). The policy of "Quantitative Easing" (QE) does not automatically lead to higher real economic growth, but it accelerates the rise in stock and other asset prices and acts in times of recession as a monetary incentive system for speculative capital, which conducts increasingly riskier business with the incoming money flows.

The influence of central banks on the credit creation of commercial banks, which is limited from the outset, declined for a while after the 2008 financial crisis. The commercial banks had ever more opportunities to obtain missing reserves from the central banks, which in turn constantly lowered the interest rates, thus facilitating the procurement of further reserves for the commercial banks, even though their lending did not increase for a time. At an interest rate of zero, central banks can no longer use the interest rate as a tool to encourage commercial banks to lend more (During the 2008 financial crisis, not only did the economy's trust in private banks diminish, but so did their trust in each other; the banks no longer lent each other reserves, so that the risk premiums on the interbank market continued to rise despite the central bank's interest rate cuts. This brought the interbank market to a standstill).[2]

The greatly increased liquidity in the financial markets in recent decades (including the constant possibility of short-term liquidity problems), the multiplication of derivative instruments, the expanded risk management, and the comprehensive credit creation of commercial banks make comprehensive money supply control (M1 to M3) by the central banks obsolete, although they can constantly make corrections through the purchase and sale of government bonds. Ultimately, especially in times of crisis, they act and intervene as an important independent economic institution for the production of financial instruments in the markets. After the financial crisis of 2008, the Fed's bond purchase programs were for a certain time no longer limited in terms of duration and volume. In 2012, the Fed held 27% of all U.S. government bonds (Stelter, 2013: Kindle Edition: 2473). The money supply is here rather to be understood as a credit volume, which is elastic today and changes dynamically over time. The policy of the central banks must inevitably orient itself to the price movements in the financial markets, where the financial companies themselves try to gain more influence on monetary and fiscal policy. And if the European Central Bank can only buy government securities issued in Europe on the secondary markets, the EU member states and their fiscal policy remain tied to the price movements in the financial markets, which in turn intensifies the debt competition between the EU states (Varoufakis, 2012: 207f.). On the other hand, the new monetary policy instruments of the central banks and the knowledge that the central banks can theoretically grant unlimited loans against collateral (purchase and payment promises) show that the system of speculative capital can temporarily stabilize again in times of crisis. The stabilizing policy of the central banks can but also lead to new destabilization. A higher repo activity of the central banks leads to more liquidity and expands the repo activity overall. This in turn requires more collateral for repo transactions, which leads to an increase in their prices. The policy of central banks thus stimulates the entire financial system and can create new spirals of asset prices and bubbles.

By keeping interest rates low to (unsuccessfully) generate economic growth, they have partly led companies and households to take on more debt. This leads to a debt trap and increasing instability. Even before the Covid pandemic many companies financed themselves with cheap loans from the commercial banks due to the loose monetary policy of the central banks, which led to an increase in corporate debt. However, the interest rates of the commercial banks have not constantly and not in every sector fallen. In 2019, private debt in the context of a falling rate of profit had already reached dimensions that made it difficult for many companies to repay their loans. Although the goal of cheaper financing options was to increase investments in the industrial sector, this did not occur, and the expansion of credit supply was also not accompanied by an increase in overall demand. The purchasing power of private households stagnated. Industrial companies continued to face declining profit prospects, while the major stock markets were at historical highs just before the outbreak of the financial crisis. Enormous amounts of money circulated in the financial markets and drove asset prices up. In the shadow banking system, liquidity buffers were reduced again. There was an increase in leveraged financial transactions, massive stock buybacks and high dividend payouts. In addition, the low interest rate policy leads to the following: The interest rate and the price of the security are inversely related. When interest rates are low, then investors can take on higher loans and invest in assets, be it derivatives, real estate, jewels, gold, and stocks, which of course further fuels asset inflation. There is today an implicit guarantee from the central banks for the hedging of securities trading, which is equivalent to a put option, with which the prices of assets cannot fall below a certain level.[3]

The liquidity in the markets can be increased by lowering the prime rate and reduced by raising it. The prime rate policy, whose goal is the regulation of money circulation and not that of financial actors, has lost its effect today and therefore are increasingly supported by balance sheet policy and other activities of central banks. The Fed has long tried, albeit without much success, to influence the lending of private banks by changing interest rates (and through minimum reserve policy). Higher prime rates are generally intended to restrict the lending of commercial banks, while lower ones are intended to promote it. If interest rates are high, commercial banks should pass on the higher interest rates to their customers. But precisely the low-interest policy of the central banks in recent years does not automatically lead to lower interest rates and to higher lending by the commercial banks, as they constantly assess the risk of lending and the creditworthiness of the borrowers/customers and calculate (for which they operate a specific risk management) and therefore can restrict lending especially in recession phases (and thereby keep interest rates high). Monetary policy is characterized here by an asymmetry between the interest rates of the central bank and the interest rates of the commercial banks. The problems that commercial banks have, especially in crisis times, are not the lack of access to cash, but the lack of lucrative investment opportunities when the demand from households and businesses for loans could be low. Companies that are affected by low profit rates during a recession usually ask for fewer loans. The credit creation potential of commercial banks is thus limited insofar as companies in a recession also reduce debt and not only take out new loans, or because the commercial banks themselves restrict lending due to the lack of profit expectations of their potential borrowers. The credit creation of the commercial banks remains tied to the processes of private capital accumulation and the development of profit rates. However, these processes must be empirically investigated, and here we can also see counter-trends in the last decade. The borrowing policy of zombie companies as a result of low interest rates is an example of this. According to data from FactSet, seven percent of the forty-five thousand listed companies in the world could not cover their interest costs over a period of three years until 2020. Given the favorable borrowing costs, even more loans were taken out during the pandemic and some companies became zombies. Their over-indebtedness became apparent in 2022.

It should also be considered that central banks can no longer unchallenged or only temporarily perform the function of a "lender of last resort", as part of the national and transnational operations of financial capital (commercial, investment and shadow banks) are carried out independently of the central bank, so that the intervention power of the central banks always remains dependent on the price movements of derivative money capital. But especially in economic crisis times, the use of the safety device "central bank" is demanded again by the endangered financial capital units themselves and also claimed. Central banks link operations such as minimum reserve formation, liquidity assurance and interest rate policy constantly with the strategies of private financial capital. In the course of the policy of "quantitative easing" (QE) and the lowering of interest rates, the expansive developments in the money and capital markets were promoted and accelerated, without the investment dynamics of industrial capital having significantly improved so far. The new monetary policy toolkit of the central banks and the knowledge that the central banks can theoretically lend unlimited loans against collateral (purchase and payment promises) leads to the system of speculative capital being able to temporarily stabilize again in crisis times. The central banks can mobilize enormous sums of money in times of crisis, as long as there is confidence in a stable money standard. This in turn depends on the strength of the national economy, generally on capital accumulation.

Already during the financial crisis of 2008, the Fed acted as a market maker and broker-dealer in the markets to restore market liquidity. The Fed granted loans or bought securities, regardless of their creditworthiness. The Fed acted as a counterparty through the establishing new facilities for both lenders and borrowers in the money and capital markets.

It purchased large quantities of mortgage-backed securities and provided liquidity to the shadow banking system. This contributed to the revival of the securitization market and the support of money market funds. The Fed's own repo transactions also stimulated the private sectors. Thus, parts of the money market were integrated into the Fed's balance sheets. However, by 2009, commercial banks were once again so saturated with reserves that active monetary policy by central banks via repo became more difficult, and they thus temporarily lost their influence on the money creation of commercial banks. This development is to be understood cyclically.

The fixation of central bank policy on liquidity risks is no longer sufficient today for the shadow banking system to stabilize it in times of crisis. In 2013, the overnight reverse repo facility for government bonds for banks and shadow banks was already converted into a permanent facility. This covered their need for safe government bonds, while the need for central bank money was not yet satisfied by a permanent facility. When discrepancies arise about the liquidity and solvency of financial institutions, the financial system is destabilized. If the prices of securities fall in certain situations and have a negative impact on repo transactions (repo rate increases), the institutions of the shadow banking system do not have sufficient funds to meet their liabilities. Normally, these funds are then provided by the private banks, while competition among the banks keeps the repo rate low. But when, for example, the Fed sold a small portion of its securities in September 2019 (to reduce its balance sheets) and did not renew the repo transactions, the repo rate rose sharply, which also reflected the higher short-term demand for liquidity from private financial actors in the shadow banking system. This showed that it had become necessary to provide the shadow banking system not only with access to safe securities, but also to funds. When the repo rate reached 10%, the Fed had to set a cap and was forced to reopen its repo facilities for commercial banks and shadow banks (demand for central bank money). Central banks now have to create market liquidity by issuing purchase promises (and not payment promises) and therefore also have to deal with the insolvency risks in the shadow banking system. Wullweber speaks at this point of a "new framing of neoliberal laissez-faire" (Wullweber, 2021: Kindle Edition 2867). It is now important to know that even actors from the shadow banking system, such as large investment funds, could receive central bank money in exchange for securities.

They can also use the central banks to liquidate securities, a privilege that was previously reserved for commercial banks.

The central bank must therefore create market liquidity and financing liquidity by issuing purchase promises and therefore also deal with the insolvency risks of the shadow banking system. Central banks are now themselves acting as traders on the financial markets, buying and selling assets to stop downward movements through their own monetary policy. They also offer financial actors a bid-ask spread in repo transactions, a buying and selling price for financial products, to secure a framework in which these can be traded. Uncertainties are to be transformed back into a calculable risk. The price of the repo funds is now increasingly determined by the market-based valuation of the collateral (not by the interest rate policy), which is constantly fluctuating. The policies of the central banks and the state are based on an acceptance of the logic of capital, that is, there is no hard regulation of finance and its logic by laws, but in times of crisis this logic must be adjusted by the central banks. The circulation of money capital is now even increasingly secured by the central banks.

The QE policy was still based on the provision of liquidity through focused on the exchange of government bonds, while central banks now intervene directly in the money and capital markets in the role of "Market Makers" and guarantee supply and demand for almost all securities. Bailouts, "Emergency Liquidity Assistance", and deposit insurance have so far been used to protect the official banking sector. The shadow banking system, on the other hand, had its own private security mechanisms, which were normally considered sufficient. But after the fall of Lehman Brothers, one of the major broker-dealers in the shadow banking system, the Fed created additional security structures, new facilities for the shadow banking system, so that it could procure money and government bonds.[4]

With the swap lines (currency swap agreements), the Fed already offered other major central banks a temporary mutual currency arrangement in 2008 to ensure worldwide liquidity in US dollars. The Fed agreed to hold a stock of dollars for trading with another central bank at a certain exchange rate. In return, the Fed received an interest premium, so the swap lines were only used when there was no more liquidity on the national markets. The dollar amounts that other central banks received from the Fed were passed on to domestic illiquid banks (who also had to bear the costs for the swap line). On October 3, 2008, the Fed granted the ECB, the Bank of England, the Bank of Japan and the Swiss

National Bank access to unlimited dollar liquidity. Within three years, the amount of credit granted under the swap facilities grew to a staggering 10 trillion dollars (Tooze, 2018: 252). Since many companies had difficulties meeting their dollar obligations due to lack of revenue in 2020, the Fed even expanded its existing currency swap lines to the previously participating central banks to ensure dollar liquidity. The Fed opened a temporary window for foreign central banks to use US Treasury bonds for repos with the Fed. The Fed once again became the world's central bank.

The Phenomenon of Repo

Repo transactions have increased immensely in recent years and have gained importance. The repo market offers a wide range of affordable financing options for private and government financial actors. The high demand for collateral for repo transactions allows governments to place their bonds on the financial markets in even larger dimensions. Central banks, in turn, use the repo market as a tool for their monetary policy, with a higher repo activity leading to more liquidity in the markets. This in turn requires more collateral for repo transactions, leading to a rise in their prices. On the one hand, there are investors who need funds to make short-term profits through trading assets with different risk profiles or to replenish capital reserves, such as hedge funds, commercial banks, and other financial companies. On the other hand, there are money market funds, asset managers, pension funds, and other institutional investors who want to invest excess capital with relatively low risks. These different actors can now be connected with each other through repos outside the private banking system.

The policy of central banks stimulates the entire financial system through repos and can at the same time set off new spirals of asset price increases. The repo market today requires the daily intervention of central banks, as there is still no trust between financial actors. The Fed alone conducts repo transactions amounting to up to 500 billion US dollars every working day to support the smooth functioning of the short-term US dollar financing markets. The market for unsecured interbank loans has lost importance, while the demand for secured repo transactions continues to increase (Wullweber, 2021: Kindle Edition 1042ff.).

Repo, in the context of the relationship between commercial and central banks, means that commercial banks sell securities to the central bank and buy them back after a certain (usually short) period of time, thereby providing the commercial banks with additional cash for a short period of time. The level of interest for the repo is determined by the difference between the selling and repurchase price of the security, both of which are set by the central bank (Cf. Binswanger, 2015; Kindle Edition: 759f.). Repos are therefore contracts in which securities are sold at a certain price to be repurchased after a certain period of time. The commercial bank must pay a risk premium on the security, which depends on the quality of the security. Repos include the promise of a trade at face value. In times of crisis, the repo rate, risk premiums, and margin calls increase. Repo transactions can become expensive.

The Federal Reserve launched an extraordinary program of repo loans to its so-called "primary dealers" on Wall Street (including JP Morgan, Goldman Sachs, Barclays, BNP Paribas, Nomura, Deutsche Bank, Bank of America, Citibank etc.) on September 17, 2019, when there were market turbulences. These were overnight loans as well as 14-day and even longer-term loans. In 2020, due to the Corona pandemic, there was an expansion of open market operations and the provision of liquidity. In this context, the Fed also reactivated the overnight repo facility for the shadow banking system (which was closed again a few years after the 2008 crisis). By securing the repo market (government bonds are of fundamental importance here), assets should not lose value excessively and at the same time the circulation of money should be ensured. On July 2, 2020, the cumulative value of this market, whose collateral mainly consisted of US Treasury securities and mortgage-backed securities, amounted to a total of 11.23 trillion US dollars (Vighi, 2022). What is striking here is the astonishing extent, which confirms that Wall Street banks were already on the brink of a disaster before the arrival of the Corona virus. Further evidence of the ongoing fragility of the credit market was provided on July 28, 2021, when the Fed announced the establishment of a "Standing Repo Facility" that provided the 24 primary dealers of the Fed and other counterparties with 500 billion dollars in backstop loans on a weekly basis.

Funds are often raised through repo transactions with a term of one day. Repo transactions are generally contracts in which securities are sold at a certain price to be repurchased at a fixed price plus interest. Repos can also be resold by the buyer of the securities and thus serve as security for the lender. The security then still belongs to the lender, while the borrower receives all interest payments on the security during the term of the loan. However, the borrower must also pay a risk premium for the security. The level of interest for the repo transaction is determined by the difference between the selling and repurchase price of the security. If the underlying securities as collateral lose value during the term of the repo transaction, additional securities must be delivered (margin call). The preferred securities for securing repo transactions are safe government bonds. The problem with repos is that this form of security can have a crisis-enhancing effect. If the value of the securities is downgraded in a crisis, there are higher risk premiums, margin calls, and higher security discounts (Wullweber, 2021: Kindle Edition 1797ff.).[5]

In good times, repo transactions increase liquidity, i.e., the ability to turn securities into cash. The trade with Repo transactions are typically conducted by so-called market makers, also known as shadow dealers, who can also engage in proprietary trading. These market makers can be major banks, clearing houses, or investment funds. For example, they borrow money from index funds or the central bank via repos and pass this on to pension funds or hedge funds by buying back these funds' assets via repos (Wullweber, 2023).

Financial companies in the shadow banking system cannot grant loans like private banks, but must finance themselves in other ways. Therefore, shadow traders need access to the money markets, otherwise they would have to finance their transactions with their own capital or take out bank loans. While the convertibility of bank loans is guaranteed by the state through various security mechanisms, repo transactions often involve private processes and securities, with the degree of security varying. Private bank deposits are protected to a certain extent by deposit insurance, while the securities in repo transactions are protected by securitized loans or swap transactions (CDS). The prices of the securities underlying the repos are determined in the market, with prices fluctuating, but a payout at face value is promised. In times of crisis, the price of securities can fall sharply because no buyers can be found, which has prompted the Fed to also create securities for the shadow banking system.

In such crises, a similar dynamic always occurs: Due to lower profit expectations, there are strong sales of securities, causing their price to fall, so now higher security discounts are demanded for repo transactions. Financial companies with high leverage run into payment difficulties because they have to provide additional collateral that they may not even own, forcing them to sell more securities and conduct fewer repo transactions. It is now becoming increasingly difficult to sell securities to finance other securities purchases. When the liquidity of securities used to secure repos falls, these become more expensive, reducing overall financing liquidity. Fewer repo transactions are conducted, and financial companies that have to repay the funds received via repo transactions must now also sell securities far below price to get any funds at all. Ultimately, central bank money is needed to be able to service existing liabilities at all.

The shadow banking system today is based on a hedging structure, at the center of which are the repos, with the securities of the repos depending on the trading of securities and their market valuation. It is assumed that individual securities serving as collateral can fall in price, but not a large amount of securities at the same time. The price decline of individual securities is also covered by credit default insurance (CDS). However, when shadow banks change the liquidity in the markets and have high leverage, they can become systemic risks, both directly and through their interconnection with the private banking system.

Repo transactions increase liquidity in the financial markets, with government bonds having the highest market liquidity, while other securities can fluctuate massively in price. When the market liquidity of these securities falls, risk premiums rise. Since the market for government bonds is also limited, increasingly other assets are used as collateral, which should be as liquid as government bonds, but are not and therefore need to be hedged through swap transactions.

The safest repos are therefore government bonds, which also have the lowest interest rates and the smallest risk premiums, with the level of risk premiums and the quality of the securities used as collateral being crucial. Repos are used both for risk hedging and for financing risky investments. In the shadow banking system, short-term loans are usually balanced with long-term liabilities, illiquid assets are made tradable through securitization, and a flexible system of Risks, maturities, and hedges are established. With the help of market makers, capital market-based loans are financed through the money market. Since the Corona crisis, central banks have again provided the shadow banking system with repo facilities and thus a security structure.

The Financial Markets and the Covid-19 Crisis (and the Consequences)

During the Covid-19 crisis, due to widespread lockdowns worldwide, there was a significant decline in supply and demand in the industrial production. Consequently, in contrast to the huge profits of Big Pharma, the large technology platforms, and some major banks, total corporate profits in the US in 2020 fell by about 30% (Tooze, 2018).

The problem in the financial markets is more complex. The nomadization of risks in the global financial markets can affect the entire financial system. On financial markets, which are driven by cheap loans from central banks, any interest rate increase is at least potentially catastrophic for banks, hedge funds, pension funds, and the entire market for government bonds, because the costs of borrowing increase and liquidity dries up. This was exactly the case during the "repocalypse" (Vighi, 2021) in September 2019: The interest rates rose within a few hours to 10.5%, and panic broke out, which affected futures, options, currencies, and markets where traders speculate with loans financed by repo transactions. The only way to defuse the contagion within the financial linkages was to pump as much liquidity as necessary into the financial system. Between September 2019 and March 2020, the Fed pumped more than 9 trillion dollars into the banking system, which is about 40% of the gross domestic product (GDP) of the USA[6] (Ibid.: 120ff.).

As disagreement about the economic impacts of Covid-19 increased in February 2020, stock indices worldwide fell sharply. Investors began to buy particularly large amounts of US government bonds, so their yields fell and their prices rose, while at the same time the prices for risky assets on the financial markets collapsed. Shortly after, the flight to cash began, as now assets were drastically liquidated. The run on the US dollar in turn intensified activities on the foreign exchange markets. Finally, even relatively safe papers like government bonds were sold to get cash. The volatility in the markets was extremely high. In March 2020, the downward dynamics in the financial markets then affected all assets, including American government bonds, which are considered the most liquid and safest papers, and with their emergency sales a further flight into the dollar began.[7] Driven by computer algorithms, bond prices fell, while the bid-ask spread[8] rose, so especially hedge funds, which make their profits with small differences between the price of government bonds and related futures, got into turbulence. Hedge funds refinance their holdings for US government bonds on the repo market, where they exchange these for cash, among other things to be able to buy more government bonds. When these transactions also turned negative, the hedge funds were confronted with margin calls and, due to a lack of own funds, were forced to liquidate positions and sell 100 billion in US government bonds. The Fed had to respond with the only means that still helped, namely the activation of almost unlimited Liquidity, that is, it had to act as a market maker (Tooze, 2021: Kindle Edition 2190ff.). Thus, it provided over 300 billion in overnight repo financing in the short term, as well as 100 billion for longer-term repo transactions.[9] The Fed found itself in the role of the global lender or the world's central bank, granting dollars to anyone who was short of cash.[10]

When the world economy fell into free fall again in 2020 at the beginning of the Covid pandemic, many governments resorted to massive and inflationary rescue actions for capital in the financial markets. The rescue, especially of financial companies (also in the shadow banking system), involved an unprecedented expansion of monetary support and incentives. In March 2020, the Fed issued emergency loans to provide private investors with short-term liquidity. It even began purchasing corporate loans worth 2.3 trillion US dollars. The Fed also bought government bonds from financial actors for about 1 trillion dollars and provided hedge funds and securities dealers with cash. In this way, the Fed secured a minimum price for the securities held as collateral and guaranteed a maximum price for the provision of liquidity (Wullweber, 2021: Kindle Edition 2837). The Fed also acted as a counterparty to creditors and debtors in the money and capital markets in repo transactions. There was a significant expansion of open market operations and further provision of liquidity.

The Bank of England, the Bank of Japan, the Swiss National Bank, and the Bank of China launched similar programs. In an unprecedented step, the ECB also launched a pandemic emergency purchase program amounting to 750 billion euros in mid-March 2020, which was later increased to 1.850 trillion euros. These funds were primarily used to buy government bonds from EU member states (Tooze, 2021: Kindle Edition 2468).

The central banks decided to provide extensive funds, pumped loans and cash into the markets, acted as traders in the financial markets, and expanded the policy of quantitative easing and repo transactions, while at the same time governments launched additional investment and economic stimulus programs with enormous sums. Despite the collapse of the world economy and the turbulence in the financial markets as a result of the Covid-19 crisis, asset prices began to rise again after their brief decline in spring 2020. In search of higher returns, financial investors turned back to risky financial products, while stock market indices rose to record levels. To achieve higher returns, many institutional funds again invested in highly leveraged, risky, and less liquid assets. The quantitative and credit policy of easing again lowered the borrowing costs for public and private borrowers. Zombies were kept alive, stock prices rose, especially those of growth and technology values, real estate prices and cryptocurrencies exploded, and high-yield corporate bonds and exotic credit instruments such as Collaterized Loan Obligations (CLOs) were in high demand. The Fed's rescue actions from March 2020 drove up the prices of all types of assets.

By the end of 2021, the boom subsided. When it turned out that inflation was persistent, the central banks ended the policy of QE and the easing of lending and began to raise interest rates. By May 2022, stock prices fell, while growth and technology values imploded. Thus, the market cooled down again over the course of 2022. Since 2022, when food and energy prices began to rise and the major economies were confronted with the problem of inflation, which we will come back to later, the Fed tries to tighten monetary conditions. It raised interest rates, and instead of buying government bonds to provide liquidity, it sold them, withdrawing monetary reserves from the financial system. The measures introduced relate to short-term interest rates and changes in the central bank's balance sheet (sale of government bonds) and vary in the respective dosages of adjustments. When central banks raise short-term interest rates, other interest rates charged for borrowing money for investments and speculation can also rise. This endeavor by central banks to regain monetary leeway can in turn have negative effects on financial markets and the real economy. If central banks end their low-interest-rate policy and real interest rates rise more strongly, many industrial companies, households, and many states, even some industrialized countries, may run into payment difficulties. The state cannot indefinitely accumulate debt, as it is constantly evaluated on secondary markets. It remains unclear in 2023 what significance the shrinking of the Federal Reserve's balance sheet will have in terms of a tighter monetary policy.

Higher interest rates from the Fed also lead to a stronger dollar and capital inflows from emerging markets to US financial markets, making these countries potentially more vulnerable to crises. The policy of the US Federal Reserve is therefore not only domestically motivated—and never was. By raising interest rates, it supports the dollar, attacks the euro and the "emerging markets", and pushes large German and Swiss banks to the brink of a crisis. At the historical moment when a non-dollar and non-euro zone is forming in Eurasia, the Federal Reserve is working to restore the global dominance of the dollar on a broad front. The world system is still dominated by the world reserve currency—the US dollar. As a result of the Fed's decision to raise the prime rate, the dollar has therefore gained in value. Consequently, capital was withdrawn from emerging markets and directed into the US dollar. This has destabilized currencies around the world. The prices for energy and pharmaceutical products are largely settled in dollars on the world markets, so the costs of importing these vital products in emerging countries have skyrocketed and they have fueled domestic inflation. So while the technocrats of the Fed raised interest rates to dampen economic activity at home and lower inflation, they simultaneously exported inflation abroad.[11] However, in 2022, the dollar's share of global reserve currencies fell ten times faster than the average of the previous two decades. In 2001, the dollar's share of global currency reserves was still 73%, subsequently falling to 55% by 2021 and finally to 47% in 2022. The causes are mainly to be found here: The BRICS countries possess many raw materials, while the USA still controls the financial markets. The USA needs foreign raw materials, while the BRICS countries can create or strengthen currencies that are also tied to tangible assets such as gold, oil, and minerals. Thus, the price formation for oil and gold is already shifting to Russia, China, and West Asia. As a result, the demand for US dollars is declining, which could reduce the purchasing power of the dollar and its exchange rate in the long term.[12] The US dollar remains dominant in international payments and as an international reserve currency. The US dollar is not gradually being replaced by the euro, the yen, or even the Chinese renminbi, but is also being attacked by a number of smaller currencies.

The world's central banks have thus responded to the possibility of an upcoming crisis, which was positively influenced by the Russian invasion in Ukraine and by speculative and inflationary developments in the global energy and food markets, with further "tightening". This also means that they continue to raise interest rates, thereby dampening domestic economic activity (employment, investments, etc.), suppressing real wages, and triggering a recession, in the hope that a slump in domestic economic activity will lower price inflation (which is primarily determined on the largely deregulated and speculative global financial markets). Since a domestic response to a global phenomenon (energy price inflation) cannot be regulated by the central banks, the markets for government and corporate bonds as well as for stocks moved downwards in 2023, as it was recognized that higher interest rates do not lead to a reduction in global energy and food prices, but primarily to a domestic recession. It should be noted at this point that in the financial markets, not only does volatility drive illiquidity, but illiquidity begins to cause volatility. If both effects occur simultaneously, a spiral can occur in which volatility increases and liquidity collapses (Tooze, 2022e, 2022f).

The Fed is in a dilemma: If it tightens monetary policy too much and raises interest rates too quickly, this could lead to an increase in the cost of borrowing, so that new investments in technologies decline, the credit-driven demand of consumers for products stalls, and a general economic downturn occurs. However, if the central bank does not act, i.e., does not reduce its money injections and does not raise interest rates, then high inflation may not be temporary. Although inflation cannot be combated with an increase in interest rates alone. It should be sufficiently clear by now that any money creation program, which is urgently needed to support the financial sector, can lead to a further erosion of purchasing power in conjunction with inflation, so that new creative methods for controlling the impoverished masses become necessary. The alternative to the scenario of cheap money would be for the central banks to raise interest rates until the market bubbles burst. The result of the delirium in the dilemma is that the Fed will look for a middle way in the medium term. The same applies to the Bank of England and the European Central Bank.

It is necessary that the constantly growing debt pressure on the financial markets is regularly somewhat alleviated. Price inflation helps by reducing overheating in the bond market, as inflation reduces the real value of debt. However, there is still the risk that the inflationary dynamic will become self-sustaining (hyperinflation). Another important point, however, is that the central banks, with their tightening policy, which is supposed to combat inflation, lead the real economy to stagnation and at the same time have to try to ensure the stability of the volatile financial sector. What must be avoided at all costs is an event in the markets triggered by the rise in debt. In the current situation, the growth of the debt bubble needs some relief, in a situation characterized by war, falling asset prices, and rising consumer price indices. This logic becomes clear when one looks at the US Margin Debt, for example, the borrowed capital with which operations are carried out on the stock exchange. Since October 2021, Margin Debt has fallen by 14.5%, while the Nasdaq has lost 17.6% (Tooze, 2022e, 2022f).

The technocrats of the central banks are currently raising interest rates despite fears of recession and continuing the sale of bonds (quantitative tightening), which is referred to as "demand destruction". The ECB has also "tightened" monetary conditions by in 2022, the prime rate was raised by 75 basis points to 1.25%. At the moment, according to Ann Pettifor, the elephants of the central banks are trampling on the livelihoods of populations around the world by intervening in the markets, raising interest rates, and destabilizing the economic system[13] (Pettifor, 2022a, b).

At the beginning of 2023, the effects of each Fed interest rate hike of 0.5% on the US real estate market are already visible. The interest rate hikes have driven up mortgage rates, putting pressure on the real estate market. The interest rates for real estate financing have more than doubled by April 2023. In addition, commercial properties are only 60 to 70% occupied. Over the next five years, more than 2.5 trillion US dollars in commercial real estate debt is due in the US, as much as never before in a five-year period. 70% of commercial real estate loans are held by smaller banks, which exacerbates the situation.

But while homebuyer sentiment is at a historic low, homebuilder sentiment remains relatively high—confirming that there is no longer a complementary correlation between real economic conditions and speculation with asset prices; after all, it was the Fed that continued to inflate the real estate bubble by buying mortgage-backed securities, even as demand is now falling (Tooze, 2022e, 2022f).

In March 2023, the Silicon Valley Bank, the sixteenth largest banking institution with intensive connections to tech companies in the US, went bankrupt and was closed by US regulatory authorities.[14] Inflation is driving interest rates up, which in turn reduces the market value of bank assets such as bonds, especially government bonds. Since government bonds are not accounted for at face value or their acquisition price, but at the current market price, and bonds make up over a quarter of US bank assets, the price decline of the bonds resulted in accounting problems for some banks, so that equity threatened to slip into the red. The problem is that the market valuation of assets and mortgages has fallen due to the increased interest rates. The interest rates for the bonds and mortgages bought a few years ago are lower than for the new mortgages and new treasury notes and bonds. When interest rates rise, the prices of the "old securities" fall. However, if the banks simply hold onto their bonds or mortgage packages, they do not have to write down the market price of their assets accordingly. They only have to disclose the market value loss if depositors withdraw their money and the bank actually has to sell these assets to raise the money to pay out its depositors.[15] Since the many corporate customers of the SVB were not covered by deposit insurance and feared intervention by the regulatory authorities, money was withdrawn from this solvent bank and reallocated. The growing gap between what investors can earn by buying risk-free treasury papers and the small money that banks paid their depositors prompted wealthier depositors to withdraw their money to achieve a higher market return elsewhere. Most investors were aware that higher interest rates would lower the price of bonds—most strongly for bonds with a long term. Asset managers avoided such price declines by reallocating their money to short-term treasury notes or money market funds, while the prices of real estate, bonds, and stocks fell.

Particularly, smaller US banks also recorded losses amounting to billions, which relate to bonds in their portfolios. After the financial crisis of 2008, US regulatory authorities had imposed on banks to hold more government bonds, that is, liquid assets, in their portfolios, whose prices now fell as a result of the increases in the prime rates by the Fed and were responsible for (so far unrealized) losses in the banks' balance sheets. Consequently, US banks heavily relied on the crisis loan programs of the US Federal Reserve. The Fed pumped $152 billion into the financial sector through its discount window in one week, clearly surpassing the previous weekly record of $111 billion, which was reached shortly after the bankruptcy of the investment bank Lehman Brothers in 2008.

However, the profits of the US banking sector reached an all-time high of around $80 billion in the first quarter of 2023, as insolvent banks were taken over by larger institutions. JP Morgan Chase, as expected, recorded the highest profit of all banks, achieving a profit of $11.7 billion in the first quarter. This is due, among other things, to interest rate increases by the Fed, which affect credit contracts with variable interest rates as well as new contracts with (rising) fixed interest rates. Higher profits also come from one-time inflows to First Citizens and Flagstar, who bought the remnants of Silicon Valley Bank and Signature Bank.

Small banks in China are also in danger, and some are already on the verge of collapse. In China, this is due to the shortage of financing in competition for deposits with larger banks and high defaults by local borrowers due to China's economic slowdown in recent years.

The share prices of the crisis-ridden Credit Suisse plummeted by double digits in March 2023. In their wake, bank shares plummeted across Europe. Five-year credit default insurance for debt securities, Credit Default Swaps (CDS), consequently shot up to 574 basis points. Credit Suisse received a liquidity line of more than $50 billion from the central bank, and the regulators stated that Credit Suisse met the Swiss capital and liquidity requirements. Credit Suisse customers continued to withdraw deposits on Thursday. The authorities provided the bank with additional liquidity of more than $150 billion. Eventually, Credit Suisse was taken over by UBS.

The question that concerns the markets at the beginning of 2023 is what happens when central banks continue to raise interest rates in response to rising inflation and continue to sell government bonds. The risk is not that government bonds suddenly become worthless because the US government defaults or hyperinflation occurs, but primarily that the financial markets no longer function because prices and yields become abnormal and trillions of dollars are churned in the portfolios, which can trigger a crisis as hedge funds, banks, and other investors now also compete for cash. However, if the markets for government debt become fragile, this is not to be underestimated, as government bonds represent the most reliable collateral. Government bonds play an important role in the financial system and for the states, which had to go further into debt in past crises to stimulate the economy through economic programs and other crisis measures. The market for US Treasuries suffered from a latent liquidity withdrawal in March 2023 and comprised securities with a face value of around $23.5 trillion.

Notes

1. The 23 trillion dollar market for US government bonds offers a smooth spectrum of homogeneous assets, which only differ in their maturity, ranging from a few weeks to 30 years. They are traded on

a curve that is oriented towards the maturity. These are safe assets without serious default risk, which therefore offer an extremely liquid market, which is the ideal platform for financial engineering, enriched with algorithmic high-frequency trading. As the largest pool of fixed-income, safe assets, the government bond market registers every economic and political news within milliseconds. The prices and yields that result from these transactions. They set the standard for all other borrowings and loans.

2. The freezing of the interbank market threatened the global banking system in 2008 and required urgent measures by the Fed and other central banks. In response, the Fed initiated a certain type of QE by buying distressed assets from banks, thereby cleaning up their balance sheets. This did not inject new money into the US economy and thus did not create inflationary pressure. But it helped private banks, at least those that had not failed to do business again on an extended scale, thereby ending the credit crunch after the rise in defaulted loans. It took about 18 months for US retail banks to boost their lending again, which led to an economic recovery after another six months.
3. Debts always become a problem when they exceed the ability of companies, states, and households to repay them in the long run. Therefore, if one wants to follow Keynes at this point, the interest rates of commercial banks should be so low that continuous repayment is possible, regardless of whether it results from income, profits, or taxes. There should also be political control of lending, as too high (real) interest rates lead to intensification and extension of working hours, pressure on profit rates, and higher taxes. Despite the low-interest policy of central banks and the oversupply of money and monetary capital, the interest rates of private banks have not fallen in recent decades, as mainstream economics would have us believe, but have risen. The interest rates of central banks and commercial banks do not necessarily have to be synchronized.
4. In recent years, both the volumes of long-term refinancing operations and the balance sheet totals of central banks have increased, and their purchases are partly covered by inferior collateral. Unsold securities were outsourced to state-founded "bad" banks and enormous bond purchase programs were launched. During the financial crisis of 2008, a large part of the bad mortgage-backed securities (MBS) were deposited with the central banks. The bloating of the

central bank balance sheets was mainly promoted by measures to save the existing financial system. In the past, central bank money was backed by gold, then by safe debt securities (government bonds), but today it is not even backed by safe debt securities, because risky stocks are among the assets of central banks. Mortgages and non-tradable loan claims of commercial banks are included.

The balance sheet of the US Federal Reserve decreased at the beginning of 2023 due to tightening, as hardly any new bonds and securities were purchased. It fell from its peak of nearly nine trillion US dollars reached in mid-2022 to 8.3 trillion in March 2023. However, after banking problems in the same month, liquidity had to be massively pumped into the markets again, causing the Fed's balance sheet to swell to more than 8.6 trillion.

5. Repos are usually short-term contracts with a term of one day (overnight repos). A risk premium is added to the price for each repo transaction. The collateral is valued at *Mark-to-Market*, its price is adjusted daily to the current market value. If there is a loss in value of the collateral, the counterparty is entitled to demand additional margin or collateral. Government bonds are primarily used as collateral, as they are considered the safest securities.
6. Vighi points out that throughout the history of the Fed, there has never been a direct link between the central bank's reserve creation and the money supply in retail banking. However, since September 2019, the reserves newly created by the Fed have been replicated dollar for dollar as deposits at the existing 4,336 US commercial banks. The expansion of the Fed's balance sheet now directly corresponded to the total money supply in the economy. According to Vighi, it must be emphasized that the financial house of cards was already on the verge of collapse in 2019 and the virus came at the right time to enable and justify the monetary flooding with the associated paradigm shift (Vighi 2022: 127).

For Vighi, there are three important consequences of this process of monetary centralization, orchestrated by the Fed in consultation with the world's most powerful asset manager: (1) Inflation, (2) further indebtedness, and (3) a totalitarian model of emergency-driven capitalism. Vighi assumes that in the course and aftermath of the Covid-19 pandemic, there is further controlled destruction of the productive economy and its infrastructure, which allows even more capital to be skimmed off from the real economy and directed into the financial markets. The immediate function of the pandemic was to curb the inflationary surge in the short term, as fear campaigns dampened spending and consumption and prevented the huge amount of money being pumped into the financial sector from circulating as real demand in the economy. The real economy is being scaled back, because the less is produced and consumed, the less money is in circulation and the lower the inflation. The lockdowns had this effect for Vighi. However, this changed after the Covid pandemic in 2022 with the emerging inflation and the rise in prime rates.

7. Even the US bond market is not immune to shocks. In September 2019, it was severely shaken by the so-called repo market crash. But the real shock came in March 2020, when the government bond market stopped functioning for several weeks (Tooze 2022d, 2022e 2022f). This triggered a panic that was even greater than in 2008 and required gigantic interventions by the Fed. In comparison with the Eurozone, it is important to emphasize that the reason for the panic in March 2020 was not concern about the solvency of the US government. The volume of government bonds has constantly increased due to the deficits accumulated in the last quarter of a century. In relation to GDP, US government debt has risen immensely due to interventions during the pandemic. But the deficits themselves are not the main problem, but the question of whether private financial actors can trade government bonds on a liquid market.

   Government bonds are either assets with which returns are realized, and/or papers that are used as collateral. But trading no longer worked in March 2020 because there were too many sellers and not enough buyers in the market, so the prices even for these safe securities collapsed. The Fed had to intervene as the buyer of last resort and offered, among other things, repo facilities, hoping that private investors would have less reason to sell their holdings if they could obtain funds through the Fed. This resulted in trillions of dollars of liquidity being flushed into the system and the sell-off was stopped.
8. It's about the bid-ask spread, the difference between the purchase and selling price. On the financial markets, new products with large bid-ask spreads are often created, because these spreads mean

high profits. Then other actors start to participate in the financial markets, and as the market grows, the spreads become narrower. The market becomes more and more liquid, i.e., the bid-ask spreads shrink.

9. One instrument that prevents liquidity from reaching the real economy is the Fed's Overnight Reverse Repo Facility (RRP). While it continues to flood the financial markets with money, the Fed, thanks to the reverse repo facility, wipes out any surplus it pumps into Wall Street. A zero-sum game of giving and taking: At night, financial actors deposit their excess liquidity with the Federal Reserve, which provides the same government bonds and mortgage-backed securities as collateral that it takes out of the market during the day as part of its QE purchases (Vighi 2021).
10. The market for government bonds can also become illiquid for other reasons. In March 2023, following the bankruptcy of Silicon Valley Bank, the Fed launched the "Bank Term Funding Program," which offers generous conditions. This is a credit program of the US central bank, in which private banks are to be quickly supplied with emergency loans against collateral even in manifest market turbulence, in order to prevent payment defaults and liquidity bottlenecks in the financial sector. It grants each "deposit institution" loans with a term of up to one year against any collateral that the Federal Reserve buys as part of open market operations. The collateral can be government bonds, mortgage-backed securities, or similar papers. The papers are to serve as collateral at their face value, not at their current market value. Normally, banks have to deposit their securities at market value as collateral when they want to receive additional liquidity from the central bank. With this program, the central bank suspends the market mechanism in order to stabilize the financial sector.

    But why should a bank that has access to this program now sell government bonds? You get a better deal if you leave them to the Fed as collateral for a loan. Suddenly, trillions of dollars in government bonds are no longer available for sale. The fact that many fewer government bonds are in circulation must have an impact on liquidity. These banks would now need a selling price that is much higher than the The purchase price is to be able to sell their securities. On the other hand, one must consider that a crisis, partly triggered by falling asset and bond prices, leads to investors fleeing into government bonds and driving prices back up. This also happened in March 2023. The extreme price movements were due, however, to the fact that the market was very thin and there were large gaps between bid and ask prices. The liquidity conditions on the government bond market were relatively poor, suggesting that any technically induced movement exaggerates yield fluctuations (probably).

11. However, one must assume a long-term devaluation of the dollar, which can also lead to a decrease in the central bank reserves held worldwide in dollars due to its use for the geopolitical goals of the USA. China is gradually ready to replace the dollar with the RMB, and other strategic rivals of the USA such as Russia are ready to abandon dollar assets and a reserve currency system based on the dollar after their currency reserves were frozen. Cryptocurrency advocates will try to displace any fiat currency with their digital money, which is an almost impossible endeavor, as such cryptocurrencies lack essential features of a real currency. The status as a world reserve currency correlates with geopolitical hegemony. If the USA continues to crack down hard with trade and financial sanctions, competitors will decouple from the dollar system in terms of trade and finance.
12. The de-dollarization has many forms, but three are particularly easy to recognize: the settlement of international transactions in currencies other than the dollar, especially the Chinese yuan, the reduction of the dollar's share in global foreign exchange reserves, and the decline in foreign holdings of US government bonds.

    In international payments, the role of the yuan (and other currencies) has experienced a massive upswing in the past year. The most obvious example is Russia, which was practically forced by Western sanctions to use the yuan for most of its international transactions. But several other large countries—including Brazil, Argentina, Pakistan, and Bangladesh—have already agreed to use the yuan or their own currencies for the settlement of their international transactions (or are currently negotiating about it).

    Looking at the composition of global currency reserves, the shift towards de-dollarization is perhaps less obvious. The US dollar still dominates with a share of around 60% of global currency reserves, while the yuan makes up less than 3%. However, according to current trends, the dollar's share of reserve currencies is shrinking at 10 times the average speed of the last two decades.

The process of de-dollarization is primarily geopolitical rather than economic in nature. It's not just about finding an efficient system, but about challenging Western currency hegemony.

13. At this point, Fabio Vighi argues that the game of supply and demand in the markets does not work at all: According to this law, the price of a bond rises when it is in high demand, while the yield falls; conversely, the price falls when the demand for bonds decreases, and the yield rises. Higher bond interest rates should deflate "hot" air in any asset bubble. The bond market is supposed to be relieved of pressure with high bond interest rates, thus preventing an overheating of the economy. However, according to Vighi, the financial system is systematically distorted by central banks, which have promoted a monster called speculative capital through the massive liquidity injections of the past decades, which is no longer controllable. The current severe turbulence in bond markets around the world, whose yields show signs of structural instability, suggest that central banks are running out of means to mend the cracks in the financial system (Vighi 2022: 127).
14. The headlines were full in March 2023 with the bankruptcy and subsequent receivership of Silicon Valley Bank (SVB) by the Federal Deposit Insurance Corp (FDIC). As expected, the share price and capitalization of parent company SVB Financial have plummeted.

First, some general remarks. When a commercial bank grants a loan, it does so by making a deposit in a customer's bank account. Loans create deposits, not the other way around. When a bank grants a loan, it also expands its balance sheet. Most money in capitalist economies like the USA is digital (over 90%), the rest of the money supply consists of physical banknotes and coins, referred to as cash. Most payments are made digitally today; we are moving closer and closer to a cashless economy as payment methods change and some places become cashless businesses. In a "run on a bank", one will probably transfer their balance to a safer financial institution. Reserves are assets of commercial banks that are held as assets at the central bank - in the case of the USA, at the Fed. Reserves decrease when people actually want to hold more cash or banknotes. However, bank loans do not come from reserves.

SVB was a Californian commercial bank that operated on both the West Coast and the East Coast. The bank was supposed to help finance start-up companies, as many new companies in the computer and technology industry were emerging in and around Silicon Valley. With the boom of the high-tech economy, the bank also evolved. In the 1990s, SVB entered the risky business of real estate loans. However, SVB's core business at this time was still lending to start-ups and acting as a venture capitalist by creating new deposits for their customers. During this phase, SVB's investors benefited from the bank's ability to grant loans and from their customers' ability to service these loans with interest. In the 2000s, more and more loans were granted, expanding the bank's customer base and SVB's balance sheet. At this time, the bank continued to focus on its niche business: tech start-ups.

It seems to be true that the bank's deposits increased during the pandemic as the profits of technology companies soared. In addition, SVB decided to buy long-term government bonds to create another source of income for the company. However, the deposits of their customers were by no means used to purchase these securities. Commercial banks are free to buy securities at their own risk by expanding their balance sheet, as they do when lending to customers. There is a difference between the loans that are converted into deposits for customers by a simple computer entry and the actual deposits of bank customers. In the first case, the loan is repaid to the bank with interest. Once the loan is repaid, the account can be considered closed. In the second operation, there is no loan, but a company simply stores its deposits in the bank's balance sheet.

The mainstream often confuses cash with digital money and loans with what are actual deposits. How did SVB go bankrupt if the bank did not use customer deposits for wild speculative purchases or risky investments? First, Firstly, there are many types of bankruptcies, but a bank bankruptcy is something special, as this institution deals with deposits and creates money as loans to customers. Deposits that are loans to customers, and deposits that are not loans (e.g., the cash flow of technology companies), are on the same side of the balance sheet. In a bankruptcy, the value of the assets falls below the value of the bank's liabilities. In the case of SVB, rising interest rates and bad investments triggered the collapse.

The bank's assets are the reserves at the central bank, the loans to customers, from which it receives interest and fees, and the additional investments in assets, derivatives, and bonds. SVB has expanded the asset side of its balance sheet by purchasing long-term government bonds and also held mortgage-backed securities. At the end of 2022, SVB held securities worth $117 billion in its books. When the Fed raised interest rates, SVB found it harder to sell bonds, as investors could buy new bonds with higher interest rates. Eventually, SVB was forced to sell bonds at a loss, significantly reducing its asset side of the balance sheet. Why would one buy a security with a return of 1.5% when one can get, for example, a security with a return of 3.5%? The value of SVB's assets fell dramatically, and alongside the loss in value of the investment assets, another source of assets dried up. With profitability problems in the technology sector, there were fewer companies demanding loans that would have expanded SVB's balance sheet on the asset and liability side. With the loss in value of the asset side, the liability side also decreased, as companies now transferred their deposits to another financial institution. For this reason, SVB's management wanted to raise more equity to balance the books, but this also failed. Eventually, liabilities exceeded assets, and SVB was declared insolvent, whereupon the FDIC took over.

With rising interest rates, older bonds will therefore lose value. Their prices fall on the money markets. This is a minor problem if one can hold the bond until the end of its term and the state pays out the bond plus return. But those who have to sell, because, like SVB or Credit Suisse, investors are withdrawing money from the bank, make losses. The current market value of old bonds is now significantly below their face value, i.e., below the value that the state pays back after expiry. In the face of high inflation, longer-term bonds also lose value.

15. When central banks raise interest rates, new government and corporate bonds are issued at higher interest rates. These higher interest rates increase the yield of the newly issued bonds. The yields of these bonds are higher the fewer new bonds come onto the market. The new, higher-rated bonds are then more profitable for investors than the many bonds that were issued under lower

interest rates. As a result, older bonds are sold as quickly as possible, as savvy investors flock to the higher yields of the scarcer, newer bonds. This price shift results in the prices of low-interest bonds falling further. Government bonds are traded at a market value that may differ from their face value at the time of issue. Interest rate development and market value of government bonds are inversely proportional. When interest rates fall, bond prices rise. Conversely, it is the case with a rising interest rate level, where bond prices fall. Bonds that were issued in a phase of low interest rates lose market value due to their lower interest rates in a high-interest phase. And these high interest rates, which the central banks introduced for the purpose of combating inflation, have led to a massive decline in the price of government bonds.

However, this does not matter if the bonds are held until maturity and there is no pressure to sell. Over time, future interest rates could fall and bond prices rise. However, if bonds were used as collateral, lenders will find that the borrower's collateral has lost value and demand more collateral to support the (often high) outstanding debts. There is a scramble to sell or to mobilize more capital to satisfy creditors.

References

Binswanger, M. (2015). *Geld aus dem Nichts. Wie Banken Wachstum ermöglichen und Krisen verursachen*. Weinheim.

Fischbach, R. (2017). *Die schöne Utopie: Paul Mason, der Postkapitalismus und der Traum vom grenzenlosen Überfluss*. Köln.

Gabor, D. (2016). The (Impossible) Repo Trinity: The Political Economy of Repo Markets. *Review of International Political Economy, 6*, 967–1000.

Gordon, R. J. (2017). *The Rise and Fall of American Growth: The U.S. Standard of Living Since the Civil War*. Princeton.

Meister, R. (2021). *Justice Is an Option: A Democratic Theory of Finance for the Twenty-First Century*. Chicago.

Pettifor, A. (2022a). Central Bankers: Engineering a Worldwide Slump and Declaring Class War. https://annpettifor.substack.com/p/central-bankers-engineering-a-worldwide

Pettifor, A. (2022b). The Sudden Paralysis of the System? Messing with a Marvellously Intricate and Fragile Global System. https://annpettifor.substack.com/p/the-sudden-paralysis-of-the-system

Stelter, D. (2013). *Die Billionen-Schuldenbombe. Wie die Krise begann und warum sie noch lange nicht zu Ende ist*. Weinheim.

Tooze, A. (2018). *Crashed: Wie zehn Jahre Finanzkrise die Welt verändert haben*. München.

Tooze, A. (2021). *Welt im Lockdown. Die globale Krise und ihre Folgen*. München.

Tooze, A. (2022d). The Regime at Risk—Macroprudentialism Faces the Test of Inflation. https://adamtooze.substack.com/p/chartbook-137-the-regime-at-risk

Tooze, A. (2022e). Zugzwang—Are We on the Brink of a Central Banking Paradigm Shift? https://adamtooze.substack.com/p/chartbook-151-zugzwang-are-we-on

Tooze, A. (2022f). The Bond Market Massacre of September 2022. https://adamtooze.substack.com/p/chartbook-157-the-bond-market-massacre?utm_source=%2Fsearch%2FLiability%2520Driven%2520Investment&utm_medium=reader2

Varoufakis, Y. (2012). *Der globale Minotaurus. Amerika und die Zukunft der Weltwirtschaft*. München.

Vighi, F. (2021). The Cental Bankers' Long Covid: An Incurable Condition. https://thephilosophicalsalon.com/the-central-bankers-long-covid-emergency-noise-and-conspiracys-best-kept-secret/?fbclid=IwAR1Nus3syvTQeO2W9w2xCvFDh9C-mTeXxS7YHdWbkooMPl8kYf3iWUnf9Zc

Vighi, F. (2022). *Unworkable. Delusions of an Imploding Civilization*. New York.

Wullweber, J. (2021). *Zentralbankkapitalismus. Transformation des globalen Finanzsystems in Krisenzeiten*. Berlin.

Wullweber, J. (2023). Der neue Staat-Finanzmarkt-Nexus. https://makroskop.eu/spotlight/bankenbeben-fehlverhalten-oder-systemcrash/der-neue-staat-finanzmarkt-nexus/

CHAPTER 9

The Phenomenon of Stagflation

The biggest non-event of the neoliberal era of capitalism is the stagnation of the economy during the phase of the fourth "industrial revolution", which has not been overcome even by digital automation and the associated productivity advances. The paradox is that the productivity growth rates in the manufacturing sector collapsed precisely when they should have been rising rapidly due to automation.[1]

A significant slowdown in economic growth is noticeable in Europe after the pandemic. The Eurozone officially entered a technical recession at the beginning of 2023. This recession is particularly pronounced in Germany. On a global level, the weak performance of capital is due, among other things, to weak domestic demand. Government spending shows a significant decline, while private consumption is stagnating against the backdrop of inflation and more restrictive credit conditions. The effects of monetary policy tightening will gradually become apparent. Corporate investments are also likely to slow down as they are hampered by rising interest rates. According to OECD forecasts, a significant slowdown in growth is to be recorded in the major Western countries.[2] Investments in productive capital have been significantly lower in these economies since 2010 than in previous decades. The case of Japan is indicative: in the 1980s, the growth of productive capital was more than 5% per year. Since 2010, it has almost dropped to zero.

A. Szepanski, *Capitalism in the Age of Catastrophe*, Palgrave Insights into Apocalypse Economics,
https://doi.org/10.1007/978-3-031-57754-3_9

It is difficult to capture the movement of profit rates based on data from national accounts and information from companies. At the moment, according to the managers of large companies, the profits of large companies have increased. Profits rose sharply in 2020 and seem to be holding up for the time being despite rising costs. Two factors were responsible for this: firstly, profits were boosted by government measures to cushion the shock of rising gas and electricity prices for companies. Secondly, companies passed on cost increases (wages and intermediate goods), thereby increasing their profits and contributing to inflation.

Let's take a closer look at the problem of stagnation in the capitalist economy. In his book *Smart Machines and Service Work*, Jason E. Smith extensively refers to the economist William Baumol, who assumes that the developed industrial countries have been divided into two major economic sectors since 1960, namely the technologically advanced sector, whose production processes are characterized by technological innovations, high accumulation rates and large-scale network processes, and the technologically stagnant sector (service sector), whose technologically stagnant structures rather prevent a significant increase in labor productivity (Smith, 2020: Kindle Edition 1132). It may be precisely the dynamics of the first sector that cause the stagnant productivity rates in the second sector, insofar as machines are used in the innovative sector over certain periods of time that enable higher output with fewer workers (even if the output remains constant, the use of new machines always involves fewer workers being used),[3] so that laid-off workers have to find employment in other sectors, today mainly in the service sector (Ibid.).

The stagnant service sector will therefore tend to increase in terms of employment numbers, with income ratios there being elastic. And because productivity in the service sector remains low for various reasons, increasing output here leads to an increase in employment. Ultimately, this development, i.e. the differentiation of productivity growth rates in the two sectors, leads to a gradient, insofar as productivity in the first sector continues to rise, while it tends to remain constant in the second sector (service sector), which in turn leads to job losses in the dynamic sector and absorption by the stagnant sector.[4] For Baumol, this trend leads to a growth rate in the entire economy that asymptotically tends towards zero. Solow's productivity paradox, which states that the computer can be found everywhere today, except in productivity statistics, would now have to be specified to the effect that the rapid computerization of the innovative sector of the economy has led to declining growth rates of productivity in the entire economy.

Numerous labor-intensive jobs in the service sector are far less subject to competitive pressure or even outsourcing to other countries than technologically developed sectors, as they must be consumed near the production sites and consumption. These jobs are often poorly paid, so there is no reason for companies to replace these precarious jobs with the use of new machines, which only pay for themselves after years. And many of these professions cannot (yet) even be replaced by the smartest AI machines because their work structure, such as in nursing, requires intuitive complexity (from haptic to affective), emotional intelligence, and dealing with uncertainty. Thus, in industrialized countries over the past decades, a polarization has solidified between a highly mechanized, capital-intensive, and productive sector and a much larger service sector with low productivity gains, so Smith's summary (Ibid.: 1742 ff.).

Smith also points out that the ubiquity of technological gadgets such as the smartphone, which combines telecommunications, shopping, video, and text in one device, in conjunction with the rise of large technology companies and new platform companies, has far-reaching effects on finance, mobility, consumption, etc., but negligible effects on the productivity of industrial jobs. In addition, there is a deep dichotomy between two separate service sectors, on the one hand, the corporate sectors, which often act as intermediaries and supply products to the industry, and the consumption sectors, which supply products to individuals and families.

In his book *Automation and the Future of Work*, Aaron Benanav also assumes an increasing deindustrialization in the developed countries of the Global North since the 1970s (Benanav, 2022). To substantiate this thesis, Benanav examines the development of productivity as the ratio between output and employment. The more output per worker is produced, the higher is the labor productivity. For all sectors, the growth rate of production minus the growth rate of labor productivity gives the growth rate of employment (Ibid.: 32 f.). If the output of cars increases by 3% and the labor productivity in the automotive industry increases by 2%, employment increases by 1%, according to Benanav. The reverse is also true. Whether changes in innovation lead to job destruction depends on the relative speed of productivity and production growth. And Benanav comes to his important thesis: If output grows slower than labor productivity, then the number of jobs will decrease. (Ibid.) This is about the question of capacities, which rather than the destruction of jobs due to technological innovations indicate the employment rate.

Although the productivity growth rates in the USA since the 1970s were high compared to those of output (which led to a decline in employment growth), this was not because the former grew faster than before (which could be a sign of increasing automation), but because output had grown much slower than before. For Benanav, this decline in production growth as a sign of deindustrialization cannot be explained solely by technological factors. He refers to positions that are more attributable to the theory of underconsumption, insofar as it is the lack of realization of goods that leads to a decline in output. Since the end of the twentieth century, one could even speak of a global "wave of deindustrialization," according to Benanav (Ibid.: 27ff.). This overlooks urgent questions about the determination of different productivities (capital and labor productivity).

The economist Robert Gordon comes to even more negative results. In the USA, labor productivity increased continuously from 1920 to 1970. However, between 1970 and 2014, this rate has dropped by more than a third. Gordon predicts a further decline to only 1.2% annually by the year 2040. (Gordon, 2013) Productivity growth in the service sector is even weaker. In the Global South, it is probably negative. Even China's spectacular growth in labor productivity—from 7.2% per year and upwards between the years 1993 and 2013—has not yet fully compensated for the country's systemic backlog. The labor and capital productivity in the Global North is still higher, and China's productivity advances have been offset by rising unit labor costs in recent years—partly due to worker unrest.

Meanwhile, Gordon speaks in his book *The Rise and Fall of American Growth* of a rapid decline in net investments of private US companies since the turn of the millennium. (Gordon, 2017) The rate of net investment relative to the capital stock has been declining since the 1970s and has been dramatically falling since 2002 (from 1970 to 2002, we recorded an average of 3.2% net investments in the USA, in 2013 it was only 1%). (Ibid.) If you also count financial expenditures for intellectual property as investments, i.e., legal titles for technologies to secure revenue streams, the investment rates for new, more efficient production methods and new organizational methods are even lower. Now, in contrast to the dynamics of industries with high and dense competition, which require constant innovations, there are non-competitive sectors (anti-markets), in which market shares are won by securing property rights.[5]

With the cost reduction of the elementary element of the computer industry, the microchip, a cheapening of machinery took place, which in principle should enable an increase in the profit rate with increasing technical composition of capital. However, the establishment of globally functioning production structures and processes requires the use of comprehensive and widespread cybernetic systems and networks. Thus, while there was indeed a reduction in the production costs of microchips themselves, at the same time there was an increase in the total costs for the extensive systems that are necessary to produce the chips and other products in the first place. The chip-producing companies became larger and at the same time more strongly automated. In 1966, a new factory still cost 14 million dollars, in 1995 already 1.5 trillion dollars and today the price amounts to 6 trillion dollars (Dyer-Whiteford, 2015: Kindle Edition 1553). When factories and offices mutate into computerized "work stations" supported by satellites, logistics, and "Point-of-Sale platforms", then the costs can increase immensely. Just updating the software of digitized management systems can cause enormous costs, so that despite the cheapening of some components of the computer industry, the organic composition of capital increases, although this can again be offset by the use of electronically coordinated supply chains, access to cheap labor, through outsourcing and unpaid work on the internet.

It can be assumed that in the analysis of unit costs, in addition to the marginal costs (of an additional unit produced), the allocation for fixed costs, which relate to the lifespan and capacity of existing machine systems, must also be taken into account. Furthermore, fully utilized machine systems require permanent maintenance, repairs, and upgrades throughout their lifespan, which also applies to complex software systems and their cycles, which are subject to an accelerated wear process due to competition and today's cult of innovation, leading to high costs when new systems have to be deployed (Fischbach, 2017: 36). A cost degression with increasing output can be observed especially in automated machine systems only within the lifespan and capacities of these systems.

The scale effects achieved through automation, that is, achieving higher output at constant costs or producing qualitatively better products, has been at the center of all rationalization pushes since the nineteenth century, with product and process innovation (power multipliers such as the mechanization of machine tools, electric motors, assembly line) releasing masses of labor; the latter will also occur with the further penetration of automation through all production areas, but sudden productivity leaps are to be doubted, as indicated not least by the current stagnation in large parts of the world economy. Overcapacities, deindustrialization, and financial capital flows can lead to a decline in productivity, as short-term profitability has replaced a longer-term approach that could combine capital and labor in a productivity-enhancing manner.

The accelerated growth driven by computer and information technologies is referred to in scientific circles as "singularity", but a distinction must be made between technical and economic singularity. Economic singularity is measured by how the substitutability between information and conventional inputs generally develops. The economist William D. Nordhaus has pointed out in a new study that economic growth depends on the extent to which materiality can be replaced by electronics. In addition, it is important to consider at the macroeconomic level that higher productivity leads to lower prices, so that an increasing share of productivity-strong sectors can only be demonstrated in total if their volume growth overcompensates for the fall in prices. Nordhaus also addresses the question of the constant substitutability of certain production factors by information at the organizational level (Cf. Nordhaus, 2015). He proves that this was not the case in the past and also predicts only slow development towards economic singularity for the twenty-first century, although capital intensity continues to increase in favor of the capital stock (compared to labor effort) and thus also the share of information capital. Nevertheless, it can be assumed that digital information and communication technologies in the new millennium have contributed to establishing a new level of productivity in production and distribution by intensifying and accelerating the exchange of goods between companies, and enabling rationalization processes in global supply chains and in the supplier industry, the reorganization of areas such as architecture, urban planning, healthcare, etc. The software that processes management methods, derivatives, and digital logistics can certainly be understood here as a basic innovation that is integrated into a new technical–economic paradigm.

We cannot go into detail here about the problems of growth, productivity, and technology of capitalist economies. Only this should be said at this point: A capitalist economy that is supposed to achieve a constant return in the long run must also grow at a certain rate. A growth rate of 3% corresponds to a doubling time of GDP of 23 years; a growth rate of

10% leads to a doubling of GDP after only 7 years. If the increase in return is the general goal is, this results in an acceleration of all processes dominated by the economy. So if the global economy were to grow by three percent annually from today, it would approach a GDP of one quadrillion dollars by the year 2100.

Let's turn to the question of stagflation or inflation. The weak economic growth of the capitalist global economy has been accompanied since 2022 by a rather unexpected inflation of energy, raw material, and food prices. With inflation, money seems to lose value or there seems to be too much money in circulation compared to the goods on the market.[6] In reality, however, it is the prices that are changing and rising. So if one wants to understand the phenomenon of inflation, one should examine price developments.[7] In contrast to the fantasy world of neoclassical economics, where companies "take" prices from the market, prices in the capitalist economy are set by companies according to power, taking into account their cost structures, sectoral profit rates, and other external macroeconomic factors (financial markets) over which the company has little influence. No matter how powerful the company is, the decision to raise prices will encounter friction. Therefore, inflation must be examined both macro- and microeconomically in the context of relations and interactions between money, power, companies, production, distribution, speculation, finance, competition, supply, and demand, etc.

We saw a steadily rising asset price inflation in the years after the 2008 financial crisis, which is now stagnating or spreading to the industrial sector in the core countries since 2022. In October 2022, the inflation rate in Germany was 4.5%, while in the USA at the same time an inflation rate of 6.2% was reached. This was the highest value in the USA for 30 years (Tooze, 2022d, 2022e). The specter of stagflation, the mix of stagnation and inflation, is now looming and initially reminds of the oil price shock of 1973, when OPEC reduced its production volumes in response to the wars in the Middle East.[8] Today, however, since the Covid-19 crisis, we are dealing with bottlenecks in global supply chains that affect the worldwide supply of goods, and as a result, with a price increase for many intermediate products, raw materials, semiconductors, and fossil energy carriers. These bottlenecks result from the Covid-19 crisis with regard to supply chains, but also from the previous overload of a partially defective and neoliberal privatized infrastructure in many capitalist core countries. Energy prices had already increased in 2021, but this increase was accelerated by Russia's invasion of Ukraine, the subsequent sanctions by Western countries, and the decision to decouple the European economies from Russian energy sources. Here, however, the speculative activities on the financial markets play an important role in the price increases of energy carriers. At the same time, the Covid-19 crisis led to massive monetary and fiscal measures, which in the context of bottlenecks and interruptions in global supply chains and rising raw material prices, caused inflation rates to rise. Severe drought periods intensified concerns about access to food, driving volatility in the financial markets. Added to this are the inflationary consequences of climate change, which lead to increases in food prices, as well as a changed dynamic of capitalist competition, namely the ability of certain large companies to exploit supply blockades to increase prices in to drive up the height.

Some authors speak at this point of a supply inflation, where prices are driven up particularly by the costs of companies and their price-setting power. Increased raw material prices also raise the prices of goods produced with them. But why have raw material prices risen? In general, the costs of raw material production have not risen in recent decades, as productivity gains in the extraction of raw materials have often even lowered them. However, material costs are also based on the prices that a company expects in the future, in order to realize high profits now. And this is where the financial markets come into play, as we will see. Currently, there are also temporary problems in the global supply chains and the energy prices that permeate all economic sectors, which, in addition to the price development driven by the financial markets, the price-setting power of large companies and the interventions of states and central banks during the Covid-19 crisis lead to price increases. In fact, it is more likely to assume that the supply side rather than the demand is driving inflation (Roberts, 2022).

Price inflation is largely supply-driven in Europe. In the case of "cost-push inflation", the driver is a cost increase such as that of energy prices, and this effect then spreads throughout the entire economy of industrial and commercial companies. Transport costs and production costs increase, and if companies have a certain price-setting power, then they raise prices and pass on the costs to customers. Normally, higher raw material prices and wages squeeze the profit margins of companies, especially when the economy is weakening. However, and contrary to what experts assumed, the profit margins of large companies in the fourth quarter of 2022 were close to a record high in relation to costs. The

Fortune 500 companies made a record profit of 1.8 trillion dollars on a turnover of 16.1 trillion dollars in 2022. People are now even talking about a “greedflation”, assuming that corporate profits account for an estimated 30% of inflation (Daniel, 2023). But isn’t this corporate policy exactly another symptom of what we call the ecstasy of an escalating surplus production, in which industrial companies are involved when they are able to exploit economic and political situations due to their market power?

The COVID-19 pandemic was clearly followed by a supply shock. In addition, there is imported inflation in Europe because the euro is losing value against the dollar, making prices for products imported from the USA more expensive. Production collapsed worldwide with the closures of factories, workers were sent home or to the hospital, traffic and trade came to a standstill; social activities and events were prevented by isolation and lockdowns. The lean structure of global supply chains deprived the complex production and logistics networks of any leeway, and this became a major trigger of the shock when shipping was also stopped and the ports emptied. And once these connections were broken, they were difficult to restore. In addition, the bottlenecks were exacerbated by companies’ strategic adjustment to the situation, leading to a “bullwhip effect”.[9] The initial bottlenecks led to an anticipation of future supply problems and thus to a precautionary hoarding along the entire supply chains. The pent-up demand was then the result of the previous supply shock, and the price increase was also accelerated because the pent-up supply did not keep up with the increase in demand. The “shock” on the supply side is also to be understood as a result of a slowdown in industrial production, international trade, corporate investment and real GDP growth, factors that were already evident in 2019 before the outbreak of the pandemic (Ibid.). This happened because the profitability of capitalist investments and the industrial profit rates in the major economies had fallen to almost historical lows.

The pandemic forced car manufacturers worldwide in March 2020 to close their factories and temporarily suspend orders from suppliers. At the same time, the electronics industry faced increased demand for mobile phones, televisions, computers, games, and household appliances from customers. Consequently, chip manufacturers redirected their deliveries to the electronics industry, which was also willing to pay more for the silicon wafers. When the automotive industry came back online faster than expected in the summer of 2020, it was found that the needed chips were not available and suppliers preferred to fulfill their more lucrative contracts with other companies. Large orders cannot be fulfilled in this industry at short notice, as it takes about three months to manufacture even the simplest semiconductors.

Without these important components, car manufacturers could not meet demand. Despite the easing of public health restrictions in 2021, the number of new registrations in the USA fell to a level not seen since the 1950s, and there was a global production deficit of an estimated over 11 million vehicles and losses of 210 billion dollars for this industry worldwide (Tooze, 2022d, 2022e). In this difficult situation, global car manufacturers began to diversify their strategies, bypass their suppliers and turn directly to the chip manufacturers, hoping that they had the strategically important input in stock. Companies like Volkswagen, BMW, and Daimler, which then reported record profits in 2022, were able to increase their margins because this was made possible by supply shortages in conjunction with robust demand. Given the scarcity of semiconductor chips, the companies focused on the production of larger cars with higher profit margins as well as on the production of electric vehicles. These can easily be sold to wealthy, less price-sensitive consumers.

Companies raise prices because it increases their profits. However, rigid price setting is only possible for companies with high market power. The large corporations have a diverse product portfolio and their revenue management and marketing are so perfected that their customers stay with them even in times of crisis. In addition, due to their global reach, they are less dependent on a single national market and also have more financing options beyond bank loans, which makes them less dependent on bank interest rates. Large companies in concentrated industries with high market power were able to raise prices during the pandemic after a long period of price stability and this supported the general inflation process. At the microeconomic level of companies, an initial phase of price increases in systemically important sectors is to be expected. Powerful companies have the power to raise prices, but they usually only do so if they expect their competitors to also raise prices. This requires a kind of implicit agreement, which can be facilitated by rising costs in certain sectors and supply shortages. Rising prices in upstream sectors (energy and raw materials) are the trigger for price increases in downstream sectors. To protect their profit margins from rising costs, the downstream sectors also raise prices, among other things due to shortages (semiconductors). There is now a phase of spreading and amplifying the cost shock. Workers respond by trying to fend off real wage cuts. Inflation by powerful companies can lead to a general price increase, which can be temporary, but under certain conditions can also contribute to self-sustaining inflation spirals.

Behind the statistically determined average inflation rate hide, as Bichler/Nitzan have shown, individual price changes of companies with different rates (Bichler/Nitzan, 2022). Inflation is always differentiated, i.e., the prices of various goods rise in all possible directions, and it is the powerful large corporations that benefit the most from it. The result is that there is no uniform inflation rate. Instead, there are different rates in the respective industries. These rates can be averaged to calculate an average measure and determine a general trend; however, this requires subjective and political decisions about which goods are included in the average calculation and how their respective price changes should be weighted. In short, the inflation rate is inherently ambiguous.

And in this sense, inflation is always and everywhere a redistribution phenomenon, and not only between classes and layers, but also between the companies themselves.[10] This means that wholesale price inflation tends to lead to a systematic redistribution of profits from smaller to larger companies. A change in the price level is never evenly distributed across the respective sectors and companies. It always leads to a change in the matrix of relative prices: some sectors and companies lose, others win. Here there are the first signs of the emergence of a new macroeconomic regime to report, which differs from the immediate supply shocks and the counter shocks on the demand side: The signs of the last two years suggest that capital has moved from the sectoral instrumentalization of asymmetric shocks to a general attack on wages.

In addition, inflation is associated with a wealth transfer, insofar as the relationship between bond prices and bond yields is inverse. When interest rates rise, bond prices fall and vice versa. When inflation rises, lenders demand higher interest rates. A ten-year bond that yields 5% interest to investors is less attractive when interest rates rise. Why should one earn 5% for years when another bond yields more? If you lend a government capital at 5% for ten years, while inflation is 4%, then the real return on the investment is 1%. However, if inflation turns out to be 10% in retrospect, the real return is negative (5%).

For powerful companies, cost-driving inflation is thus a great opportunity to raise prices. Producers in certain sectors even benefit from supply chain bottlenecks and the increase in energy prices, as they can excessively increase their profit margins. The extraordinary profits of some energy and shipping companies in recent years are a typical example of this.[11]

The price increases in certain industries are accompanied by a rising demand for raw materials, such as sand, which is needed for the booming real estate industry in many countries, especially China. The debt-financed, resource-, and energy-intensive construction of real estate is the driving force for China's economy. At the same time, the demand for fossil raw materials as well as those needed for the green transformation is increasing, and supply bottlenecks are also emerging here.

Some authors now also speak of demand inflation. But the current price increases for many products, especially energy, electricity, gasoline, and food, have less to do with the demand for the products having increased. They are also not solely due to the war in Ukraine, but, as we will further elaborate, particularly due to speculative activities in the financial markets (Pettifor, 2022c). For households with low income, demand cannot have increased because more goods cannot be demanded due to a lack of available money. Here, consumers are robbed of real income through higher prices (Ibid.). In the USA, however, there was indeed a kind of demand inflation, because the massive economic stimulus from Biden temporarily increased the demand of both the population and companies. Because the savings rate of the US population is relatively low, the money was used directly to purchase goods, so the multiplier was high.

The Corona pandemic did not cause inflation, but at least exacerbated it, because (1) demand was pent up among consumers with higher incomes, with these households using up their savings that they had accumulated during the pandemic, and (2) supply bottlenecks arose—these bottlenecks were partly caused by restrictions on international transport of goods. (3) The newly created money no longer remained exclusively in the financial system, but also partly arrived in the real economy. This names some symptoms of inflation, but not the causes.[12]

For Michael Roberts, the inflation of prices ultimately depends on what happens in the future with the creation of new products in an economy—and this in turn depends on the rate of capital accumulation, the profit rate, and the profitability of capital. (Roberts, 2022) For Marx, due to increasing labor productivity, which lowers prices per unit, there was a long-term deflationary pressure on the prices of goods. However, for Marx there were countervailing factors that could exert long-term upward pressure on prices, such as the intervention of monetary authorities with their attempts to control the money supply.[13]

Inflation rates reached post-war lows in the 2010s despite the policy of "quantitative easing" because inflation remained in the financial sector and real GDP growth slowed along with investment and productivity growth. When banking experts analyzed the Fed's extensive QE program at the end of 2008, many feared it would lead to a return of inflation. However, this was not the case—also because bank lending to private customers had declined sharply in the wake of the implosion of the inter-bank market and because the Fed took over the part of the QE program that did not increase the money supply through new bank loans.

If the current inflation rise in certain industry sectors were solely due to problems in global supply chains and the Ukraine war, it would indeed be a temporary phenomenon. However, it must also be noted that, for example, energy prices are primarily regulated on the financial markets, which was then also partly responsible for their price increase.

Wolfgang Edelmüller writes in an article *War Economy and Economic War* the following aptly: "The price formation on the spot markets for fossil energy raw materials and their derivatives, which play an important role in the supply of fuels and heat energy carriers, is not so much influenced by real shortages with actual supply bottlenecks, but by the speculative expectation of possible shortages in the near future, which is reflected in the pricing of relevant futures contracts on the financial markets.The energy price explosion, which has clearly dominated the general inflation shock for more than a year alongside the pandemic-related supply chain disruptions, is noticeably driven by the economic war and its entourage of speculators and profiteers. Inflation is therefore to a large extent a speculation and profit inflation, which originates on the futures markets for energy raw materials and finds its continuation in the real price-setting power of energy corporations. The exploding profits are paid for by the mass of consumers in the inflation-threatened end consumer markets, where the working population suffers real income losses from wages and monetary transfers, so that poverty and the risk of poverty continue to spread" (Edelmüller, 2022).

Thus, today's inflationary pressure, which means a loss of purchasing power for the broad masses, is not simply a consequence of the problems with global supply chains, but is primarily also the result of the oversupply of fictitious and speculative money.

The war in Ukraine and the economic war of the West and the embargo behavior of the EU in trade with fossil fuels from Russia created deep uncertainty in the financial markets in 2022, thereby opening up a wide field of speculation for speculative capital, which usually led to price increases. The energy price explosion, which, in addition to the pandemic-related supply chain disruptions and the money flooding by the central banks, is currently driving inflation, is driven by the economic war of the West, which in turn motivates the speculators in the financial markets with the latter being the main causes of the increase in energy prices. Inflation is therefore to a large extent also a speculative inflation, which originates in the financial markets, specifically in the futures markets for energy raw materials, and finds its continuation in the price-setting power of the energy corporations as profit inflation, however, only to a limited extent (Pettifor, 2022c). In the last 10 years, the major oil and gas corporations have suffered enormous losses. The five Super-Majors ("Big Oil")—ExxonMobil, BP, Shell, Chevron, and Total—lost a staggering 76 billion dollars in 2020. (Ibid.) Oil prices plunged into negative territory in 2020, but recovered in 2022.

While supply and demand in traditional markets play a certain role in the dramatic fluctuations of oil, gas, and food prices, the much more important cause for rising high prices (and their subsequent crashes) lies in the financial markets. Understanding this is important because the rise in oil prices has already had serious, sometimes catastrophic consequences, it has also accelerated the collapse of the climate. Prices are therefore primarily determined on the global futures, options, and derivatives markets, where investors and traders speculate on the development of gas and oil prices and thus influence the (current) spot price. To put it bluntly, the prices for commodities are mainly determined by the speculators on Wall Street and at the Chicago Mercantile Exchange—not by politicians in Washington or Moscow. Not by the CEOs of global oil companies like BP or EXXON. Not even by increasing demand, because the price formation on the spot markets for fossil energy raw materials, which are important for the supply of fuels and heat energy carriers, is less influenced by real shortages and supply bottlenecks but by the speculative expectations of potential shortages in the near future, projections that are reflected in the pricing of futures contracts and derivatives in the financial markets show. (Ibid.) Capitalization today means discounting, that is, one seeks the calculated (discounted) present value of the risk-adjusted profits of an economic unit expected in the future. The discount rate is used to estimate the present value of the liabilities oriented towards the future.

As the *US Energy Information Administration* explains, there are differences between the participants in the various markets for oil. Commercial traders (oil producers and airlines) buy and sell physical quantities of oil. Non-commercial traders (banks, hedge funds, commodity trading advisors etc.) do not buy or sell oil, but they speculate in the financial markets only with financial instruments (futures contracts and derivatives) on the price of oil. (Ibid.) Putin or EXXON executives can influence the oil supply, but both have little influence on the price of a barrel of oil. Putin was right when he claimed in June 2022 that Russia does not set oil prices. (Part of Putin's power also relies on the financial markets. It is estimated that between 2002 and 2012, Russia received up to 560 billion dollars from financial speculators, most of which came from Wall Street and the City of London.)

As even a 2006 US Senate report states, the financial market operates outside the reach of producers and outside the regulatory systems of most governments. At the same time as there was a massive influx of speculative dollars into energy commodities, the ability of US national control authorities to monitor the nature, extent, and impact of these speculations has decreased. Above all, trading in US energy commodities on exchanges not regulated by the CFTC (Commodity Futures Trading Commission) has exploded. (Ibid.)

The power of speculative capital has further increased with the passage of US legislation in 2000, because commodities such as oil and wheat, which had previously been traded on traditional markets, could now be financialized due to the deregulation under the "Commodities Futures Modernisation Act". Speculators operating on the Chicago Mercantile Exchange and the New York Mercantile Exchange owe the Clinton administration the gift of the "Commodities Futures Modernisation Act". This deregulation of commodity markets was based on a report prepared by Alan Greenspan, Larry Summers, and Robert Rubin. New derivative instruments such as Credit Default Swaps were no longer regulated as "futures" under the "Commodity Exchange Act" of 1936 (CEA) or as "securities" under federal securities laws (Ibid.).

It is the derivatives that are now at the center of speculation, and they are to some extent separated from the price of the underlying asset such as oil, although not completely decoupled. Now, far more derivatives and futures contracts are bought and sold than barrels of oil are traded.

Thus, speculative financial instruments make up between 25 and 50 times the total value of the oil on which they (increasingly only tangentially) are based. Commodity prices are now subject to a volatile arms race of financial markets, leading to wild swings in prices up or down.

To summarize: In the first phase of inflation in 2022, energy prices and agricultural commodity prices were primarily responsible for the rise in inflation. In the second phase, increases in basic prices were responsible for cost increases for many consumer goods and services, which were highest where market concentration is greatest. The rise in prices for raw materials is not primarily due to supply or demand conditions in the market for these goods, but to the conditions prevailing in the international financial markets. These markets determine the prices for commodities and most energy products.

The prices set on international markets are often tied to the expectations of market participants, and since most transactions do not need to be financed to take place, they can reflect a fictitious supply and demand that does not correspond to the actual supply and demand in the real markets. Most of the time, it is speculation that is responsible for the strong fluctuations in commodity prices. The prices of commodity derivatives, which often affect the price of real goods, depend on the strategies of the actors in these markets and on international financial regulations. Most price increases in futures contracts, which then affect spot prices, are due to an excess demand for futures contracts, which in turn depends on the hedging strategies of financial and non-financial companies. Some companies have to hedge the entire planned production in advance through the sale of futures on the market.[14]

The state of the world economy, even in China, is more than fragile in 2023. The risk of a global recession is so great that the energy markets are already reacting to it. The oil price has fallen in the year 2023. The barrel is traded at around 90 dollars at the beginning of 2023, after it had cost 120 dollars in June.

When the German Minister of Economy, Habeck, talks about Germany becoming poorer, this is to be specified, that due to the speculation-driven inflation at the consumer markets, the many consumers of the lower and middle income groups become poorer, but richer are especially the financial actors who profit from the speculation with fossil fuels and the associated appropriation of the increased prices.

The western economic war for the oil and gas exports important for Putin's war of aggression, on which the energy supply of several countries in the EU depends, also increases the uncertainty that leads to further speculative escalations of prices on the financial markets. This economic war is intended to produce the double effect of reducing dependence on Russian energy raw materials and accelerating the decarbonization of the economy.

Behind the latter argument lies the neoliberal belief in the efficient steering competence of the capitalist market price system. Accordingly, the price elasticity of demand leads to a reduction in the quantity demanded for fossil fuels when prices are sufficiently high. The loss of price advantages creates diversion effects, so that the energy and mobility transition can be achieved through market processes. However, if, for example, social security measures against the risk of poverty are taken by the state through bonus payments, this is also restricted again. Households with higher incomes, who are at the top in terms of fossil energy consumption, can easily absorb the price increase. Direct steering via the market thus does not work.

The price elasticity of demand depends on the level of income off. In the lower and middle income range, the price elasticity of energy demand is high, while it decreases with higher incomes. This is related to income-dependent restrictions, as households with low and middle incomes have a direct effect of the price increase on consumption and spending behavior. Since these households cannot afford the energy price increases and do not have the means for energy-saving investments such as changing the heating system, they are forced to make direct savings and suffer real income losses. The compensation payments are for the lower layers like a drop in the bucket. Social policy is now like politics itself. It is administered to the masses in homeopathic doses, diluted so far that it becomes vanishingly small in relation to the overall solution, until it finally almost completely disappears and leaves only a trace that is so small that it can hardly be perceived anymore, but finally survives as a simulation (as a policy of well-intentioned advice on how to save money). When social policy, as the distribution of alms, is also bound to the right of the state donor to control the private life of the recipient in detail, then its simulation does not even need this control anymore, because it seeps into everything until it has created the universal consumer-patient.

Back to the question of central banks and financial markets. If the inflation continues to rise in the coming years, the central banks have to raise the prime rates further and thus risk a massive debt crisis. However, if they maintain a policy of cheap money or return to it, there could occur a stagflation, while problems in the supply sector persist. But even if they continue the second strategy, a debt crisis could follow, as private debt in the advanced economies could become unbearable. Highly indebted companies would go bankrupt, followed by indebted households and a part of the shadow banking and private banking systems.

The Fed, as already mentioned above, is in a dilemma. If it tightens monetary policy too much and raises interest rates too quickly, this could lead to the cost of borrowing for investments or expenditures rising so sharply that new investments in technology decline, consumer demand for products stalls, and a recession occurs. However, if the central bank does not act and continues its policy of cheap money, high inflation may not be temporary at all. However, the current inflation trends, which are among other things the result of rising energy prices and disruptions in global supply chains cannot be solved by raising interest rates, because there is no interest rate that can untangle the supply chains or lower the energy costs. However, an interest rate increase does affect the demand side by making borrowing more expensive, reducing investments and job creation, and causing a recession and higher unemployment. Under these circumstances, workers lose their ability to negotiate higher wages, and suffer from a decline in their purchasing power, which further lowers demand.[15]

Central banks, armed with the core monetarist theses, assume that it is inflation expectations that need to be fought first and foremost by aligning them with the desired price stability. This requires a reliable monetary policy of the central bank, which leads to low inflation expectations. However, the immediate question arises as to how inflation expectations should be measured and thus predicted. To do this, one would need to know how the large, powerful companies (outside the financial sector) in the sense of Bichler/Nitzan, who really have pricing power, price their expectations. However, for these companies, the significant costs are their own costs and not the aggregated price level or national inflation expectations. (As of January 2023 the overall inflation rates have somewhat decreased, but the so-called core inflation, which excludes energy and food, remains high. This is mainly due to the increase in the cost of services and industrial goods. In May 2023, food inflation in Europe is in the double-digit range (EU average 19.17%), in Germany at 21.2%, in the United Kingdom at 19.1% and in Turkey at 67.89%).

As for the cost of borrowing and servicing existing debt, the US Federal Reserve and other central banks are currently implementing a strict monetary tightening by raising their prime rates, which form the lower limit for other loan interest rates, further and reducing the available money supply for borrowing. This can lead to a shortage of credit and liquidity. In addition to increasing the number of bank loans, there has been an explosive increase in "subprime" loans before the tightening, which has brought the debt burden of American companies to a record level. The total stock of "subprime" corporate debt (junk bonds, leveraged loans, etc.) has reached 5 billion US dollars in the USA. According to national accounts, the total debt of companies outside the financial sector (bonds and loans) amounts to 12.7 billion US dollars, with the share of subprime debt making up 40% of the total amount. (Tooze, 2022d, 2022e) These debts finance very speculative or highly indebted companies either in the form of loans ("Leveraged Loans") or with bonds without investment-grade rating ("junk bonds"), but they also include corporate loans that are sold as part of securitizations, the so-called "Collateralized Loan Obligations" (CLOs), as well as loans that are privately granted by non-banks and are completely unregulated.

It can be assumed that the large debt overhang can never be fully repaid. After the First and Second World War, debt levels were reduced through a combination of robust economic growth, which led to higher tax revenues, and actual defaults, either informally through inflation or formally through a debt restructuring. If productivity (and thus growth) in the industrialized countries does not improve much stronger than currently seems plausible, then inflation could now take over a large part of the debt reduction. The question for investors is whether the central banks, if they react to the rising inflation pressure with interest rate hikes, will not trigger a shock in the markets. But the central banks also know that they cannot keep interest rates low because they would induce even more bad debt.

Higher inflation can, however, to a rather small extent also be the result of high government deficits increasingly being financed by the central banks. The expansion of central bank reserves and their operations as well as their policy of Quantitative Easing (QE) can then intensify price inflation for consumer goods as soon as the commercial banks grant more loans in the course of this policy, i.e. channel debt (and cash) into the economy. It is an illusion that the mass of fictitious and speculative capital remains entirely in the financial sector, it can indeed affect the real economy and influence the purchasing power of the masses. However, the question arises why the policy of QE, which began after the financial crisis of 2008, only led to inflationary pressure in the real sector in 2022. Inflation should have set in the real sector much earlier, but instead we only saw asset price inflation in the financial sector to record. Daniela Gabor shows that the policy of QE has primarily supported the financial system, which constantly needs liquidity and in which money markets, assets, derivatives, and other high-risk instruments are increasingly dependent on collateral (Gabor, 2016). For Gabor, as we have already seen above, the policy of states and central banks includes, among other things, the transformation of the market for government bonds into a "collateral factory" for the money markets. The hedging of the repo market supports the market-based financial system, which relies on safe securities, and at the same time stabilizes the monetary policy transmission processes itself. Only the government bonds of the leading imperialist countries are to be understood as collateral in times of crisis. When central banks buy securities, their prices change. Through increased repo transactions, central banks can also channel higher liquidity into the markets. This expansion of liquidity allows market makers to conduct more repo transactions, which in turn increases the demand for collateral, leading to a rise in their prices and other financial products. Thus, monetary policy has effects not only on the money market, but also on the prices of assets in the capital markets.

The policy of the central bank also determines today which securities are traded as collateral for repo transactions and which actors are accepted as contract partners. Since the global financial crisis of 2008, the number of financial actors with whom the central banks conduct repo transactions has been significantly expanded and now includes, for example, money market funds. At the same time, the quality criteria for the securities that the central banks accept as collateral have been significantly lowered since the financial crisis and later again in the COVID-19 crisis. The securities accepted by the central bank as collateral are preferably used as a basis for repos between private actors, as they have a very low haircut. The central bank policy stimulates in this way significantly the banking *and* the shadow banking system, including new liquidity spirals and asset price bubbles. The *stabilizing* monetary policy of the central bank thus also has a *destabilizing* effect.

After the 2008 crisis, central banks did not print money that flowed into industrial companies, households, or government budgets. If we link this insight with the problem of declining productivity (and thus lower returns on capital investments), it becomes clear that QE policy must be seen as necessary for the stability of the financial system, without being able to generate industrial growth or promote a return to state-led fiscal dominance. However, it can never be completely ruled out that the money does not only circulate in the financial system. It depends on which variants of QE are preferred by the central banks.[16]

The internal limitation of real accumulation by inflation (lack of demand) acts like a factor driving capital into the virtual space of transnational circulation of financial assets, which in turn is characterized by growing debt masses. This is by no means to be understood as a pathological distortion of the original capitalist model, but as the logical consequence of its structural crisis. (Vighi, 2022) A hypertrophic and ecstatic financial system of the current scale cannot easily coexist with real growth, i.e., flourishing mass consumption and mass production. If today's volume of fictitious and speculative capital were to circulate freely on all markets, it could trigger hyperinflation—which has so far been exported to the neglected peripheries of the globalized world.[17]

Even though the global liquidity index deteriorated rapidly in 2022, the last day of the year 2022 saw a record high in reverse repo deposits at the New York Fed: 2.5 trillion dollars from 113 parties. This meant that investors parked excessively large amounts of money at the Fed, as the reverse repo facility guaranteed higher returns than, for example, industrial investments (the repo rate was 4.3% at the end of 2022). And this also means that large amounts of liquidity, which have a massive potential for inflation, were at least temporarily floating again on the financial markets and thus did not appear directly as real demand—exactly the strategy that has been used since the 1990s to suppress inflation. But this solution must eventually raise problems, as the fictitious and speculative capital has swelled to a size that can no longer be easily contained, although counter-trends are noticeable in 2023. In fact, financial capital has long since begun to cannibalize the real economy. (Ibid.)

Finally, two questions arise: what is the significance of inflation for the financial industry and how should its relative weakening in 2023 be assessed? Inflation works for and against finance. On the one hand, inflation requires a restrictive monetary policy and a reduction in liquidity, which deprives the financial markets of the continuous support they have received over the past years in the form of government bailouts and quantitative easing by central banks; it could even provoke a sudden drying up of liquidity and the outbreak of a financial panic. On the other hand, inflation devalues the price of accumulated debt and the real interest rate, shifting the relationship between debtor and creditor in favor of the former. The loss in value of the debts means that the amount that the debtor has to repay, actually decreases, causing creditors to lose correspondingly. Also, companies can repay loans more easily due to inflation, because the borrowed amount decreases in value. For commercial banks, rising interest rates have a positive effect, and for wealthy households, rising interest rates mean that they can further increase their money assets by buying securities such as bonds and benefiting from the rising interest rates.

However, a new trend has also emerged since 2023. A spiral of rapid debt disinflation is emerging, in which debts are no longer repaid, written off or no longer serviced, while borrowing is declining. The price of assets is falling, but the price of debt in relation to assets is rising. This development, which is triggered by high real interest rates and low real wages worldwide, in turn leads to a fall in the price of goods and services and, above all, assets—primarily because it reduces demand for these goods and assets.

The hegemony of the financial industry seems to be diminished in 2023. Even if its hegemony temporarily weakens, finance remains a powerful structural formation with a central position in the world economy. Despite the restrictive measures of the central banks, the real credit costs—i.e., the nominal interest rate minus the inflation rate—on both sides of the Atlantic are still not far above the negative range. However, the signals for financial distress are already increasing. The Goldman Sachs index, which reflects the availability of financial resources and which takes into account not only interest rates but also exchange rates and stock fluctuations, reached a level at the end of 2022 that has not been achieved since the low point of 2009 (Durand, 2023).

Can the relative and temporary, but by no means structural, loss of importance of finance be measured? If one imagines importance as a balance of power—both within the capital factions themselves and of financial capital against workers and the state—then financial hegemony cannot be captured with a single measure. However, one way to estimate its intensity in an approximation is to look at the extent of the expected valorization, measured by the value of financial assets in relation to the nominal size of the economy. The turnaround in the stock markets after a decade-long boom was a first indication in this regard. Since November 2021, the FT Wiltshire 5000—the broadest index of the US investment market—has fallen by 17.5%. The total market capitalization in the US fell from 200% of GDP to 150%, thus below the level before the pandemic. In Europe, the trend is similar: The STOXX Europe 600 fell by 12.6% over the same period. (Ibid.)

Another indication of the temporarily weaker position of the financial sector is the decline in its share of total profits. In the US, the profits of the financial sector have fallen from a peak of 27% in early 2019 to 15% in the second quarter of 2022; in the Eurozone, a decline from 10 to 6% is recorded. On a deeper level, the power of finance lies in liquidity; it implies the ability of the financial industry to discipline companies and state institutions by playing them off against each other. The greater the reach of liquidity, i.e., the more fluid and integrated the financial markets are, the greater their power. The outflow of liquidity in the new inflationary context also negatively affects financial hegemony. The shift in the composition of the Fed's balance sheet from bank reserves to short-term liabilities also leads to a liquidity outflow from a broadly based banking system to a very narrow, risk-prone one. The shift in the composition of the balance sheets of commercial banks from the financial cycle to the industrial cycle also reduces the liquidity available to the financial markets.

With regard to derivatives, stocks, and other financial instruments, there was a decline in prices in 2022. Public and private capital, growth stocks, technology values, cryptocurrencies have fallen in price, while credit spreads have risen and thus the price of debt has fallen. Even cash yielded a negative real return due to inflation. And if one is heavily leveraged—for private households this means mortgages, credit cards, car loans, student loans, personal loans, for the corporate sector business loans, bank loans, corporate debt in the form of bonds—then the ability to repay debts to be extinguished in danger. There can be a systemic debt crisis and banks can get into financial trouble themselves. The losses are then socialized, and there is an increase in public debt. Private debts thus become public debts.

The current rise in inflation shows that the monetary stabilization of financial capital by central banks can be fragile can be. Thus, the grammar of the new inflation is certainly not on the pandemic and the war in Ukraine to reduce, because to a certain extent, it is also the result of the interventions of central banks after the financial crisis of 2008 and the subsequent financial boom in the 2010s, which was fueled by an unconventional monetary policy. Through the devaluation of financial assets in 2023, the excessively accumulated fictitious and speculative capital is slowly and at least partially reduced, but all this is tied to cyclical movements and by no means signifies the loss of hegemony of financial capital. The inflation figures in March 2023 from the USA show that inflation has now been reduced to six percent. The slightly lower core inflation rate of 5.5%, which excludes the prices of energy carriers and food, shows that inflation is only to a lesser extent due to the war in Ukraine and the pandemic.

How are the future prospects to be assessed if, like Nouriel Roubini, one predicts a prolonged period of stagnation? Roubini cites several key points for this (Roubini, 2022): The shrinking supply of young workers in the West leads to increase in wages and thus to rising costs, which reduces the accumulation rate of capital. Deglobalization as a result of restriction of global trade in goods, services, technologies, data, and investments leads to higher import prices, rising production costs. This also weakens growth. The relocation of production from still cost-effective countries like China to more expensive industrial countries will lead to further cost and price increases. In this context, the competition between the USA and China threatens to freeze into a cold war, so that among other things, intense technology wars (semiconductors) could break out. If China takes a leading role in the technologies and industries of the future such as AI, then it could offer many emerging countries in the areas of e-commerce, platforms for digital payment systems, and 5G networks lucrative offers. The Russian invasion in Ukraine has increased the prices of energy, food, and other commodities, which are important for global supply chains and consumer and production processes. Global climate change will increase the stagflationary pressure as a result of water shortages in certain parts of the world, an insufficient supply of green energy, pandemics, and natural disasters. Increasingly frequent cyber attacks disrupt supply chains, power grids, and financial infrastructures. The power of the dollar could dwindle if China pursues a competitive economic, trade, investment, technology, currency, and financial policy. The role of the US dollar as an important reserve currency is declining and the resulting devaluation can lead to strong inflation and stagflation, as most commodities are priced in dollars and the devaluation leads to a price increase leads. The demand for dollars, which results from their status as a global reserve currency, means that the USA can take out cheaper loans to finance their high budget and trade deficits. But if the budget and current account deficit of the USA is getting bigger and bigger, while the dollar is increasingly used as a weapon for foreign policy and national security goals, this could very soon lead to a loss of power of the dollar. Trade and financial sanctions can disrupt global supply chains, which depend on the financing and payment transactions in dollars, as well as the smooth functioning of global financial markets, think of the functioning of SWIFT, further disrupt. Finally, financial wars lead to further stagflationary financial disruptions.

Notes

1. In recent decades, the growth of the manufacturing industry and thus economic development has focused on East Asia, especially China. In most of the poor world—Latin America, South Asia, the Middle East and Africa south of the Sahara—the economies have undergone negative development simultaneously de-agrarianization and deindustrialization, especially in the years after 1980.

   Industrialization in East Asia has statistically compensated for the stagnation in almost all other countries—with the East Asian industrialization partly responsible for the loss of the production base in other countries. This was the case even when incomes in most poor countries rose, mainly due to the commodity supercycle from 2000 to 2015, which was partly driven by the explosively growing demand in the Chinese market, which in turn has helped to set the emerging countries on a technological export profile.
2. The poorest countries are in the most difficult situation. After three decades of strong decline, extreme poverty has been on the rise again in the last three years. The resurgence of inflation, exacerbated by the war in Ukraine, has been making the situation difficult since the fall of 2020. Rising interest rates are causing these countries to be further strangled. The interest rate differences to the US government bonds have exploded. A large part of their public revenues are used for debt service. The disruption of supply chains (due to Covid-19, war in Ukraine and the climate disaster) has driven up food and energy prices and driven the spiral of misery. As interest rates have been rising for a year, some states are threatened with bankruptcy due to their debt burden. According to the World Bank, 60% of global extreme poverty is concentrated in Sub-Saharan Africa today, and the number of people living in extreme poverty continues to increase.

3. From an entrepreneur's perspective, labor productivity does not appear as a calculation of measurable output over working hours, but as a measurement of output over labor costs. What ultimately counts for the entrepreneur are the costs of labor. A reduction in wages or a decrease in the total number of employees results in an increase in (monetary measured) labor productivity by reducing unit labor costs.
4. Smith, however, sees not only a productivity divergence between a technologically advanced and a stagnating sector, but points to the divergence between the growth of unproductive and productive labor in the Marxian sense, which exerts a downward pressure on the profit rate. The rising share of unproductive workers, who work in administration, circulation and surveillance, represents a an increasing burden on the system as a whole, as a significant part of the wage sum includes personnel who perform activities that do not produce value and whose wages must be paid from the surplus value that is produced by productive workers elsewhere in the economy. A discussion should now begin on what is meant by productive work. We have had this discussion at another place (Szepanski, 2014a, 2014b).
5. Another approach is offered by the French economist Durand (Durand, 2023). He points out that profits in the advanced capitalist economies have at least temporarily risen since the 1980s (masses of profit), but the profit rates and investments stagnated or declined. At this point, the cyclical movements must be empirically examined. Numerous explanations have been put forward for these developments, including the maximization of shareholder value, the increasing monopolization of transnational companies or the toxic effects of the ever accelerating financialization. Durand does not offer any significantly new causal factors for this development, instead, he argues that the puzzle of profits without accumulation is at least partly an artificial one, a statistical illusion, created by the inability to capture the effects of globalization. The factors of globalization and digitalization should now allow companies in the Global North to exploit their position at the top of the global supply chains to demand low prices for end or intermediate products from companies at the lower end of the supply chains in the Global South. On the other hand, the investments of transnational

companies from the Global North are increasingly going into the Global South.

With the term "Techno-feudalism", Durand also joins the growing number of those who want to explain the puzzle of this dynamic by emphasizing the role of intellectual property rights and intangible goods, which allow US companies to extract enormous profits from their supply chains. With the term "Techno-feudalism", Durand argues that the emergence of intangible goods has led to the creation of four new types of rents: The legal rents from intellectual property (rents from patents, copyrights and trademarks) and the monopoly rents (companies that have the ability to integrate a supply chain and provide the necessary infrastructures), as well as dynamic innovation rents and intangible differential rents. Innovation rents refer to valuable data sets that are in the exclusive possession of these companies, while differential rents characterize the ability of companies within a single supply chain to expand their activities. Equipped with these categories, Durand sees only neo-feudal rentiers everywhere. The rise of tech companies, according to Durand, feeds a gigantic rent economy and leads to stagnation. (Ibid.).

6. This notion not only implies the existence of a supposedly optimal ratio between money and goods/services, while other factors are ignored (including financialization), but it also says nothing about the causes of inflation: How does such an imbalance between "too much money" and "too few goods" come about? Was there an increase in the demand for more goods or a decrease in supply?
7. In the official measurement of inflation (which is used by the central banks, the state and other financial authorities), the consumer price index (CPI) is used, i.e. a basket of certain goods that are regularly consumed by households. This means that other prices are not taken into account: for example, rental costs are included in the CPI, but the rise in real estate prices (which are considered investment goods) are not.
8. Oil price shocks, like all negative shocks, reduce potential growth and increase production costs. This puts pressure on companies that consume oil; they have to cut jobs and/or increase prices. A loose monetary policy lowers the capital costs and helps companies maintain the number of employees until demand picks up again. But it leads to further costs and price increases.

9. The same forces that have amplified the "bullwhip effect" could also lead to a price drop once the bottlenecks are eliminated and the inventories along the supply chains are replenished; a ceasefire and negotiations to end the war in Ukraine could eventually lower energy prices, especially if accompanied by a slowdown in China.
10. Today, workers assume that inflation harms them because it reduces their purchasing power. However, this is not a characteristic of inflation itself, but a characteristic of class struggle. The wage decline is a sign that the workers, when companies raise prices, are not able to increase their income. Historically, this lack of power was not the norm.
11. According to Bichler/Nitzan, stagflation is a business strategy, it is one of two ways to make profits. (Bichler/Nitzan, 2022) The first way to make profits for companies is to keep prices constant, while trying to sell more goods. The second way is to drive up prices. Since the latter option often requires a restriction of the flow of resources (what flows freely, cannot be expensive), Bichler/Nitzan conclude that inflation goes hand in hand with economic stagnation. In principle, a company could pursue both strategies at the same time, i.e. increase prices and sell more products at the same time. In practice, however, the two strategies usually exclude each other. If a company wants to sell more goods, a strategy that Bichler/Nitzan call "breadth", it is easiest to lower the price of the goods. If the company wants to raise prices, a strategy that Bichler/Nitzan call "depth", it must restrict access to the goods it sells, because things that flow freely cannot be expensive. (Ibid.) According to World Bank data, higher inflation tends to go hand in hand with a stagnating energy consumption. The stagflation thesis of Bichler/Nitzan thus seems to be confirmed, at least for the last half century.
12. It seems that even the Fed today no longer views the rise in inflation as temporary, but assumes that it will probably continue for some time, even though the median forecasts assume that the personal consumption inflation rate will fall to 2.1% by 2024.

    Moreover, there has never been an inflation that was primarily caused by rising wages. In fact, real wages have only increased by an average of 0.4% per year over the last 20 years until 2020, which is less than the average annual real GDP growth of around 2%. It is the share of GDP growth that is attributable to profits that has increased (Roberts 2022). Marx argued that rising wages do not lead to price increases, but to falling profits, and this is the real reason why mainstream economics brings wage-driven inflation into play.

13. Regarding the question of inflation, Anwar Shaikh initially assumes that competition determines relative prices through the balancing movements of profit rates (Shaikh, 2016). The growth of aggregate demand can be fueled by new purchasing power, where the modern credit system can at least virtually stimulate purchasing power unlimitedly, raising the question of the limits of supply. For Shaikh, the limits arise from the fact that no economy can generate a higher accumulation rate than the one at which the entire economic surplus is reinvested (greater than the profit rate). Shaikh compares Ricardo's corn-corn model with Marx's schemes of extended reproduction as well as with von Neumann's and Kaldor's models. (Ibid.: 695) It is about how the maximum growth potential of an economy can be utilized (growth-benefit index). Since the profit rate is the rate of profit to capital, and the accumulation rate is the rate of investment to capital, the growth-benefit index is the share of investment in profit.

    The case of increased demand due to new purchasing power with limited supply is to be considered. An increase in demand will express itself in expanded production and/or higher prices, i.e. in a nominally higher gross amount. The growth rate of GDP is then a function of the new purchasing power in relation to GDP. On the supply side, it should be noted that real growth is increasingly dampened as the current growth rate gradually reaches the maximum growth rate. This is consistent with Keynes' statement that at full employment, the new demand is less absorbed by the new output but leads to price increases. These statements are used by Shaikh for his theory of inflation (Ibid.: 676ff.).

    If real growth positively correlates with net purchasing power and net profitability (marginal net profit rate, profit on new investment) and negatively with the degree of utilization of growth and eventually reaches a critical point, then we always have a non linear function in the relation between both moments. If the inflation rate is equal to the difference between the growth rate of nominal and real output, and the former is a function of the new relative purchasing power, then inflation positively correlates with the new purchasing power and the net profitability and negatively with the unused growth potential. A possible fall in net profitability can be compensated to a certain extent by an increase in demand, so that the growth rate falls less sharply than the profit rate. A fall in the growth rate leads to unemployment, while an increase in the growth-capacity rate makes the economy more susceptible to inflation. This is the secret of stagflation. The rates can only vary within certain limits, but in a system with fiat money there are apparently fewer limits to the growth of purchasing power. (Ibid. 678) If the rate of increase in purchasing power is low, then the impact on inflation is still small, at high rates it becomes different. Thus, inflation can be defined as a function of new borrowings (demand through consumer credit), net profitability and the degree of unused capacity utilization. Empirically, a strong relation between credit growth and the growth of nominal GDP can be registered today, where at at the peak points, the growth of the GDP is less than that of the credits, which is a sign that the increased demand leads to an inflation of securities and bond prices and to currency speculation.

14. In contrast to the spot market, on the futures market the conclusion and fulfillment of a transaction are separated in time. A future can be settled by delivery of the sold or purchased goods but in most cases, the delivery does not take place. The buyer of the future can free himself from the delivery obligation by selling a future with the same characteristics before the expiration date as the purchased future, and the seller can buy another future. The increase in index investments and new positions of institutional investors in commodities requires this rollover (swap) of the futures. Rollover means that the long positions in the expiring contracts are closed and new long positions with later maturity dates are entered. The shape of the futures curve determines the profits or losses from the rollover. The curve can either be inclined upwards or downwards, when the futures prices rise/fall with the maturity of the underlying contract. Since the curve has been positively inclined for most commodities since the beginning of the 2000s, this meant a rollover profit for sellers and a rollover loss for buyers. The buyers were the banks on behalf of the institutional investors in index funds and the sellers were money managers,

hedge funds, and banks. The profit or loss is defined as the difference between the price of the expiring contract and the price of the deferred contract within a certain time unit. If the actions of the index funds affect the price, the spread decreases during the rollover period, as the price of the expiring contract falls, while the price of the deferred contract rises. Speculators take advantage of the narrowing of the spread by entering the same positions as the index swap traders a few days in advance. Then the speculators go short positions in the expiring contracts and long positions in the deferred contracts. At the time of the rollover, they close their positions and realize the profit. The profit depends in no way on the development of the spot price of the commodities, but only on the margin between the prices of two futures contracts, which expire at different rates and are registered within a certain time window.

During the crisis, derivative positions lost a lot of value, and companies were asked to pay huge margin calls immediately in cash to clearing houses, which are owned by the largest international banks. If borrowing to settle the margin calls was too expensive, the companies tried to get rid of the short positions by building up a long position, i.e., by buying new futures. The latter increased the already high demand for futures and the prices for energy products. There are automatic feedback mechanisms that tend to increase the pressure on prices. Many energy companies were financed in various forms by the states despite their high profits, to make the margin payments. Most agricultural and energy prices have therefore not risen due to an excess demand on the goods market.

Since inflation expectations are measured at various metrics for example, at the prices of assets and derivatives on the financial markets, events on the financial markets that have an impact on monetary policy decisions can contribute to a further feedback effect. For example, the spot prices for oil and gas have fallen, while the prices for futures with longer maturities are still high. If inflation expectations include these futures prices, this justifies a further increase in interest rates to dampen inflation expectations. In this way, the central bank will not control the markets, but will be subject to their rules.

15. The effect of interest rate increases on prices peaks after at least two years, with significant impacts on real economic activity only

appearing in the fourth year. If central banks are understood as instruments of class power, a logic emerges with their policy of tightening: If the long-term trend of the economy is in declining productivity and profitability and companies are in a competitive struggle to increase their market share in a shrinking market environment, while at the same time a potential for strengthening the working class emerges, then triggering a recession, in which it is difficult to enforce wage increases, is a specifically political way to intervene in this conflict.

16. The Fed preferred a specific version of QE in 2020, namely the purchase of assets outside the banking sector, which gave companies and financial institutions that had sold to the Fed new purchasing power. This also forced the private customer banks to create new loans, leading to a massive increase in the money supply. (The other version of QE can also focus on buying up government bonds to correct the balance sheets of companies.).

    BlackRock had previously argued that the next downturn would force central banks to create new money and find ways to get central bank money directly into the hands of public and private institutions, that is, bypassing the private banks. The Fed knew that this would favor inflation, as BlackRock later confirmed in a paper, stating that the Fed is now committed to driving inflation above the target for some time. This was implemented in March 2020. In doing so, the Fed commissioned a private company to purchase assets, namely none other than BlackRock. By proceeding directly, the Fed now massively expanded credit creation, the money supply, and new spending.

    Meanwhile, the Covid measures imposed by governments also focused on the credit creation of private banks. The banks were instructed to expand lending to businesses, with governments guaranteeing these loans. Dismissed workers were paid stimulus checks, and both the central banks and the commercial banks increasingly bought government bonds. Both the central banks, but also, crucially for inflation in the real sector, the commercial banks increased the money supply, with a large part of the money being used for general consumption and not for productive purposes (loans to businesses). As a result, the money supply ballooned to a record high. In the USA, the broad money supply M3 increased by 19.1% in 2020, the strongest increase ever. In the Eurozone, the money supply M1 increased by 15.6% in December 2020 (Richard Werner). However, since February 2021, the growth of the M3 money supply in euros has been declining. The narrower money supply M1, which only includes cash and demand deposits that can be withdrawn at any time, has been shrinking since the beginning of 2023.

17. Former Finance Minister Larry Summers and the former chief economist of the IMF Olivier Blanchard both warned in 2022 that the passage of the proposed $1.9 trillion spending package by the US Congress, in addition to the $900 billion stimulus program, risked causing inflation. The combination of loose monetary policy, accumulated consumer savings, which were unable to be spent during the pandemic, and an already declining unemployment rate can contribute to rising inflationary pressure. On the other hand, zombie companies contribute to deflationary pressure due to favorable financing conditions and overcapacity.

References

Benanav, A. (2022). *Automation and the Future of Work*. Verso.

Bichler, S., & Nitzan, J. (2022). The Stagflation Norm. https://capitalaspower.com/casp-forum/topic/the-stagflation-norm/

Daniel, W. (2023). 'We May Be Looking at the End of Capitalism': One of the World's Oldest and Largest Investment Banks Warns 'Greedflation' Has Gone Too Far. https://fortune.com/2023/04/05/end-of-capitalism-inflation-greedflation-societe-generale-corporate-profits/

Durand, C. D. (2023). The End of Financial Hegemony? The New Left Review. https://newleftreview.org/issues/ii138/articles/cedric-durand-the-end-of-financial-hegemony

Dyer-Whitheford, N. (2015). *Cyber-Proletariat: Global Labour in the Digital Vortex*. London.

Edelmüller, W. (2022). Kriegswirtschaft und Wirtschaftskrieg. https://makroskop.eu/spotlight/versailles-durch-die-hintertur/war-economy-and-economic-war/

Fischbach, R. (2017). *Die schöne Utopie: Paul Mason, der Postkapitalismus und der Traum vom grenzenlosen Überfluss*. Köln.

Gabor, D. (2016). The (Impossible) Repo Trinity: The Political Economy of Repo Markets. *Review of International Political Economy, 6*, 967–1000.

Gordon, R. J. (2013). *Is US Economic Growth Over? Faltering Innovation Confronts the Six*. http://www.voxeu.org/article/us-economic-growth-over

Gordon, R. J. (2017). *The Rise and Fall of American Growth: The U.S. Standard of Living Since the Civil War*. Princeton.

Nordhaus, W. D. (2015). NBER Working Paper No. 21547. September 2015. http://www.nber.org/papers/w21547.pdf

Pettifor, A. (2022c). Grain Inflation: Starve the Poor, Feed the Rich. The War and Inflation—Who Is Winning? https://annpettifor.substack.com/p/grain-inflation-starve-the-poor-feed

Roberts, M. (2022). The Inflation Conundrum. https://thenextrecession.wordpress.com/2022/10/28/the-inflation-conundrum/

Roubini, N. (2022). *MegaThreats: Ten Dangerous Trends That Imperil Our Future, And How to Survive Them*. Boston.

Shaikh, A. (2016). *Capitalism. Competition. Conflict. Crises*. New York.

Smith, J. E. (2020). *Smart Machines and Service Work*. Chicago.

Szepanski, A. (2014a). *Kapitalisierung Bd.1. Marx' Non-Ökonomie*. Hamburg.

Szepanski, A. (2014b). *Kapitalisierung Bd.2. Non-Ökonomie des gegenwärtigen Kapitalismus*. Hamburg.

Tooze, A. (2022d). The Regime at Risk—Macroprudentialism Faces the Test of Inflation. https://adamtooze.substack.com/p/chartbook-137-the-regime-at-risk

Tooze, A. (2022e). Zugzwang—Are We on the Brink of a Central Banking Paradigm Shift? https://adamtooze.substack.com/p/chartbook-151-zugzwang-are-we-on

Vighi, F. (2022). *Unworkable. Delusions of an Imploding Civilization*. New York.

CHAPTER 10

Debt as a phenomenon of the Over

The phenomenon of *excess* is also evident in the rising global debt, which today affects households, companies, and states alike.[1] However, the capital company is indebted in a unique way. When a company uses its own capital, it must also be appropriately interest-bearing, with companies constantly having to compare alternative investments with their current interest rates, upon which the company's investment activity depends. The inherent compulsion to pay interest only becomes fully visible to the company when the capital to be invested has actually been generated as borrowed capital through a loan or a bond. Peter Ruben summarized these processes in his definition of capital as follows: "Thinking of capital formation as debt production is the requirement that economic understanding must meet if it wants to arrive at a clear concept of capital." (Ruben, 1998: 50–51) For Pistor, debts are even the asset per se, mainly because they can be easily converted into state money by an investor. Claims for future payments must be encoded in property law and at the same time enable convertibility into cash (Pistor, 2020).

It is the commercial banks that exercise a very special power in the corporate universe, insofar as they can create new book money as interest-bearing debts through credit creation. The largest part of a country's money supply is created today when commercial banks grant loans to borrowers, namely to governments, companies, and households; they are

A. Szepanski, *Capitalism in the Age of Catastrophe*, Palgrave Insights into Apocalypse Economics,
https://doi.org/10.1007/978-3-031-57754-3_10

simply "debt traders" who create the necessary money as book money via the granting of loans and thus produce and allocate debts. (Szepanski, 2018a, 2018b 2022) The power of private banks to create new money in the form of loans includes a structural, redistributive, and allocative power. Currently, besides the central banks, only commercial banks are allowed to create new money as interest-bearing debt securities.

The indebtedness of households, companies, and states reached a global all-time high of 281 trillion dollars in 2020; this is more than 355% of the total gross world product (GWP) (Maki, 2021). In the advanced economies, it was already 420% of the GWP in 2022, with a rising trend. In China, it is three hundred percent of GDP. The Institute for International Finance warns that if global debt continues to grow at the average pace of the last 15 years, global debt could rise to over 360 trillion by 2030. This would increase the debt ratio to more than four times the global economic output, a level that could choke off economic growth under the massive costs of debt service. For the future, neither the expected return to repay the debts nor the period in which they can be paid is known. It is known that stagnant future economic growth will further exacerbate the debt problem, as the repayment of debts and interest payments become even more precarious. The big question regarding the expected capital returns in all possible forms, with which debts can be paid, is whether these can be generated and realized at all in the future.

In the last forty years, the boom-bust cycles have always followed the same pattern, insofar as easy money and cheap loans were created to clear up each crisis. Therefore, global debt ratios climbed from 2.2 times GDP in 1999 to 3.2 times in 2019. They even rose to 3.5 times GDP after the COVID-19 crisis. While the debt ratios were high, the debt service ratios were low due to zero interest rates, negative prime rates, quantitative easing, and credit easing. However, when interest rates rise, actors with high debt ratios must also again expect high debt service ratios. Interest is constantly due, which can lead to an increase in the debt service ratio leading to insolvencies and a severe recession. As global growth in income and even wealth is slowing down, states, companies, banks, and households are holding even more debt that they can hardly repay in the future. Debts that arise at zero or negative interest rates and were still manageable, are increasingly precarious and non-repayable when central banks have to raise the prime rates, as is currently necessary to combat inflation.

In December 2022, the BIS also warned of the dizzying 80 trillion dollars in off-balance sheet debt held by financial institutions and funds—an amount larger than the circulating dollar-denominated treasury bills, repo, and commercial papers (BIS, 2022). These are derivative debts that are not captured by official statistics, usually complex speculative instruments such as foreign exchange swaps and forward contracts. The BIS claims that these invisible debts have grown from 55 trillion dollars to 80 trillion dollars within a decade, with daily foreign exchange swap transactions amounting to 5 trillion dollars per day. US financial institutions and pension funds have twice as many dollar obligations resulting from foreign exchange swaps as the dollar debts reported in their balance sheets. Foreign banks have derivative debts of 39 trillion dollars, which are also not reported. This debt burden is a ticking time bomb within the networks of the global economy.

A capital economy that is intensively driven by debt, inherently requires the creation of more and more debt. More debt in turn requires more growth, perhaps even non-linear growth of various forms of capital, to generate the profits and returns to pay off interest. Even if maintaining economic growth has negative external effects such as environmental destruction and dysfunctional social relationships, growth or expanded capital accumulation is absolutely necessary to ensure that even parts of the debt can be settled.[2] According to Robbins/Di Muzio, every economic transaction today contains interest, whether it's the purchase of a good, a rent or mortgage payment, a meal in a restaurant, or payment for a service, that is, interest that is someone's debt.[3] (Robbins/Di Muzio, 2015: 113–114)

Especially excessive borrowing to finance expensive facilities and assets carries a significant risk. If, for example, a borrower takes out billions for the construction of a fiber optic network and the stock price shoots up due to speculation about future profits, the borrower might be convinced that he is investing in the future. But if no revenues are generated in the near future that could service his debts, then the investments can drive the borrower into ruin and thereby harm various companies involved in the construction or even drive them into ruin as well.[4]

Under these economic conditions, is there a possibility to ever repay debts? To answer this question, three limitations must be mentioned first: Firstly, an economy that exhibits exponential growth would have to double at a growth rate of 3% every twenty-three years (Ibid.: 14). Regardless, every growth triggers an acceleration of all processes initiated and dominated by the economy. Money must flow faster, people must work faster, and even food crops and animals must grow faster; through the use of growth hormones, antibiotics, and feed, for example, cattle today reach their slaughter weight in fourteen months, instead of three to four years as in the past. Time becomes an enemy to be overcome (and which cannot be overcome). Even when maintaining a constant and low growth rate, one must now expect that institutional investors and banks are always looking for more profitable investment opportunities, about 80% of which are debt securities. Currently, global assets amount to around 293 trillion US dollars, with 100 trillion US dollars alone being managed by institutional investors, whether they are pension funds or insurance companies. It is becoming increasingly difficult to find investments in which this money can be invested in order to achieve the long-term average capital return of 4 to 6%—and this requires an ever-increasing willingness to take risks (Di Muzio, 2020).

Secondly, the private money creation of banks through loans/debts, but without creating the money that will pay the interest, leads to there being more debt in the system than the potential to repay it. For example, if a bank lends $1,000 at 10% interest, it does not create the money to pay this interest—that would be $100. The bank creates just $1,000 and not $1,100 (Robbins/Di Muzio, 2015: 20). The question must therefore be: Where does the interest come from? The only possible answer is that the interest comes from the realization of capital in the future—that is, there is currently never enough money in the system to pay off all debts. In this sense, for creditors, the potential of debt as a technology of power lies in its temporal permanence. In order for there to be a return on the invested capital, there must be an inherent compulsion or an obligation from someone to produce an amount that is greater than the invested amount. Whether the return is interest, rent, or profit, it must be greater than the original loan and capital investment. The integration of various money capitalists into the chains of money and payment flows, which all include the creditor-debtor relationship, leads at least temporarily to the additive increase of the initial capitals; money capital functions in these processes/flows as a self-referential relation, whose code is profit/non-profit.[5] Temporarily, the structural gap can be partially closed if institutions take on more debt with a later due date than there are currently loans that have been granted to earlier parties. This structural feature of global capital in the context of private credit creation by commercial banks promotes competition for larger return differences, so that the debts can be repaid.

Thirdly, economic growth is still largely dependent on fossil energy sources to this day, and this type of energy is a non-renewable resource, the costs of which are likely to rise further in the course of the twenty-first century. The question of a possible enforcement of renewable energies cannot be discussed further here. It is only worth mentioning that the investment push necessary for the transition to a carbon-free economy raises a material problem: on the one hand, dirty activities—especially in mining or metal production—become unprofitable due to increased regulation or higher carbon prices, on the other hand, investments for the greening of infrastructure still require such resources to expand the infrastructural capacities for green technologies. In addition, companies would have to be regulated with the specification of concrete decarbonization targets in food production, energy generation, and transport, which would lead to a reduction in profits and macroeconomic indicators for the accumulation of capital. This would require massive political interventions to push back the extractive economies and their industrial and logistical sectors, as well as the financial system that capitalizes on raw materials, oil, and rare earths. It is also hardly conceivable that the "integrated world capitalism" (Guattari) would allow a very high tax burden on capital gains and wealth in favor of climate protection. This would be accompanied by the weakening of the large financial companies, which would go hand in hand with de-financialization and a loss of power.

Robbins/Di Muzio speak of an energy-debt-money nexus, where the creation of interest-bearing loans is supported (not determined) by the energy of fossil fuels (Ibid.:14). The current level of indebtedness in the context of globalization would not have been possible without fossil fuels. The capitals of various countries—especially the empires of England and later the USA—were able to expand precisely because of the energy surplus provided by fossil fuels. Fossil capital continues to drive economic growth to this day[6]; and with drastic ecological consequences, just think of the climate change caused by the greenhouse effect. There are three main obstacles to mention here, which stand in the way of further growth: (1) The planet is finite and resources are being depleted at an accelerated pace. (2) Fossil fuels are not renewable and their combustion contributes excessively to global warming. (3) There has never been an example of continuous exponential growth on Earth. The difficulty in maintaining growth is that capitalization depends not only on the power of companies but also on the ability to capitalize various aspects of nature (Ibid.: 20).

Notes

1. Debts contain a temporal relation, they are defined by time: They require the promise to pay at a time that has not yet been reached, namely in the future, and thus the present is deferred in favor of a contractually regulated future, which is known before it occurs. Regarding time, debts operate with a double movement: The promise to pay includes deferral and anticipation.
2. Michel Foucault, for example, describes economic growth as the "only true and fundamental social policy" of neoliberalism, which he also calls the "truth regime of the market".
3. The question is, who gets the interest portion of the price? The interest portion contained in the prices does not benefit all households and certainly not the weaker ones. The majority goes to those who have the most interest-bearing assets. The richer you are, that is, the more interest bearing real and money capital you own, the larger is the share that you get from the pot of collected interest. The greatest loss is borne by those households that do not own any interest-bearing assets or at least none that is significant. They only pay in, without ever getting anything back.

   Robbins/Di Muzio write that about 35–40% of everything we buy goes as interest to bankers, financiers, and bondholders (Robbins/Di Muzio 2015: 114). This explains how wealth is systematically transferred from the majority to the minority at the top of the income pyramid. Debt as a technology of power means that wealth is mathematically encoded into the system through the redistribution of money to the already rich. Consequently, we have constructed a debt-based money system, divided into an economy of net debtors and net creditors, with the latter making up at most 1–5% of the population.
4. A loan is a contract. The interest must be serviced in good and bad times, and due debts must be repaid at maturity or refinanced through a new loan. The comparison of interest rates between two bonds that mature at the same time shows the investor the default risk. The higher the risk, the higher the interest rates or returns.

Since it is unlikely that the US government will default, its securities and bonds offer a risk-free benchmark return. Other debtors—households, companies, cities, states, or countries—must offer a higher return for their debts to attract lenders. The spread between two yields indicates the default risk. For example, a company issues a ten-year bond with a yield of 8%. If a ten-year US Treasury bond yields 2%, the spread is 6%. This means that investors are not willing to buy the company's bonds unless these bonds yield significantly more money than a safe government bond. The higher the spread, the more the market doubts the solvency of the bond issuer. Higher spreads, however, attract investors who are looking for high returns to compensate for the risk of default. More and more risky debts are now being accumulated, as higher spreads compensate for the risk of default.

5. Baudrillard has written an excellent essay on the debt problem (Baudrillard 2023). He refers to the electronic scoreboard at Times Square, which displays the amount of American national debt, which, as he says, can never be settled.

   When one looks at the billboard with its flying figures, Baudrillard says, one gets the impression that the debts are taking off to reach the stratosphere. (Ibid.) This concerns the number in light years of a galaxy that disappears into the cosmos. The debts circulate in their own orbit, which is stocked with money capital that is now free from any economic investment and moves in a parallel universe (the acceleration of money capital has freed money from its entanglements with the everyday universe of production, value, and utility). For Baudrillard, monetary circulation is ex-orbital and ex-centric. Therefore, the debts can never be settled. Accordingly, we need at least a virtual time insurance, because our future is about to dissolve in real time.

   Today, global or planetary debts act as a collective and symbolic credit line, through which people, companies, and nations are bound together. People are bound together by their virtual bankruptcy (this also applies to banks), just as accomplices are bound together by their crimes. Everyone is sure to exist for the other in the shadow of unredeemable debts, because the total sum of global debts is much larger today than the total sum of available capital.

   The true artificial satellites, according to Baudrillard, are the global debts, the capital flows, and the nuclear threats that orbit the earth in an orbital dance. As pure artifacts with a sidereal speed and an instantaneous ability to reverse, they have found their true place. It is the orbit where they rise and set like artificial suns.

6. However, it should not go unmentioned that in 2022, investments in solar plants boomed in Europe. Almost 32 gigawatts of solar capacity were installed across Europe, representing a growth of 33% compared to 2021. Solar and wind energy have thus overtaken all other forms of electricity generation in Europe—gas, nuclear power, or coal.

References

Baudrillard, J. (2023). Global Debt and Parallel Universe. https://non.copyriot.com/global-debt-and-parallel-universe/

BIS. (2022). Quarterly Review December 2022. https://www.bis.org/press/p221205_de.htm

Di Muzio, T. (2020). Capitalized Money, Austerity and the Math of Capitalism. https://www.academia.edu/41619254/Capitalized_Money_Austerity_and_the_Math_of_Capitalism

Di Muzio, T., & Robbins, R. H. (2015). *Debt as Power: Theory for a Global Age*. Manchester.

Maki, S. (2021). World's $281 Trillion Debt Pile is Set to Rise Again in 2021. *Bloomberg*, 17 February. https://www.bloomberg.com/news/articles/2021-02-17/global-debt-hits-all-time-high-as-pandemic-boosts-spending-need. Accessed on 30 April 2021.

Pistor, K. (2020). *The Code of Capital: How the Law Creates Wealth and Inequality*. Princeton.

Robbins, R. H., & Di Muzio, T. (2016). *Debt as Power*. Manchester.

Ruben, P. (1998). Was bleibt übrig von Marx' ökonomischer Theorie? In U. Hedtke & C. Warnke (Eds.), *Philosophical Writings*. Online Edition: www.peter-ruben.de

Szepanski, A. (2018a). *Kapital und Macht im 21. Jahrhundert*. Hamburg.

Szepanski, A. (2018b). *Imperialismus, Staatsfaschisierung und die Kriegsmaschinen des Kapitals–Drei Essays*. Hamburg.

Szepanski, A. (2022). *Financial Capital in the 21th Century*. New York.

CHAPTER 11

Finance, World Market, and Imperialism

Maurizio Lazzarato argues in his book *Capital hates Everyone*, that the state has lost power, weight, and importance to capital since the mid-twentieth century. (Lazzarato, 2021: 43) In particular, the transnational operations of large corporations and the interplay of finance and logistics at a global level would permanently weaken the state vis-à-vis capital. The twentieth century, as a result of comprehensive capitalization, has undermined the formation of the state as a nation-state, so that a new paradigm of Schmittian imprint could emerge, which should secure the survival of the modern state. This paradigm understands the modern state as an imperial union of intertwined nations. According to Kojève, the modern state is only truly a state when it is an empire. The Cold War was the paradigmatic beginning of the era of empires, in which empires are transnational political units, composed of (culturally or economically) intertwined nations.

William I. Robinson also assumes the dominance of transnational corporations over states in the world market, especially of financial corporations, which not only operate in the financial sector itself, but also invest heavily in media, industrial, and commercial companies as well as in the global military-industrial security complex. (Robinson, 2022: 16f.) Neoliberalism is characterized by a transnational class of billionaires, who are not only able to dominate the political process, but also to take it over.

A. Szepanski, *Capitalism in the Age of Catastrophe*, Palgrave Insights into Apocalypse Economics,
https://doi.org/10.1007/978-3-031-57754-3_11

In addition, the enormous concentration of economic power is evident in the existence of globally influential political power complexes, which include, among others, the IMF, World Bank, BIS, WTO, G7, and G20 states. Members of the transnational capital also hold important positions in national governments, particularly in the finance, economic, and often also in the defense ministries.

Robinson discusses in his book *The Global Police State* a new transnational capitalist class that has emerged from the leading capitalist groups in the highly industrialized world and today represents the hegemonic faction of capital on a global scale. (Robinson, 2021) This class consists of the owners and managers of transnational corporations, especially of tech and finance companies, which dominate and drive the world economy. The large corporations have internationalized the markets through dense networks that go far beyond national borders. They operate largely independently of their original states and territories. Although initially this development was about the "Atlantic Ruling Class" that formed the majority of the transnational capital, today hyper-rich capital factions and elites from almost all continents are part of this transnational class. It should not be concealed that the Communist Party of China now plays an important role for this transnational capitalist class. It must also be added that the fusion of transnational capital with national, right-wing populist political forces can further fuel the new fascism of the twenty-first century. This new fascism must be understood as a preemptive strike against the proletariat, in the form of the global police state. (Robinson) The project of twenty-first century fascism attempts to establish a mass base among the privileged sectors of the global working class, such as the white workers in the Gobal North and the middle classes in the Global South and North, the latter of which are exposed to increased insecurity and decreasing mobility as well as socio-economic destabilization.

However, one should not assume a linear tendency towards monopolization of power by transnational capital and its class on a global scale, as there are always sectoral dispersions and heterogeneity that affect both industrial, tech, and finance companies as well as the states. Adam Tooze has pointed out that, for example, the globalization of textile production today takes place in the form of relatively manageable China-Asia networks, while the automotive industry has a multipolar structure with the USA, Japan, Europe, and Korea operating complex regional and national networks. The globalization of corporate networks in the IT sector, on the other hand, comprises a network of connections between

Japanese, Chinese, Korean, and American companies. (Tooze, 2023b) The world economy thus consists of a very specific patchwork, that is, networks that connect certain nodes in a way that is vertically, but also not uniformly organized. Globalization does show hegemonic trade or financial flows, but the different sectors mainly differ from each other in their network effects.[1] Tooze, however, emphasizes the factor of network heterogeneity too much, without taking into account the hierarchical and vertical dimensions of capital power.

Beyond all neoliberal theories of market fundamentalism, capital still needs the capitalist state, while conversely, the state is structurally dependent on capital. Thus transnational capital and its representatives instrumentalize states around the world, so that almost every country in the world is now integrated into the circuits of transnational capital. In this context, states must create favorable location conditions for capital accumulation, i.e., on the one hand, a good climate for profits and, on the other hand, repressive rules for the proletariat. It is now the new transnationalist class that constantly tries to translate its structural power in the global economy into a supranational political authority, a kind of transnational state apparatus, which does not have a global government, but can at least be understood as a loose network of transnational and supranational organizations that cooperate with the Nation-states when it comes to securing the conditions of transnational capital accumulation. This is an institutional network in which nation-states do not disappear because, on the one hand, they create the conditions for global capital accumulation and, on the other hand, they must preserve their political legitimacy as a nation. (Robinson, 2021)

The large transnational companies of the capitalist core countries still invest in industrial capacities today, but less in their own economies. The liberalization of world trade, the collapse of the Soviet Union, and the development of logistics have enabled the large corporations of the capitalist core countries to tap into new sources of profit and investment opportunities in the Global South, while the prices for their inputs are falling due to cheap imports from the South. The economic power centers on the world market are based on a complex interplay between the imperialist states, which provide the launch platforms for developed capital by providing material and social infrastructure, and the large financialized transnational corporations, whose money capital constantly flows ecstatically around the globe. In the final analysis, the states are now dominated by a transnational capitalist war machine.[2] (Lazzarato, 2021)

Global financial capital constructs its war machinery on the basis of the circulation of speculative and fictitious capital; there is no externality, no parasitic function of finance against the "real economy" to report, on the contrary, thanks to its degree of deterritorialization, thanks to the speed and constant acceleration, finance regulates the globalized production.

The economic power relations between the leading capitalist economies remain strictly hierarchical, but the relative power of individual countries, companies, and their economies can shift again and again. For Tony Norfield the result is a division of the world based on the expansive exercise of economic, political, and military power by financial capital, the states, and the transnational corporations. (Norfield, 2016: Kindle Edition: 189f.) The creation of the global world market in the course of neoliberal globalization since the 1980s shows that the world market is more than just the aggregation of states and companies, namely a complex structure, a chain of international political relations, commodity, and money capital flows, and monetary networks, which are based on the various national states as well as the various systems of financialized capital power, but the complex structure of the world market develops a certain independence and yet there is no uniform economic structure of the same. (Milios/Sotiropoulos, 2009) The world economy is not simply the sum of national parts, but it is itself a hierarchically differentiated structure as a (open) totality, within which today in particular the growth of capital exports of the companies of the leading imperialist states is promoted, the space for capital circulation and the financial industry is expanded and a complex relationship between leading and subaltern nations is established within the framework of complicated networks of information transmission and politics. In addition, there is an expansion of international credit relations, foreign exchange, and derivative trading. Emerging countries and some countries of the Third World are gradually integrated into the capitalist world economy by the dynamics emanating from the capitalist centers, by opening them up as markets or as cost-effective production locations.

It can be assumed that the transnational corporations are in competition with each other, but there are also overlaps in their strategies, insofar as they have no interest in states that make access to their markets difficult or even deny it. Rather, they are interested in states where wage levels are low, low taxes have to be paid and from which they do not expect nationalizations. Already in the 1980s, the World Bank played a central role in Africa by replacing the "colonial administrations" and initiating a special program called "structural adjustment": In exchange for growth-oriented loans, a country now had to guarantee the liberalization of imports, the privatization of state industries, the abolition of all restrictions on currency exchange and commodity prices, all subsidy programs, and all workers' rights and social securities. The Washington Consensus, a doctrine from the late 1980s developed by the IMF, the World Bank, and the US Treasury as an economic recipe for emerging countries in Latin America, was based on the relaxation of capital and import restrictions, the privatization of state-owned enterprises, the liberalization of the local economy, the enforcement of tax discipline, and a monetary policy aimed at low inflation. Governments were to achieve new development goals by transforming public services into investment opportunities for private financing. Although there were partial prosperity effects for the working classes in these countries, unrestrained capital mobility caused enormous economic and financial boom-bust cycles. During the booms, money flowed into the emerging economies and during the recessions it flowed out, causing severe financial crises.[3]

The states that have the largest volumes of direct investments, trade turnovers, foreign loans, and foreign assets are also integrated into the economic policy of the debtor countries, and they do not leave the management of the national deficits of the underdeveloped countries to the responsible governments, but are only willing to exchange financial aid for access rights to state property and to the national disposal mass of the capital of the economically underdeveloped country. This results in strictly hierarchically structured power relations between the leading world economic powers and the many weak countries that are notorious losers on the world market. Overall, it can be said at this point: The transnational companies of the imperialist countries remain at the top of the hierarchy of the world market, their mergers, and acquisitions reinforce the tendency towards oligopolization, they have the largest price mark-ups and their increasing market power often goes hand in hand with a decline in investments and an increase in financial activities.

Robinson assumes that the world economy remained internationally based from 1945 to 1973 (large corporations operated on the world market from national territories), while from 1973 onwards one can speak of a transnational economy in which state territories are not the basis, but can even be hindering factors for big capital. For Robinson, there is a transition from a world economy to a global economy here.

(Robinson, 2022: 16) While in the stage of the world economy, countries, and regions were connected to each other through trade and financial flows on an international market, in the new global economy, nations and corporations are organically interconnected through the transnationalization of production processes, finances, and the cycles of capital accumulation. It is particularly about the free flow of globalized money capital, about flows of speculative capital, money, and information, about geostrategies, and industrial-political-military hegemonies. The production processes are now fully integrated into the global circulation networks, which stake out new dimensions of space–time accumulation and also bring about new forms of warfare that transcend nation-states and their borders. All networks of the circulation of goods, money, capital, and information, but also all networks of social reproduction, are today parts of a global economic machine, i.e., the reorganization of national economies under the directives of a transnational capitalist war machine. (Lazzarato, 2021: 33).

The "globalization" of the economy today subjects anything with few exceptions to the code of capitalization which leads to new orders of time and space. Where they are touched by transnational speculative capital, the weak economies in the Global South merely mutate into the folkloric accessories of its hegemony. The fictitious and speculative capital then only passes through their territories to dissolve them in their independence. This also describes the process of "deterritorialization" (Deleuze), because now "globalization" takes place everywhere, just no longer on territories that once could be assembled into a globe as independent parts. Globalization has long since left this globe. At least it no longer knows any geographical centers. (Lenger, 2004) At the same time, however, one can also speak with Bruno Latour of a "minus-globalization" that refers to the closure or suspension of other perspectives than those of capital. (Latour, 2018: 22) Since 1989, there has been a hyperglobalization, in the course of which most emerging countries opened up to freer trade and capital traffic, so that cross-border traffic of goods, services, capital, investments, labor, technology, data, and information increased dramatically. Sloterdijk has spoken early in this context of a total mobilization, with the availability and the already accelerating circulation of goods, fictitious and speculative capital, information and raw materials, not least human labor, and natural resources in kinetic processes around the globe. (Sloterdijk, 1989) However, such globalization would have to be offset by a planetarization, which wants to restore the generation and production of diversity, locality, and fragmentation, be it biodiversity, technodiversity, or noodiversity. (Frey/ Hui, 2023: 115) Instead, the crashes, the errors, and the costs of hyperglobalization trigger quite different counter-reactions, which accelerated after the global financial crisis of 2008. Recently, as a result of the Covid-19 crisis and the resulting interruptions of global supply chains and logistics and transport networks, demands for reshoring or friendshoring of manufacturing processes and global supply chains have become louder again.

Thanks to the triumph of digitized logistics and the global supply chains it enables, the factory is now fragmented, distributed, scattered among the various territories of the planet, so that a single product can contain a multitude of parts from all over the world.[4] While Marx still understood the factory as the "engine" and the beginning of every value chain, individual goods are now produced across the entire global logistical space and not in a single location. Global logistics (management of goods transport and information transport) has enabled flexible supply chains and timely just-in-time production, and it is now circulation that maintains and secures the global exploitation of a workforce scattered across the entire planet in distributed workspaces. Since capital itself is not a physical object, but a movement, and the increase in the speed of this movement from G to G‘ leads to increases, intensifications, and more concentrated periods of circulation, a more fluid connectivity and the flexible management of supply chains over distant areas is absolutely necessary. The logistical development in the second half of the twentieth century has increasingly blurred the boundaries between manufacturing and movement—production and distribution. Growth now no longer simply arises from producing more goods to sell them on new markets, but also requires a denser networking of global supply chains as well as the intensification or acceleration of existing cycles of both goods and money circulation. With Marx, one could now speak as a counter-tendency of a form determination of value creation by the use value, which is characterized by a kind of return of the repressed physical boundaries of the spaces that limit the form of accumulation and value increase in historically specific ways.

For Harney/Moten, the logistics of capital is characterized by movement and access. Logistics takes place along the line that moves with people and goods, and by moving through people and goods, it accesses people and goods to move, and moves people and goods to access.

(Harney/Moten, 2022: 66) However, one must also emphasize the political aspects of the global enforcement of logistics, understanding logistics as a result of the counterpower of workers, which was established in the Fordist factories of the 1960s. Added to this were conflicts that affected social reproduction and the welfare state (feminist and anti-racist movements) as well as struggles in the peripheries for decolonization, which brought about a new global composition of the proletariat. Thus, one must understand the enforcement of logistics and the primacy of circulation also as a response to political conflicts that led to the unraveling and global dispersion of production, thereby blowing up the centered spatiality of the factory in the core countries and organizing the production processes along global supply chains including a new international division of labor and a new geography of capital. Globalization has hurt low-skilled workers in advanced economies. In the near future, accountants, lawyers, and even doctors could increasingly face competition in emerging countries and virtual competition through AI. Competitors in China and Asia have long since developed. With more than 2.5 billion citizens in China and India and many more in other emerging countries who belong to the global working population, now even the more skilled workers in advanced economies must compete.

John Smith points out that today about 80% of world trade (measured in gross exports) is connected with the international production networks of transnational corporations, with according to UNCTAD about 60% of world trade consisting of trade with intermediate goods and services that flow into various stages in the production process of goods and services for end consumption. (Smith, 2016: 34) Smith further argues, that outsourcing production to the Global South was from the outset also a strategy of capitalist companies to push back union organizations in developed countries and to lower wages there. It is an important feature of today's globalization that a large and growing share of the workforce within the global supply chains is located in the emerging and developing countries of the Global South. To sharpen the concept of super-exploitation, Smith tries with various empirical evidence to show that it is the wages pushed below the value of labor in the production processes of the countries of the Global South that are primarily responsible for the high profits of transnational corporations.[5] (Ibid.: 187 ff.) This explanation is asserted as the main characteristic of twenty-first century imperialism and partly opposes positions that start from the financial hegemony (Milios, Norfield, Robinson) of transnational corporations or the dispossession by capital (Harvey) as an essential feature of imperialism. In any case, super-exploitation represents another moment of the ecstasy of transnational capital.

For Smith, corporate outsourcing is the most important transformation of neoliberal globalization, namely the worldwide distribution of production processes due to the demand of transnational corporations, headquartered in the imperialist countries, for low-wage labor, which is recruited in the countries of the Global South. (Ibid.: 39ff.) Wage arbitrage is for Smith thus the main driving force for the outsourcing decisions of transnational corporations.

Smith tries to reconcile this with Marx's theory of surplus value. For Smith, capitalism began with the exploitation of labor power through absolute surplus value (extension and intensification of the working day). With the development of capital, there was an increase in the production of relative surplus value or the introduction of labor-saving technologies to reduce the value of labor power while keeping the working day the same length. In the twenty-first century, Smith argues, the super-exploitation of workers in the Global South occurs less through an expansion of absolute and relative surplus value, but rather through the lowering of wages below the value of labor power. (Ibid.: 197f.) In *Capital*, Marx recognizes the latter method as an important form of surplus value production, but argues that capitalism could also extract surplus value without this form of exploitation. Marx believed that among the factors counteracting the tendency of the falling rate of profit, not only an increasing rate of surplus value or decreasing costs of technology or increasing foreign trade and the financialization of capital are included, but also the lowering of wages below the value of labor power (super-exploitation in Smith's words). Marx excluded this factor in his abstract analysis of the laws of motion of capital.

Now, however, Smith argues, all three types of surplus value extraction can be found today in globalized production processes, with the third being most significant in the Global South because the imperialist North considers this the most profitable way to appropriate surplus value. It should be noted, however, that in addition to super-exploitation, the methods of absolute surplus value, but also the use of the latest technology to save labor (relative surplus value) are applied in the Global South. Foxconn may pay its workers low wages, but it also uses the latest technologies.

Against Smith, it could also be argued at this point that it is not only the low wages in the less developed countries, but above all also the productivity of investments (capital productivity) of Western capital as well as social relations that determine the direction of international trade and capital flows. It was not only the large distribution companies that benefited from outsourcing the production of textiles and other goods to the less developed countries in Asia, but also American electronics companies like Cisco, Sun Microsystems, and AT&T outsourcing their production, driven by highly technologized competition with Japanese companies. The outsourcing of production to Taiwan and South Korea at the highest technological level helped American electronics companies reduce production costs and gave export-oriented industrialization in the so-called "emerging countries" a powerful boost. Electronics and other high-tech industries were at the forefront of the outsourcing wave, which picked up again after the financial crisis of 2007.

In their book *Rethinking Imperialism*, Milios/Sotiropolous pose the important question of how to explain that the percentage of international capital sums flowing to the Global South, compared to the shares remaining within the developed capitalist countries, is still relatively low. (Milios/Sotiropolous, 2009) A striking feature of the imperialist world economy is that companies in the North compete less with those in the South, but still more with other companies from the North. Apple competes with Samsung, but not with Foxconn or the Taiwan Semiconductor Manufacturing Company (TSMC) and other suppliers. The relationship of imperialist companies to their suppliers is therefore to be seen as complementary and not as competitive, even though this complementarity is very unevenly structured. The issue is who can outsource production to low-wage countries the fastest and most effectively. Meanwhile, the countries of the South compete fiercely with each other to maintain their market position.

Especially the emerging countries, which attract foreign direct investments and other forms of capital investment to a large extent, are characterized by processes of rapid and catching-up economic development (China in the current historical phase, Southeast Asian countries like Taiwan and South Korea in the 1980s and 1990s). These are countries that manage to narrow the development gap between themselves and the more advanced countries, or in some cases even close it completely. This empirical evidence not only relativizes what can be called Smith's *super-exploitation approach*, but also the *capital surplus approach* of classical imperialism theories, which remains in some modern approaches. It is worth remembering at this point that (a) in industrialized countries, according to the capital surplus approach, the volume of capital destined for accumulation increases rapidly, while investment opportunities continue to shrink, so that capital must be exported, while (b) according to the approach of extra profits or super-exploitation, underdeveloped low-wage countries become a source of extra profits by lowering the cost price of industrial products, so that these countries are likely to attract international capital movements.

The new form of imperialism is based in particular on an implicit pact between the financial capital of the leading countries and the economies of the emerging countries. While the latter countries gain access to the goods markets in the West and at the same time receive a flood of direct investments from large multinational companies, the former countries have concluded agreements (TRIPS, GATT, GATS) to protect the patents and property rights of domestic companies, create markets for services, and open foreign markets for their own corporate controls. The emerging countries, in turn, were able to exploit the competitive costs of wages; they mainly produce "low-tech" consumer goods with the imported technologies, then export these to the capitalist core countries and ruthlessly combat the weaker companies there. But they are increasingly investing in research, which still mainly relies on creative imitation and adaptation, but also aims to promote such innovations that should reduce the technological gap with the highly technologized core countries. In key industries such as AI, robotics, the IT industry, space, air and sea travel, renewable energies, and electromobility, China wants to catch up technologically with the Western core countries by 2035. China's total expenditure on research and development in 2022 amounts to almost 3.09 trillion RMB (about 456 billion US dollars), an increase of 10.4% compared to 2021. China's share of global technology spending has risen from 5% in 2000 to 23% in 2020. In addition, China already accounts for about 60% of the world's production capacities for solar modules, components of wind turbines and batteries. Without China, the transformation to green energy in Europe and the USA would not be possible. In addition, Chinese companies have increased labor productivity and yet kept labor costs relatively low. We are now observing the emergence of hyper-capitalized centers in emerging countries and peripheries, while at the same time "Third World zones" are emerging in the metropolises of the North and the wage shares and working conditions of workers there are deteriorating. China is now investing heavily in high-tech and infrastructure projects at home and abroad. Experts estimate the costs at 180 billion dollars just for the development of 5G capacities in 2014 and 2015. (Roubini, 2022) To expand its international power and presence, China launched the Belt and Road Initiative (BRI), making China the main financier for major infrastructure and development efforts in dozens of low- and middle-income countries in Asia, the Middle East, Latin America, and Africa. The Chinese economy is a system of state capitalism, in which the controller enjoys almost unassailable political authority.

The companies of the imperialist core countries continue to build their economic power on the world markets also through the export of capital. Direct investments abroad are primarily today conducted by companies from North America, Europe, and Japan, but increasingly also by such countries as China, Russia, India, and Brazil. The export of capital from the leading industrial countries prevents, on the one hand, the destruction of less productive capital domestically, and on the other hand, the more productive companies benefit from new extra profits or super profits by transferring their money capital abroad. For the capital exporting companies, the corresponding transactions demonstrate the company's power to generate investments in other countries, but they also have to take into account the expectations that financial investors from all over the world place on them. There are two forms of capital export: on the one hand, foreign direct investments, where the production process is relocated abroad but remains as property within the company itself, and on the other hand, companies that outsource part or all of the production process to an independent company, independent in the sense that the leading company does not own any means of production, even if it controls the activities in production in many ways.[6] The transnational corporations, which still have their headquarters in the imperialist countries, are today the strongest driving forces of the globalization of production. Their structuring of the production processes in the low-wage countries takes on two basic forms: firstly, the "in-house" relationship between the parent company and its foreign subsidiary, and secondly, an "arm's-length" relationship with formally independent suppliers. (Smith, 2016: 68ff.)

In summary, Smith cites four reasons why outsourcing firms might prefer an "arm's-length" relationship with their low-wage suppliers over direct investments: (1) Foreign investors often pay higher wages than domestic companies. (2) They shift the responsibility for all possible processes to the companies of the less-developed countries. (3) Transfer of risks. (4) Avoidance of direct investments in favor of what UNCTAD calls a "non-equity mode", which in turn releases further funds for the large corporations for investments in the financial markets or for financing acquisitions and share buybacks. (Ibid.: 79).

In many cases today, therefore, direct intra-company relationships with a subsidiary are transformed into business relationships with independent suppliers by simply signing legal documents, without changing the working conditions or work procedures, the prices for the inputs, or the profits that accrue from the sale of the production. (Ibid.) A Western company can also buy machines and pass them on as capital contribution to a local company in emerging countries, where the machines are installed. The local company can in turn use the machines as security for a local bank loan and thus has the opportunity to bring money out of the country. This is not the only way in which financial surpluses change the production relationships, by reinvesting transferred profits, for example, in financial assets. It can be assumed that today, in general, many of the higher profits achieved through outsourcing are not reinvested in production, but serve to leverage assets or are invested in the financial markets to achieve speculative profits and thus promote the financialization of the imperialist economies.

Smith describes four types of direct investments, (a) the efficiency-oriented formation, which implies a reduction in costs, especially labor costs, (b) the market-oriented investment, which mainly takes place between the imperialist countries themselves and relies on the proximity of the production sites to the consumers, (c) the resource-seeking direct investment in the extractive (fossil) industries, and (d) the direct investment based on technology transfer, which almost exclusively takes place between imperialist countries. (Ibid.: 82)

The export of capital from a country with higher labor productivity into a country with lower one leads to, on the one hand, the acceleration of the accumulation process in the capital-importing country, which results in an above-average increase in the rate of profit there. On the other hand, the repatriation of a portion of the profits to the capital-exporting country can also lead to an increase in the rate of profit in that country. This indeed leads to a reduction in the differences between the overall rate of profit of the more developed capital-exporting country and the overall rate of profit of the less developed industrial country that imports capital. We should bear in mind that this is a process that exclusively affects the developed capitalist countries and emerging economies. In contrast, the least developed countries continue to play a marginal role in international capital movements and thus in the international tendency to equalize national profit rates. We should further consider that this international tendency to equalize profit rates is a much weaker process than the corresponding process (existence of a general rate of profit) within a unified national formation. The organization of capital at the level of the nation-state, which is expressed, among other things, in the existence of a specific national currency for each country, excludes the formation of uniform international production prices (lack of a uniform international currency for all countries) and thus the formation of an international general rate of profit at the level of the world market. The rate of profit is therefore different from country to country and is only subject to a process of equalization among the developed capitalist countries based on constantly growing volumes of international investments. This process is reinforced by the rapid growth of the globalized financial sphere. The underdeveloped countries, on the other hand, are at the lower levels in the international hierarchy of profit rates, which is due to the weakness of domestic capital against pre-capitalist and pre-industrial production, and consequently leads to low productivity of labor in these countries. The underdeveloped countries are only weakly integrated into international trade and only slightly involved in capital traffic.

The liberation of the financial system from the barriers of purely national money is an important component of the monetary entanglement of the war machines of capital on the world market and leads to a comprehensive internationalization of the financial system. The rise of the transnational financial industry is perhaps the most important historical event in the era of globalization—this refers to the construction of a monstrous global financial complex, which leads to a new concentration of socio-economic power. The owners, managers, and directors of financial corporations are today at the center of the nodes of globalized economy networks. The global stock market, for example, has more than doubled from 2003 to 2017 and surpassed the 100 trillion dollar mark. The states themselves must create certain conditions for the international transactions of the financial system by enacting rules for payment transactions between national payment systems; they offer insurance for certain transactions or provide guarantees for the regular payment of exports and grant licenses to foreign financial companies for business activities in their own country. In addition, the national central banks control foreign exchange trading according to the rules of the national exchange rate. To smooth out erratic price movements on the world markets, a whole range of other measures are taken. The balance of trade, the balance of payments, and the exchange rate development are important parameters that indicate the constant efforts of an economy and its companies in the competition for the realization of the money capital circulating on the world market.

Companies whose growth is limited due to lack of demand in their own country and therefore need to expand on the world market require a developed global banking system that organizes the circulation of the respective national currencies. The services of private banks for exporting and importing companies are expanded by their own credit business, with which they take on special risks for companies in foreign business, by, for example, assessing the creditworthiness of domestic companies against foreign ones. guarantee business partners according to the rules of their country and at the same time protect the rights of domestic companies against foreign business partners. However, private banks not only act as service providers for export and import businesses, but primarily as organizations for their own profitable credit businesses. They engage in currency arbitrage by buying cheaply across currency borders and selling at a high price. With freely fluctuating exchange rates, private banks constantly reassess the valuation of currencies against each other with their international money movements.

Speculative uncertainty or risk always remains part of capital accumulation, which in turn is a resource for insurance business and derivatives trading. Various indicators, indices, and parameters can become the subject of financial speculation. The national differences between growth rates, interest rates, government debt ratios, inflation rates, exchange rates etc., and their fluctuations contain a risk potential that is managed by trading securities and derivatives, i.e., there is a molecular valuation of monetary performance and flow sizes, which are fundamentally uncertain and therefore must be hedged with a variety of derivative instruments (which can be a profitable business for some companies, but not necessarily). With these processes, the international financial system creates a turnover volume of enormous dimensions, drives capital accumulation on a global scale forward evaluates and influences the hierarchy of states and their currencies as well as that of transnational companies in global competition. One must distinguish between the powerful nations, whose economies function more or less smoothly both as a source of credit and as an investment sphere for money capital (successful financial centers), and the less powerful nations, whose economies do not have such capacities. Certain financial companies conduct speculative stress tests for countries, where doubts about their creditworthiness arise, whether fundamental data such as inflation rates or the increase in government debt in relation to economic growth are alarming or whether the speculations about the future growth of the respective territory are overheated, which is why the financial institutions then react with higher interest rates on government bonds. The power with which the financial industry functionalizes states and companies for their own businesses always also exists in the form of currencies, which in turn are strongly influenced by imperialist states. In general, all countries must strive to make profits abroad so that their companies can earn foreign exchange.

In analyzing the world market, the respective access of transnational companies to the global financial industry must always be taken into account. Because globally operating companies need various financial services for their strategies—think here of the stability of international payment systems, the role of currencies in international trade, long-term investments, trading in securities and derivatives, short-term loans, and generally the exchange of money for money. The important functions of the financial system for the capital economy can only be fully understood today in an international context. While within the financial system itself there is a differentiated division of labor (e.g. bank lending, securities management, foreign exchange trading, stock and bond markets, etc.), its most important organizations and operations are concentrated in just a few developed countries. The financial capital is an important tool for the leading imperialist countries and their companies to maintain and improve their privileged position in the world market, with the financial industries managing assets and income from all possible countries. In economically developed countries, it is not only the famous 1% of the super-rich who benefit from the financial position of their country in the world market, but a much larger part of the population, even privileged workers and employees still own financial securities, which in turn are traded on the world markets. Also, high-turnover financial institutions like insurance companies and pension funds are usually located in rich countries, as there groups that are financially capable of investing in such funds.

Smooth access to one's own currency through a local central bank can significantly increase the economic influence of (financial) companies on other countries. A US bank, for example, that is based in France, is subject to certain restrictions there, but due to its connections to US financial capital and the Fed, it can offer more favorable access to the dollar in France. Financial companies have better chances of expanding on the world market if their countries already have a dominant position in world trade, direct investments, and securities trading, and if financial transactions are largely carried out in their own currency. Economic power also lies in the ability to grant large loan amounts and to have easy access to credit markets, which in turn means that one can borrow money at relatively low interest rates anywhere in the world. All in all, this means taking an influential position in global financial networks. This also depends on the state to which a financial company belongs, as the state provides the technological infrastructure that is absolutely necessary for the company's economic expansion.

Tony Norfield identifies three key factors that show why the financial sector plays a dominant role in the economy of an imperialist country and particularly in the world economy (Norfield, 2016: Kindle Edition: 2926ff.):

a. The use of funds from abroad for lending to domestic companies and the state. This can be done today particularly by US financial companies (due to the dollar in its function as a world reserve currency) and by the London banking system.
b. The financing of investments that domestic companies make abroad to set up surplus production processes there. This can be done through bank financing or via the stock markets, which allows for further concentration of capital across national borders.
c. The appropriation of a part of the surplus produced worldwide, by the large private banks and investment funds of the imperialist states granting loans and other financial securities to domestic and foreign companies and states. Each of these financial advantages of the companies of an imperialist state also depends on their privileged relationships with certain other privileged states.

The disruption of trade during the peak of the Corona pandemic led some scientists and experts to declare that the world was now in a phase of deglobalization. But instead of continuing to shrink, global merchandise trade reached an all-time high in 2021 as economies quickly recovered from the pandemic-induced trade implosion, according to a report by the United Nations Conference on Trade and Development. While trade temporarily recovered, the global transport and logistics network was ultimately unable to keep up with the sudden surge in pent-up demand for consumer and production goods. Because the direction of development regarding globalization is far from decided, people are now also talking about "Slowbalisation" or "multiple plateaus of globalization".[7] (Tooze, 2023a) Above all, the trade trends between China and the rest of the world and between emerging countries among themselves hardly suggest a sudden end to globalization. This dynamic of integration continues.

The transnational capitalist class relies on an open and integrated world economy for the continued accumulation of capital and power on a global scale, so that capital can no longer completely retreat to the territories of the national economies. It is therefore expected that transnational companies will by no means withdraw from globalization, but rather intensify the diversification of supply chains and the "nearshoring" of production processes that were previously outsourced abroad. With vertical integration, corporations are once again making greater efforts to gain direct control over supply chains and the entire production and distribution process. Tesla, for example, manufactures batteries, control software, car seats, and electric motors within the group. In addition to vertical integration, other strategies are being used by the groups, such as building up larger warehouse capacities again or establishing production sites in several regions of the world in order to be able to cushion regional crises. The same applies to the trend towards concluding long-term contracts with several raw material suppliers. In particular, the transnational capitalist class and governments will establish new nodes in the global distribution networks to reduce dependence on a few key nodes and reduce the volatility of supply chains that has become apparent in recent months. (Robinson, 2022: 60f.) Companies have already begun to relocate their production and distribution networks closer to the markets they serve. According to an industry report titled *The State of the Freight 2021*, nearly 90% of shippers have begun to diversify their suppliers. (State of the Freight, 2021)

The disruption of global supply chains as a result of Covid accelerated the digitally driven restructuring of the global economy, which had already begun before the outbreak of the pandemic. The computer and information technologies introduced in the 1980s formed the technological basis for globalization. They enabled the transnational capitalist class to coordinate and synchronize decentralized global production processes, thus creating the globally integrated production, finance, and service system. After Covid-19, the technologies of the so-called fourth industrial revolution—including artificial intelligence, big data, machine learning, and autonomously controlled land, air, and water vehicles—are driving a new era of global capitalist restructuring. This restructuring will also include the digitization of supply and logistics networks.

The global economy may recover from the depths of the pandemic-induced implosion. Unless unforeseen events occur, global supply is likely to catch up with and surpass global demand. However, given the underlying structural crisis of global capitalism, global economic turbulence will continue. On the eve of the pandemic, growth in some European Union countries had already shrunk to zero, much of Latin America and Sub-Saharan Africa was in recession, growth rates in Asia were steadily declining, and North America was facing a slowdown. After decades in which globalization seemed an unstoppable force, protectionism, trade wars, and sanctions are accelerating the reshaping of the world market towards a more fragmented model in the wake of the Covid-19 crisis. The decoupling of the USA from China (and Russia) seems to be gaining momentum, and it will cause significant economic damage to both sides. The geopolitically induced balkanization of the global economy, or deglobalization, reduces trade in goods, but also the international flow of services, labor, data, technology, and information is stalling. For example, the US government allegedly does not want to buy Huawei's 5G technology for its telecommunications systems because of possible surveillance by China.

Social polarization and economic inequality had already reached unprecedented levels worldwide before the pandemic: today, just one percent of humanity controls more than half of the world's wealth, the top 20% 94.5%, while the remaining 80% have to make do with just 5.5%. (Oxfam) In almost all countries of the world, social and economic inequality has increased during the pandemic. The new digital technologies that now form the core of the global economy have significantly increased productivity and corporate profits in the core countries, while the global economic restructuring enabled by these technologies has led to a growing mass of underemployed, unemployed, precariously employed, and an increase in the surplus population worldwide. Given the extreme inequality, the global market is unable to absorb the production of the global economy, leading to chronic stagnation accompanied by sharp structural crises.

When we talk about multipolarity today, what is mainly meant economic and especially geopolitical shifts on the globe are meant (BRICS), then one must also acknowledge that the USA, with its globalized financial system, the dollar, and the industrial-military complex, will remain the leading hegemonic power for the time being. Nevertheless, something is emerging that could be called the "fifth world war" or the "second cold war" in the course of post-globalization and the developments towards multipolarity. Deleuze/Guattari spoke of the third world war as a technological war, in which politics is the extension of a warlike peace. Baudrillard spoke of a fourth world war, ignited by the war on terror. In the sign of a conflict-laden world order, which oscillates between "unipolarity versus multipolarity", the war in Ukraine has already been negotiated, and it is not to be excluded that the new war over Gaza will take on unforeseen international dimensions. At the same time, there is talk of a "Second Cold War", which is primarily taking place between the USA and China.

The end of globalization has been announced several times. It has not yet occurred, while the processes of globalization have indeed transformed. These can now proceed with various frictions and local crises and generate heterogeneous political, economic, and social conditions in different places around the world. At the same time, there are cross-border factors for global processes to consider, such as infrastructures, energy distribution systems, digitalization, logistics, finance, and artificial intelligence. The development of artificial intelligence is certainly not free from sanctions, restrictions, and trade wars. Nevertheless, it seems to define the upcoming technological standard around which capitalism is being reorganized at a global level. Standard and variation are constitutive elements of the operations of capital on a global level and both moments generate a high degree of heterogeneity on the one hand, but on the other hand, they do not lead to solidification in specific capitalist formations that could clearly distinguish themselves from each other.

The hegemonic transitions and transformations that characterize the change of the capitalist world system have always been determined by a sequence of wars. Today, it is necessary to consider the diagnosis of a crisis of global hegemony of the USA made by Giovanni Arrighi in the 1990s and the catastrophic turbulences that characterize the current global economic situation, especially in view of the wars currently raging. This does not mean to design scenarios of the decline of the USA, but to acknowledge, that the West is currently trying to consolidate its dominant position, which, however, should not be equated with a lasting influence outside of the West.

The term "centrifugal multipolarism", proposed by Adam Tooze to characterize this development, shows the turbulent and potentially catastrophic features of the current world system. In this process, established poles start to drift: states, great powers, and empires still play an important role in the formation of the poles, but an increasingly multipolar world is not exclusively organized according to territorial aspects. Global processes, such as those of transnational capital, go beyond sovereignly defined territories to varying degrees and decentralize the process of pole formation. The centrifugal multipolarity is primarily characterized by transnational capital and its actors, which combine the logic of capital accumulation with a political rationality in the production of times and spaces and the control of populations.

The world economy is not simply the sum of national parts, but it is a differentiated system, within which today the growth of capital exports of companies from the leading imperialist states is promoted, the space for capital circulation and the financial industry is expanded, and a complex relationship between leading and subaltern nations is established within complicated networks of information transmission. In addition, international credit relations are expanded, transnational corporations are formed, international derivative sales are extended, and peripheral countries are successively integrated into the capitalist world economy through the dynamics emanating from the capitalist centers, by being developed as markets or as cost-effective production locations.

The relationship between the USA and China deteriorated in 2023 to the lowest point since their rapprochement in the 1970s. People now speak of a "Second Cold War". Both the USA and China have installed restorative political projects in the wake of the 2008 financial crisis. These projects mutually exclude each other and at the same time revive today's global geopolitics. Unlike the first Cold War, in which the superpowers tried to consolidate their territory in blocks, the USA and China are now competing for supremacy in intertwined and connected global networks on a global level.

The spatial logic of the Second Cold War is focused on the control of networks and their structures. The Second Cold War differs from the first Cold War in the competition for supremacy in infrastructure, digital, production, and financial networks. The networks that are the subject of great power rivalry are closely linked. Today, the oceans are crisscrossed by internet cables, which are important components of digital and infrastructural networks. The infrastructure and digital networks are supported and underpinned by financial networks, which in turn revive the global production networks. The USA is trying to undermine China's privileged position in the infrastructure networks by playing out its power in the financial networks. Similarly, China is trying to use its superior position in the digital networks to achieve an improvement in payment systems and to consolidate the project of the digital Yuan.

Factors such as interconnectivity and interdependence are among the key principles of network structures, with geopolitical rivalry focused on controlling nonlinear and not necessarily hierarchical nodes in topological networks, which do not have to be overtly territorial. However, the USA and China continue to operate within the logic of world capital, and their economies are closely intertwined in certain areas. Therefore, it is not possible for the USA to contain China's influence in the long term, and Beijing can hardly hope to take a homogeneous block of states out of the reach of Washington's influence. Nevertheless, the USA and China continue to try to establish themselves in networks through which they can exercise geopolitical and geo-economic power. In practice, this is done through a series of strategies, such as setting rules that determine how networks are integrated or who can participate in them.

The control or attempt to regulate the flows of capital, goods, money, labor, knowledge, data, technical standards, etc. has always been a strategy of geopolitical power coordination, but the development of these strategies has gained urgency in light of the network-based structure of today's capitalist world economy. As a result of global financial integration, the transnationalization of production activities, the increasing complexity of international division of labor, and the rapid development of digital technologies, the world economy is increasingly organized as a heterogeneous formation of complexly structured networks that extend across territorial borders. By controlling key nodes, capitalist actors can gain privileged access to strategic inputs, control the circulation of information, optimize division of labor and logistics, set standards, and include or exclude competitors.

At the same time, financial risks are rather amplified than mitigated by the comprehensive use of Fourth Industrial Revolution technologies (artificial intelligence and robotics and quantum computers) for the organization and management of economic networks by companies and states. Therefore, states and companies use a range of tools to reduce vulnerability to threats and weaknesses, starting with decoupling through the relocation of vulnerable value chains to other countries and the integration of tech giants into the defense sector.

This is primarily about networks of infrastructure, digitality, production, logistics, and finance. We can only address the latter here. The global financial and monetary architecture has developed parallel to the consolidation of American hegemony. The USA owns most of the most powerful financial institutions and world financial centers, which centralize control over the global financial system and host the deepest and most liquid financial markets. The US dollar still tops the global currency system. Most global financial and trade transactions and the major commodity markets are settled in dollars. US government bonds are the world's main currency reserves and the linchpin of the global financial system. A major obstacle to the internationalization of the Chinese economy and efforts to take a central position in other networks is precisely that many of the internationally active Chinese companies still use the US dollar for their trade and business activities.

China has pursued a multi-track strategy in recent years to improve its position in global financial networks. The policy of controlled liberalization of financial markets and limited opening of capital movements aims to reduce the risks and costs of integration into US-centered global financial markets. While China-led multilateral initiatives such as the New Development Bank of the BRICS countries and the Asian Infrastructure Investment Bank are gaining importance, they remain insignificant actors compared to the bilateral lending of China's two main policy banks, the Chinese Development Bank (CBD) and the Chinese Export–Import Bank (CHEXIM). Together, the CBD and the CHEXIM granted almost half a trillion dollars in international loans between 2008 and 2019, thereby catching up with the World Bank over the same period. Most of this goes to financing infrastructure projects around the world. Although Chinese lending has contributed to the current sovereign debt crisis, its origin primarily lies in the fact that many regions of the world have been increasingly exposed to cyclical dollar financing conditions since 2008. The ultra-loose monetary policy in the USA and in large parts of the Global

North in the 2010s triggered greater risk appetite among institutional investors. In return, more and more states were able to borrow on the global capital markets, often at high interest rates.

China's hesitation to fully liberalize its capital account seemed to rule out the prospects for the Renminbi as a dollar competitor for a long time. A series of measures to promote the internationalization of the Renminbi in recent years, as well as China's status as the most important trading partner for the majority of the world's countries, increase the incentives for states and investors to hold Renminbi-denominated assets. Of particular importance are commodity derivatives, as they serve as benchmark prices tied to a specific currency and give the issuer of this currency significant power in the commodity markets. In addition, the concerted Chinese efforts to take a leading role in the introduction of digital currencies by central banks represent another means by which China could displace some dollar transactions.

The USA's preeminence in the global financial system is currently not being questioned, although recent events could rather weaken American hegemony. Financial sanctions against countries like Cuba, Iran, and North Korea have been in place for several decades, but the willingness of the USA and its allies to deny Russia access to currency reserves, the SWIFT payment system, and the correspondent banking network seems to be a sign of a change in the way the USA exercises its financial power. If the USA continues to use the denial of access to financial networks as an economic weapon, it is likely more actors are pursuing alternatives that lie beyond the reach of America. However, the financial institutions based in China do not constitute a fully-fledged alternative financial system. Nevertheless, they are likely to be the main beneficiaries if the share of the world economy threatened by exclusion from US networks grows.

As the rivalry of the great powers focuses on the centrality of networks, it is hard to imagine that either side will achieve a decisive victory. Many countries orient themselves towards both the USA and China—for example, financial networks can be connected to Wall Street and domestic companies can be integrated into networks coordinated by American multinational corporations, while Huawei and other Chinese technology companies expand digital networks and Chinese state-owned companies build roads, ports, and energy networks all over the world.

The networked nature of this rivalry favors the possibility for third countries to pursue independent goals to a certain extent. Since countries can align some networks with China and others with the USA for the time being, there is also little incentive to choose a side. The stronger the compulsion to choose between membership in US- or Chinese-influenced networks, the more likely the formation of territorial blocs reminiscent of the first Cold War becomes.

Notes

1. Dynamic, flexible, and networked systems do not maintain their stability through a rigid control structure, but maximize their ability to tolerate variability, and manage their stability through the strategic generation and maintenance of instabilities or through the management of a permanent state of crisis. This change in the modalities of power proves to be that of financialized capitalism, is evident in the networked form of computing, and in the use of algorithms and artificial intelligence.
2. After the industrial wars in the first half of the twentieth century, war and state have increasingly become functions and components of the war machine of capital since the 1970s. In general, a war machine cuts, transforms, codes, and recodes streams of all kinds. War machines are always associated with structures of work and energy that destroy matter, obstacles, and barriers or convert matter into pure energy. They are also machines that decrypt or destroy information.

   Seizure, conquest, and appropriation are no longer the exclusive prerogatives of the state, which has also partly lost its monopoly on violence and its application. (Lazzarato, 2021: 33) Violence is increasingly also exercised by "civilian" institutions. Today there are private security companies, private armies, mercenary companies, and other private economic and social instruments that can be more effective in protecting capital than large-scale bombings. (Robinson, 2021) The wars led by the USA in Iraq and Afghanistan in particular opened up enormous opportunities for private military and security companies. A new global industry has developed that is no longer limited to specific geographical territories or any state. Many of these private military companies are part of transnational corporations. For example, Vinnell, a division of Braddock, Dunn & McDonald, a military contractor, which is in turn held by the Carlyle Group, one of the largest private equity holdings, integrates investors from 75 countries and cross-investments from hundreds of companies around the world. These private companies work for anyone who pays them. Their clients include states, companies, landowners, non-governmental organizations, and even Mexican and Colombian drug cartels. The largest client is the Pentagon, which between 1994 and 2002 alone concluded more than 3000 contracts with US-based companies worth 300 billion dollars. In 2018, these companies employed 15 million people worldwide to protect private property, provide security personnel for transnational corporations, collect data, organize police units, conduct counterinsurgency and surveillance operations, manage prisons, and suppress protests, etc. (Ibid.).

At the same time, the military expenditures of the imperialist states are increasing, especially since the Ukraine war, and despite continuous technological improvements of the weapons systems, they testify to a development that Mary Kaldor refers to as "arms baroque". She writes: "The arms baroque artificially prolongs the life of industries that would otherwise have long since shrunk. It ties up resources that are needed for investments and innovations in newer, more dynamic industries. […] As the weapons system continues to perfect itself along the lines drawn by manufacturers and buyers, it has apparently already overreached. It has become oversized, costly, overbred, and increasingly less functional. Its social sense is to create an ever more complicated network of dependencies between soldiers, sailors, officers, managers, designers, workers, and bureaucrats. In addition, it still spreads a certain pomp, a kind of social reverence, as baroque art, baroque architecture, and baroque technology have always radiated—a pomp, however, that is probably already a sign of decline." (Kaldor, 1981: 25)

The reversibility of war and power continues to return as a leitmotif in the work of military strategists and finds in finance an important example of the imposition of coercion through economic violence. The financial system can now, as the most deterritorialized form of capital, connect with the most deterritorialized form of state sovereignty, war. This is by no means about the disappearance of the state, but about its integration into the strategies of capital. The state exercises its "power" in a "partnership" with other forces, which in turn subject it to their strategies. What all strategic theories emphasize is the fact that the destructive effect of violence can very well have an economic and above all financial origin. When military strategists think of war today, they do not think of the "front", of regular armies, of confrontations between states as in the time of total wars, which have colonized our imagination.

Lazzarato/Alliez show in their book *Wars and Capital,* that a first theoretical approach to the new functions of war, which are also understood as components of the war machine of financial capital, took place in the book published in 1999 *Unrestricted Warfare*, which was written by two colonels of the Chinese Air Force, Qiao Liang and Wang Xiangsui. (Alliez/Lazzarato, 2018) In the context of the rivalry between China and the United States flaring up after the Cold War, the authors see international financial activities including the sanctions of the leading imperialist countries and capitals as a "bloodless war" that can have comparable effects to a "bloody war". The financial system is therefore today an integral part of non-conventional warfare. Today, the authors note, the factors that threaten "national" security are less to be found in the military forces of an enemy state, but in the plundering of resources, the struggle for markets, the control of capital, trade sanctions, and other economic elements. With this paradigm shift, it becomes apparent that damage caused by new non-military weapons can be as dangerous as the damage caused by military weapons. Total war has transformed into a global war, in the sense that it represents the other face of globalization, the military aspect of the "civil" actions of the world market. It is endemic, sporadic, always ready to break out, but against the backdrop of a war against the population. The war in Syria, the war for the control and "final elimination" of migrants, the war for the privatization of welfare are certainly not the same, but there is a continuity between them, a political transversality: In today's capitalism, war is essentially always a civil war, a war against the population. (Lazzarato, 2021: 12) The war of capital, unlike the war led by the state, does not aim to confirm and expand sovereignty, but the subjugation of humans and non-humans to the production of profit.

3. Governments of emerging countries have difficulty achieving an appropriate price for their assets when investors are not willing to spend money on risky projects abroad. Likewise, governments and development banks that securitize their infrastructure assets in emerging countries must ensure that the risk-adjusted returns match or exceed those of dollar-denominated assets in order to maintain

investor interest. Under today's volatile conditions in the world markets, investors must be given a reason (higher returns) to invest in an emerging country, rather than putting their money in less risky US assets.

4. It is a scandal that the official statistics do not disclose the profits of American, European, and Japanese corporations, which are based on the super-exploitation of workers in the Global South, but rather the huge markups on the production costs appear as profits produced in the USA, UK, and other imperialist countries, even though the goods are only consumed there, and this then results in, for example, every piece of clothing increasing the gross national product of the country in which it is consumed far more than that of the country in which it is produced.

Let's take another look at the impressive numbers that John Smith provides regarding the exploitation of Apple's iPhone. (Smith, 2016: 21ff.) In 2006, the 30-GB iPod was sold in retail for 299 US dollars, while the total production costs, (with the production being completely carried out overseas) amounted to 144.40 dollars, resulting in a gross profit margin of 52%. The gross profit is divided between Apple, its retailers, and distributors, and is partly forwarded to the US government through taxes on sales, profits, and wages. In official statistics, the gross profit is treated as value added in the USA and contributes to the American gross national product. The offshore jobs are mostly located in the low-wage sector, while the jobs in the USA are distributed between highly paid engineers and managers and lower-paid retail and non-professional workers. Research and development accounted for more than two-thirds of the total wage sum in the USA and the workers involved received an average of 85,000 dollars per year. Meanwhile, 12,250 Chinese production workers received 1,540 dollars per year or 30 dollars per week—only 6% of the average wages of US retail workers, 3.2% of the wages of US production workers, and 1.85% of the salaries of US skilled workers.

Smith also mentions an example of textile workers in Bangladesh, where a T-shirt that is produced there is sold in Germany for 4.95 euros by H&M. (Ibid.: 13f.) H&M pays the manufacturer in Bangladesh 1.35 euros for each T-shirt (which is 28% of the final selling price, of which 4 cents cover the costs for 400 g of raw cotton material imported from the USA; shipping to Hamburg adds another 6 cents per T-shirt). Thus, 0.95 euros of the final selling price remain in Bangladesh and are divided between the company, the workers, the suppliers of preliminary products and services, and the government of Bangladesh, thereby increasing the gross domestic product of Bangladesh by this amount. The remaining 3.54 euros are added to the gross national product of Germany, the country where the T-shirt is consumed. This is composed as follows: 2.05 euros represent the costs and profits of German transporters, wholesalers, retailers, advertising etc. (part of which flows back to the state through various taxes). Finally, H&M makes a profit of 60 cents per shirt, while the German state receives 79 cents of the selling price through the value-added tax of 19%; 16 cents cover various "other items". (Ibid.)

5. To explain these processes, it is necessary to consider, on the one hand, the global labor arbitrage, and on the other hand, the existence of a massive global reserve army, which makes the world system of extreme exploitation possible. Labor arbitrage involves the enforcement of extremely low wages abroad, especially in poor countries, by transnational corporations. It is therefore an unequal exchange process. For Smith, it is this super-exploitation that is behind much of the production expansion in the Global South. The fact that this was the basis for the rapid economic growth of some emerging countries, especially China, does not change the fact that enormous imperial returns were created for multinational corporations in the Global South.

   According to Smith, the fact that exploitation now takes the form of super-exploitation is partly due to the fact that in countries with a rapidly growing, formerly peasant workforce, authoritarian regimes in the South and powerful multinational corporations from the North were able to enforce low wages and long working hours, so that wages could be kept below the value of labor power (the costs of reproduction). Smith also emphasizes that the suppression of the international mobility of labor by the Global North has also contributed to this. (Smith, 2016: 93)

   By shifting the production of certain goods to less developed and emerging countries, the costs of their production are reduced, precisely because wages remain exceptionally low there. According to Smith, the inexhaustible dynamism of cheap labor is the key factor for the shift of production to the Global South. It is also facilitated by the breakdown of the production process into individual operations through the introduction of new technologies. Many of these processes can now be carried out by non-specialized workers. And developments in transportation and communication, or logistics, make it possible for the entire production process to be distributed across a larger number of countries.

In addition, super-exploitation is visible today even in imperialist economies, consider zero-hour contracts, where workers must be available around the clock for minimal wages. In all of Southern Europe, where youth unemployment is at 40–50%, young people are forced to live with their parents and earn miserable sums in low-wage jobs in retail and the leisure industry. And the data also shows that poverty for the bottom 10% of households in the Global North (including the USA) has increased since the 1980s.

Against Smith, it must be objected here on a general level that for capital it is not primarily about the expansion of the market for consumer goods and thus the level of wages, but primarily about the expansion of productive and above all financial capital exploitation and therefore the money capital cycles as a whole must be examined at the international level.

6. One reason why transnational corporations increasingly prefer to outsource their business activities to independent companies is that these are forced into intense competition with each other, which is an effective way to depress wages and intensify work. Another incentive for "deverticalization", i.e., the transition from a vertical parent-daughter relationship to a horizontal contractual relationship between formally equal partners, is for transnational corporations to pass on direct responsibility for environmental pollution, poverty wages, and the suppression of unions to poor countries. Smith cites the example of Coca-Cola in Colombia, the center of the Latin American soft drink empire, where the food workers' union, Sinal-Trainal, accuses the company's management of collaborating with death squads that have murdered nine union members and leaders since 1990 and forced many others into exile. 80% of Coca-Cola's workforce now consists of non-union temporary workers, and their wages are only a quarter as high as the wages their unionized colleagues earn. (Smith, 2016)
7. Tooze points out that since 2008, global goods exports as a proportion of GDP have returned to the level of 2000. (Tooze, 2023b)

This regression in trade can be linked to a parallel regression in the degree of financial globalization, measured by global cross-border bank loans. In 2008, this figure was 60% of global GDP and has now fallen to about 37%. The "real" and financial globalization are not separate processes, but are closely linked.

References

Alliez, E., & Lazzarato, M. (2018). *Wars and Capital*. Cambridge.

Harney, S., & Moten, F. (2022). *Allseits unvollkommen. Plantokratie und schwarzes Studium*. Wien.

Hui, Y., & Frey, J. (2023). *Kosmotechnik und Kommunismus*. Matthes & Seitz.

Kaldor, M. (1981). *Rüstungsbarock*. Berlin.

Latour, B. (2018). *Das terrestrische Manifest*. Berlin.

Lazzarato, M. (2012). *Die Fabrikation des verschuldeten Menschen. Ein Essay über das neoliberale Leben*. Berlin.

Lenger, H.-J. (2004). *Marx zufolge. Die unmögliche Revolution*. Bielefeld.

Milios, J., & Sotiropoulos, D. (2009). *Rethinking Imperialism: A Study of Capitalist Rule*. London.

Norfield, T. (2016). *The City. London and the Global Power of Finance*. London/New York.

Robinson, W. I. (2022). *Global Civil War: Capitalism Post-Pandemic (Kairos)*. Oakland.

Robinson, W. I. (2021). *The Global Police State*. London.

Roubini, N. (2022). *MegaThreats: Ten Dangerous Trends That Imperil Our Future, And How to Survive Them*. Boston.

Sloterdijk, P. (1989). *Eurotaoismus. Zur Kritik der politischen Kinetik*. Frankfurt/M.

Smith, J. (2016). *Imperialism in the Twenty-First Century: Globalization, Super-Exploitation, and Capitalism's Final Crisis*. New York.

State of the Freight. (2021). https://www.supplychainquarterly.com/articles/4495-the-state-of-the-freight-2021

Tooze, A. (2023a). On Deglobalisation and Polycrisis. https://adamtooze.substack.com/p/chartbook-192-on-deglobalisation?utm_source=%2Fsearch%2Fslowbalization&utm_medium=reader2

Tooze, A. (2023b). Globalization: The Shifting Patchwork. https://adamtooze.substack.com/p/chartbook-198-globalization-the-shifting?utm_source=post-email-title&publication_id=192845&post_id=105142155&isFreemail=true&utm_medium=email

CHAPTER 12

The Capitalization of Nature

Both the ecstatic extraction of natural resources by capital and the simulative processes of nature conservation have ostensibly nothing to do with overproduction. It is precisely the scarcity of natural resources and the associated increase in commodity prices that contributes to the capitalization of nature, insofar as financial capital speculates on their appreciation. This involves, on the one hand, the financialization of the extraction of natural resources and, on the other hand, the conservation of nature, which is not achieved through labor and production, but through circulating financial capital. Scarcity, in turn, is related not only to the finite availability of natural resources but also to the institutional creation of private property rights.

Financial actors with different trading strategies appear on the financial markets, provide liquidity, stimulate trade, and transform the first nature into a portfolio investment. In addition, commodities/natural resources serve not only to speculate on internal price developments but also to hedge positions of other assets. By far the most important financial instruments for the capitalization of commodities/natural resources are derivatives. (LiPuma/Lee, 2005)Derivatives aim here not only to hedge expected cash flows as in traditional project financing but also to securitize the expected future output of the project/company.

A. Szepanski, *Capitalism in the Age of Catastrophe*, Palgrave Insights into Apocalypse Economics,
https://doi.org/10.1007/978-3-031-57754-3_12

Both the trade in physical commodities and the associated trade in derivatives for both hedging and speculative purposes have increased in recent years, bringing the phenomenon of *over* back into focus at this point. The large trading companies increasingly resemble financial holdings with a broad range of financial services and financial investments. They place risk management at the center of their core competencies and own their own research departments and futures brokers, which act both as traders of physical commodities and as financial investors who constantly diversify their portfolios. Transnational commodity trading companies are constantly involved in speculative hedging transactions.

An important instrument on the markets are commodity indices, which are used by a variety of financial actors such as banks and hedge funds. Commodity/natural resource indices combine several commodities/natural resources into a single financial instrument. In this context, financial investors enter into a commitment in commodity indices, by entering into a bilateral financial agreement, usually a swap, with a bank. The investor buys a portion of the commodity index from the bank, and the bank in turn hedges its risk associated with the swap agreement through futures contracts on a commodity exchange. This strategy of index funds has led several authors to claim that these instruments have contributed to the strong price fluctuations in the commodity markets in recent years. Moreover, the prices of seemingly unrelated commodities correlate. By bundling various commodities into one asset class, commodity indices convey the idea that commodities possess a unique risk premium and represent a homogeneous investment class. This in turn facilitates the assessment of the risk-return of commodity/natural resource instruments and makes them accessible to a wide range of different investors.

A particular focus of the financial industry today is the carbon markets, which are intended to control the dynamics of fossil capital through specific control instruments. While in the case of other natural resources physical goods are actually present and the state issues property rights to them, the commodity in the case of carbon markets is created by the state itself. We see here a capitalization of nature beyond physical goods. Carbon markets have decontextualized and mathematized the climate problem to such an extent that little relevance for global warming remains.

The creation of private property rights in the form of emission certificates has turned the right to pollute into a commodity that can be traded across borders. In principle, every country has the same right to a certain level of pollution. However, it can be assumed that for industrialized countries the costs of reducing CO2 emissions are much higher than for developing and emerging countries. Thus, it can be assumed that industrialized countries tend to buy emission rights from developing countries in order to maintain their own industrial production. This results in financial resources from the capitalist core countries being invested in the alleged preservation of natural resources based on the economic logic of maximum profit-seeking in the periphery, in order to continue to have lucrative investment opportunities at home, while the environmental impacts of these activities are also shifted to less developed areas.

This allows the production of carbon as industrial emissions in one place to be "offset" with its storage in tropical forests. Once a certain piece of forest has been certified so that it can deliver a certain amount of carbon credits, these credits are detached from the direct connection with the forests and can be purchased by actors at any location for the purpose of emission offsetting and emission reduction. The credits can be further traded and serve as collateral for other investments and be packaged with other environmental 'products'. Over time, their value will therefore deviate from the value of the forest parcel from which it originally came.

Such economic innovations turn the earth into a carbon matrix, in which production is reduced to the profitable exchange of the chemical element carbon. Speculation can also lead to excessive price fluctuations and possibly to a strategic hoarding of certificates by large investment funds, to further increase prices.

Jason W. Moore writes that the capitalization of nature represents an attempt to forego the conversion of commodities into money in capital accumulation and to pursue a direct G-G′ transaction. (Moore, 2016) This was facilitated by the idea of nature as a provider of environmental services. As Büscher further describes, financial instruments that refer to natural resources also stand for the increasing abstraction of nature conservation efforts from the attachment to a specific place and enable the generation of values from afar and freely around the world. to circulate. Büscher calls the financialization of offset-oriented natural capital a "fictitious conservation". (Büscher, 2015)

Financial capitalization is necessary to free capital from the constraints of investing in constant capital such as machinery. Natural protected areas, like agriculture and forestry and other forms of supposedly sustainable resource use, still require substantial investments in fixed capital. Even ecotourism, which requires the movement of consumers to travel destinations, requires high investments in fixed capital at certain locations. Capitalization initiates a process that allows buyers at one location to connect remotely with services at another location. (McAfee, 2012) With the creation of carbon markets and other new financial mechanisms, however, this restriction is lifted: speculative capital is now completely location-independent and can be exchanged worldwide. Derivatives can therefore be considered a kind of transition strategy that enables the transition from production at the location to the "free" circulation of money capital around the world. All of this overall facilitates the process of capital accumulation by reducing the friction caused by transaction costs.

The conceptualization of certain aspects of the earth's productivity as a resource of profitable substitutability leads to an understanding of the "global environment" as a kind of abstract matrix that can be broken down into newly conceived, interchangeable parts. Technologies, especially the connectivity of new information and communication technologies and the internet, played a crucial role in facilitating these innovations and structuring the results.

Today, more and more investment funds are emerging that offer products and services that utilize the discourse on environmental protection and sustainability. (Büscher, 2015) These investment trends are accompanied by an expansion of environmental indices, which are intended to serve as a guide and to improve investment strategies. The construction of nature as a "service provider" is a significant conceptual step that enables financial investments in markets for nature conservation. Conservation biologists have been using the language of ecosystem services since the 1970s. Such language fabricates nature as a service-providing unit. However, the resulting payments for its services do not flow back to nature, but to those who annex it. The question of which nature work can become "billable" at all and who can collect payments or profit from speculations on their future value through enforceable property or possession rights is then of importance.

The implied Wall Street Consensus is also supported by the imperial states and the multilateral development banks, which direct the trillions managed by the private finance industry into the asset classes of climate or sustainable development goals. The state uses public funds to align the risk-return profile of these assets with the preferences of investors. The conversion of climate or nature into asset classes requires the capitalization of public goods and social infrastructures, which go beyond water, electricity, and transport. It also includes housing, education, and health care; these must generate cash flows that pay institutional investors. The consensus sees the state as a risk reducer: its fiscal arm enters into public–private partnerships to make them bankable by transferring part of the risks to the state's balance sheet, while its monetary arm protects investors from liquidity and exchange rate risks.

References

Büscher, B. (2015, December). Nature on the Move I: The Value and Circulation of Liquid Nature and the Emergence of Fictitious Conservation. *Journal of Marxism and Interdisciplinary Inquiry, 6*(1–2), 20–36.

LiPuma, E. (2017). *The Social Life of Financial Derivatives: Markets, Risk, and Time*. Durham/London.

McAfee, K. (2012). Nature in the Market-World: Ecosystem Services and Inequality. *Development, 55*, 25–33. https://doi.org/10.1057/dev.2011.105

Moore, J. W. (2015). *Capitalism in the Web of Life. Ecology and the Accumulation of Capital*. London.

CHAPTER 13

The Capitalocene and Fossil Capital (Overpollution)

It is pandemic outbreaks, fires, floods, superstorms, droughts, and heatwaves, whose frequency today makes global warming as identifies a "wild ecology". The multiplication of these ecological events—and the associated impending collapse of the infrastructure of hospitals, medical aid, funeral services, food and water supply, transport, and energy and communication networks—provides the material evidence that the existing system has taken an "exterminist" direction. At the same time, established ecology allows industrial systems to maintain an appearance of ethics, while potentially catastrophic processes continue unabated. Each year seems to establish a new normal for the various climate parameters—which means that anomalies have become the norm. We live in a time of catastrophic points and curves. Record high temperatures are increasingly followed by record low temperatures in certain places, even if the global trend is upward. Local and global overlap and blur into each other: The rise in sea levels is not globally uniform; climate change is a global phenomenon, but extreme weather events occur here and there, making their prediction and the prevention of their effects increasingly difficult.

In 2012, global CO_2 emissions were 58% higher than in 1990.[1] This had the consequence, among other things, that hurricanes became stronger due to higher temperatures in the catchment areas of oceans and the Arctic ecosystems reached a series of tipping points. The threshold

A. Szepanski, *Capitalism in the Age of Catastrophe*, Palgrave Insights into Apocalypse Economics,
https://doi.org/10.1007/978-3-031-57754-3_13

at which the ice sheet in Greenland irreversibly melts and a rise in sea levels of up to six meters can be reached, is now not at a further global warming of 3.1 degrees, but of 1.6 degrees. Melting ice intensifies warming because the exposed darker sea surface absorbs more solar heat than the ice and later releases it to the atmosphere, which in turn accelerates the shrinkage of the remaining ice. This mechanism is a classic example of a self-reinforcing process: The same phenomenon, namely ice loss, is both a consequence and a part of the cause of temperature increase. This "ice-albedo feedback" plays a major role in ice loss in Greenland, which has increased significantly in recent years.

The temperature increase caused by capital, along with factors such as the reduction of biodiversity, the acidification of the seas, extreme weather conditions, precarious drinking water supply, chemical pollution, and the change in soil conditions, to name just a few, can no longer be denied. The goal of keeping global warming below two degrees Celsius is now far off, while constant investment is being made in new oil fields, coal-powered factories, new airports, new highways, etc. In 1990, the annual increase in warming was one percent, and since the year 2000 we have been dealing with a rate of 3.1 percent. (Malm, 2016: 3) It is a bleak fact: The more knowledge about the consequences of global warming there is, the more fossil fuels are burned. The facts are well known and they can also be interpreted. *They are the product of a fossil capital economy.*[2] (ibid.)

The first industrial revolution was, among other things, about the implementation of a technology based on fossil fuels, a poisoned fruit of history to this day, according to Andreas Malm. The current climate is a product of ongoing CO_2 emissions in the past. The transfer of carbon, which originated from geological reserves and led to fireplaces, only to be emitted into the atmosphere, set the process in motion. It takes time, until a certain quantity of CO_2 emissions was recognized as heat yield and before it affected the planetary ecosystem. With each new emission added to past emissions, the concentration of CO_2 in the atmosphere increases (CO_2 remains in the atmosphere for several thousand years) and global warming accelerates, that is, *emissions are cumulative.* (ibid.: 11) The emission of one ton of CO_2 would not be so dangerous if there were not already trillions of tons of CO_2 in the atmosphere; it is therefore the total accumulation that causes temperatures to rise, and the more CO_2 is emitted, the less likely it is to be able to slow down the ongoing increase at all.

If a certain increase in global warming, say two degrees Celsius, is to be maintained, logically only a very specific amount of CO_2 can be emitted. Even if the fossil economy were to be stopped in one fell swoop, it would still continue to cast its shadow into the future. A warmed sea causes the ice of Antarctica to melt and destabilizes the permafrost soils, to set further feedback processes in motion—all in all, climate change is also a dirty mix of time scales. So one must not forget that the "1.5 degree limit", as set by the IPCC and the UN, still allows for global warming that results in more intense and frequent hurricanes, storms, and other weather events. Rising floods and drought periods, reduced crop yields, declining fish stocks—while sea levels rise—are the result. This forces the migration of people living on islands or in low regions. Finally, there are higher death rates among animals and humans and the growing devastation of parts of the earth. Climate change causes tens of thousands of deaths per year, so the "1.5 degree limit" can be described as a "death sentence" for many indigenous peoples and island dwellers. (ibid.)

One of the disturbing findings of climate science is that global warming may not occur gradually, representable as a uniformly ascending line on a graph, but must be understood as a series of ecstatic accelerations, in which various tipping points are reached and exceeded. These tipping points could take the form of a cascade.[3] (ibid.: 11)

The Amazon suffers from recurring drought and forest death. In the northern coniferous belts, rising temperatures lead to marked forest fires, permafrost soils thaw and release methane; in the tropics, coral reefs disappear and thus affect the ecosystems of the oceans. Long ago, not all physical interactions are understood and represented in climate models. Global warming does not necessarily have to lead to an increase in temperatures all over the globe. Thus, the global average temperature is a measure that refers to the determination of the further course of climate change, it is a scientific construction that works with probability theory. This measure describes the total increase in heat energy in certain layers of the atmosphere, but it is by no means clear how the higher energy affects seasonally and locally. This depends on a whole range of other factors, such as the specific distribution of land, ice, and sea, the structure of the mountains and the large vegetation areas.

It is widely known that only 10% of humanity is responsible for half of all current CO_2 emissions that come from consumption. The richest 1% has a CO_2 footprint that is 175 times larger than that of the poorest

10% of the world's population. The emissions from the wealthiest residents in the USA, Saudi Arabia, and Luxembourg are two thousand times higher than those of the poorest residents of Honduras, Mozambique, or Rwanda. However, the biggest air polluter in the world is the American military. If it were a country, it would rank 47th in the world for fossil fuel consumption, making it one of the largest emitters of greenhouse gases. Consider the historical inefficiency of the US military, the planet's largest oil consumer and, unsurprisingly, also its most important oil policeman. The Pentagon is an accounting black hole, from which no light emerges. (ibid.)

Most will say that the answer to all these problems is taxing dirty energy or a complete ban on CO_2 emissions, as well as subsidizing clean energy. A reasonably applied CO_2 tax could accelerate the introduction of renewable energy until it is able to completely replace fossil fuels. New fossil sources and infrastructures could be banned, and the revenue from CO_2 taxes could be used to fund the research of new technologies. But in any conceivable scenario of this warmed planet, every Green New Deal also fails due to the logic of capital. Because in capitalism, the class of owners and managers is forced to make a series of decisions about where and what to invest in, taking into account prices, wages, profitability, and other fundamental determinants of the economy. Even if these owners wanted to prevent the sinking cities and billions of migrants by 2070 with high investments in climate protection, they could not. The drive for relentless growth and thus increasing energy consumption is not chosen, but is structurally enforced by capital.

The "derisking" state sees climate policy as a matter of "mobilizing" private capital, i.e. pushing back the market rather than replacing it. The aim is to make green infrastructure assets "investable" or green production facilities profitable in order to meet capitalists' demands for risk calculability in the face of unprecedented uncertainty. To this end, the derisking state redistributes risk from private investors to its own balance sheet via specific strategies. The weak derisking state works with institutional capital to create infrastructure asset classes. The institutional capital either directly or indirectly owns these infrastructure assets by holding the financial liabilities used to "buy" these assets (e.g. loans or bonds to finance a PPP hospital). The robust derisking state works with industrial capital to incentivize the creation of new industrial assets in strategic industries such as cleantech. It may also choose to derisk infrastructure asset classes for private capital (and vice versa for the weak derisking state), but the main target of derisking interventions is green manufacturing capacity.

Andreas Malm poses the crucial question for his book *Fossil Capital I* in these contexts: *What is meant by a fossil economy*? (ibid.: 14) A simple answer would be: An economy with sustainable, structurally induced growth, which is based on an increasing consumption of fossil fuels and therefore generates a continued increase of CO_2 in the atmosphere. (ibid.) In accordance with the laws of thermodynamics, it is known that no growth can permanently feed itself, it always relies on the dissipation of natural resources. Modern capitalist growth is so far unimaginable without fossil energies, although according to Jason W. Moore, focusing solely on these in the context of the growth dynamics of capital equates to technological determinism, which does not take into account other factors of the growth explosion, the "Four Cheaps", which we will return to later. (Moore, 2015)

Malm translates Marx's thesis of the rising organic composition of capital (value composition between constant and variable capital) into a rising fossil composition of capital. (Malm, 2016: 422) Over a longer period of time, the tendency of capital to reduce the proportion of human labor compared to that of machines in production can be translated into the law of an increasing concentration of CO_2 in the atmosphere. This dynamic was first found in England in the nineteenth century during the consumption of coal, which was necessary for the textile trade and production.

The tendency of (industrial) capital to increase its mobility and flexibility in competition requires more and more fixed capital to be invested in means of production, infrastructures, and means of transport. When capital employs new fixed capital, it wants to use it until its value has been amortized. The fossil economy is a socio-ecological structure in which a certain economic process and a certain form of Energy is interwoven with each other. From a certain point in the nineteenth century, entrepreneurs in England obtained the energy for their businesses from the nearest lignite field and did not build any more water mills. They transported their products on merchant ships, not sailing ships, and later preferred the car and airplane as options for travel and transport. All in all, fossil energy has a historical substance. (ibid.)

The fossil economy therefore undeniably has its birthplace in England: The country was responsible for 80% of global CO_2 emissions in 1825 and for 62% in 1850. At the beginning, the transition from the consumption of natural resources (water) to that of fossil energies (coal) was slow. This transformation required new technologies, labor, scientific research, etc. It was initially the profit motives of small and medium-sized enterprises that drove innovations in the energy sector. The material was initially coal, which had been burned in Britain for hundreds of years, but it was the industrial revolution that led to a rapid increase in the combustion of coal in factories. The transformation of heat into motion, or the conversion of thermal energy into mechanical energy, was achieved through the means of production steam engine. In the first steam engines, coal was burned to move the piston up and down in vertical motion. In a steam generator, which is part of the machine, energy is generated by combustion, with the heat energy contained in the steam being converted into mechanical work by means of a piston.

Another source of propulsion was the continuous rotation of wheels. It was James Watts who discovered the usability of burning coal for wheels. The piston produced a continuous circular motion, making the engine useful for the production of all kinds of products. The rotating engine could now drive a machine, which was the starting point of sustainable economic growth that increased output per capita, i.e., improved labor productivity. As a source of thermal energy, coal was useful for a number of processes, but only as a source of rotating mechanical energy could it drive the production of all sorts of products. (ibid.: 218ff.) A rotating machine could also drive a vehicle—the second moment of sustainable growth—that allowed trips over land and sea to transport goods to and from the mill. The heat could act on materials with certain chemical properties, pumps could move liquids, machines and vehicles could produce and transport a range of goods, and powered by the combustion of coal, it was the steam engine that made fossil fuels ubiquitous in the production of goods. It should be noted that thermodynamic power and social power are not separate areas. *Fossil fuels are primarily a materialization of social relations.* (ibid.) And fossil fuels require human labor as a condition of their existence. It is labor that brings people and nature together and allows biophysical resources to flow into the cycles of social metabolism. *Workers are the first interface between economy and nature.* (ibid.: 23)

It was initially water power that was used for the production of cotton in England before the steam engine was used in factories for the production of textiles. Malm attempts to provide a historical explanation for why and how steam power replaced water as the "prime mover" of the emerging industrial age.[4] During the first industrial revolution, the water mill hindered the conditions necessary for capital, insofar as natural properties such as weather conditions and landscape did not allow for urban concentration and discipline of work in the factory. Instead of continuing being exposed to the conditions of nature, capital created its own matrix with points and arteries, which set a cycle in motion and created a new space, the abstract mathematical space, the factory, which enabled the cooperative accumulation of workers and the possibility of capital accumulation.

Analogously, we are dealing with an abstract temporality, with the right of the capitalist to fix and use the labor force in production for a certain period of time. During this period, the worker is subjected to the dictate of intensifying productivity (the output measured within a fixed unit of time). Abstract time inherits time as a mathematical unit and must be considered an incorporeal event that is not based on natural fluctuations or changing weather. If the work was performed faster and more intensively, this also had to happen with the "prime mover" (steam engine) and all pores of production interruption had to be eliminated. The increase in labor productivity was therefore also based on the steam engine, and this was in line with the necessities for capital, that the machines could be switched on and off ad hoc and could be increased in speed if necessary. Abstract space and abstract time together form what Malm calls a distinctive space–time of the capitalist mode of production. (ibid.; 357) Capital does not circulate in space and through time as if there were two fixed axes along which it develops, rather it produces its own abstract space–time. The necessary substrate for this space–time are the fossil fuels. They represent the geological compression of time and space, and their dense energy allows capital to produce its own space–time to extract the surplus of nature. And space–time began to influence the atmosphere sustainably with the mining of coal. The depth of capital's dependence on nature is fully developed when the CO_2 produced by the combustion of fossil fuels is equipped with a transformative power like no other anthropogenic substance. *Steam power was also a manifestation of the class power of capital*. (ibid.; 145f.)

Malm clearly shows that in the initial phase of the industrial revolution there was neither a shortage of water, and water was not more expensive than steam power or technically inferior to it. Engines based on steam power at this time still required expensive coal and were often unpredictable due to disastrous collapses. (ibid.: 369ff.) However, steam power also had its advantages over water in that the management of water power depended on the cooperation between competing mill owners, while steam engines, although they were still more expensive than water mills at this time, could operate independently of each other. The owners of mills powered by steam were also independent of geographical conditions and this in turn allowed the concentration of production in the cities, where there was also a sufficient contingent of available cheap workers at this time. The existence of a fully integrated factory therefore required a large concentration of workers. In addition, a semi-functional infrastructure could be provided in the cities.

In *Capital Vol. 2*, Marx assumes three circuits of industrial capital, namely money capital, productive capital (constant and variable capital) and commodity capital, summarizing the entire circuit of capital in the process formula G – W (PM, AK) … P … W' – G' (G for money, W for commodities and P for production; AK for labor power, PM for means of production). Foreign or own money capital is the engine for industrial enterprises that buy goods (means of production, buildings, energy, raw materials, software etc.) and hire labor forces, so that products enriched with surplus value can be produced and also realized, leading to the formation of new money capital. Machinery, energy, products, or production processes are not capital in themselves. Marx has shown that the above formula is the decisive expression of all economic relations appropriate to capital, and of course, production is included in this, which functions as a purely functional process, a process for the generation of profit. Capital ties the production process to its monetary metamorphoses or to the (monetary) total circulation, i.e., production is to be understood as a function and phase of the circulation of capital (in the second comprehensive sense), whose general form can be written down in the following formula:

G-W–P-W'-G'.

This also spans the conceptual difference between labor power and labor to explain surplus value. Not labor, but labor power is bought and sold, Marx writes, and labor power is bought at its value and its use in the production process as labor results in a greater value than it itself has. Marx considers this to be the crucial point of his economic analyses, which lead to the concept of surplus value. And labor transforms into dynamis or living potentiality regarding the production of surplus only where a capitalist techne or technology, among other things, accesses it as a transformation of labor power into labor. And the economy of time strikes when the use of labor power in the production process generates greater value than it itself costs. As time beyond that time which its reproduction requires, labor power performs unpaid labor, the result of which is represented in surplus value. From the outset, surplus value is therefore to be understood as the result of the simultaneity of a non-simultaneity, insofar as the exchange and use of labor power interlock as symmetry and asymmetry; surplus value arises from the asymmetry-in-the-symmetry. For capital, production is a simple mediation, a nasty necessity that has to be accepted. And the cycles of capital are boundless, so that after the return of profit, the cycle must be repeated on an expanded scale:

$$G\text{-}W\text{-}G'\text{-}\ G'\text{-}W'\text{-}G''\text{-}G''\text{-}W''\text{-}G'''$$

The money must be constantly reinvested to maintain capital accumulation or expanded reproduction. This also requires production at a higher level, so that capital production can be assumed to be a spiral. For each further cycle, capital also requires a larger amount of natural materials, or, to put it another way, the accumulation of capital is realized by increasing the productive consumption of the material, that is, by higher reserves and resources of biophysical substances, which are extracted from nature to return to the world's landfills at the end of the cycle. And this spiral is, so to speak, sustainable: The more biophysical resources are extracted from the earth, the more resources the next expanded round of production requires. The capitalist property relations are therefore characterized by the following factors: (a) the seemingly infinite potential for profit production, (b) the compulsion, mediated through the competition of companies among each other, to operate this profit production incessantly, and (c) the necessity of productive consumption of ever more natural materials. Capital, in its search for the cheap fours (labor, raw materials, energy, food; see Moore, 2015), does not want to register any limits in nature, but to circulate like an ascending perpetuum mobile.

Building on these insights, Malm develops the general formula of fossil capital. At a certain stage of the development of capital accumulation, fossil fuels become a necessary material substrate for the production of surplus value, that is, they are used as material across the entire range of production. If F stands for fossil fuels as part of the means of production, then it can be written (ibid.: 343):

$$G–W…P…F\text{-}G^{‘}$$

Fossil fuels are now within the metabolism of the productive consumption in ever increasing quantities in circulation, and this with a necessary by-product, the existence of which Marx and Engels were also aware of: Higher quantities of CO_2 in the atmosphere are part of production. The formula is now:

$$G\text{-}W…P\ (CO_2)\ …G^{‘}$$

Since fossil energy now feeds the perpetuum mobile of capital accumulation, a raw material that seemingly never runs out, the formula on an extended scale is:

$$G\text{-}W…P\ (CO_2)\ …G^{‘}\text{-}\ G^{‘}\text{-}W^{‘}…P^{‘}(CO_2{}')…G^{‘‘}$$

It is about the triangular relationship between capital, labor, and non-human nature, and also about a process that at each stage involves the productive consumption of higher quantities of fossil fuels.

The cycle of individual consumption of fossil fuels, for example of driving a car, is:

$$W\text{-}G\text{-}W(F/CO_2)$$

The F in the formulas must of course come from somewhere, it must be offered as a dead thing by a capitalist on the market. A capitalist for whom fossil fuels are not an input, but an output. This applies to the business of extracting gas, oil, and coal. The formula for this primitive accumulation of fossil capital is:

$G\text{-}W…P…\ G^{‘}\ (F)$ (ibid.: 346).

In order to consume fossil fuels productively as an industrial enterprise, or to operate the private consumption of fuels, it therefore requires a company that specializes in the production of these fuels and for which this is a process of profit production. Within a fossil economy, the cycles of productive and individual consumption of fossil fuels are inextricably intertwined.

Jason W. Moore has presented an expanded and comprehensive conception of the capitalization of nature. His thesis of the Capitalocene identifies the origins of capitalism and capitalogenic environmental design in the revolutions of labor and landscape between 1492 and 1750. Capitalism became a geological force in these centuries, creating a modern constitution of biological flows through the globalizing infrastructures of capital, empire, and class formation. For Malm, the rise of capitalism is a question of an Anglo-centric history, shaped by the geographies of class struggle, technical innovation, and the coal revolution. For Moore, on the other hand, it is the epochal land and labor revolution after 1492 that produced a capitalist world ecology. Malm's description of fossil capital is for Moore an important element of a longer history. Moore does not agree with Malm's periodization because it does not take into account the constitutive geohistorical relationships that preceded and accompanied large industry after 1800: The intertwining of plantation complex and transatlantic class dynamics and their contribution to capital formation in industrializing Britain. The productive forces are understood by Moore as configurations of capital, class and technique, and are integrated into the imperialist dynamics of accumulation.

Moore calls in his writings to finally overcome the philosophical dualism that sees economy and ecology as separate areas, and instead to focus on the relations between both areas. (Moore, 2015: 16) If one understood that the (capitalist) relations and not the relata were central, then one would understand, for example, how and why Wall Street is always also a mode of organizing nature. One would finally understand how the turbulences on the stock markets are connected with the problems of the climate and life on this planet in a way that has not yet been even noticed by radical left economists.

The currently highly regarded theory of the Anthropocene is for Moore a theory that remains within the society-nature dualism. Accordingly, the decisive economic development for humanity begins in eighteenth century England with the steam engine and coal. Long before this, and this is to be understood as a critique of Malm, according to Moore, at least the potential of capital to transform the environment exists. This concerns speed, scope, and measurement of environmental factors. Consider the first plantations in Madeira. In addition, transformations in ecology cannot be attributed to an abstract category like humanity as the cause. This is a deeply anthropocentric and Eurocentric view of things. Therefore, Moore replaces the term "Anthropocene" consistently with "Capitalocene". (ibid. 176) This is also supported by the fact that capital in the period between 1700 and 2008 has increased by a factor of 134, while in the same period the population only grew by a factor of 10. The dynamics of ecological Earth transformation in the last three centuries is therefore primarily due to capital accumulation and the appropriation of cheap nature by capital.

For Moore, capitalism is always more than just an economy or a system, namely a way of organizing nature. He speaks of capitalism as a world-ecology, which establishes and organizes the connection between capital accumulation, the pursuit of power, and the co-production of nature. (ibid.; 161) In doing so, Moore initially opposes the statements of René Descartes, which are still considered relevant today. The currently still quoted dualistic-Cartesian narrative, according to Moore, states the following: Capitalism emerges from nature, draws wealth from nature, and thus degrades nature. And at some point, the catastrophe comes, nature collapses, and takes revenge on man. This perspective on nature as a factor external to man is a fundamental condition for the affirmation of capitalist accumulation. Capitalism as a historical project tries to code, quantify, and rationalize nature, which is understood as external, to ensure constant economic growth. Nature must therefore be dominated, and this is done by applying the laws of nature with the help of technology. This view goes back to Newton.

On the other hand, Moore makes it clear from the outset that he is concerned with a completely different conception of nature. What he calls "Web of Life" is nature around us, as us, and in us. "Web of Life" is the complex interplay of organic and inorganic as a permanently changing and altering relation; it is about multilayered relations, in which there are no antagonistic basic units (human versus nature), but only networks in networks of relations. Worlds within worlds. (ibid.: 40, 63, 123) At this point echoes of Bruno Latour's network theory can be found, which aims to crystallize the network dispositif as the hegemonic mode of operation of current systems. If one understands the network as a metanarrative, as Alexander Galloway has pointed out, one quickly ends up with a kind of network fundamentalism ("everything is a network"). Everything then exists in the form of a system, an ecology, a montage, in short, as a network.

Everything that people do, for Moore, takes place in a stream of streams, in which nature constantly surrounds and traverses man, who is himself part of nature. Moore speaks, to distinguish himself from the theory of the Anthropocene, of streams of power and capital into nature, and of streams of nature into power and capital. Instead of a "metabolic rift", as Bellamy Foster writes, Moore speaks of a "metabolic shift". (Moore, 2015: 25) Fundamentally, Moore then introduces the term "Oeikos". This refers to the creative, historical, and dialectical relation between humans and extra-human natures. The Oeikos enables the history of capital accumulation in the "Web of Life". The relationship between humans and nature is to be understood as a stream of streams; humans internalize the entire nature and this internalizes the differences and coherences of man. Moore brings into play on this general level Marx's term "metabolism" of man with nature, a game of ever-changing relations and interpenetrations, with which new environments are created—environments, for Moore, are not only forests and fields, but also factories, office towers, airports etc.

Moore is initially concerned with the destruction of dualistic thinking, which revolves around nature and man as separate entities; he is interested in the relations and intra-actions between culture/human and nature, with which diverse configurations are co-produced; he speaks of the configurations of man-in-nature, regarding organisms and environments, regarding life and water, of land and air. Nature is not only existent (first nature), but it is also historically present (second nature; it includes human organizations, non-human currents, techniques, relations, and substances—and the web of life). In this sense, history is always one of a double internality: man-in-nature and nature-in-human. (ibid.: 17) However, it should be added at this point with Yuk Hui that the overcoming of the dualism of culture and nature is always also a question of technology, which is necessary to enable a coexistence of nature and culture. (Frey/Hui, 2023: 61) For Hui, in order to escape the deadly destructiveness of cybernetic systems and their inherent progress and perfectionism, a new cosmotechnics must come into play, which brings the cosmic order and the human orders into harmony through techniques. (ibid.: 65) With Simondon, he notes that technology cannot be completely subsumed by culture. Technical objects possess their own mode of existence and specific relations to other existences. It is, to use

Karen Barad's term, intra-activities, in which capital, humans, techniques, apparatuses, and nature are interwoven.

Moore speaks, without emphasizing technology, of a co-produced world-ecology of capital, power, and nature. It is not just about asking what capital does to man and nature, but also about what nature does for capital: The formula then is "capitalism-in-nature/nature-in-capitalism". (ibid.: 37) It is ultimately about the question of how nature and energy are converted into value and capital. Capitalism has not only destroyed nature in its long phases, but also developed it through a multitude of projects, including those that force humans (as part of nature) to work (as oeikos), partly for free or at least for low wages. And this, Moore predicts, would become increasingly difficult for capital in the future.

In a time of rapid transformation of networks—urbanization, labor markets, financialization—it is an important task to examine the flows of capital, power, and energy, which are under the dominance or under the grid of capital accumulation and their spatio-temporal actualizations. Capital always implies the active domination of time over space, and this in the course of accelerating its turnover times. Each of these accelerations simultaneously implies the production of a new space, which is fixed and variable at the same time. Space is not simply out there, but it diffuses into social relations and forms environments, which always also open up possibilities for contingencies. Capital, non-human flows, relations, and substances, and the web of life are in an interpenetrating relationship.

At this point, Moore introduces the term "nature-as-matrix". (ibid.: 175) The nature-as-matrix is the basis, condition and constituting agent in the history of civilizations. Nature is thus understood more as a matrix than as a resource. As a matrix, in and through which human activities unfold—nature is the field on which historical "agencies" act. "Agencies", and here again there is an echo of Latour, Moore initially defines quite generally as relational and emergent properties between complexes of human and non-human natures, whereby the latter also produce specific configurations of human activities. Even the climate is to be understood as a complex of determinations, which indicate transformations in specific historical contexts. The climate is a historical vector, one that is to be located within the "oeikos". Thus, the co-production of nature, the pursuit of power and capital accumulation are by no means to be understood as independent blocks, whose relations might only be held together by feedback mechanisms. Rather, these three blocks interpenetrate in various relations and thus shape a specific historical capitalism. Moore thus implicitly recurs again and again to the Actor-Network Theory of Latour, according to which there can be no objects that are not in relation to each other.[5]

For Moore, nature can neither be destroyed nor saved, but only transformed or reconfigured, that is, nature is not a static field, but it renews itself in cycles and changes cumulatively. Historical natures are both producers and products of capitalist development. Moore distinguishes between "nature in general" and "historical nature". While nature in general has been inevitably there for billions of years, the capitalist historical nature is defined by the law of cheap nature and reproduced by the capitalist revolutionizing of nature and the parallel sequence of historical natures.

Moore differentiates two simultaneous relations and processes: On the one hand, the economic relations between capital and labor produce the socially necessary abstract labor time as a result of the extraction of surplus value, and on the other hand, the relations of the partly violent appropriation of cheap nature produce the abstract social nature. This refers to the processes by which capital and states map, code, quantify, and measure the human and extra-human nature for the purposes of capital accumulation. (ibid.:)

Moore rightly distinguishes here between capital as project/logic and capitalism as historical world ecology, the latter understood as a history of capital, power, and nature shaped according to a specific pattern—an (open) totality, in and with which, however, many determinations operate. As we have depicted in *Capitalization Vol. 1* it is necessary to make a conceptual distinction between capital and capitalism. (Szepanski 2014a, 2014b) Capitalism is to be understood as a—under economic, political, and cultural aspects—quite heterogeneous historical formation, a world ecology of capital, power, and (re)production in the web of nature, but essentially determined by the production and circulation logics of capital. In capitalism, besides the dominant mode of production of capital, one also finds non-capital-determined modes of production, be they neo-feudal, slum-like, corrupt, and criminal economies, but also cooperative economies, which are only partially or not at all linked to capital. We consider capital as a conceptual logic or as a differential system, whose production and circulation cycles follow a specific immanent lawfulness that keeps the system in balance, as it also makes it crisis-prone. Capital and its own method of capitalization function, so to speak, as the engine (which cannot be separated from a relation) of the formation "capitalism", in which the economy ultimately determines all other areas such as politics, culture, art, science etc.

For Moore, the law of value within the framework of capital logic is a gravitational field that exerts a lasting influence on the capitalist world ecology over long patterns, but also allows significant contingencies. Anwar Shaikh speaks in his book *Capitalism: Competition, Conflict, Crises* similarly speaks of order-in-and-through-disorder, a systemic mode of turbulent regulation, which takes the form of repetition occurring according to certain patterns. A wide range of phenomena, according to Shaikh, can ultimately be explained by a small set of operating principles that ensure that current events revolve around the centers of gravity. (Shaikh, 2016: 55ff.) This type of eventfulness, Moore notes again, cannot be understood as an economic phenomenon alone, but must be understood as a systemic problem with crucial economic and ecological moments.

For Moore, the capitalization or the capital accumulation always also relies on the appropriation of unpaid labor outside of capital circulation, an appropriation that remains within the reach of capitalist power and logic. (Moore, 2015: 177) The limits and configurations of cheap nature are therefore also actively produced by symbolic practices and material transformations that fall within the power domain of capital. Thus, the capitalization of everything and everyone not only requires the constant revolutionizing of the productive forces (within the capitalist mode of production and in relation to the relations of production), but also the reproduction of capitalism as world-ecology, and the latter cuts between the boundaries of paid and unpaid labor and human and non-human resources.

Capital requires the production of cheap nature, the four "cheaps": cheap food, cheap energy, cheap labor, and cheap raw materials. (ibid.: 188ff.) Cheap nature is then produced when "agencies" such as capital, the sciences, and the empire succeed in releasing cheap sources in and from nature for capital production, cheap also in the historical sense, insofar as the four cheap "cheaps" contribute to reducing the socially necessary abstract labor time. The concept of appropriation in Moore refers to such extra-economic processes that apply unpaid or cheap labor outside of the capital system and channel it into capital circulation. (ibid.: 64) The appropriation of unpaid or cheap labor increases the general rate of profit and thus appropriation is also to be understood as a productive activity. It not only provides raw materials, but it co-determines the socially necessary societal labor time. If abstract labor concerns the capital-wage labor relation, through which surplus value is produced, then social nature denotes the relation capital-cheap/unpaid labor, through which an increasing productivity for capital over longer periods of time becomes possible at all. At this point, Moore's substantialist reading of the value theory, which is based on the basis of the "substance" of labor time, becomes apparent again when he mentions abstract labor.[6] The interpretation of labor as substance[7] and as the exclusive source of surplus value complicates the examination of important phenomena of the contemporary global economy such as intangible assets, financial markets, and the biophysical limits of capitalism. More interesting in Moore is the concept of appropriation. It channels human and non-human sources of unpaid labor/energy towards capital circulation, without necessarily having to capitalize the sources. If capital can appropriate large amounts of unpaid labor/energy, the costs of production definitely decrease. In these times, there is a high world-ecological surplus,whereas the ecological surplus is the rate between the mass of capital and the appropriated mass of unpaid labor/energy.

The appropriation of cheap resources, but also of cheap waste, does not produce capital, but the spaces, relations, and energies that first made it possible for capital accumulation to take place so extensively over long historical periods. Moore simply asserts that for the stabilization of the capital relationship, the appropriation of cheap nature is of even greater importance than capitalization. However, this is doubtful.

The dialectic of productivity and plunder—the accumulation through capitalization and the accumulation through appropriation—has allowed capitalism to survive to this day, thus being able to reproduce itself over six centuries. Moore tries to justify this with Marxist categories. When the technical composition of capital increases, the organic composition of capital usually also increases over longer periods, except, according to Moore, under the conditions of a rapid appropriation of cheap nature. (ibid.) Moore goes so far as to see the level or fall of the organic composition of capital decisively constituted by the production of cheap nature (even the cheapening of constant capital can lead to such a fall). The technical composition of capital can therefore, as is the case in capitalism, increase while the organic composition of capital decreases, in Moore's case due to the appropriation of cheap nature, and counteracts the fall in the rate of profit. However, there are a number of factors that Moore leaves unmentioned.

Constant capital can be divided into fixed (machines) and circulating constant capital (raw materials). The latter is again to be distinguished from the circulation of capital. In this context, Moore speaks of underproduction; capital is constantly trying to reduce the value share of raw materials or circulating capital in relation to machines and buildings (fixed capital), even if (pushed by increasing productivity) the material throughput of raw materials in production increases. This is done through the appropriation of cheap raw materials. If one places more weight on the development of circulating capital than on fixed capital, this also has implications for the law of the falling rate of profit. The appropriation of cheap nature counteracts the fall in the rate of profit. The rate of profit is inversely proportional to the value of raw materials. The overproduction of fixed capital finds its counterpart in the underproduction of circulating constant capital, or to put it another way, capital tries to lower the price of raw materials relative to fixed capital while simultaneously increasing the physical throughput of raw materials (which in turn drives global warming). Malm also mentions this latter point, but without referring to the cheap four "cheaps". In order to increase its own profitability and to beat other companies, a company must not only invest in machines, but also increase labor productivity and intensity with each step. Increased labor productivity also means increased material throughput of raw materials per unit of working time. Production is therefore directly linked to the systems of forestry, energy, mining, and agriculture. In addition, the cheap appropriation of raw materials and energy can not only lower the prices for circulating, but also for fixed capital. Cheap metals also lower the prices of machines.

If one considers technology in the context of the rate of profit, technically better machines, the increase in organizational efficiency, the influence of communication, information, and logistics lead to an increased output of goods and the rate of profit rises. It also increases if wages rise slower than productivity. This was the case in Fordism, while it can also lead to a temporary increase in the rate of profit with a slow increase in wages and a slow increase in productivity, as is sometimes the case in neoliberalism. But even in the analysis of early capitalism, Moore sees further additions as necessary. In the mines, textile production, and agriculture, new techniques and the processes of making nature usable lead to an increase in labor productivity. In early capitalism, technical innovation, systemic violence, and symbolic innovation were mobilized in projects to both extend the working day, increase the intensity of work, and produce and appropriate cheap nature. Polish grain, slaves, and the Norwegian forests, the appropriation of natural fertility functioned for capital like an increase in the production of relative surplus value. (ibid.: 99) There are historical–geographical connections between the increase in labor productivity and the necessary conditions for the reproduction of capital, which for Moore are unimaginable without the appropriation of cheap nature. And these conditions depend on the massive addition of unpaid or cheap labor outside the capital system and wage labor. Appropriated nature itself becomes a productive force. However, the inner logic of capital accumulation deteriorates over time those conditions of production that allow it to provide cheap input for the same. Therefore, new boundaries of appropriation must always be found and overcome in order to set long waves of accumulation in motion. Technological progress, the power of capital, and the sciences open up the possibility for new appropriation surges.

Appropriation deals with how capital can reduce the basic external costs of its production. World-ecological revolutions provide an increasing ecological surplus which represents the gap between the appropriated and the capitalized natures in the end. An ecological revolution takes place precisely when the innovations of capital, the sciences, and the empire enforce a new unity of abstract labor, social nature, and primitive accumulation. Moore refers to this unity as a "world-ecological regime". Technological and organizational innovations allow increasing productivity, while the mapping, quantification, and discovery of new historical natures allow an increasing appropriation of unpaid labor and energy (supported by new imperialisms and land grabs, agro-industrial and scientific revolutions, unpaid labor, soil fertility etc.) Thus, capital constantly asks for labor that is required to make the free resources of nature usable.

However, there is another free effect for capital, which lies in the capital fixe and to which Hans-Joachim Lenger has pointed out. (Lenger, 2004) This is about the "mathesis" of ratio numbers as a technology of information, into which productive labor is inscribed. To put it differently: The industrial dispositives need technological control logics that constantly interfere with the monetary logics of capital. These technologies not only accelerate and revolutionize production and circulation, thus allowing relative surplus value to grow, but they also intervene in the productive and cooperative body of labor and produce a media-structured assemblage that obeys the laws of difference, relation, and speed.

Marx writes about this: "Just as increased exploitation of the wealth of nature by merely higher tension of labor power, science and technology form a power of its expansion independent of the given size of the functioning capital." (MEW 23: 631) In the context of technosciences, Marx also comes to speak of the "free appropriation". To be "free" implies in the economic logic of capital not to be absorbed and to be outside the structures of value and price relations. This free size springs from a difference that does not immediately have an economic status, but remains indispensable to enable capitalization. At this point, Marx distinguishes between general and communal labor. Both merge into each other in the production process, but they also differ. General labor includes, among other things, scientific labor. What Marx calls "general labor" is constituted in differential relations that every technique goes through and objectifies as combinatorial logic in the capital fixe, to form as "mathesis" of machine programs the prerequisite for a cooperation of many workers. (Lenger, 2004) The latter then refers to communal labor as the cooperation of the workers. The free resources arise for capital also through the latter. Thus, economic progress does not take place exclusively in the medium of capital itself, rather it possesses a potency relatively "independent" of capital (nature, science, and cooperation), which capital appropriates "for free". Like a reserve or resource that capital does not need to invest in and yet appropriates, nature, knowledge, and technology appear here as if they were naturally "free".

However, the free appropriation also returns as devastation. Capital, according to Marx, "creates conditions that cause an incurable rift in the connection of the social and the material exchange prescribed by the laws of life, as a result of which the soil power is squandered and this squandering is carried far beyond the borders of one's own country by trade." (MEW 25: 821) The temporality of capital and its logic constantly unleash devastations, which also amount to a hostage-taking of future generations, because their free labor is already presupposed. (Lenger, 2004)

The globe has today become a garbage dump of production sites and the consumption processors of hypermarkets. Regarding the long-standing devastation of the globe, Moore speaks of a "general law of over-pollution" and highlights three aspects (Moore, 2022a, 2022b): First, the law specifies the relational asymmetry between surplus value and over-pollution, with the latter being considered an unbearable form of poisoning. Over-pollution implies a tendency towards non-linear shifts and increases in all kinds of socio-ecological systems. Second, the law emphasizes the central importance of the limits of cheap nature for global accumulation, insofar as every limit in the production of products today also implies a waste limit. In this way, an inseparable connection is established between escalating over-pollution and the imperial projects of waste disposal. Third, the non-linear development of over-pollution in the history of capitalism is shown, with each new ecological regime not only producing more waste, but also qualitatively new and more toxic forms of waste. (ibid.)

Thus, quantitative economic growth in capitalism incessantly drives pollution, leading to qualitative state shifts, among other things, in the biosphere. Carbon dioxide accumulates in the atmosphere, plastic waste in the entire biosphere, nuclear power plants continuously spit out highly toxic radioactive waste without a single final repository existing in the world, and even in space, the earth is encased by a floating garbage dump of rocket and satellite debris. This is no longer about the entropic output of organisms or the earth system, but about the technologized garbage production, which indicates an exosomatic metabolism in modern economy. (Schlaudt, 2021: 50) Schlaudt thus aims at a technologically constituted metabolism of man with nature, with which the production of waste also takes on a new historical-economic dimension. This applies both to the inevitable excretions of the products (waste heat, dust, etc.) and to the products themselves, which are thrown away in masses after consumption (electronic gadgets, etc.). There is now talk of the *toxic world*.

Carbon dioxide is initially just a bundle of molecules, but under certain power and capital relations, it becomes a greenhouse gas. Moore now speaks of the age of the "Wasteocene". (Moore, 2022a, 2022b) Poisoning is therefore not a capitalist accident, but part of the design of capital. And as capital grows, so does waste production, yes it becomes more toxic and "at the same time a growing humanity takes up more and more space, so that the social metabolism no longer has an ›outside space‹ more for the trash, but everything becomes part of the *milieu intérieur*." (Schlaudt, 2021) It is easy to see that capitalism also shapes itself through strategies of cheap nature, which activate qualitatively new potentials of poisoning and trigger potential state shifts of waste production on multiple and increasingly global levels. For Moore, these processes can no longer be stopped or balanced today. The waste limits have been exceeded, but this also means that they have disappeared. We remember Baudrillard's excesses of disappearance, and this applies to the waste limits not only in the sense that the limits become invisible, no, they disappear quite realistically.

At this point, Moore introduces his concept of the rise of negative value, which results from the crossing of the "planetary boundaries" by capital. (Moore 2018) This crossing results from a mix of factors that indicate the dynamics of an impending and catastrophic change for capital, namely a radical increase in production costs. Moore calls the crossing itself a continuous transit from "surplus" to "negative value". The core processes of capital accumulation now increasingly generate direct and immediate obstacles to the extended reproduction of capital. According to Moore, negative value stands for the catastrophic multiplication of biophysical limits for capital in the web of life, which prevent the cheap or cost-effective production of the four cheaps: food, labor, energy, and raw materials. (ibid.: 22) The negative value also crosses the boundaries between the human and the non-human realm and now directly flows into the production costs. The increasing organic composition of capital has the increasingly capitalized composition of global nature as consequence, which in turn promotes negative value. While the increasing organic composition of capital intensifies the tendency towards a falling rate of profit, the capitalization of nature brings with it a number of new problems. One thinks, among other things, of the scarcity of resources, the destabilization of the biosphere, and the associated rising production costs. Negative value touches both capitalization and the processes of appropriation.

The consequences of over-pollution excesses are managed in an increasingly violent way. Negative value now operates in a temporally discontinuous, but tendentially increasing form. Herbicide-resistant superweeds, antibiotic-resistant infections, rampant pandemics, not to mention climate change generated by capital. In short, negative value is not an arithmetic or a subtraction, but a negation of living conditions. (Moore, 2022a, 2022b) The "Wasteocene" illuminates the tendential activation of the general law of overproduction in the history of capitalism. Many wastes in capitalism are not fundamentally toxic, and in modest amounts, they are even necessary by-products of production, just think of the manure produced by livestock farming. However, modern waste has a different quality, in that it indicates a unique negative tendency: decay, death, infection, and contamination. Plastic, with its properties—moldable, easy to process, and light—has driven the trend towards disposable consumption. Many countries are vying for waste today, especially Thailand, Vietnam, and Malaysia. Because what German consumers simply consider plastic waste has long since become a globally traded economic good. Even eco-products do not escape the law of waste: Isn't it premature or unreasonable to put a solar system on a roof, which is the most advanced today, when tomorrow's development will have surpassed it? Every *seized* opportunity is a defeat, every *made* decision is a decision for waste. In this accelerating continuum of waste through the circulation of quasi-objects, the phases of distinction finding, interruption, and reflection are to be further reduced, which also corresponds to an increasing control and appropriation of lived time. Horizontal communication and vertical control.

Already in the 1960s, Günther Anders spoke of a throwaway society or a global cesspool, which for him was still closely tied to industrial mass production. (Anders, 1961) Similar statements can be found in Pierre Klossowski, who associates with mass production a mindset that no longer knows the durability of things. (Klossowski, 1999) In his book *The Living Currency*, Klossowski characterized industrial production with the principle of a production-to-the-extreme, which demands a consumption-to-the-extreme, namely to produce products in series for short-term wear and tear, in order to consequently accustom the consumer, who must pick up on this short-term nature, to completely lose the idea of a durable object. (ibid.) The destruction of durability by machine innovation, by means of which not only the machines, but the consumer products are replaced by others ever faster, is thus already part of industrial and serial mass production. This intensifies the transience and loss of the object and is intended to eliminate any thought of the durability of the objects, whereby they mutate into quasi-objects in their commodity finiteness, that is, they have become calculable and quantifiable and short-term replaceable and are thus as objects null. The objects mutate into non-things. They are nothing. In other words: Every object is now potentially garbage, yes the object is garbage. (Only the price keeps the object alive).

For Klossowski, therefore, one must simply conclude, garbage is not an inevitable side effect of industrial production, but its main purpose, insofar as the manufactured industrial goods are entirely subject to the growth compulsion of capital, which absolutely demands their rapid obsolescence and uselessness as well as their immediate disposal, so that one must indeed come to the conclusion that the real purpose of the goods can only be to be garbage. If marketing today labels every product as new, even as brand new or as a never-before-seen sensation, then in the optimal case the moment of the product's appearance coincides with its disappearance, at least the product is subject to a rapid decay process, because—produced in series—it can only be the precursor of an even newer product. The product thus inherently carries the stigma or the deficiency of the outdated and deficient, its half-life tends towards zero. And garbage is therefore not only what rots on the garbage dumps of the world, but also the huge range of goods on the shelves of supermarkets and in the online shops of Amazon. Commodity garbage is the coming abject, which is not perceived as such. "Waste is the dark, shameful secret of all production. It should preferably remain a secret." (Bauman, 2005: 42)

And it must not be forgotten that this kind of toxic waste is often enough accompanied by an aseptic hyper-hygiene, think for example of the dead food of the food industry, which is made durable by chemical stabilizers. Baudrillard writes: "Once everything will have been cleansed, once an end will have put to all viral processes and to all social and bacillary contamination, then only the virus of sadness will remain, in this universe of deadly cleanliness and sophistication" (Baudrillard 2012b: 37). The perfect consumer good, according to Schlaudt, would then be money itself, "with which we pay for the perishable goods: sterile, wear-free, and eternally durable. Money is the commodity purified of all earthly residue, the purity itself ... Money is therefore the most sublimated twin of garbage, which in turn finds its highest form of intensification in the absolute, unrecyclable residual garbage. With money and garbage, the two poles of the Manichaeism of consumer society are named." (Schlaudt, 2021) And in the end or after the end, only the virus of sadness remains.

Notes

1. Today, China generates more than half of the worldwide steel and cement production, and these two sectors alone are responsible for about 14 percent of global CO_2 emissions. Chinese steel and cement production has become more efficient over the last ten years, but their emissions have nevertheless skyrocketed because production volumes have increased many times over—for cement by three times and for steel by five times compared to fifteen years ago.

2. Automobiles rely on fossil energy (which is a legacy of photosynthesis that dates back hundreds of millions of years) and their spread was enforced in the twentieth century in wide areas and zones of the earth. Moreover, their existence relies on an infrastructure equipped with oil terminals, petroleum refineries, networks of roads, lobbying groups etc., factors that have emerged over longer periods of time.
3. A new study suggests that changes in the circulation of the oceans, which moves the air around the world and is responsible for warming, could be such a driver of a cascade. The melting Greenland ice in a warmer Arctic is a key component of ocean circulation. A further calming of the circulation could lead to a shift in heat production across the globe as well as a collapse of the rainforest in the Amazon, to permanent drought in Africa's Sahel zone, to an influence on the Asian monsoons and a rapid warming of the southern ocean. This could in turn lead to an acute rise in global sea levels, while the West Antarctic ice sheet could break and eventually bring about a shift towards a new climate regime that researchers call "Hothouse Earth". It should be noted that the rise in sea level is not uniform in all regions of the oceans, because it varies with the circulation of the sea, the structure of the coasts and also with the measures for coastal protection.
4. Malm distinguishes three forms of energy: (a) streams of energy that are not captured by photosynthesis and are suitable for the concentrated use of machinery, but remain dependent on landscapes and weather, (b) life force refers to energy sources that are embodied in living creatures and shaped by the imperatives of metabolism, and (c) energy as a stock consists of the relics of stored solar energy from the past that must be extracted from the ground by humans. (Malm, 2016) The history of the industrial revolution shows the replacement of the first two forms of energy by the latter, under very specific economic conditions and phases of class struggles. The early industrialization in England was still based on life force and water in terms of energies, specifically on water mills, while the combustion of coal in this period was merely to provide heat for factories and homes.
5. The problem with this theory, which certainly has references to Carlo Rovelli's relational quantum theory, is that the relationships, by preceding and exceeding the objects, completely determine

these. But how can the object then introduce new and generative movements into such relationships? Thomas Nail, on the other hand, assumes that objects are singular and cannot be completely reduced to relationships (although relations are primary). (Nail, 2018) However, this is because the movements of matter, from which the objects consist of, are not fundamentally determined. Matter is "indefinite fluctuation" at its smallest level. However, these fluctuations are not objects. Movement is indefinite and relationships are indefinite relationships. The constant indefinite movement is a fundamental characteristic of nature. Objects are just as "true" as fluctuating fields, and the idea of replacing one with the other makes no sense, as objects themselves are metastable fields.

6. Philip Mirowski (Mirowski, 1986) has shown how Marx extracted certain parts from the scientific models that were hegemonic in his time to explain the emergence of value, namely parts from thermodynamics and from Newton's physics. Thus, Marx introduced a double measurement of value; the first is based on the working hours per day, the second on the average socially necessary, socially-abstract labor. There is therefore a thermodynamic (Carnot) and a gravitational measurement (Newton), a metric and a topological, one based on horsepower, and one based on a field of forces, a more substantial and a more relational measurement. But this parallelization of the two physics and the associated measurements, which are finally "synthesized" via money and capital, remains insufficient in their specific reduction.
7. We have had the debate about the labor theory of value elsewhere. (Szepanski, 2014a, 2014b)

References

Anders, G. (1961). *Die Antiquiertheit des Menschen 1. Über die Zerstörung des Lebens im Zeitalter der dritten industriellen Revolution*. München.

Baudrillard, J. (2012a). *Von der Verführung*. Berlin.

Baudrillard, J. (2012b). *The Ecstasy of Communication*. Cambridge.

Bauman, Z. (2005). *Verworfenes Leben*. Hamburg.

Klossowski, P. (1999). *Die lebende Münze*. Berlin.

Hui, Y., & Frey, J. (2023). *Kosmotechnik und Kommunismus*. Berlin.

Lenger, H.-J. (2004). *Marx zufolge. Die unmögliche Revolution*. Bielefeld.

Malm, A. (2016). *Fossil Capital: The Rise of Steam Power and the Roots of Global Warming*. London.

Mirowski, P. (1986). *The Reconstruction of Economic Theory*. Cham.

Moore, J. W. (2015). *Capitalism in the Web of Life. Ecology and the Accumulation of Capital*. London.

Moore, J. W. (2018). Cheap Food and Bad Climate: From Surplus Value to Negative Value in the Capitalist World-Ecology. https://jasonwmoore.com/wp-content/uploads/2017/08/Moore-Cheap-Food-and-Bad-Climate-2015-CHS.pdf

Moore, J. W. (2022a). How to Read Capitalism in the Web of Life: Towards a World-Historical Materialism in the Web of Life. https://www.academia.edu/76654904/How_to_Read_Capitalism_in_the_Web_of_Life_Towards_a_World_Historical_Materialism_in_the_Web_of_Life

Moore, J. W. (2022b). Waste in the Limits to Capital: How Capitalism Lays Waste to the Web of Life, and Why It Can't Stop. *Emancipations, 2*(1/4), 1–45.

Nail, T. (2018). *Being and Motion*. Oxford.

Schlaudt, O. (2021). *Müll-Philosophie. Des Teufels Staub und der Engel Anteil*. Merkur. Heft 870. November 2021.

Shaikh, A. (2016). *Capitalism. Competition. Conflict. Crises*. New York.

Szepanski, A. (2014a). *Kapitalisierung Bd.1. Marx' Non-Ökonomie*. Hamburg.

Szepanski, A. (2014b). *Kapitalisierung Bd.2. Non-Ökonomie des gegenwärtigen Kapitalismus*. Hamburg.

CHAPTER 14

The Ecstasy of Information: Big Tech and Platforms

Ecstatic financial speculation, high debt, significantly overvalued tech stocks, massive central bank interventions and, in some territories, state-organized militarized accumulation have kept the global economy running and masked its instability in the face of chronic stagnation in industrial production in recent years, with the exception of China.

While the first phase of capitalist globalization from the 1970s onwards mainly involved the creation of a globally integrated production and financial system supported by logistics, the new waves of digitalization and the rise of big tech and platform companies since the 2008 financial crisis have enabled a very rapid transnationalization of digitally based services. In 2017, these services accounted for around 70 percent of total gross world product and included communications, computing, digital and platform technologies, e-commerce, financial services, and a variety of other non-tangible products such as film and music. (Robinson 2022a) In Western countries, financial companies have jumped on the financial technology (fintech) bandwagon in order to use technically mature models and escape the impending crisis. While Silicon Valley enjoyed unrivaled status for a long time, Chinese tech companies entered the market in the 2010s and have continued to mature under the tutelage of the Chinese Communist Party (CCP). This also provided the impetus for Trump's trade war, which should be seen as a tech war to protect Silicon Valley.

A. Szepanski, *Capitalism in the Age of Catastrophe*, Palgrave Insights into Apocalypse Economics,
https://doi.org/10.1007/978-3-031-57754-3_14

The second cold war between the US and China is primarily about fifth-generation mobile communications (5G) and artificial intelligence (AI) systems, on the basis of which the future data-driven economy is to be organized.

The current digital restructuring of the global economy is progressing at breakneck speed following the coronavirus shock strategy. According to the United Nations, the "sharing economy"—i.e. activities mediated via platforms—will increase to a turnover of 335 billion dollars by 2025. Global shipments of 3D printers reached 6.7 million by the end of 2020 The global value of e-commerce reached an estimated $29 trillion in 2017, equivalent to 36% of global GDP. Exports of digitally delivered services amounted to USD 2.9 trillion in 2018, which in turn accounted for 50% of global services exports. In 2019, the volume of global internet traffic was 66 times the total global internet traffic in 2005, while global internet protocol (IP) traffic, a proxy for data flows, increased from around 100 gigabytes (GB) per day in 1992 to more than 45,000 GB per second in 2017. (UNCTAD: 2019) Machine-to-machine connectivity, specifically blockchain, requires even higher speeds (up to gigabits per second) for the extensive collection and processing of data. In addition to 5G technology, cloud computing will also be necessary.

The coronavirus pandemic has shown just how central digital services have become for the global economy. The pandemic and its consequences, which have accelerated digital restructuring, are leading to a huge expansion of labour-reduced digital services, including all kinds of new teleworking arrangements, drone deliveries, cashless commerce, digitized finance, tracking, and automated medical and legal services. The pandemic has intensified efforts by technology companies to move more and more areas of the economy into these new digital realms. In addition to pharmaceutical companies, it was technology companies in particular that saw a further boost during the pandemic, as their digital services became crucial to the economy when hundreds of millions of workers worldwide had to work from home.

But the new phase of restructuring began after the financial collapse of 2008 and was spearheaded by the big tech companies—including Microsoft, Apple, Amazon, Tencent, Alibaba, Facebook, and Google, who have now been joined by Zoom and other companies that have been boosted by the pandemic. Robinson refers to this as a new block of capital. Apple and Microsoft each had a market capitalization of 1.4 trillion dollars in 2020, followed by Amazon with 1.04 trillion dollars,

Alphabet (Google's parent company) with 1.03 trillion dollars, Samsung with 983 billion dollars, Facebook with 604 trillion dollars and Alibaba and Tencent with around 600 billion and 500 billion dollars respectively. To give you an idea of how quickly these tech giants have grown, you only have to look at Google's market capitalization, which rose from less than 200 billion dollars at the end of 2008 to over one trillion dollars at the beginning of 2020. In just two years, from 2015 to 2017, the total value of all platform companies with a market capitalization of more than USD 100 million increased by 67% to more than USD 7 trillion. (Robinson, 2022b: 64ff.)

A handful of mostly US-based tech companies that generate, extract, and process data have absorbed huge amounts of money from transnational investors from around the world who are desperate for new investment opportunities and have poured billions of dollars into the tech and platform giants as an outlet for their excess accumulated capital. Annual investment in the IT sector rose from $17 billion in 1970 to $65 billion in 1980, then to $175 billion in 1990, $465 billion in 2000 and $654 billion in 2016, before reaching the $800 billion mark in 2019. (ibid.: 65) The big global banks and investment funds are becoming even more closely intertwined with tech capital, as are companies from all over the world that specialize in cloud computing and AI.

Anyone who works with data, whether doctors, lawyers, teachers, or brokers, will have to compete with an algorithmic computing engine that scans, stores, and processes vast amounts of data and may even suggest unconventional answers as a result of the rapid development of AI. The AI revolution could be the first technological revolution to destroy jobs and wages on a large scale. AI affects jobs in many industries and it affects cognitive workers as much as less skilled workers. By allowing machines to scan text and perform their own pattern analysis, distinguishing AI-generated text, images, and audio from human products will become increasingly difficult over time, at least in terms of standards. As a result, a large number of white-collar jobs that require a higher level of cognition will become obsolete. Indeed, AI has initially replaced routine work, but will increasingly be able to take on creative tasks as well.

The next phase of digitization will require large investments that can only be made by the big tech companies. In recent decades, computerization has already increased fixed capital costs, which has had a negative impact on profit rates in many countries. Since digitized machines are expensive, we can expect further attempts by capital to lower wage rates. Because automated machines can work for twenty-four hours but require at least expert supervision, new issues of working time regulation and organization arise. A wave of deindustrialization could now also hit the Global South if production outsourcing to developing countries is reversed and production facilities are relocated back to the capitalist core countries.

The rise of the digital economy goes hand in hand with the merging of the Silicon Valley empire with transnational finance capital and the military-industrial-security complex, creating a new capital bloc that appears to form the core of the emerging post-pandemic paradigm. This new bloc will be even more powerful than it was at the beginning of the pandemic, driving a vast new centralization and concentration of capital on a global scale. (ibid.)

Familiar things like satellite surveillance, enormous computing capacity on silicon chips, sensors, networks, and predictive analytics are now part of the global digital systems that are currently also comprehensively quantifying, analysing, evaluating, and capitalizing on the lives and behaviour of populations. These are no longer technologies of power and energy, but media technologies that store, process, transmit, and display information. The excess of these media technologies leads to a superfluous overflow, the operational and at the same time delirious stuffing of systems with information that is to be stored and recorded down to the last piece of information. Baudrillard speaks of an obesity of simulation. (Baudrillard, 1991: 32).

Under pressure from the financial markets, Google, for example, feels compelled to constantly increase the effectiveness of its data tracking and its analyses generated by machine intelligence and, for this very reason, to combat any user claim to privacy protection with the most diverse means. Thanks to a range of devices such as laptops and smartphones, cameras and sensors, computers are now ubiquitous in capitalized everyday life; they are sign-living machines that execute algorithms (calculable, formally unambiguous procedural instructions) and only develop their full power in the context of digital media networking, for which the program-controlled design, transformation and reproduction of all media formats is a prerequisite. In this game, social networks in particular enable a type of economy that has established a new algorithmic governance based on the extraction of personal data, which leads to the construction of metadata, cookies, tags, and other tracking technologies. This development has become known primarily as "big data", a system based on networking, databases and high computer performance and capacity. Since the 2010s, data has been generated in new dimensions—2.5 trillion (quintillion) bytes per day in 2018.[1] In the years 2016–2018 alone, 90 percent of the data volumes generated worldwide in human history up to that point were generated. It should also be noted that AI is by no means immaterial. By 2027, AI could be responsible for 4.2 to 6.6 billion cubic meters of water extraction. That's more than the entire annual water withdrawal of Denmark.

Like all governance, if we think of it in Foucault's terms, algorithmic governance also implements specific technologies of power, but today they are no longer based on statistics relating to the average or the norm; instead, we are dealing with an automated, atomic, pulsating, and probability-based artificial machine intelligence, which operates forensics and data mining independently of the respective medium—automatic computing collects, records, and capitalizes data on the behaviour of market participants, who are controlled by means of the extraction of their data by tech companies and whose behaviour is also capitalized on, at a rapid speed, close to that of light, using the methods of artificial machine intelligence. The digital machines that continuously collect data and read and evaluate data traces thus mobilize an a-normative and a-political rationality that insists on the automatic analysis and monetary valorization of enormous amounts of data by modelling, anticipating, and thus influencing the behaviour of agents.[2] Today, this is trivially referred to as ubiquitous computing, in which tech capital no longer only extracts user behavior and produces the prediction products created by the algorithms on this basis on the Internet, but also in the real world, in order to then constantly diversify and deepen the prediction products using special processes. For example, signals from cars, fridges, houses, and bodies etc. are constantly flowing as data into the digital networks, which are sold to advertising customers who run targeted advertising. (Zuboff, 2018: 225).

For Zuboff, companies such as Google and Facebook automate the purchasing behavior of consumers by channeling it through the feedback loops of AI machines and targeting it to those companies that are advertisers of these companies. However, the targeting of advertisers remains imprecise to this day. The sales-promoting behavioral modifications that are to be achieved among users are based on machine processes and techniques such as tuning (adaptation to a system), herding (tailoring of the masses), and conditioning (training of stimulus–response patterns), which guide the behavior of users in such a way that the machine-generated prediction products actually drive their actions in the direction of the intentions guaranteed by Google or Facebook. (ibid.) The predictability of user behavior is now a genuine source of profit: the consumer who uses a fitness app should ideally buy a healthy beverage product at the moment of maximum receptivity, for example after jogging, which is made palatable to them through targeted advertising. Sportswear manufacturer Nike, for example, has bought the data analysis company Zodiac and uses it in its stores in New York. When a customer with the Nike app on their smartphone enters a store, they are recognized and categorized by the geofencing software. The start page of the app changes immediately and instead of online offers, the new items in the store appear on the screen, i.e. special offers and recommendations tailored to the customer. Particularly loyal customers receive small gifts in the store and can even have the desired goods delivered to their changing room via smartphone.

Systems theory assumes that psychological systems cannot observe the rhizomatic arrangement of meaning on the internet. The meaning-referencing operations mechanized by hyperlinks produce one thing above all, namely incoherence, a fluid system that can no longer be brought to unity, which externalizes knowledge and information on hard drives. (Fuchs, 2023: 259) As a system whose center can be anywhere and whose boundary is nowhere, the Internet constantly offers new possibilities for fakes, ressentiment, and the reinforcement of imposance, which virtually challenge the disinhibition of communication and simulation, because there are hardly any stop rules or stopping points in the network. The metaphor of surfing refers to a fragile and wild trip with which psychological systems are socialized on the Internet in order to repeat what the simulation operates socially on a psychological level by learning to perceive the relationship between reality and fiction, as Fuchs says, as blurring. (ibid.: 267) This blurring takes place without any depth and leads to those borderline blurs that Baudrillard plays around with his concept of simulation—by means of operations that seemingly wildly and repeatedly create the difference between before and after, whereby it is not entirely certain whether psychic systems can even perceive this de-ontologized hyperreality (as a hyper-a-social system).[3] In surfing, we experience effects serially, accumulating them in a way that intensifies and creates resonances and interference patterns that move through the successive links. Link after link, we click into a lull. This lull is an expression of transductive momentum—the impulse to continue the transition—and explains the strange attraction of surfing.

Tech capital is no longer just about selling advertising; rather, it quickly became the model for capital accumulation in Silicon Valley, adopted by nearly every start-up to this day. But the model is not limited to individual companies or the Internet sector, but has spread to a large number of companies across various sectors and industries, including insurance, healthcare, finance, cultural industries, transportation, etc. Almost every product or service that starts with the word "smart" or "personalized", every internet-connected device, every "digital assistant" represents an interface in the corporate supply chain for the invisible flow of behavioral data on the way to predicting the future in a surveillance economy.

In the role of investor, Google quickly abandoned its avowed antipathy to advertising, opting instead to increase profits by leveraging exclusive access to user data waste in combination with analytical capabilities and high computing power to generate predictions about user click-through rates, which can be seen as a signal of the relevance of an advertisement. Operationally, Google transformed its growing data volumes to "work" as behavioral data surplus, while simultaneously developing new methods to aggressively skim behavioral surplus. This includes data-intensive cloud services.

It is no longer enough to automate the information streams that illuminate the population in the present; the goal is now to predict the population's future behavior as accurately as possible. These processes are constantly being redesigned to eliminate any possibility of user self-determination, which is not insignificant for the capital markets if the predictions about the behavior of populations are not only probable, but approach the certainty that the desired behavior will occur. However, such adjustment processes are never likely to be completely successful. However, the more behavioral surplus one acquires, the more accurate the predictions are, and the more the surplus can be varied, the higher the predictive value. This new drive of the economy leads from desktops via smartphones into the real world—you drive, walk, store, look for a parking space, your blood circulates and you show your face—everything is to be recorded, localized, and marketed.

The resources of workers who have already been cheapened by capital can now also be tapped. The workers who work in Amazon's centers are tracked and observed, providing the double amount of time for the company, which profits monetarily from the work on the one hand, while accumulating data on the movement of bodies in space on the other. This magical trick of collecting data as a by-product of various types of cheap labor is a major coup for capital and another opportunity for the extraction of any human residue. As Jason E. Moore says, the four cheapies (labor here) allow new strategies to survive crises because the exploitation of cheap data helps reduce stagnant productivity by capturing all kinds of existing work as a service to data-producing machines. (Moore, 2015) The rise of cheap data is not just about the data pulled from human behavioral processes. As Google and Facebook work to manipulate clicks and behaviors, data is being collected from the movement of machines to the growth of plants to the movement of interest rates. This data is used in various ways to train learning machine systems to manipulate populations or create new markets.[4]

Behavioral surpluses also arise from rendering more behavioral data than necessary to feed into artificial machines (ranking, statistical modeling, prediction, speech recognition, and visual transformation) that then produce predictions about user behavior. Zuboff describes these predictions as quasi-derivatives that tech capital sells to the highest bidders on the behavioral futures markets. (Zuboff, 2018: 105) It can be concluded that algorithmic operations with data generate such profitable products, which aim to predict and monetize the future behaviour of users, for very specific companies: Google's important customers are those who need advertising and pay Google to provide them with an effective range of predictive products, which in turn are based on the comprehensive monitoring of users. These products are therefore based on Google trying to predict exactly what users are doing, thinking, and feeling now and in the near future (ibid.: 119), which is also intended to limit the risk for advertisers so that relatively safe bets can be made on future behavior. However, the addressees of the markets in which Google sells prediction products are not exclusively advertising customers, but ultimately everyone who has an interest in purchasing "probabilistic information," (ibid.: 120) including, for example, states, especially their intelligence services, which therefore maintain a close relationship with the companies in Silicon Valley.

The prediction machines are a kind of black box whose internal processes are far beyond the capacity of human perception. At this point, Zuboff speaks of a shadow text in which the machines provide the relevant instructions for action, which are mostly aimed at influencing user consumption. For example, the algorithmized selection of images that Instagram shows a user includes streams of that user's behavioral data, the data of their friends, data of people who follow the same account as the user, as well as data and links of their activities on Facebook. (ibid.: 555) There is a multitude of data and operations that even the programmers of the machines can no longer understand.

However, when Zuboff focuses so much on the area of expropriation, extraction, and control of data, she largely limits her arguments to a critique of surveillance and thus does not provide a deeper analysis of the relationship between capital and labor. Zuboff logically distances herself from theories of "digital labor." Accordingly, Zuboff does not have much to say about the extraction of surplus value in the digital realm. AI is claimed to be the continuation of data analysis techniques first promoted by government agencies and the military, cultivated by intelligence agencies, and finally developed by internet companies into a planetary business of surveillance and prediction. These techniques produce actors who are understood merely as passive subjects of measurement and control (not as collective actors). Zuboff bases it on Harvey's theory of "accumulation by dispossession" and presents it as an ongoing process in the digital industries as well. When Zuboff analyses Google's procedures for the extraction and expropriation of user data in detail and correctly, she writes of a parasitic economic logic, but without considering further capitalization strategies for data. And Zuboff cannot imagine that the expropriation of user data is not the sole source of Google's exorbitant profits. Talk of surveillance capitalism only describes one aspect of digitalization. In digital capitalism, the processes of capital accumulation and the constitution of power are organized by means of digital technologies and lead to digital goods and digital structures. Computers are integrated into networks in which texts, video images, websites, and platforms are linked on the basis of relational structures and algorithms. Digital practices and digital structures are formed as modes of existence of technical networks and objects (Simondon), which have their own logic and development in the areas of production, distribution, and circulation. The server farms of Facebook and Google are technological structures that store large amounts of personal data, but at the same time the practices of searching, clicking, liking, and uploading remain important.

What Zuboff continues to largely ignore: Google produces a commodity—real-time access to vast amounts of human knowledge—that is cheap to produce, insofar as Google does not pay the publishers and creators of content whose pages are indexed for their production and their products. (Morozov, 2022) Google gives away its search functions for free, which in turn enables it to sell a highly profitable product—the attention of its users—to advertisers. Zuboff writes of indexed information that Google's web crawlers take without payment. It is easy to see why this function does not meet Zuboff's own definition of expropriation, because no users are involved. (ibid.) The enormous success of Google's business model suggests that the company's practices are not characterized by "information feudalism" but, as Morozov writes, are advertised as "information communism." (ibid.) Thus, one can justify the lofty goal of unlimited, free indexing of information produced by others, as if there were no property rights—including rights of access and use.

There is often talk of a kind of techno-feudalism whose agents draw rents. What gives the digital economy its neo—and techno-feudal character is the fact that, like the feudal lords, it manages to appropriate huge portions of the global mass of surplus value without ever being directly involved in the exploitation of labor or the production process. The French economist Durand also draws on Zuboff's work to demonstrate the hidden domination exercised by the producers of big data, arguing that the secret of Google's success lies in its ability to extract, compile, and profit from a multitude of data sets. Due to network effects and impressive economies of scale, Google enjoys an effective monopoly: the company will profit more from new data sets than a start-up company, making competition much more difficult. (Durand, 2023).

However, the basic tenor of the argument here is too user-centric, as Durand, like Zuboff, ignores the crucial role of indexing in Google's overall operations. The third-party sites that Google links to in order to produce its search results remain the property of their publishers; Google does not own the information it indexes. Theoretically, any other well-funded company could develop web crawling technology for its indexing. However, this could be extremely expensive, but one should not confuse such obstacles with a rent-like situation: What's expensive for a Berlin start-up might be relatively affordable for a big bank. You can't pretend, Morozov says, that Google's business is all about extracting data, that Google is purely a rentier—and not also a capitalist company. (Morozov, 2022 Enforceable property rights, which allow the owner of productive resources such as land to exclude other capitalists from access to these resources, create "rents." These rents are part of the surplus value generated in capitalist production, although they have no direct relation to the exploitation of productive labor power. The owner of land resources such as fields, waterfalls, mineral and hydrocarbon deposits, etc. has a free advantage in his function as a rentier when he brings resources into play to share in the surplus value generated by productive wage labor. But if, by analogy, tech companies are just rentiers generating profits virtually for free by exploiting intellectual property rights and network effects, why are they investing so much money in what can be called a kind of production? Alphabet's R&D spending in 2017, 2018, 2019 and 2020 amounted to $16.6 billion, $21.4 billion, $26 billion and $27.5 billion respectively. (ibid.)[5] If one accepts that Google is engaged in the production of goods with search results—a process that requires massive capital investment—there is no great difficulty, Morozov argues, in treating Google as a capitalist company engaged in capitalist production. This is not to say that the digital giants do not employ other strategies and tactics to consolidate their power.[6]

However, Morozov asks too little about the specificity of these new tech companies. Originating from the military-industrial complex and driven by the search for new markets, cyber-capitalism operates through a material ensemble of social practices, meanings and technological apparatuses; it is a global conglomerate of multiple layers of systems and standards, machines and management, commodities and communication, ideologies and interoperability, products and protocols. These layers are integrated via cybernetic feedback loops. The cyber-tech sector is capitalistically structured and driven by profit extraction, competition, investment, and innovation; it is subject to speculative bubbles and booms that did not exist under feudalism—even if it is characterized by supposedly non-capitalist but quite familiar practices such as monopolization, market manipulation, nationalism, and proximity to the military-industrial complex. Each of the big tech companies has its own strategically diversified businesses, ranging from social media advertising to business logistics, video games, and semiconductor manufacturing. These companies are also subject to a high degree of volatility. Behind their rise today are large asset management firms such as Vanguard Group and BlackRock. These companies are also shaped by cybernetics, digitality, and quantum theory. BlackRock attributes much of its success to its big data system, Aladdin, which manages huge investment portfolios not only for BlackRock, but also for its competitors Vanguard and State Street, as well as Alphabet, Apple, Microsoft, and the major insurance companies. Through Aladdin, BlackRock controls a key component of the financial sector's digital infrastructure. This fusion of financial power and techno-scientific domination elevates finance itself to an even more abstract level and can be considered a key component of cyber-capitalism.

Platforms

The English term "platform" comes from the software industry and refers to the technology of the application (hardware) or to an operating system, which in turn leads to a specific software development. In the context of the Internet, the concept of the platform is a result of the dotcom crash in 2001, when highly valued IT companies in particular were unable to meet the profit expectations set by the financial markets, threatening the IT industry with a comprehensive financial and symbolic collapse, to which platform companies were introduced in response in order to reorganize the sector.

Platforms are initially to be understood as companies that provide online offerings or offer a specific service. To this end, the companies provide a digital infrastructure and architecture through which communication and interaction between two or more players can be mediated: Drivers, customers, advertisers, service providers, producers, logistics companies, and physical objects. The platforms generate their economic success through the exploitation of data and the utilization of third-party activities. They are part of the "sharing economy", within which services such as cab rides (Uber), food deliveries (Deliveroo), apartments and rooms (Airbnb) etc. are organized via applications in such a way that customers can book certain services via their smartphone. To do this, the platforms absolutely need the formally independent service providers/ employees and the users (crowd) and their activities on the internet in order to generate customers, while their employees have to provide their own work equipment. Material costs and risks are thus outsourced to the employees, who can therefore also be described as "contingency workers".

The platforms are not responsible for the content produced on their websites, but provide the technical infrastructure and thus control the form. The platforms function as algorithmized and automated online markets and act as intermediaries, although it cannot be ruled out that they would be superfluous if suppliers and consumers met directly. Therefore, they are structurally forced to control the data flows produced by users and to oligopolize communications with so-called lock-in strategies. In the course of specific competitive mechanisms, platforms often push themselves between producers and customers with cheap offers, and the corresponding network effects can lead to massive oligopolization. All platforms reserve the right to change the structures of their business at any time.

The platforms can be roughly categorized. Companies such as Ali-baba and Amazon access users from two sides. On the one hand, they monetize their data and demand, and on the other, they advertise their products and services by selling them. There are also platforms that finance themselves mainly through advertising (Google, Facebook) by extracting information and data from users in order to analyze it and use the results to offer advertising space.

There are also cloud platforms (AWS, Salesforce), which identify themselves as owners of the hardware and software of digital businesses and rent them out when there is demand. Another type is industrial platforms (GE, Siemens), which produce hardware and software to transform traditional production processes into processes based on the internet and thus reduce production costs, i.e. transforming products into digital services. There are product platforms (Rolls Royce, Spotify) that generate profits by using other platforms to convert a product into a service and charging rents or fees for this. Finally, there are platforms (Uber, Airbnb) that operate with almost no ownership of assets.

Amazon, Apple, and Facebook are among the largest companies in the world in terms of market capitalization, although they are distanced from what is usually referred to as the productive sphere of the capitalist economy, in which goods and services are produced. At least Apple produces smartphones among other products, although its "production" is more a design of a number of products that other companies produce and that Apple, as an oligopolist, can sell in a barely controlled market structure, not to mention its extensive activities in the financial markets. Alibaba and Amazon are in the e-commerce business as platforms that sell other companies' products for a fee. Alibaba is also heavily involved in financial transactions, while Amazon is a big player in cloud computing services. What these rapidly expanding companies have in common, apart from Alibaba, is that they are based in the USA. The dominance of the US as a territory for these top companies is based on a large and relatively affluent population, which enables a market in which start-ups can still grow into corporations because very wealthy individuals invest large sums of money in potentially successful ideas. Even today, more than half of Google/Alphabet's revenues come from the US. This is a mechanism by which existing privileges secure future privileges.

In the "sharing economy", the digital interfaces, which are now called platforms, control and manage work in a completely restructured labor market. The drivers and bicycle couriers of new platforms such as Uber and Wolt differ from the dependent employees of traditional companies in that they offer a service themselves, whereby the means to carry out the service that a platform app provides them with must be provided by themselves, be it a car or a bicycle and in any case a smartphone. What is worn out during the performance of the service is therefore the property of the drivers and couriers. The drivers, who are allowed to pick up passengers by Uber, for example, are under strict digitalized control and are also forced to follow the platform's algorithms in terms of location. The routes they take are dictated by the GPS system, while their efficiency, availability, and interaction with passengers are subject to constant evaluation, which then determines how, when and where the drivers are deployed.

The drivers and couriers do not act as official employees, but are private contractors to the platform companies. Far from offering an alternative to precarious work, those who ultimately provide the service for customers oscillate between the restrictive conditions of wage labor and the risk of self-employment. This means that the service providers who use the platforms' offerings are freed from the repression of wage labor, but also from the social guarantees that come with it (because the platforms often do not pay social security contributions). In this way, they seem to represent the epitome of neoliberal subjects. At least the personal dependency on a boss who sweetens a working day with all kinds of orders disappears, because the drivers have little to do with the organizers of the platform, even in an emergency it is hardly possible to contact them. So it is apparently up to the drivers themselves how they organize their working day, but they are never allowed to slow down while working and they have to keep up with the competition at all costs, so they simply have to pedal as hard as they can.

The companies always increase the hourly wage for the most effective of their drivers, but this means nothing other than that the permanent monitoring and automated evaluation of the drivers' performance ensures competition, comparison, and scaling in the long term. In the case of self-employed drivers, earnings are measured by the number of deliveries made. And this usually also increases the willingness to take risks while driving and thus, incidentally, the drivers' demand for accident insurance benefits; the rising insurance premiums reflect the courage to take risks, which in turn boosts the drivers' performance, because they also have to earn the money for the accident insurance. If no orders are received during a shift, the drivers do not receive a wage, but their working time is seamlessly transformed into free time. However, because the couriers can't do anything with this free time and don't want to—who wants to eat their way through the paralyzing mash of everyday life—not only are the really stressful shifts the most popular with self-employed drivers, but they are also constantly asking for new shifts. As a rule, drivers reliably clear the market and, due to their own lack of financial resources, are constantly reporting a need for further shifts, thereby increasing the demand for courier jobs, which is why the algorithm can further worsen the financial conditions for its customers with every update, although this in no way leads to a noticeable drop in demand.

For many theorists, the large platforms are nothing more than the assemblage of commercial contracts between a "principal authority", which concludes contracts on behalf of the company, and a multiplicity of agents who independently provide services for the companies. The platforms thus multiply partnerships that are based on purely commercial encounters and on the basis of which services are offered to third parties without regulated employment contracts and wage labor. (However, it is still virtually impossible for a number of companies in various sectors to produce without hiring wage labor). Finally, employees are not only dependent on their own work, but also on their integration into social networks that are structured by ratings and rankings and other ordering procedures, and this also means that the exploitation of their labor resources and their risk management ultimately depend on evaluations that are favored by positive ratings and whose accumulation must necessarily succeed. Thus, a driver's own work performance and the promotion of their skills in the course of self-marketing constantly require positive evaluation and recognition from customers, which manifests itself in scores, likes, friends, and followers, and optimizing these ratings is an important task for a driver. The accumulation of reputational capital must necessarily result in an efficient credit score in order to gain the trust of banks and insurance companies. The sustainability of the service providers' operations thus depends much more on the approval of lenders and sponsors than on the entrepreneurial ethos emphasized by neoliberal ideologues or the price of human capital to be increased, whereby the sponsors are mostly financial speculators who use means of production based on digital machines for the extraction and forecasting of certain resources and raw materials (in this case the behavior of users), which serve to profitably modify the behavior of customers, which in turn cannot be achieved without total control of the drivers.

On the platforms'webpages, the platforms assign their service providers a specific set of assets to be continuously evaluated, which the employees must combine, move and manage as part of their "reputational capital". Some theorists see the management of "reputational capital" as the main resource that the mobile players have to cultivate in order to rise up the company hierarchy or simply survive. Eventually, service providers, such as drivers or couriers, will have to maintain a Facebook hyperpage themselves, where the various recommendations from friends, mentors, lenders, sponsors, customers, and service providers are documented. These open profile portfolios, designed by algorithms, make it possible to show the attractiveness and trustworthiness of a person, to determine their reputational value and thus their suitability for a job, a credit line or a partnership. Obviously, private asset managers now have to speculate on their own reputational capital or follow the speculation of others.

Notes

1. According to Bernard Stiegler, the processes involved are those of "grammatization". (Stiegler 2016: 19) In the digital stage, these lead to individuals being guided through a world in which their behaviour is grammatized when they interact with computer systems that operate in real time. For Stiegler, however, grammatization begins with cave paintings and leads via the media of cuneiform writing, photography, film, and television to the computer, the internet, and the smartphone. The result of all this is that the data paths and traces generated by today's technologies of computerization constitute ternary attention-reducing retentions or mnemonics that include specific time procedures and individuation processes, i.e. "industrialization processes of memory" or a "political and industrial economy based on the industrial exploitation of consciousness times". (ibid.: 160f.) According to Stiegler, the digitalization of data paths and processes, which today function intrusively by means of sensors, interfaces, and other means and are basically generated as binary numbers and calculable data, creates an automated social body in which even human life is transformed into an agent of the hyper-industrial economy of capital. Deleuze already foresaw this development in his famous essay on control societies, but the forms of control will only reach their full potential when digital

calculation integrates the modulations of control techniques identified by Deleuze into algorithmic governance, which also includes the automation of all existences, ways of life, and cognitions.

2. The new automated systems model the social in real time, contextualizing and personalizing social interactions, whether in healthcare, business, or administration. The new algorithmic governance includes technologies with territorial and spatial dimensions, which are used, for example, in the "Smart and Sensored Cities" programs. With Google's Street View, Google is turning public space into an impersonal space of spectacle, transforming it into a living tourist brochure with the sole aim of monitoring and extracting data from users (Zuboff 2018: 169), so that ultimately we can even speak of an expropriation of paths and space, precisely because Google succeeds beyond the exploitation of online data sources in monitoring the real world more and more comprehensively across the board, when people are permanently tracked along certain paths and at the same time still steered to certain destinations via behavior modification machines. These smart instruments are based on "automatic computing" and "ambient computing", i.e. on technologies whose invisibility makes individuals even more active and efficient, because these technologies weave themselves into the factory of life unnoticed and yet at the same time stimulating and reinforcing behavior until they are indistinguishable from it. Algorithmic governance focuses entirely on relations, on relations of relations, which in turn are reduced to correlations, because the models of artificial neural networks determine correlations and patterns in particular, but never causes or the explanation of causalities; they serve to classify, bundle, and optimize behaviour. They are based on stochastic random walk models or sequence generators. In their essay on algorithmic governance, the sociologists Berns and Rouvroy show that the size, speed. and performativity of algorithms - elements that relate to relational data processing - far exceed the capacities of human decision-making. They describe this governance, characterized by technological performativity, as a certain kind of (a)normative or (a)political rationality based on the automated collection, aggregation, and analysis of big data in order to model, anticipate, and preemptively influence possible behaviours. (Berns/Rouvroy 2013: 177f.) Google can easily predict that someone will probably want to buy a suit in the near future, and if this person is near a shop

window behind which suits are on display, an advertisement pops up on their cell phone recommending the purchase of a suit on display. Life itself is immersed in data production, in a pulsating blaze of information, but beyond that we ourselves have become data in relation to machines that capture, assimilate. and process our lives, as if we ourselves were parts that are modulated and held ready for machine intelligences. All this no longer needs to be made explicit, because it is part of the habitus through which subjects themselves are machinized as they stream, update, capture, share, link, verify, map, secure, troll, and trash, even if it produces the ultimate boredom. The investments that affect the dividuum today extend to genetic manipulation. Neurotransmitters, organs, biological components, and somatic identities are available for exchange. Also worth mentioning are the military implementation of robotics and artificial intelligence research, the process of a second evolutionary epoch through artificial life research, and the technical access to the genetic basis of the human body through molecular biology as described by Baudrillard. A rapid ecstasy of risk production sets in. In line with Baudrillard, Thomas Metzinger speaks of a multilayered momentum of these processes, which are largely unreflected and politically uncontrolled. (Metzinger 2023) This is why, especially today, because we know that the brain is "extim" for the self, it is important to consider what a neuronal correlate of consciousness means. Metzinger cites here, for example, the problem of cosmetic psychopharmacology in the form of the long-term use of suitable mood enhancers. In general, it can be assumed with Bifo Berardi, Metzinger. and Baudrillard that the human brain today drifts in a flow of media complexes from radio, television, and the Internet; these are systems and their environments that are characterized by immense dynamics of their own, constant growth and increasing transmission speeds. While Metzinger speaks here of a jungle for which our brains were not created, Baudrillard calls this the ecstasy of simulation. What's more, technical systems are now beginning to reconfigure human brains. It degenerates into an all-encompassing enthusiasm for freedom when the body is constantly cannibalized in relation to the monetary. Even the body mutates into a profitable company, think of implants, transplants, and surgical interventions, and sales are made with it, be it organs, blood, or germ cells. "Self-tracking"—the extraction, collection, counting, and evaluation of data on all conceivable characteristics and functions of one's own body using various apps and processes - describes a new form of self-optimization. Such apps and technologies can automatically record, catalog and then graphically display all kinds of data.

3. The problem that the state and traditional mass media have with the Internet is that their own disinhibition exaggerations put them in competition with a wild, disinhibited hyperreality to which they are inherently inferior. Now, for the first time, the state, which is always on the verge of encroachment (the police work in this dark zone), is losing its monopoly. The internet offers structurally uninhibited communication, it does not set any stopping points and it is simply impossible (despite algorithmic power) to control its escalation orgies. You can only switch it off, which is what happens in an emergency.
4. A company like Google needs to obtain certain levels of diversification resources when collecting data that reflects user behavior and is also used to track excess behavior (Google's data exhaust) in order to effectively convert the data into predictive products using its machine intelligence and sell them to advertising customers in a targeted manner. The products go after the user like "heat-seeking missiles" (Zuboff) in order to suggest exactly the right fitness product via displayed advertising when the user has a pulse of 78, for example. Thus, with increasing diversification, a broad diversification of monitorable topics in the virtual world must be achieved on the one hand, and extraction operations must be shifted from the network to the real world on the other. In addition, algorithmic operations must gain depth, i.e. they must target the intimacy of users in order to intervene in their behavior in a controlling and formative way, for example by displaying pay buttons on the smartphone at the right time and in the right place or automatically blocking a car if the person concerned has not paid certain insurance amounts on time. The wealth of data that tech capital's analysts can now draw on is infinite. They know exactly who complains to companies, calls hotlines, or complains about a company on online portals and how often. We know the favorite stores, restaurants, and pubs of many consumers, the number of their "friends" on Facebook, the creator of ads that social media users have clicked on. We know the color of a person's skin, their gender, their financial situation, their physical illnesses, and mental health problems.

5. Amazon also spent 42.7 billion dollars on research and development in 2020 alone and employed over one million people worldwide. (Morozov, 2022) In the USA, the company employs more people than the entire residential construction industry. Morozov asks whether tech capitalists are really outside of production when they spend large sums of money on research and development. Even more telling, a close analysis of the balance sheets of Google, Amazon. and Facebook shows that they own fewer intangible assets than other large companies—in fact, they own fewer intangible assets today than they did ten to fifteen years ago.
6. The behavioral surplus model and the metaphors that are supposed to characterize it, describing the data as fluid, cascading, and overflowing, also partly ignores the production of cheap data, which is often enough characterized by concentrated, but at the same time cheap and tedious work. When users voluntarily upload thousands of images of faces, which are then used by the owners of the platforms, these images often need additional tagging or categorization in order to be useful for commercial purposes, because the images do not describe themselves. This is where cheap labor comes into play. The digital piecework of workers like those employed by Amazon's Me-chanical Turk is essential to producing the cheap data collections that many AI systems and research projects require. ImageNet, the main database of images using visual object recognition software development, relies on the work of MTurk workers who sort and tag millions of images every day to compile them into datasets used by military research or companies like IBM, Alibaba, and Sensetime, the latter two companies providing the technology the Chinese government uses to control the minority Uyghur population, for example. New research has highlighted the stress and horror of workers employed in digital factories when they have to sort out images of ISIS crimes, for example, or spend days scanning social platforms for hate speech and violent videos. Like all cheap things, cheap data relies on massive externalities to mitigate risk where possible or shift it to other people and natures, while profits flow in the opposite direction. But the mental damage to workers is only one of the externalities that arise from the hunt for cheap data. The cheap energy required to train AI models and massively transfer large amounts of data to and from the cloud is less visible than the exploited workers, but the cumulative effects are enormous. Studies

estimate that the energy needed to train a single AI model has five times the CO2 emissions of the average car over its lifetime. The hardware needed to handle all these models and collect the data requires a high amount of valuable metals and plastic. Cheap nature is needed when extracted from cheap labor to make the fiber optic cables and computers that collect and connect data. (Moore, 2015)

References

Baudrillard, J. (1991). *Die fatalen Strategien*. Semiotext(e).

Durand, C. D. (2023). The End of Financial Hegemony? The New Left Review. https://newleftreview.org/issues/ii138/articles/cedric-durand-the-end-of-financial-hegemony

Fuchs, P. (2023). *Das System Selbst*. Velbrück.

Metzinger, T. (2023). *Bewusstseinskultur. Spiritualität, intellektuelle Redlichkeit und die planetare Krise*. München.

Moore, J. W. (2015). *Capitalism in the Web of Life. Ecology and the Accumulation of Capital*. London.

Morozov, E. (2022). Critique of Techno-Feudal Reason. https://newleftreview.org/issues/ii133/articles/evgeny-morozov-critique-of-techno-feudal-reason

Robinson, W. I. (2022a). *Can Global Capitalism Endure?* SCB Distributors.

Robinson, W. I. (2022b). *Global Civil War: Capitalism Post-Pandemic (Kairos)*. Oakland.

Stiegler, B. (2016). *The Automated Society. The Future of Work*. Polity.

UNCTAD. (2019). United Nations Conference on Trade and Development (UNCTAD). *Digital Economy Report 2019* (New York). https://unctad.org/en/PublicationsLibrary/der2019_en.pdf

Zuboff, S. (2018). *Das Zeitalter des Überwachungskapitalismus*. Frankfurt/M.

CHAPTER 15

Surplus Population

While the accumulation of capital at the beginning of the twentieth century brought about a shift of the working population from agriculture to industry, at the end of the twentieth century, at least in the capitalist core countries, there was a transfer of capital from industrial production areas to the financial, service, and information sectors, thereby causing deindustrialization. At this point, one should remember Marx's law of capitalist accumulation, which states that with increasing capital accumulation, both an industrial reserve army, which is in relation to official wage labor, and a surplus population outside the official labor markets develop, with the first population group being subsidized by the state for a long time, while the surplus population tries to secure its reproduction with slave labor, part-time jobs, and activities in the informal sector. The important membrane here is between the industrial reserve army (as part of the official labor market) and the surplus population, which is located outside the official labor market and is pushed worldwide, but especially in the Global South, into informational, semi-legal, or illegal economies. Marx already introduces the terms of relative and absolute surplus population. On the one hand, he speaks of the industrial reserve army as a cyclical phenomenon, insofar as it flows into or falls out of production depending on the degree of capital accumulation (relative). Marx also believes in a long-term tendency that leads to a disproportionate growth

A. Szepanski, *Capitalism in the Age of Catastrophe*, Palgrave Insights into Apocalypse Economics,
https://doi.org/10.1007/978-3-031-57754-3_15

of the industrial reserve army compared to the entire working population. If this reserve army grows strongly in the long term, part of it must eventually fall out of the wage labor relationship due to the technical development of production and disappear from the official labor market, so it can no longer be used as variable capital at all (absolute). This development should also be empirically investigated based on technological developments at the level of the world market. The global proletariat today, in addition to the wage-dependent, collectively secured working class with relatively high wages (core staff) in the Western countries, also includes the precariat and a surplus population of over a billion, who are denied any access to the official labor markets and must reproduce in informal and non-capitalist economies or vegetate in slums, that is, exist as accumulated corpse-like existence.[1] It is these totally dispossessed, the masses of unemployed, the day laborers, and the Asian and African migrant workers exploited under proto-industrial conditions, the post-colonial army of slaves, the old and sick, but also the superfluous young people, who are trained by an education system that focuses mainly on the daily evaluation of everyone by everyone, for jobs that will not exist in the future—all in all the global lumpenproletariat, which is outside the official work system. The surplus population today vegetates mainly in the Global South on the narrow ridge between survival and total liquidation. The Buddhist economist Karl Heinz Brodbeck writes about the Global South: "There is probably a teleological, but no factual difference between what is produced on the one hand at the global market barriers in terms of hunger, death, and misery and on the other hand in the camps of Hitler, Stalin, Mao, as well as the enclosures and camps of the US empire and its satellites. Certainly, in the camps there is naked and intended violence, guided by the intention to torture and kill specifically. The victims of the markets are probably not intended, but they are precisely and literally accepted. The madness of both actions, the production of victims or their acceptance, nevertheless has a common form: The enforcement of an abstraction without regard to the means, guided by the stupid pride of a ruling ignorance. It is therefore not a coincidence that an instrumental convergence between totalitarian violence and the abstract rule of money is increasingly emerging, and the difference between the misery in the slums and the terror in the modern torture chambers is being leveled." (Brodbeck, 2012: 1232–1233)

In his book *Cyber-Proletariat*, Nick Dyer-Witheford examines in detail the composition of the global proletariat (in its relationship to cybernetics), which he calls a "multifaceted multiverse" composed of those layers that can still sell or rent their labor power to capital to secure reproduction, an industrial reserve army without work supported by the welfare state, and a surplus population divided into those who work in the informal sectors of the subsistence economy and those who are denied any employment and have thus become completely useless not only for capital but increasingly for any kind of production. (Dyer-Witheford, 2015: 126f.) The surplus population continues to grow today both in the informal sectors of the economy and in the minimal subsistence economy, while at the same time precarious wage labor is expanding in a diffuse service sector; we also see the mobilization of women for paid and unpaid work in the reproduction sector and the escalation of underemployment and unpaid or insecure work. In the peripheries of the Global South, in addition to the informal sectors that are still connected to the circuits of capital,[2] (home work and work without contract), there are also non-capitalist modes of production such as slavery or subsistence economy. There are productions in which labor power is integrated into the commodity-money-commodity cycle, where the first commodity is labor power itself, which is bought for money and integrated into a production process, the products of which, when realized on the market, bring in just enough money to purchase the goods necessary for the reproduction of labor power and a small surplus for the entrepreneur.

The collective *Théorie Communiste* speaks today of three zones on the capitalist world market: (1) The hyperzones of capital with high functional performances in the area of labor markets and production sites (finance, technology, and research). (2) Secondary zones with intermediate industries and technologies (logistics and communication). (3) Crisis zones of informational industries with low-paid jobs or zones where no work is done at all. (Dyer-Witheford, 2015: 126f.) In the first zone, high-paid wage labor including private risk coverage meets such work in which certain aspects of Fordism remain, while other workers struggle with precarious conditions. In the second zone, precarious, low-paid work is the norm, mixed with islands of contractually paid work, with migration and the lack of social risk coverage. In the third zone, the survival of the proletariat depends on humanitarian aid, illegal trade and mafia structures, on agriculture, but also on small communities. This layering and stratification must be understood as a volatile and porous process, permeated by constant global migration movements of the proletariat and the restructurings by capital. What is modern on a global level is not universal progress towards prosperity and the rule of law, but an accelerated descent into informality, precariousness, and pure superfluity. Instead of upward mobility, there is only a staircase down to report for part of humanity, over which laid-off workers and dismissed public employees of the formal sector descend into the shadow economy, and this not only in the Global South. This development has also gained momentum in the imperialist countries and has since the 2008 financial crisis and the Corona pandemic have given a new massive boost.

The growth of the informal economy not only coincides with neoliberal globalization, but is further driven by a rapid transition from state regulation to new laissez-faire regimes. As the ILO notes, it is now widely recognized that the stabilization and structural adjustment policies of the 1980s and 1990s, which led to increasing poverty, unemployment, and underemployment in many countries, contributed to the spread of the informal economy. (ILO, 2018) The existence of informal work allows capitalists to cut costs and increase flexibility, among other things through forced overtime, layoffs, and the absence of regulations and legal protection, so that the risks and costs of adapting to demand are transferred to the workers. Part of the informal proletariat remains a labor pool for the formal economy and its networks, which reach deep into slums.

Thus, the official unemployment rates in the countries in the Global South are already very high, but they hide the true extent of the number of people living on the edge of or below the subsistence minimum, and that without any possibility of earning their livelihood. These dispossessed workers are on the one hand former farmers, who would flock back to the countryside in millions, especially in Asia, if there were farmland and cheap credits available for them, on the other hand unemployed people who vegetate in the slums or perform fragmented work. Generally, it is the case that workers are released by stronger technological development in one sector and can find employment in new sectors. However, the current development in China shows that even in these new sectors, the most advanced production methods are used, so they absorb less labor than with old production methods. Thus, today the rise of some emerging countries is not only based on cheap labor, as John Smith often assumes, but also on modern technology, so that the productive absorption of labor is less than the high growth rates in China, for example, suggest.

William I. Robinson identifies three forms of surplus proletariat: a floating, a latent, and a stagnant surplus proletariat. The first two forms are groups that can still enter and exit the wage-dependent production process according to the cycles of capital accumulation and are integrated by new forms of division of labor (industrial reserve army). The third group are those who are structurally outside the production process. (Robinson, 2021) Marx tried to capture this group under the term of the lumpenproletariat, but he could not foresee the processes in and with which, for example, through the replacement of work by technologies, but also through other processes, the existence of the surplus population would become a structural problem for the world economy. Apart from Marx's largely negative qualification of the lumpenproletariat, this is now a structural moment that stands for the marginalization of the outcasts in the capitalist world system.

The surplus population, especially in the Global South, has long become a structural category of political economy; it is a huge population group that suffers from long-term underemployment, has to generate a vital income in the informal economy of the slums of megacities and is supplemented by internationally migrating refugees who flee wars, oppression, and natural disasters and have to live as labor migrants in the non-places of the world. The surplus population of the Global South has mainly concentrated in the "planet of slums", as Mike Davis has documented in his book of the same name, where hundreds of millions of people live in total misery. The spectacular growth of urban slums is also a result of the deep crisis in the countryside. As Mike Davis notes, urbanization in the Global South is rapidly advancing despite falling real wages, rising prices, and exploding unemployment. (Davis, 2007)

Gilles Deleuze, as early as the 1990s, presciently spoke of the universally indebted human being, but quickly added, against any ontologization of debt, that the powers of control always face the danger of uprisings—the indebted and the excluded are one and the same. They are the same global surplus, with the indebted as microcredit borrowers still having an economic function for financial capital, while larger parts of the surplus population vegetate as human waste in the slums of the southern metropolises, functionless for capital. Today, capital must constantly find new agents capable of incurring debt, students, homeowners, and part-time workers, without being able to reduce the surplus population on a global scale even remotely.

If today the uprising is not only a collective action but a form of class struggle, then the surplus population must also possess an explanatory power in this; it is to be understood as a constitutive part of the global proletariat, whose historical task lies in the negation of capital. The more the better-off and collectively secured parts of the working class in the western metropolises affirm capital in order to be able to reproduce themselves at a relatively comfortable economic and social level, the more massive the political significance of a globally expanding proletariat that largely no longer has access to traditional forms of reproduction. According to Joshua Clover, we are in the midst of a long-lasting exodus of the propertyless from all continents to the western world, driven by increasing geopolitical volatility, wars, and the inability of capital to adequately absorb the workforce in the countries of the Global South—a diaspora of an expanding suprafluidity and at the same time immobile and abandoned surplus population. (Clover, 2021)

If the everyday life of a part of the world's population in the Global South increasingly takes place in informal economies, then this part itself becomes surplus and is confronted with the conditions of its reproduction beyond the wage labor relationship, and in this conflict-ridden situation, which then also shows up on the streets, any unauthorized gathering of a group at the corner, on a public square, or just in the streets can be understood as a potential riot. In contrast to the strike, it is difficult to find out when the riot starts or when it ends. On the one hand, it is a particular event, on the other hand, it is the holographic miniature of a complete situation, a world-picture.

The riot seems to maintain or affirm nothing, perhaps a shared antagonism, a shared misery, and a shared negation. Often it does not even possess the positive language of a program or a demand, but only the negative language of vandalism, destruction, and aimlessness. But still, it is not lacking in determination. Clover speaks of the overdetermination of the riot by historical transformations that make the antagonism, especially the struggles in circulation, necessary. The welfare state, which still accompanied the accumulation of capital in Fordism, has disappeared, and with it the possibilities of capital and the state to ensure social and economic improvements for wage earners. Capital and labor are increasingly moving into circulation, while the surplus population is in the informal economy. The new uprisings in circulation do not necessarily have to be carried by workers, because in principle anyone can liberate a marketplace, close a street, or occupy a port. The insurgents may be workers, but they do not function as workers in the riot, because the participants are unified here not by their jobs, but in their function as dispossessed.[3]

While the early riot hardly confronted the police and the armed state (it took place in the economic space), this has changed with the post-industrial riot. On the one hand, one directly sees the ensemble of goods in the local supermarkets, on the other hand, when it comes to the pricing of goods, one is confronted with capital economy as an invisible planetary logistics and a barely graspable financial industry. Only the police can be spotted at every corner. An important moment of the uprising is surprisingly made by Joshua Clover in the concept of surplus, whereas the uprising is usually understood in the context of deprivation, lack, and deficit, while for Clover it precisely indicates the lived experience of surplus, such as surplus danger, surplus instruments, and surplus affects. The most important surplus is the actively negating, resistant population in the breaking moments of mass mobilization, which condense into an event in which the uprising bursts the police management of a concrete situation and at the same time radically decouples from everyday life. However, this type of insurgent surplus production always remains confronted with the conditions of socio-economic processes and transformations that respond to crises or constitute them in the first place. All of this shows the uprising not only as a purely contingent, but also as a necessary form of political struggle. In view of the existence of a huge surplus population and the insurgent politics of surplus, Clover comes to an important conclusion: The uprising is the modality through which the surplus is lived. (ibid.) Primary circulation is today primary uprising, which is the surplus life—however short-term—itself; The latter is the subject of politics and thus at the same time the object of state violence. The violence of the police now becomes part of the uprising itself, or, to put it another way, the flashing coalition of the insurgent surplus exists in an economy of state violence.

Notes

1. The "economically active population" of the world grew from 1.9 billion in 1980 to 3.1 billion in 2006 and is now approximately 3.5 billion. This is by no means solely the result of global population growth, but also a result of the deepening of global capital accumulation and markets. Almost all numerical growth of the working

population took place in the emerging countries, where today 84% of the global working population live.

2. The informal sector in the economy was first defined by the ILO in 1972 and thus includes all work that is not legally recognized, not registered, and not protected, or not regulated by the authorities. (ILO) The informal economy is not regulated by the state, so no taxation, no workplace inspection etc. takes place. Informal workers are not legally recognized and therefore receive no legal or social protection and are not able to enforce contracts. Although the state is not entirely absent here, it has retreated to primitive forms of coercion. In addition, the informal economy promotes state corruption, replacing taxes with bribery and protection money and the rule of law with cooperation between police and gang leaders to maintain control over the slums and protect market monopolies. Today, 2 billion people work in the informal sector (ILO, 2018).
3. We discussed this in detail in the riot book about Hamburg (Dellwo et al., 2018).

References

Brodbeck, K.-H. (2009). *Die Herrschaft des Geldes: Geschichte und Systematik*. Darmstadt.

Clover, J. (2021). *Riot.Strike.Riot: Die neue Ära der Aufstände*. Hamburg.

Davis, M. (2007). *Planet der Slums*. Hamburg.

Dellwo, K.-H., Szepanski, A., & Weiler, P. (2018). *RIOT—Was war da los in Hamburg? Theorie und Praxis der kollektiven Aktion*. Hamburg.

Dyer-Whitheford, N. (2015). *Cyber-Proletariat: Global Labour in the Digital Vortex*. London.

ILO. (2018). Mehr als 60 Prozent der globalen Erwerbsbevölkerung arbeiten in der informellen Wirtschaft. https://www.ilo.org/berlin/presseinformationen/WCMS_627629/lang--de/index.htm

Robinson, W. I. (2021). *The Global Police State*. London.

References

Agamben, G. (2023). Die zwei Gesichter der Macht: Anarchie und Politik. https://non.copyriot.com/die-zwei-gesichter-der-macht-anarchie-und-politik/
Aglietta, M. (2000). *Eine neues Akkumulationsregime. Die Regulationstheorie auf dem Prüfstand*. Hamburg.
Alliez, E., & Lazzarato, M. (2018). *Wars and Capital*. Cambridge.
Altvater, E. (2010). *Der große Krach oder die Jahrhundertkrise von Wirtschaft und Finanzen, von Politik und Natur*. Münster.
Altvater, E., Hoffmann, J., & Semmler, W. (1979). *Vom Wirtschaftswunder zur Wirtschaftskrise. Ökonomie und Politik in der Bundesrepublik*. Berlin.
Armand, L. (2023). *Entropology*. London.
Amin, S. (2012). *Das globalisierte Wertgesetz*. Hamburg.
Anders, G. (1961). *Die Antiquiertheit des Menschen 1. Über die Zerstörung des Lebens im Zeitalter der dritten industriellen Revolution*. München.
Arnoldi, J. (2009). *Alles Geld verdampft. Finanzkrise in der Weltrisikogesellschaft*. Frankfurt/M.
Arrighi, G. (2008). *Adam Smith in Beijing*. Hamburg.
Asher, I. (2016). *Portfolio Society: On the Capitalist Mode of Prediction*. New York.
Arthur, C. J. (2022). *The Spectre of Capital: Idea and Reality*. Leiden.
Arthur, C. J. (2023). *Global Debt and Parallel Universe*. https://non.copyriot.com/global-debt-and-parallel-universe/
Ayache, E. (2005). The »non-Greek« non-foundation of derivative Pricing. http://www.ito33.com/sites/default/files/articles/0509_ayache.pdf

A. Szepanski, *Capitalism in the Age of Catastrophe*, Palgrave Insights into Apocalypse Economics,
https://doi.org/10.1007/978-3-031-57754-3

Ayache, E. (2008). The French Theory of Speculation. Part I: Necessity of Contingency. http://www.ito33.com/sites/default/files/articles/0803_nail.pdf

Ayache, E. (2010a). *The Blank Swan: The End of Probability*. London.

Ayache, E. (2010b). The Turning. http://www.ito33.com/sites/default/files/articles/1007_ayache.pdf

Ayache, E. (2010c). The End of Probability. http://www.ito33.com/sites/default/files/articles/1011_ayache_0.pdf

Bank für internationalen Zahlungsausgleich. (2013). https://www.bis.org/publ/qtrpdf/r_qt1312_de.htm

Bataille, G. (1985). *Die Aufhebung der Ökonomie*. Berlin.

Bataille, G. (2019). *Der Fluch der Ökonomie*. Berlin.

Bataille, G. (2021). *Der verfemte Teil*. Berlin.

Baudrillard, J. (1975). *The Mirror of Production*. St. Louis.

Baudrillard, J. (2021). *Der verfemte Teil*. Berlin.

Baudrillard, J. (1976). *Der symbolische Tausch und der Tod*. München.

Baudrillard, J. (1990). *Cool Memories*. London/New York.

Baudrillard, J. (1991). *Die fatalen Strategien*. München.

Baudrillard, J. (1992a). *Das perfekte Verbrechen*. München.

Baudrillard, J. (1992b). *Transparenz des Bösen. Ein Essay über extreme Phänomene*. Berlin.

Baudrillard, J. (1994). *Simulation and Simulacra*. Michigan.

Baudrillard, J. (2000). *Der unmögliche Tausch*. Berlin.

Baudrillard, J. (2001). *Das System der Dinge. Über unser Verhältnis zu alltäglichen Gegenständen*. Frankfurt a. M./New York.

Baudrillard, J. (2002). *Paßwörter*. Berlin.

Baudrillard, J. (2012a). *Von der Verführung*. Berlin.

Baudrillard, J. (2012b). *The Ecstasy of Communication*. Cambridge.

Baudrillard, J. (2015). *Die Konsumgesellschaft. Ihre Mythen, Ihre Strukturen*. Cham.

Baudrillard, J. (2023). Global Debt and Parallel Universe. https://non.copyriot.com/global-debt-and-parallel-universe/

Bauman, Z. (2005). *Verworfenes Leben*. Hamburg.

Beck, M., Samuel, K., & Sgambati, S. (2022). Leveraging Financial Claims: Transatlantic Bank Struggles and the Power of US Finance. In B. Braun & K. Koddenbrock (Eds.), *Capital Claims: Power and Global Finance*. London.

Beller, J. (2021). *The World Computer: Derivative Conditions of Racial Capitalism*. Durham.

Benanav, A. (2022). *Automation and the Future of Work*. London.

Bericht des Europäischen Ausschusses für Systemrisiken (ESRB) (2016): https://www.esrb.europa.eu/pub/pdf/ar/2017/esrb.ar2016.de.pdf

Bichler, S., & Nitzan, J. (2009). *Capital as Power: A Study of Order and Creator*. Florence.

Bichler, S., & Nitzan, J. (2013). Differential Accumulation. http://bnarchives.yorku.ca/323/03/20121200_bn_da_ft_lexicon_web.htm

Bichler, S., & Nitzan, J. (2015). *Capital Accumulation: Fiction and Reality*. Philosophers for Change. http://philosophersforchange.org/

Bichler, S., & Nitzan, J. (2022). The Stagflation Norm. https://capitalaspower.com/casp-forum/topic/the-stagflation-norm/

Binswanger, M. (2015). *Geld aus dem Nichts. Wie Banken Wachstum ermöglichen und Krisen verursachen*. Weinheim.

Binswanger, M. (2019). *Der Wachstumszwang. Warum die Volkswirtschaft immer weiterwachsen muss, selbst wenn wir genug haben*. Weinheim.

BIS. (2022). Quarterly Review December 2022. https://www.bis.org/press/p221205_de.htm

Bockelmann, E. (2004). *Im Takt des Geldes. Zur Genese des Modernen Denkens*. Springe.

Bockelmann, E. (2020). *Das Geld. Was es ist, das uns beherrscht*. Berlin.

Braun, B. (2021). Asset Manager Capitalism as a Corporate Governance Regime. In J. Hacker et al. (Eds.), *American Political Economy: Politics, Markets and Power*. Cambridge/New York.

Braun, B., & Koddenbrock, K. (2022). *Capital Claims: Power and Global Finance*. London.

Brodbeck, K.-H. (2009). *Die Herrschaft des Geldes: Geschichte und Systematik*. Darmstadt.

Brodbeck, K.-H. (2013). Phänomenologie des Geldes. https://khbrodbeck.homepage.t-online.de/phaenom.pdf

Brodbeck, K.-H. (2023). *Phänomenologie des Geldes*. Zürich.

Bryan, D., & Rafferty, M. (2006). *Capitalism with Derivatives: A Political Economy of Financial Derivatives, Capital and Class*. London.

Butler, R. (1999). *Jean Baudrillard: The Defense of the Real*. London.

Büscher, B. (2015, December). Nature on the Move I: The Value and Circulation of Liquid Nature and the Emergence of Fictitious Conservation. *Journal of Marxism and Interdisciplinary Inquiry*, *6*(1–2), 20–36.

Callinicos, A. (2023). *The New Age of Catastrophe*. Cambridge.

Campbell, C. (2023). Quantum Computers Could Solve Countless Problems—And Create a Lot of New Ones. *Time*. https://time.com/6249784/quantum-computing-revolution/

Cherizola, J. S. (2021). From Commodities to Assets: Capital as Power and the Ontology of Finance. https://capitalaspower.com/2021/05/cherizola-from-commodities-to-assets/

Chesnais, F. (2016). *Finance Capital Today: Corporations and Banks in the Lasting Global Slump*. Leiden.

Christophers, B. (2023). *Our Lives in Their Portfolios: Why Asset Managers Own the World*. London.

Clover, J. (2021). *Riot.Strike.Riot: Die neue Ära der Aufstände*. Hamburg.
Crary, J. (2013). *24/7: Schlaflos im Spätkapitalismus*. Berlin.
Cziesla, F. (2022). *Von der Biopolitik zur Nekro-Ökonomie. Für eine genealogische Kritik der politischen Ökonomie des Todes*. Bielefeld.
Daniel, W. (2023). 'We May Be Looking at the End of Capitalism': One of the World's Oldest and Largest Investment Banks Warns 'Greedflation' Has Gone Too Far. https://fortune.com/2023/04/05/end-of-capitalism-inflation-greedflation-societe-generale-corporate-profits/
Danowski, D., & de Castro, E. V. (2016). *The End of the Worlds*. Cambridge.
Davis, A. (2018). Defining Speculative Value in the Age of Financialized Capitalism. *The Sociological Review, 66*(1), 3–19.
Davis, M. (2007). *Planet der Slums*. Hamburg.
De Brunhoff, S. (2015). *Marx on Money*. London/New York.
Deleuze, G. (1993). *Logik des Sinns*. Frankfurt/M.
Deleuze, G., & Guattari, F. (1981). *Anti-Ödipus. Kapitalismus und Schizophrenie*. Frankfurt/M.
Deleuze, G., & Guattari, F. (1992). *Tausend Plateaus. Kapitalismus und Schizophrenie*. Berlin.
Deleuze, G., & Guattari, F. (1996). *Was ist Philosophie*. Frankfurt/M.
Derrida, J. (1988). *Randgänge der Philosophie*. Wien.
Dellwo, K.-H., Szepanski, A., & Weiler, P. (2018). *RIOT—Was war da los in Hamburg? Theorie und Praxis der kollektiven Aktion*. Hamburg.
Di Muzio, T. (2020). Capitalized Money, Austerity and the Math of Capitalism. https://www.academia.edu/41619254/Capitalized_Money_Austerity_and_the_Math_of_Capitalism
Di Muzio, T., & Robbins, R. H. (2015). *Debt as Power: Theory for a Global Age*. Manchester.
Durand, C. D. (2017). *Fictitious Capital: How Finance Is Appropriating Our Future*. London/New York.
Durand, C. D. (2023). The End of Financial Hegemony? The New Left Review. https://newleftreview.org/issues/ii138/articles/cedric-durand-the-end-of-financial-hegemony
Durbin, M. (2010). *All About High-Frequency Trading*. New York.
Duta, S. J. (2022). Countering Financial Claims: On the Political Economy of Definancialisation. In B. Braun & K. Koddenbrock (Eds.), *Capital Claims: Power and Global Finance*. London.
Dyer-Whitheford, N. (2015). *Cyber-Proletariat: Global Labour in the Digital Vortex*. London.
Dyer-Witheford, N., Kjøsen, A. M., & Steinhoff, J. (2019). *Inhuman Power: Artificial Intelligence and the Future of Capitalism, Digital Barricades: Interventions in Digital Culture and Politics*. London.

Edelmüller, W. (2022). Kriegswirtschaft und Wirtschaftskrieg. https://makroskop.eu/spotlight/versailles-durch-die-hintertur/war-economy-and-economic-war/

Ehrenhauser, M. (2018). *Die Geldroboter: Wie Hochfrequenzmaschinen unser Erspartes einkassieren und Finanzmärkte destabilisieren*. Wien.

Esposito, E. (2010). *Die Zukunft der Futures. Die Zeit des Geldes in Finanzwelt und Gesellschaft*. Heidelberg.

Fichtner, J., Heemskerk, E., & Petry, J. (2022). The New Gatekeepers of Financial Claims: States, Passive Markets, and the Growing Power of Index Providers. In B. Braun & K. Koddenbrock (Eds.), *Capital Claims: Power and Global Finance*. London.

Fischbach, R. (2017). *Die schöne Utopie: Paul Mason, der Postkapitalismus und der Traum vom grenzenlosen Überfluss*. Köln.

Freiburghaus, D., & Müller, H.-P. (1973). *Zur Struktur des Krisenproblems bei Karl Marx*. In: Mehrwert. Beiträge zur politischen Ökonomie 5. Berlin.

Fuchs, P. (2023). *Das System Selbst*. Velbrück.

Gabor, D. (2016). The (Impossible) Repo Trinity: The Political Economy of Repo Markets. *Review of International Political Economy, 6*, 967–1000.

Gabor, D. (2021). The Wall Street Consensus. *Development and Change, 52*(3), 429–459.

Gabor, D., & Vestergaard, J. (2021). Central Banks Caught Between Market Liquidity and Fiscal Disciplining: A Money View Perspective on Collateral Policy. https://www.ineteconomics.org/research/research-papers/central-banks-caught-between-market-liquidity-and-fiscal-disciplining-a-money-view-perspective-on-collateral-policy

Gentili, D. (2020). *Krise als Regierungskunst*. Leipzig.

Global Risks Report. (2023). https://www.weforum.org/reports/global-risks-report-2023/

Gordon, R. J. (2013). *Is US Economic Growth Over? Faltering Innovation Confronts the Six*. http://www.voxeu.org/article/us-economic-growth-over

Gordon, R. J. (2017). *The Rise and Fall of American Growth: The U.S. Standard of Living Since the Civil War*. Princeton.

Harney, S., & Moten, F. (2022). *Allseits unvollkommen. Plantokratie und schwarzes Studium*. Wien.

Heidegger, M. (2006). *Sein und Zeit*. Tübingen.

Hui, Y., & Frey, J. (2023). *Kosmotechnik und Kommunismus*. Berlin.

ILO. (2018). Mehr als 60 Prozent der globalen Erwerbsbevölkerung arbeiten in der informellen Wirtschaft. https://www.ilo.org/berlin/presseinformationen/WCMS_627629/lang--de/index.htm

Itoh, M., & Lapavitsas, C. (1999). *Political Economy of Money and Finance*. Houndmills.

Kaldor, M. (1981). *Rüstungsbarock*. Berlin.

Kallert, A. (2017). *Die Bankenrettungen während der Finanzkrise 2000–2009 in Deutschland* .

Kaplan, A. D. H., Dirlam, J. B., & Lanzillotti, R. F. (1958). *Pricing in Big Business*. Washington.

Keynes, J. M. (1983). *Allgemeine Theorie der Beschäftigung, des Zinses und des Geldes*. Berlin.

Kindleberger, C. P. (1978). *Manias, Panic, and Crashes: A History of Financial Crises*. New York.

Klossowski, P. (1999). *Die lebende Münze*. Berlin.

Kroker, A. (1998). *Das besessene Individuum. Technologie und französische Postmoderne*. Wien.

Kroker, A. (2004). *The Will to Technology and the Culture of Nihilism: Heidegger, Nietzsche & Marx*. Toronto.

Kroker, A., Kroker, M., & Cook, D. (1999). *Panik-Enzyklopädie*. Wien.

Kurz, R. (2012). *Geld ohne Wert. Grundrisse zu einer Transformation der Kritik der politischen Ökonomie*. Berlin.

Land, N. (2010). *Fanged Noumena: Collected Writings 1987–2007*. London.

Latour, B. (2018). *Das terrestrische Manifest*. Berlin.

Lazzarato, M. (2012). *Die Fabrikation des verschuldeten Menschen. Ein Essay über das neoliberale Leben*. Berlin.

Lazzarato, M. (2014). *Signs and Machines: Capitalism and the Production of Subjectivity*. Los Angeles.

Lazzarato, M. (2021). *Capital Hates Everyone: Fascism or Revolution*. Cambridge.

Lee, B., & Martin, R. (Eds.). (2016). *Derivatives and the Wealth of Societies*. Chicago/London.

Lenger, H.-J. (2004). *Marx zufolge. Die unmögliche Revolution*. Bielefeld.

Lenger, H.-J. (2007). Eine différance der Werte. Marx mit Derrida. http://www.hjlenger.de

Lenger, H.-J. (2010). Die Mutter aller verrückten Formen. Marx, die Schrift und die Spekulation. In: Lethen, Helmut/Löschenköhl, Birte/Schmieder, Falko (Hrsg.): *Der sich selbst entfremdete und wiedergefundene Marx*, 193–207. München.

LiPuma, E. (2017). *The Social Life of Financial Derivatives: Markets, Risk, and Time*. Durham/London.

LiPuma, E., & Lee, B. (2004). *Financial Derivatives and the Globalization of Risk*. Darham.

Lohoff, E., & Trenkle, N. (2012). *Die große Entwertung. Warum Spekulation und Staatsverschuldung nicht die Ursache der Krise sind*. Münster.

Lozano, B. (2014). Of Synthetic Finance: 3 Essays of Speculative Materialism. http://speculativematerialism.files.wordpress.com/2012/12/ofsynthetic-finance-complete-text.pdf

Lyotard, J.-F. (1989). *Der Widerstreit*. München.
Maher, S. (2021). The New Finance Capital: Corporate Governance, Financial Power, and the State. https://journals.sagepub.com/doi/full/10.1177/0896920521994170
Malik, S. (2014). Ontology of Finance: Price, Power and the Arkhéderivative. In R. MacKay (Ed.), *Collapse Vol. VIII: Casino Real* (pp. 303–480).
Malm, A. (2016). *Fossil Capital: The Rise of Steam Power and the Roots of Global Warming*. London.
Malm, A. (2020). *The Progress of This Storm: Nature and Society in a Warming World*. London.
Maki, S. (2021). World's $281 Trillion Debt Pile is Set to Rise Again in 2021. *Bloomberg*, 17 February. https://www.bloomberg.com/news/articles/2021-02-17/global-debt-hits-all-time-high-as-pandemic-boosts-spending-need. Accessed on 30 April 2021.
Martin, R. (2009). The Twin Tower of Financialization: Entanglements of Political and Cultural Economies. *The Global South, 3*(1), 108–125.
Martin, R. (2015). *Knowledge Ltd: Toward a Social Logic of the Derivative*. Philadelphia.
Marx, K. (1974). *Grundrisse der Kritik der politischen Ökonomie*. Berlin/DDR
Marx, K. (1975). *Das Kapital. Kritik der politischen Ökonomie*. Zweiter Band. Hrsg. v. Engels, Friedrich, MEW, Bd. 24, Berlin/DDR.
Marx, K. (1975). *Das Kapital. Kritik der politischen Ökonomie*. Dritter Band. Hrsg. v. Engels, Friedrich, MEW, Bd. 25. Berlin/DDR.
Marx, K. (1975). *MEW: Marx-Engels Werke, Bd. 1–42*. Hrsg. v. Institut für Marxismus-Leninismus beim ZK der SED, Berlin/DDR.
Marx, K. (1992). *MEGA: Marx-Engels Gesamtausgabe*. Hrsg. v. Institut für Marxismus-Leninismus beim ZK der KPdSU und v. Institut für Marxismus-Leninismus beim ZK der SED. Berlin/DDR/Moskau 1975-1989, ab 1992 hrsg. v. d. Internationalen Marx-Engels-Stiftung Amsterdam. Berlin/Amsterdam.
McKinsey Quarterly. (2018). A Decade After the Crisis, It's a Different World. https://www.mckinsey.com/~/media/McKinsey/Industries/Financial%20Services/Our%20Insights/A%20decade%20after%20the%20crisis%20its%20a%20different%20world/A%20decade%20after%20the%20crisis%20its%20a%20different%20world.pdf
McAfee, K. (2012). Nature in the Market-World: Ecosystem Services and Inequality. *Development, 55*, 25–33. https://doi.org/10.1057/dev.2011.105
Meillassoux, Q. (2008). *Nach der Endlichkeit*. Zürich/Berlin.
Meillassoux, Q. (2011). Potentiality and Virtuality. In L. R. Bryant, N. Snirzek, G. Harman (Eds.), *The Speculative Turn: Continental Materialism and Realism*. Melbourne.
Meister, R. (2016). Liquidity. In B. Lee & R. Martin (Eds.), *Derivatives and the Wealth of Societies* (pp. 2702–3299). Chicago.

Meister, R. (2021). *Justice Is an Option: A Democratic Theory of Finance for the Twenty-First Century*. Chicago.
Metzinger, T. (2023). *Bewusstseinskultur. Spiritualität, intellektuelle Redlichkeit und die planetare Krise*. München.
Milios, J. (2003). Zur Darstellung von Marx' Krisentheorie im dritten Band des Kapital (pp. 47–60). In *Beitrage zur Marx-Engels-Forschung*. Neue Folge 1998.
Milios, J. (2004). Die Marxsche Werttheorie und das Geld. Zur Verteidigung der These über den endogenen Charakter des Geldes. In (pp. 95–114). Neue Folge.
Milios, J. (2018). *The Origins of Capitalism as a Social System: The Prevalence of an Aleatory Encounter*. London.
Milios, J. (2019). Value, Fictitious Capital and Finance: The Timeliness of Karl Marx's *Capital*. http://users.ntua.gr/jmilios/8124-Article_Text-22400-1-10-20200311.pdf
Milios, J. (2023). Die Marxsche Wert-, und Kapitaltheorie und die kardinale Rolle des Finanzsystems. http://users.ntua.gr/jmilios/Milios_Berlin-2-1-23_Fin.pdf
Milios, J., & Sotiropoulos, D. (2009). *Rethinking Imperialism: A Study of Capitalist Rule*. London.
Minsky, H. P. (2011). *Instabilität und Kapitalismus*. Zürich/Berlin.
Mirowski, P. (1986). *The Reconstruction of Economic Theory*. Cham.
Moore, J. W. (2015). *Capitalism in the Web of Life. Ecology and the Accumulation of Capital*. London.
Moore, J. W. (2018). Cheap Food and Bad Climate: From Surplus Value to Negative Value in the Capitalist World-Ecology. https://jasonwmoore.com/wp-content/uploads/2017/08/Moore-Cheap-Food-and-Bad-Climate-2015-CHS.pdf
Moore, J. W. (2022a). How to Read Capitalism in the Web of Life: Towards a World-Historical Materialism in the Web of Life. https://www.academia.edu/76654904/How_to_Read_Capitalism_in_the_Web_of_Life_Towards_a_World_Historical_Materialism_in_the_Web_of_Life
Moore, J. W. (2022b). Waste in the Limits to Capital: How Capitalism Lays Waste to the Web of Life, and Why It Can't Stop. *Emancipations*, *2*(1/4), 1–45.
Morozov, E. (2022). Critique of Techno-Feudal Reason. https://newleftreview.org/issues/ii133/articles/evgeny-morozov-critique-of-techno-feudal-reason
Mühlmann, H. (2013). *Europa im Weltwirtschaftskrieg. Philosophie der Blasenwirtschaft*. Paderborn.
Nail, T. (2018). *Being and Motion*. Oxford.
Nordhaus, W. D. (2015). NBER Working Paper No. 21547. September 2015. http://www.nber.org/papers/w21547.pdf

Norfield, T. (2016). *The City. London and the Global Power of Finance*. London/New York.
Orléan, A. (1999). *Le Pouvoir de la finance*. Paris.
Pettifor, A. (2017). *The Production of Money: How to Break the Power of Bankers*. London.
Pettifor, A. (2022a). Central Bankers: Engineering a Worldwide Slump and Declaring Class War. https://annpettifor.substack.com/p/central-bankers-engineering-a-worldwide
Pettifor, A. (2022b). The Sudden Paralysis of the System? Messing with a Marvellously Intricate and Fragile Global System. https://annpettifor.substack.com/p/the-sudden-paralysis-of-the-system
Pettifor, A. (2022c). Grain Inflation: Starve the Poor, Feed the Rich. The War and Inflation—Who Is Winning? https://annpettifor.substack.com/p/grain-inflation-starve-the-poor-feed
Pistor, K. (2020). *The Code of Capital: How the Law Creates Wealth and Inequality*. Princeton.
Pistor, K. (2022). The Rise of Autonomous Financial Power. In B. Braun & K. Koddenbrock (Eds.), *Capital Claims. Power and Global Finance*. London.
Plotnitsky, A. (1994). *Complementarity: Anti-Epistemology after Bohr and Derrida*. Durham.
Raunig, G. (2018). Dividend. https://transversal.at/transversal/0318/dividend/en
Report of the European Systemic Risk Board (ESRB). (2016). https://www.esrb.europa.eu/pub/pdf/ar/2017/esrb.ar2016.de.pdf
Reuten, G. (2019). *The Unity of the Capitalist Economy and State. A Systematic-Dialectical Exposition of the Capitalist System*. Leiden.
Robinson, W. I. (2021). *The Global Police State*. London.
Robinson, W. I. (2022a). *Can Global Capitalism Endure?* Atlanta.
Robinson, W. I. (2022b). *Global Civil War: Capitalism Post-Pandemic (Kairos)*. Oakland.
Robbins, R. H., & Di Muzio, T. (2016). *Debt as Power*. Manchester.
Roberts, M. (2022). The Inflation Conundrum. https://thenextrecession.wordpress.com/2022/10/28/the-inflation-conundrum/
Roberts, M. (2023). Polycrisis and Depression in the 21th Century. https://thenextrecession.wordpress.com/2023/01/05/polycrisis-and-depression-in-the-21st-century/
Röttgers, K. (2022). *Monetäre Textualität*. Marburg.
Roubini, N. (2022). *MegaThreats: Ten Dangerous Trends That Imperil Our Future, And How to Survive Them*. Boston.
Ruben, P. (1995). Ist die Arbeitskraft eine Ware? In U. Hedtke & C. Warnke (Eds.), *Philosophische Schriften*. Online Edition: www.peter-ruben.de

Ruben, P. (1998). Was bleibt übrig von Marx' ökonomischer Theorie? In U. Hedtke & C. Warnke (Eds.), *Philosophical Writings*. Online Edition: www.peter-ruben.de

Rubin, I. I. (1973). *Studien zur Marxschen Werttheorie*. Frankfurt/M.

Sahr, A. (2017). *Das Versprechen des Geldes. Eine Praxistheorie des Kredits*. Hamburg.

Salle, G. (2022). *Superyachten. Luxus und Stille im Kapitalozän*. Hamburg.

Schinckus, C. (2008). The Financial Simulacrum: The Consequences of the Symbolization and the Computerization of the Financial Market. *Journal of Socio-Economics, 37*(3), 1076–1089.

Schlaudt, O. (2021). *Müll-Philosophie. Des Teufels Staub und der Engel Anteil*. Merkur. Heft 870. November 2021.

Schlaudt, O. (2022). *Das Technozän*. Frankfurt/M.

Schwengel, H. (1978). *Jenseits der Ideologie des Zentrums. Eine strukturale Revision der Marx'schen Gesellschaftstheorie. Reihe Metro. Bd.1.* Marburg.

Shaikh, A. (2016). *Capitalism. Competition. Conflict. Crises*. New York.

Sloterdijk, P. (1989). *Eurotaoismus. Zur Kritik der politischen Kinetik*. Frankfurt/M.

Smith, J. E. (2020). *Smart Machines and Service Work*. Chicago.

Smith, J. (2016). *Imperialism in the Twenty-First Century: Globalization, Super-Exploitation, and Capitalism's Final Crisis*. New York.

Sotiropoulos, D. P., Milios, J., & Lapatsioras, S. (2013). *A Political Economy of Contemporary Capitalism and its Crisis*. New York.

Sotiropoulos, D. P., Milios, J., & Lapatsioras, S. (2014). Marxist Theory, Financial System and Crisis of 2008. http://www.iippe.org/wiki/images/5/5f/CONF_CRISIS_Lapatsioras.pdf

Spiegel, M. (2022). *Hyperrealität und Transhumanismus. Der Mensch in der simulierten Gesellschaft*. Wiesbaden.

Stamatis, G. (1977). *The "spezifisch kapitalistischen Produktionsmethoden" und der tendenzielle Fall der allgemeinen Profitrate bei Karl Marx*. Berlin.

State of the Freight. (2021). https://www.supplychainquarterly.com/articles/4495-the-state-of-the-freight-2021

Stelter, D. (2013). *Die Billionen-Schuldenbombe. Wie die Krise begann und warum sie noch lange nicht zu Ende ist*. Weinheim.

Stiegler, B. (2016). *The Automated Society. The Future of Work*. Polity.

Stiegler, B. (2017). *Automatic Society. Volume 1: The Future of Work*. Chichester.

Strauß, H. (2013). *Signifikationen der Arbeit. Die Geltung des Differenzianten »Wert«*. Berlin.

Streeck, W. (2015). *Gekaufte Zeit. Die vertagte Krise des demokratischen Kapitalismus*. Berlin.

Sweezy, P. M. (1971). *Theorie der kapitalistischen Entwicklung*. Frankfurt.

Szepanski, A. (2014a). *Kapitalisierung Bd.1. Marx' Non-Ökonomie*. Hamburg.

Szepanski, A. (2014b). *Kapitalisierung Bd.2. Non-Ökonomie des gegenwärtigen Kapitalismus*. Hamburg.
Szepanski, A. (2016). *Der Non-Marxismus – Finance, Maschinen, Dividuum*. Hamburg.
Szepanski, A. (2018a). *Kapital und Macht im 21. Jahrhundert*. Hamburg.
Szepanski, A. (2018b). *Imperialismus, Staatsfaschisierung und die Kriegsmaschinen des Kapitals–Drei Essays*. Hamburg.
Szepanski, A. (2022). *Financial Capital in the 21th Century*. New York.
Szepanski, A. (2024). *Im Delirium der Simulation. Aufsätze zu Baudrillard*. Hamburg.
Taleb, N. N. (2010). *Der schwarze Schwan*. München.
Thiemann, M. (2022). The Benefits of Network Centrality: Central Counterparties, the Enforceability of Claims, and the Securing of Extra-Profits. In B. Braun & K. Koddenbrock (Eds.), *Capital Claims: Power and Global Finance*. London.
Tooze, A. (2018). *Crashed: Wie zehn Jahre Finanzkrise die Welt verändert haben*. München.
Tooze, A. (2021). *Welt im Lockdown. Die globale Krise und ihre Folgen*. München.
Tooze, A. (2022a). Polycrisis—Thinking on the Tightrope. https://adamtooze.substack.com/p/chartbook-165-polycrisis-thinking?utm_source=%2Fsearch%2Fpolycrisis&utm_medium=reader2
Tooze, A. (2022b). Finance and the Polycrisis (5) The Hunt for the Next Market Fracture. https://adamtooze.substack.com/p/chartbook-179-finance-and-the-polycrisis
Tooze, A. (2022c). Finance and the Polycrisis (1): What Bends? What Breaks? What Implodes? https://adamtooze.substack.com/p/chartbook-170-finance-and-the-polycrisis
Tooze, A. (2022d). The Regime at Risk—Macroprudentialism Faces the Test of Inflation. https://adamtooze.substack.com/p/chartbook-137-the-regime-at-risk
Tooze, A. (2022e). Zugzwang—Are We on the Brink of a Central Banking Paradigm Shift? https://adamtooze.substack.com/p/chartbook-151-zugzwang-are-we-on
Tooze, A. (2022f). The Bond Market Massacre of September 2022. https://adamtooze.substack.com/p/chartbook-157-the-bond-market-massacre?utm_source=%2Fsearch%2FLiability%2520Driven%2520Investment&utm_medium=reader2
Tooze, A. (2023a). On Deglobalisation and Polycrisis. https://adamtooze.substack.com/p/chartbook-192-on-deglobalisation?utm_source=%2Fsearch%2Fslowbalization&utm_medium=reader2

Tooze, A. (2023b). Globalization: The Shifting Patchwork. https://adamtooze.substack.com/p/chartbook-198-globalization-the-shifting?utm_source=post-email-title&publication_id=192845&post_id=105142155&isFreemail=true&utm_medium=email

UNCTAD. (2019). United Nations Conference on Trade and Development (UNCTAD). *Digital Economy Report 2019* (New York). https://unctad.org/en/PublicationsLibrary/der2019_en.pdf

Varoufakis, Y. (2012). *Der globale Minotaurus. Amerika und die Zukunft der Weltwirtschaft*. München.

Vighi, F. (2021). The Cental Bankers' Long Covid: An Incurable Condition. https://thephilosophicalsalon.com/the-central-bankers-long-covid-emergency-noise-and-conspiracys-best-kept-secret/?fbclid=IwAR1Nus3syvTQeO2W9w2xCvFDh9C-mTeXxS7YHdWbkooMPl8kYf3iWUnf9Zc

Vighi, F. (2022). *Unworkable. Delusions of an Imploding Civilization*. New York.

Vighi, F. (2023). Senile Economics: Bubble Ontology and the Pull of Gravity. https://thephilosophicalsalon.com/senile-economics-bubble-ontology-and-the-pull-of-gravity/

Virilio, P. (1988). *Geschwindigkeit und Politik. Ein Essay zur Dromologie*. Berlin.

Virilio, P. (1993). *Revolutionen der Geschwindigkeit*. Berlin.

Virilio, P. (2012). *The Great Accelerator*. Cambridge.

Werner, R. A. (2017). Can Banks Individually Create Money Out of Nothing? The Theories and the Empirical Evidence. http://www.sciencedirect.com/science/article/pii/S1057521914001070

Wilkins, I., & Dragos, B. (2013). Destructive Destruction? An Ecological Study of High Frequency Trading. http://www.metamute.org/editorial/articles/destructive-destruction-ecological-study-high-frequency-trading

Windolf, P. (2017). Was ist Finanzmarkt-Kapitalismus? https://www.uni-trier.de/fileadmin/fb4/prof/SOZ/APO/19-019_01.pdf

Wray, R. L. (2000). *Modern Money Theory: A Primer on Macroeconomics for Sovereign Monetary Systems*. New York.

Wullweber, J. (2021). *Zentralbankkapitalismus. Transformation des globalen Finanzsystems in Krisenzeiten*. Berlin.

Wullweber, J. (2023). Der neue Staat-Finanzmarkt-Nexus. https://makroskop.eu/spotlight/bankenbeben-fehlverhalten-oder-systemcrash/der-neue-staat-finanzmarkt-nexus/

Zhexi Zhang, G. (2023). *Catastrophe Time!* London.

Zuboff, S. (2018). *Das Zeitalter des Überwachungskapitalismus*. Frankfurt/M.

Index

A. Szepanski, *Capitalism in the Age of Catastrophe*, Palgrave Insights into Apocalypse Economics,
https://doi.org/10.1007/978-3-031-57754-3

D

E

F

M

N

O

P

The manufacturer's authorised representative in the EU is Springer Nature Customer Service Centre GmbH, Europaplatz 3, 69115 Heidelberg, Germany. If you have any concerns regarding our products, please contact ProductSafety@springernature.com

Printed and bound by CPI Group (UK) Ltd, Croydon, CR0 4YY
28/09/2026
02224083-0006